An Anthology of Tolstoy's Spiritual Economics

Courtesy of the Henry George Foundation of America,
Columbia, MD.

The Henry George
Centennial Trilogy

Volume One: *An Anthology of Henry George's Thought*
ISBN 1–878822–81–0

Volume Two: *An Anthology of Tolstoy's Spiritual Economics*
ISBN 1–878822–91–8

Volume Three: *An Anthology of Single Land Tax Thought*
ISBN 1–878822–92–6

An Anthology of Tolstoy's Spiritual Economics

Volume II
of the Henry George
Centennial Trilogy

Kenneth C. Wenzer

 University of Rochester Press

First published 1997

University of Rochester Press
34–36 Administration Building, University of Rochester
Rochester, New York, 14627, USA
and at P.O. Box 9, Woodbridge, Suffolk IP12 3DF, UK

ISBN 1–878822–91–8

Library of Congress Cataloging-in-Publication Data

Tolstoy, Leo, graf, 1828–1910.
  [Selections, English, 1997]
  An anthology of Tolstoy's spiritual economics / Kenneth C. Wenzer.
      p.   cm.—(Volume II of the Henry George centennial trilogy)
  Includes bibliographical references (p. 261).
  isbn 1–878822–91–8 (alk. paper)
  1. Peasantry—Russia—Economic conditions. 2. Peasantry—Russia— Social conditions. 3. Socialism, Christian—Russia. 4. Russia— Economic policy. I. Wenzer, Kenneth C., 1950– . II. Title. III. Series: George, Henry, 1839–1897. Selections,   1997 ; v. 2.
  HD1536.R9T64213   1997
  335.4—dc21   97-4167
                                                                   CIP

British Library Cataloguing-in-Publication Data

A catalogue record for this book
is available from the British Library

Typeset by Cornerstone Composition Services
This publication is printed on acid-free paper
Printed in the United States of America

For
Clifford,
George,
and Donald

Contents

Preface

Shortly after the turn of the century the Russian Empire was a colossus, sprawled across half the globe, populated by tens of millions, and ruled by the most powerful monarch. Underneath the surface, however, she was rent by numerous antipodal forces.

The peasant population had grown between 1860 and 1900 from fifty to about eighty millions, crowding the land and tilling it with archaic tools and methods. Hemmed in by law and poverty, the peasants were also subject to harsh taxes (the nobility paid 1/10 the amount for the same area of land) and exorbitant land payments for the overpriced plots they received from the Emancipation of 1861. Starvation, drought, and famine were recurrent. The very personality of rural folk was at contraries: outbursts of rebellion would sometime punctuate lives of daily religious resignation. The beginnings of an artificially-induced industrialization swelled cities with an industrial work force, slightly less impoverished, perhaps, than the peasantry but suffering from social dislocation and unprotected from capitalist exploitation. Their condition worsened during times of periodic depression. And finally, various groups of peoples, especially the Jews, were subjected to a miserable existence, pogroms, and forced policies of russification. By 1900, the proletariat, the peasantry, the middle class, and different nationalities were in a state of turmoil.

Three great forces vied for the mind, heart, and soul of the Russian people. Each one attempted for its own reason to shape thought in a specific fashion. In a certain sense the three not only represented but were three distinct Russias.

There was the Russia of the Romanov dynasty. For three hundred years these tsars had been on the throne, and for two centuries the influential Russian Orthodox Church had been administratively controlled as a department of state. The ruling powers sought, in this multicultural empire, to maintain a homogenous population, a strong nobility, and a subservient peasantry adhering to the dictates of autocracy, Orthodoxy, and nationality. The gentry, the mainstay of the autocracy, resisted any social, economic, and political change. Although increasingly marginalized, it was still a potent force. These components congealed into a world frozen in time and sometimes executed in the most brutal fashion.

There was also the Russia of the developing middle-class. Much of its membership was passive; others filled the ranks of the *intelligentsia*.[1] This element was more or less alien to Russia, looking to the intellectual and political movements of post-Enlightenment Western Europe. Denied direct access to political power, the intelligentsia lacked even a consultative voice, and the nobility looked down on it and the rest of the middle class. They were determined to remake their homeland in a Western image, some through liberal constitutional reforms, others by a socialist transformation. It is, however, the latter who are best remembered, for they were driven to revolutionary extremes, and eventual success.

Then there was the Russia of Lev Nikolaevich Tolstoy, the internationally acclaimed author of *War and Peace, Anna Karenina*, and other works. Just as Tchaikovsky's music stirred hearts, so did Tolstoy's graceful yet monumental literary imagination move countless people to seek a better world. Like other social critics, he spoke for the wretched peasantry and denounced the injustices of the autocracy and nobility. But unlike them, he also condemned Western democracy for moral debasement of the individual and the proliferation of war and imperialism, that, he insisted, would sever the individual from his own human nature. He also warned against any change by violent means. Tolstoy feared that Russia would be ripped apart and then refashioned into something foreign, something quite monstrous. His fear was certainly prescient.

In Tolstoy's spiritual search for purified souls and society, the political economy of the American social critic and reformer Henry George held a prominent place. This sage of an exhausted, demoralized Old World appointed himself the spokesman for the energetic, confident New World beyond the Atlantic. At first sceptical of George's philosophy as a practical solution to the Russian peasants' suffering and land maldistribution, Tolstoy came to perceive it as a means to higher morality, and as a transitional stage to a perfected world. Sharing with the noted American reformer a simple faith on devout ethical foundations, a passion for justice, and a horror of poverty and exploitation, Tolstoy was fascinated with George's single tax.

> George's radical program of land reform first inspired the "hermit of Yasnaya Polyana" to come out in the open in defense of any kind of legislation and law, since he always had spoken, both in fiction and other publications, with disgust, bitterness, and mocking contempt of legal or constitutional thinkers, as well as reformers and judges. For decades he had fanatically condemned law for distorting morals; however, Henry George conquered the soul and heart of Leo Tolstoy, as a conscience-stricken landlord worried about the fate of the Russian peasantry.[2]

It must have seemed a godsend. George's philosophy welded together with simplicity the diverse components of Tolstoy's anarchism, promising at once an end to economic and moral suffering and a diminution of government, revering land as the sustainer of life, a divine gift to be used in common by the community—not as a private possession. During the 1880s and 1890s Tolstoy, often viewed as an impractical theorist, turned to George for a reasoned economic basis for a transition to his perfected future.

It is common for historians secluded in their study to draw parallels between ideas, movements, and people in different regions or across time. The similarities between George and Tolstoy are striking, the more so because they differed greatly in culture.

George was a product of a vibrant and growing country flexing her muscles in all directions, unbounded by preconceived notions, exalting individuality. Only a few dissenters doubted the beneficence of material progress. Men sweating in factories over the flying of sparks and cities expanding over the land embodied this growth. Advances in technology were to bring a better life through a judicious capitalism and, at times, political reform. A child of his environment, George respected material expansion as an expression of the human mind and ingenuity. It was the land that formed the bricks for the factories, gave the iron transformed into the steel of intricate machinery. He understood it as land not violated but refashioned into something wondrous by God's greatest creation, man. Insisting that land and nature must be common property, he would insure private ownership of whatever represents the laborer's effort, taxing for the public good the value of land on which that effort is expended. Just economic conditions would elevate morality. The individual as individual acquiring riches, but working harmoniously in an ethical free market society (without monopolies), would coexist with a government shorn of the military and police, carrying out purely administrative functions.

In Tolstoy's Russia the peasant majority had suffered for eons, and patterns of life had frozen amidst the endless progression of seasons. The struggle to eke out a living had made for communal arrangements pulling labor and lives together. Tolstoy's world view was conditioned by circumstances in his homeland. On the one hand was the poverty of the peasant, politically and socially oppressed, hungering for land to survive upon. On the other was the industrialization, drawing masses to unhealthy cities to work in factories, and the lure of amenities that Tolstoy perceived as corrupting to the simple spirit of the rural people. The technology that for George meant the rejuvenation and flourishing of human energy, purpose, and creativity Tolstoy abhorred for its violence to the land and its patterns of life. Only a return to an ethical agricultural life, he insisted, would solve his country's ills. The individual working in unison and sharing his bounties communally with others was his hope. The commune would be the foundation of a perfected world unfettered by property and any government or power whatsoever. George's single tax upon land values and making the bounties of the land common property, was to be the transitional means to a better society, but the main power of change must come with a conscious effort of every person to strive for perfection through an inner spiritual transformation. Tolstoy asked of people just to turn around a bit—just one single step: he knew that the simplest thing to do in the world is the hardest and most imperative.

Both George and Tolstoy looked to a progressive awakening of social consciousness even in a world torn by seemingly ungovernable changes. Both revered nature and the land as God's gift, the source of life, the object of work, and source of everything. Poverty was not a product of God but of man himself especially in the monopolization of land. Each was convinced that all values are spiritual and that inner harmony depends on a correct relationship with them. An optimistic picture of the future with a compassion for people—especially for the laborer or farmer—is apparent in both their writings.

Neither would categorize himself as utopian in the search for a better life. Each believed that the system he sought was not a product of human invention but an articulation of innate and divinely-inspired natural laws. For neither did the materialistic dialectic of socialism hold any appeal but would only foster animosities. Both George and Tolstoy were pacifists, even denying the efficacy of strikes, and relying on a comprehensive reform of society.

Each had undergone a mystical transformation and in his heart of hearts was convinced, maybe more so than most, that he was right. Although they were condemned by mainstream thought as too radical, both men were devoutly religious, preferring to creeds and churches a personal relationship to God. Each in his role as a harbinger of a new era attracted fervent disciples. Colonies were even founded by members of both groups.[3]

The Roman Catholic Church harassed numerous Georgists and had excommunicated Father Edward McGlynn, and even the Papal *Rerum Novarum* of 1891 was aimed at the single tax movement.[4] George replied to Rome with an eloquent essay. Observing the continuance of poverty and degradation, he asks the Vatican, "Is it any wonder that the masses of men are losing faith?"

> Now what is the prayer of Christendom—the universal prayer; the prayer that goes up daily and hourly wherever the name of Christ is honored; that ascends from your Holiness at the high altar of St. Peter's, and that is repeated by the youngest child that the poorest Christian mothers has taught to lisp a request to her Father in Heaven? It is, "Give us this day our daily bread!"

Yet where this prayer goes up, daily and hourly, men lack bread. Is it not the business of religion to say why? If it cannot do so, shall not scoffers mock its ministers as Elias mocked the prophets of Baal, saying "Cry with a louder voice, for he is a god; and perhaps he is talking, or is in an inn, or on a journey, or perhaps he is asleep, and must be awaked!" What answer can those ministers give? Either there is no God, or he is asleep, or else he does give men their daily bread, and it is in some way intercepted.

Here is the answer, the only true answer: if men lack bread it is not that God has not done his part in providing it. If men willing to labor are cursed with poverty, it is not that the storehouse that God owes men has failed; the daily supply he has promised for the daily wants of his children is not here in abundance. It is, that impiously violating the benevolent intentions of their Creator, men have made the land private property, and thus given into the exclusive ownership of the few the provision that a bountiful Father has made for all.

Any other answer than that, no matter how it may be shrouded in the mere forms of religion, is practically an atheistical answer.[5]

George had to contend with the Holy See; for Tolstoy it was the Holy Synod. The Imperial Russian state and the Orthodox religion, which had been refashioned into a subservient department of the government, hounded the Tolstoyans more doggedly into exile, prison, or the military. Tolstoy was left untouched, for officials did not desire a martyr. When in 1901 excommunication of the beloved heretical teacher did transpire, protests abounded and he became even more popular.[6] To this bureaucratic body, Tolstoy responded with an indignation and cry for fraternal justice and love the American would have approved, if he had lived a few years more.

. . . I believe in God, whom I understand as Spirit, as love, as the Source of all. I believe that He is in me and I in Him. I believe that the will of God is most clearly and intelligibly expressed in the teaching of the man Jesus, whom to consider as God and pray to, I esteem the greatest blasphemy. I believe that man's true welfare lies in fulfilling God's will, and His will is that men should love one another and should consequently do to others as they wish others to do to them—of which it is said in the Gospels that in this is the law and the prophets. I believe therefore that the meaning of the life of every man is to be found only in increasing the love that is in him; that this increase of love leads man, even in this life, to ever greater and greater blessedness, and after death gives him the more blessedness the more love he has, and helps more than anything else toward the establishment of the Kingdom of God on earth: that is, to the establishment of an order of life in which the discord, deception, and violence that now rule will be replaced by free accord, by truth, and by the brotherly love of one for another.[7]

Tolstoy was probably the last man assigned the role as the world's moral conscience. Not only was his literary stature supreme, but, whatever misgivings there were about his shortcomings (especially by those contemporary elements who desire to recast history for their own purposes), he served as inspiration for countless people from all corners of the globe. He is still available to whoever wants a reconstruction of society on a moral basis. His call for social and economic justice based on a deep reverence of God the Father and on Georgist political economy speaks strongly to the imagination as to the conscience. His cry against land and industrial slavery continues along with forces for depersonalization. Tinderbox economic conditions, compounded by a greater dependence on the state as source of justice; formicary-like lives driven by machines, electricity, and greed; loss of personal responsibility, along with spurious group identifications, exacerbated by a crushing of education and perversion of knowledge; a sleeping but callous consciousness with a distortion of morality: such would have been Tolstoy's appraisal of the present, and he would have dismissed as palliatives all reform, that do not lead to a full ethical resurrection. Tolstoy's fear of replacing moral and spiritual progress by technology made him a tortured Prometheus, trying to grab back his premature gift to children playing with fire. A rereading of these lesser known Tolstoyan works, which are for the most part ignored in the West, can only arouse our deadened minds and pettiness to a saner life, a higher calling, and an inward transformation. The Romanov Empire is long buried and the Bolshevik workers' state no longer exists, but as long as man has a heart, a soul, and a mind Tolstoy will endure not just as an artist, but as a social reformer and moral thinker.

After his psychological crisis in 1878-1879, all Tolstoy's writings became more oriented to religion. Then George's thought brought him to see that spirituality might express itself in a practical economics. A primary mandate of this work is to preserve Tolstoy's economic treatises in one volume. Pertinent selections from such easily available books have not been included, although I have discussed *Resurrection* in chapter two.

Such translators as Aylmer and Louise Maude, Leo Weiner, and Vladimir Chertkov have bequeathed to us a rare treasure trove of Tolstoy's works. Their endless hours of painstaking labor merit great respect. But their efforts came between 1900 and 1930, and since then the English language and its readership have changed. I have modernized spelling, reworked, at times, too literal a rendition, and deleted without ellipses repetitious wording and phrases which Tolstoy used to drive home a particular point in his moralizing. Here are two examples. The first contains minor changes; the second required a bit more retooling. Leo Weiner has accurately translated from *The Only Means* this paragraph:

Does not the same happen with the working people? The working people are worn out, crushed, turned into slaves and they ruin their own lives and those of their brothers only for the sake of insignificant advantage. The working people complain of the landowners, the government, the manufacturers, and the army.

I have slightly recast it as:

Does not the same happen with the working people? They are worn out, crushed, turned into slaves and they ruin their own lives and those of their brothers only for the sake of insignificant advantage. They complain of the landowners, the government, the manufacturers, and the army.

In *To the Working People* Weiner has also correctly rendered Tolstoy's Russian into English as:

The working men have tried, each one separately, to free themselves by supporting the illegality of the ownership of land, which they themselves condemn, and if the condition of a few, and that, too, not always and but for a brief time, is improved by such a participation in an evil thing, the condition of all only gets worse from it. This is due to the fact that what permanently improves the condition of men (not of one man, but of a society of men) is the activity which is in conformity with the rule that we should do unto others as we wish that others should do unto us. But all three means which so far have been employed by the working men have not been in conformity with the rule about doing unto others as we wish that others should do unto us.

I have opted for this variant:

Working men have tried to free themselves individually by supporting illegitimate landownership which they themselves have condemned. If the condition of a few is improved for a brief time by participating in this evil their lot will only get worse. What permanently improves the condition of men (not of one man but of the society of men) is an activity which is in conformity with the rule that we should do unto others as we wish that others should do unto us. None of the three means which they have employed so far have been in conformity with it.

As Maude has pointed out, sometimes Tolstoy himself was a bit too hasty to get material to press.[8] His choice of words could be misleading. For instance, though he considered the ownership of land a sin he used the words "owner" or "ownership" favorably when he meant that the "owner" is only a trustee, obliged to use the land wisely under divine authority. I have not rendered as "guardianship" or "tenureship" the Russian for "ownership" [*vladenie*]. My goal in my reediting (which I have compared with the original Russian) was to preserve the construction and development of thought, the nuance and meaning and impact of Tolstoy's ideas as these appear in the works of the previous translators. Some of them, including Aylmer Maude and Vladimir Chertkov, were close friends and associates of Tolstoy. Their particular translations have been duly acknowledged. Those works that I have myself translated are not indicated in the footnotes. I must, of course, shoulder the burden for any mistakes in the reedited pieces as well as in these. My transliterations are based on the Library of Congress system without the ligatures.

On September 16, 1891 Tolstoy renounced all rights to his works produced and translated after 1881. Whenever possible the publishers of current reprints were contacted for permission to use particular translated works even though they have been in the public domain for some time.

My treatment of Russian history employs not the Gregorian but the Julian calendar. For the nineteenth century the Julian calendar lags twelve days behind the Gregorian and for the twentieth century, it is thirteen days. The Bolsheviks did not replace it until February 1/14, 1918. For any material written in the West dates are in the Gregorian reckoning. Russian names traditionally rendered in English, such as Tolstoy in contrast to Tolstoi, or Tchaikovsky in contrast to Chaikovskii, will here hold to their customary Anglicized spelling.[9]

This anthology owes a great debt not only to the earlier translators but to my friends and colleagues, whose moral and professional support has given me the courage to work. To the Robert Schalkenbach Foundation for their financial support of my work on the Trilogy. At the Henry George Foundation of America: Dr. Steven Cord, Joshua Vincent, and Sharon Feinman. Gratitude must also be extended to this organization for financial support. At the Henry George School of Social Sciences: George Collins and Simon Winters. At George Mason University: Dr. Leo Hecht. At McKeldin Library (University of Maryland, College Park): Lily Griner, Patricia Heron, the inter-library loan staff for their help, and the staff of the Maryland Room for their guardianship of Tolstoy's ninety-one volume collected works.[10] Dr. William Pencak, Lindy Davies, John Blanpied, and Victor Zabolotny must also be thanked for their help. For my knowledge of Russian history and belief in myself I am indebted to Dr. Clifford Foust and Dr. George Majeska of the University of Maryland. Without Dr. Donald Hitchcock, also of the University of Maryland, who patiently guided me through the Russian language, the translations would have been unthinkable. The professional editorial touches of my friend Dr. Thomas West of the Catholic University of America have helped made this book come alive. Without the love and vigilance of my stalwart companions Oliver, Raisonique, and Clio, surviving the *mal hiver* and the long hours would have been impossible.

Notes

1. For nineteenth-century Russians,"intelligentsia" referred to a self-conscious group of concerned thinkers who desired to effect some form of social and political change (some of whom espoused revolutionary ideas). Sir Isaiah Berlin observes that the "concept of intelligentsia must not be confused with the notion of intellectuals. Its members thought of themselves as united by something more than mere interest in ideas; they conceived themselves as being a dedicated order, almost a secular priesthood, devoted to the spreading of a specific attitude to life, something like a gospel" *Russian Thinkers* (New York: Penguin Books,1986), 117. For more details see the essay in Berlin's book entitled "Birth of the Russian Intelligentsia" (Ibid., 114-135).

2. Max M. Laserson, *The American Impact on Russia: Diplomatic and Ideological, 1784-1917* (New York: The Macmillan Co., 1950), 281. See page 106, note no.7 for more details explaining Tolstoy's acceptance of a state on a transitional basis.

3. Arthur N. Young, *The Single Tax Movement in the United States* (Princeton: Princeton University Press, 1916), 250-256 and Ernest J. Simmons, *Leo Tolstoy: The Years of Maturity*, vol. 2 (New York: Vintage Books, 1960), 99-100.

4. See George R. Geiger, *The Philosophy of Henry George* (New York: The Macmillan Co., 1933), 336 -380; Charles A. Barker, *Henry George* (New York: Oxford University Press, 1955), 485-493 and 571-577; Stephen Bell, *Rebel, Priest, and Prophet: A Biography of Dr. Edward McGlynn* (New York: Robert Schalkenbach Foundation, 1968); and Pope Leo XIII, "Encyclical Letter of Pope Leo XIII," in *The Land Question* (New York: Robert Schalkenbach Foundation, 1982), 107-151.

5. Henry George, "Condition of Labor," in *The Land Question*, 100-101.

6. Simmons, *Leo Tolstoy*, 303-309.

7. Ernest J. Simmons, *Introduction to Tolstoy's Writings* (Chicago: University of Chicago Press, 1968), 111. See Lev N. Tolstoy, *Otvet na opredelenie sinoda ot 20-22 fevraliia i na poluchennye mnoiu po etomu sluchaiu pis'ma* [Response to the decision of the synod of February 20-22 and on the receipt of the letter by me on this occasion], *PSS*, 34: 245-253. The quotation is on 251-252. Translation by Simmons.

8. Aylmer Maude, *Tolstoy and His Problems* (New York: Funk & Wagnalls Co., 1911), 62.

9. The last name of the Populist Chaikovskii will be spelled differently than the composer's. The spelling for Tsar Nicholas II will be retained, but for his cousin, Nikolai will appear.

10. The extent of Tolstoy's writing is an amazing feat, for he lived in age before modern electronic methods. The last volume is an index.

Abbreviations
used in notes

CWCT   Leo Weiner, trans., *The Complete Works of Count Tolstoy* (J. M. Dent and Sons, Ltd., 1905; reprint, New York: AMS Press, 1968).

GR   General Research Division of the New York Public Library; Astor, Lenox, and Tilden Foundation.

HGP   Henry George Papers, Rare Books and Manuscript Division of The New York Public Library; Astor, Lenox, and Tilden Foundation.

HGS   Henry George School of Social Sciences, New York.

PSS   Lev Nikolaevich Tolstoy, *Polnoe sobranie sochinenii* (Complete works) (Moscow: Gosudarstvennoe izdatel'stvo khudozhestvennoi literatury, 1928–1964).

PSSL   Vladimir Ilyich Lenin, *Polnoe sobranie sochinenii* (Complete works) (Moscow: Gosudarstvennoe izdatel'stvo politicheskoi literatury, 1958-1965).

PSSC   Nikolai Gavrilovich Chernyshevskii, *Polnoe sobranie sochinenii v pyatnadtsati tomakh* (Complete works in fifteen volumes) (Moscow: Gosudarstvennoe izdatel'stvo khudozhestvennoi literatury, 1939-1953).

SB   Slavic and Baltic Division of the New York Public Library; Astor, Lenox, and Tilden Foundations.

SSH   Alexander Ivanovich Herzen, *Sobranie sochinenii v tridsati tomakh* (Complete works in thirteen volumes) (Moscow: Akademiia nauk SSSR, 1954-1964).

PART ONE—
INTRODUCTION

Lev Nikolaevich Tolstoy—"Russia's Great Single Taxer."
(Photo taken from the *National Single Taxer*, vol. 8, no. 7,
New York, July 1899; courtesy of the Henry George School of Social
Sciences, New York.)

Chapter 1

An Introductory Essay: Tolstoy's Russia

Modern Russian history can be traced from the reign of Peter the Great (1682-1725). This tsar had replaced the hallowed ideals of Byzantium with new models from Europe. The innovations that he forced on the country created a chasm between the refashioned aristocrats and the masses of the "dark people," maintaining the old pious ways. Russia in the eighteenth century was two distinct worlds, the service aristocracy and the peasantry. The gentry carried on a distorted version of European life, were uninterested in their homeland and resentful of it, virtually foreigners in thought. Catherine II (1762-1796) freed them from state service obligations. By the end of the eighteenth century, a growing minority of them took to enlightened European ideas. The members of the thinking gentry were isolated from the government and intellectually alienated from the peasantry even on their own estates. Some of the nobility did became aware of the harsh reality of serfdom, which further increased their rootlessness and distress.

It had been the persistent belief of the "dark people" of Russia, living in not much better than abject slavery, that while their bodies belonged to the nobility or the state, the land was theirs. "We are yours, but the land is ours" was a common phrase. But no mechanism existed to enforce peasant rights. Serfdom was the most noticeable feature of a backward and autocratic Russia incapable of competing with western Europe before the Emancipation of 1861.[1] The injustices of state policies and a heartless bureaucracy incensed the conscience of an intelligentsia sprung into life by the imported mentality of the Enlightenment. An autocratic regime allowed no room for legal political organization. Some turned to romantic or radical visions of recreating the world. A new type of individual was being created, the intellectual basis for the transformation of Russia.

The French Revolution and the Napoleonic wars in Europe exposed the lack of cohesiveness in the Empire. In the beginning of the nineteenth century, according to Lev Nikolaievich Tolstoy in *War and Peace*, millions "rush around from one side of Europe to another, plunder, slaughter one another, celebrate and despair, and the whole course of life is transformed and displays an intensifying motion. . . ."[2] Russia was a victor and for decades she would enjoy a heightened prestige. The aristocratic guards,some of whom became known as the Decembrists, personally exposed to Western Europe, noted the discrepancies between other countries and their homeland. Especially when it seemed that Alexander I (1801-1825) was prepared to remold Russia, reformist concepts and societies multiplied. They desired to end serfdom and introduce a liberal constitution.

In 1825, during what history has called the Decembrist revolt, the aspirations of the reformers were destroyed in the streets of St. Petersburg by Nicholas I (1825-1855), the new tsar. The executions that followed, Alexander I. Herzen, was to write, "finally provoked the childish dream of my soul."[3] The first martyrs in the history of Russian radical thought were to serve well into the twentieth century as examples of selfless devotion to the revolutionary cause. Peter A. Kropotkin like many other radicals was an avid reader of Herzen's journalistic salvos in the *Northern Star* [*Polarnaia zvezda*], awestruck whenever he gazed at its masthead with the busts of the five executed Decembrists.[4]

Tsar Nicholas I had believed that his throne and Russian society were endangered by any idea from the West that had to do with change. The "gendarme of Europe" endeavored to shut in Russia behind her first iron curtain. This metal was annealed further after the revolutionary outbursts of 1830. Censorship tightened against action and thought. The reign of Nicholas I was marked, especially during his latter years, by severe repressions. The Bible itself became subject to government scrutiny.[5]

But even the omnipresent administrative apparatus of Nicholas was not enough. Russia had been exposed to Western ideas for about a century. The works of the German Idealists and Romantics, then a recast phenomenon, were having a pronounced influence on the intelligentsia. In the phrase coined by P. V. Annenkov, "the extraordinary decade" of the 1840s was coming to birth.

In all-night philosophical discussions over Hegel, Schelling, Fichte, Saint-Simon, and other European philosophers, educated Russians explored the terms of a just society. Peter I. Chaadaev's pronouncement that the Russians have been placed" as if outside of time, [and] have not been touched by the universal education [truths and traditions] of the human race"[6] expressed the convictions of the intelligentsia at war within itself. This conflict in the early 1840s would become especially heated. The Westerners looked to Europe for Russia's inspiration. They regarded Peter the Great as a harbinger of Russia's new path of modernization enabling her to compete with the West. The Slavophiles looked to the period before his reign as a "golden age" and revered her past before the introduction of secularized and decadent Western innovations by this tsar. Both parties, however, worked from the assumption that Russia, although endowed with a special mission and spirit, was profoundly ill.

The writings of the Slavophiles, such as I. V. Kireevskii, K. S. Aksakov, and A. S. Khomiakov, present for the first time the role of Russia's special destiny couched in modern terms. These aristocrats revived the Third Rome Theory, which held that after the fall of the two world empires, Rome and Byzantium, the temporal authority and true spirituality of the universal empire [*imperii translatio*] would be transferred to Russia.[7] This Muscovite theory drew upon the newly arisen romantic patriotism called forth by the Napoleonic Wars. The subsequent Nicolaevan repression transmogrified this concept into something quite different. Now the Russian people, rather than the state, had the special destiny. Strengthened by their suffering, they were to carry messianic religious truth and redemption to all mankind. Khomiakov wrote:

> Within thy bosom, Russia mine,
> There is a bright and gentle spring
> Which pours out living waters, thine;
> Hidden, unknown, a mighty thing.[8]

The Slavophile views of the peasant and the commune [*obshchina*] were to have portentous consequences for the different elements of the intelligentsia, including critics and revolutionaries far to the left of its adherents. They were the first group of thinkers in Russia to engender a genuine love for their homeland.

The Slavophiles had wanted to make of Russian society a mystical communality based in the village commune and sustained by a devout peasantry. These ideas filtered into the consciousness of the radical intelligentsia, and found expression in Russian Populism (*narodnichestvo*).[9] The Narodniki too celebrated the peasant commune, but identified its cooperative ethos with that of Western radicalism. Bakunin and Herzen and their left-wing radical heirs, such as Nikolai G. Chernyshevskii, brought the parlor talk of the Westernizers into practical agitation. French utopianism contributed to the vision of a cooperative society and German Idealism to the sense of Russia as the unfolding of a single idea, the progressive realization of Russianness.[10] Many members of the intelligentsia—at first the nobility in the late eighteenth and the early nineteenth century, and later the *raznochintsy*—were a part of this growing movement.[11]

Among the most important radicals was Michael A. Bakunin. He craved nothing less then a radical transformation of reality. Bakunin was the first

Russian whose utopianism was uncompromisingly revolutionary. An early exponent of anarchism, he brought to it a conviction that society requires destruction. This vision of total change, along with his philosophical materialism, contributed to the thought of subsequent radicals, including the Narodniki and later the Marxists, bearing fruit in the Revolution of 1917.

Bakunin is honored as a founding father of narodnichestvo.[12] Of the different permutations of Populism, it has been suggested that only Bakuninism fully articulated its idealization of the peasantry. Bakunin hated political authority and called for a peasant social revolution, or *pugachevshchina*. He denounced faith in savants and scientists proclaiming a panacea for society's ills: their rule would be "a monstrosity."[13] Declaring that life must be lived in concordance with ideas, Bakunin made of philosophy a yardstick of reality, moral judgment, and psychological introspection.[14] Radicals, then, cannot merely romanticize the peasants; they must live like them.[15] Bakunin initiated a totally new approach to life in Russian Populism by bringing the realm of abstract ideas down to earth.

Another major contributor to Russian radical thought was Alexander I. Herzen. His writings were standard fare for the Narodniki. Establishing a free Russian press outside the Empire, he was the first journalist to denounce persistently the cruelty of the Russian autocracy. His broadsides against injustice made him a bridge between the older generation who had warred over issues in the salons and the younger impatient one, depicted in Turgenev's novel *Fathers and Sons* (1862).[16] Like the Slavophiles on the right and his fellow champions of uncoerced community on the left, he exalted the suffering Russian masses and their ancestors. Herzen's optimistic nascent anarcho-communism was the forerunner of much that was to characterize the Russian Populist radical movement. In the pages of *The Bell* [*Kolokol*], Herzen sounded the tocsin to the youth of Russia and declared that

> from all corners of our vast motherland . . . a groan is growing, a murmur is arising—this is the initial roar of an ocean wave . . . pregnant with storms. . . . Into the people! to the people—here is your place, banished ones of science . . . from which will issue forth from you not *scribblers* . . . but warriors of the Russian people![17]

Herzen's call for remaking Russia on the basis of a virtuous and liberated people influenced several generations of youth.

With the failure of the Crimean War and the freeing of the serfs under the new Tsar Alexander II (1855-1881), Herzen's fervent optimism resonated through much of liberal and radical Russia. The tsar's famous rationale was that "it would be better to reform from above than have it come from below." But his decision awakened hope of further change. The Emancipation of 1861 failed to provide justice and protect the peasants' use of the land.[18] They were provided with only meager land allotments scattered in strips, sometimes at great distances apart, for they were divided according to soil quality. These plots were redistributed every few years, and that contributed to the inefficiency of an archaic agriculture using techniques without enough work animals. Crops from the Russian land lagged behind Western yields, and drought and famine were not uncommon. The nobility retained the best land. The peasants endured periodically unjust communal control mandated by the state, which in effect became the new serf master, and they were weighed down with burdensome redemption payments based on inflated prices into which was figured the loss of wages to the nobles. Taxes on commodities even exceeded that of direct taxation. Arrears mounted close to 119 million rubles and exceeded the yearly amount of assessments by the end of the century. Insolvency was widespread, and despite an increase of available lands—much of it rented out by nobles creating social and economic dependence—life was worsened by a growing birth rate: the population increased from from fifty to about eighty million in 1900. When the Empire increasingly became part of the world market, grain prices fell. Peasants forced to earn wages through cottage industry or flight to the cities had to endure the caprices of the factory system and depressions. Disenchantment grew over the decades.[19] Subsequent political and social reforms that did not bring the peasantry true freedom frustrated the radicals.

One leading radical was Nikolai G. Chernyshevskii, who could be considered a Populist leaning to anarchism. He was among a number of intellectuals who could not tolerate the vacillations of the exiled salon radicals out of touch with their homeland or cautioning temperance. Revolution was the only answer. Chernyshevskii, like other Narodniki, wanted to found society on the village communes; these native institutions he would ultimately federate into autonomous groupings. But he did not believe that the commune was indigenous solely to Russia, and his works contain no idolization nor mystification of the masses. He rejected the concept of Russia's messianic mission and special path that even portions of the left shared with the Slavophile right, and he fused Western empiricism with the Russian social conscience, insisting that scientific knowledge was to be studied not *in vitro*, but to serve the revolution and the commune.

Chernyshevskii's most famous work, *What Is To Be Done?* (1863), profoundly influenced Russian revolutionaries.[20] The young lawyer Vladimir I. Ulyanov, known to history as Lenin, stirred to the pronouncement that it was up to "the pick of the best . . . the movers of the movers . . . the salt of the salt of the earth" to effect great changes.[21] Many a youth emulated the relationships of the fictional Vera P. Rozalskaia and her two husbands, Dmitrii S. Lopukhov and Alexander M. Kirsanov. Lenin's marriage to Nadezhda

Krupskaia was esteemed for its high revolutionary principles. Cherny-shevskii's characters belong to egalitarian cooperative associations and abstain from antiquated and superfluous "bourgeois activities."

Chernyshevskii's trumped-up sentence, subsequent martyrdom in prison, and banned writings brought him virtual canonization in his own lifetime. There were a number of attempts to free this proclaimed social conscience from prison. Chernyshevskii's selflessness inspired the first public revolutionary demonstration in Russia. A disciple named Ishutin exclaimed: "'There have been three great men in the world . . . Jesus Christ, Paul the Apostle, and Chernyshevsky.'"[22] Karl Marx referred to Chernyshevskii as "the great Russian scholar and critic"[23] and wanted to learn Russian in order to read his works. Marx thought that the commune could possibly be the means by which Russia, unlike more advanced countries, could skip the capitalist phase and establish communism.[24]

In the 1860's the radical intelligentsia was poring over Cherny-shevsksii's *What Is To Be Done?*, inspired by his martyrdom, aroused by Herzen's summons to action, burning with Bakunin's revolutionary ardor. Numbers of Populist organizations sprang up. Among them was Mark A. Natanson's circle, established in 1869 in the capital.

Natanson, in the description offered by the revolutionary Vera N. Figner, was a man of "indefatigable energy, who possessed an unusual ability to attract people, to organize and to rally them for work, a man of wide-ranging enterprise, one who had a plan for large-scale all-Russian activity."[25] Distinguished by erudition, he organized self-education and propaganda activities. Natanson was the real founder of the circle that is named after a prominent member, Nikolai V. Chaikovskii.[26] His primary concern was to establish a link between the people and the intellgentsia: to create a real people's party. The Chaikovskii circle would be remembered as the avant-garde of the 1870's and deemed later by one radical as "the flower of the youth of those times." Many members were recruited from universities and other schools. "Their historical importance," writes Franco Venturi, "lies in the fact that they wanted to live in complete accordance with the idea of a duty to the people."[27] They set for their own lives standards of moral severity that accorded with the simple and virtuous future they imagined, thereby establishing a practical basis of Narodnichestvo. Aiming to evoke the revolutionary potential of the peasantry, they were also the first group of intellectuals to establish ties with urban workers. Through Natanson's influence "forbidden books" were disseminated and other circles were started in many cities. He was also in contact with revolutionaries abroad. The Third Section of the Imperial Chancery, a forerunner of subsequent tsarist as well as Soviet secret police, considered him a "most dangerous man."

Many Populists, however, ignored the idealistic but cautious policies

Natanson counselled. The propagandistic methods he had espoused went beyond his intentions. The members of the circles resolved to become one with the masses and bring the bounty of a perfect world to the peasant's impoverished hearths. In 1874 this determination resulted in the event known as "going to the people."[28] The peasants were not ready for a utopia that eager idealists of the more privileged classes pictured to them; most of the Narodniki had to flee or were turned over to the authorities.

After return from exile in 1875 Natanson was once more instrumental in the formation of a group, which eventually became known as Land and Liberty [*Zemlia i volia*]. The Narodniki split in 1879 after Natanson was again arrested in 1877. One group, Black Repartition [*Chernii peredel*], maintained faith in propaganda. But the exasperating failure of "Going to the People" encouraged terrorism and violent revolution. The People's Will [*Narodnaia volia*], the other spin-off from Land and Liberty, espoused violence, and rather than work with the masses, the People's Will would be their instrument. Discarding Natanson's caution, it carried out numerous attacks, even targeting the imperial family. Reprisals by the government escalated, initiating a major reactionary drift in official circles. Terrorist attacks culminated in the assassination of Alexander II in 1881.

The ideas of narodnichestvo were now in disrepute among many of its former adherents and sympathizers. The repression by the government, which forced many radicals into exile or hiding, apparently turned meaningless the amorphous methods and ideology of Populism. Some of the remaining radicals, such as Georgii V. Plekhanov and Pavel B. Akselrod, turned to Marxism. Marx's writings had been a part of the "forbidden books" since 1869, but other than his critique of capitalism and his stress on economic factors they had not greatly influenced the Narodniki. Now the metamorphosis was to be effected by the proletariat, not the peasantry. Marxism, which seemed to the recent converts a verifiable logical progression in thought, could serve as a basis for action, and above all gave new meaning to their lives. Their adoption of Marxism altered the course of Russian history.

Count Witte, the minister of finance,[29] spearheaded rapid industrialization, railroad construction, and growth of capital fueled by large foreign loans. But though advances in industrial indices and production of various commodities and goods were impressive, Russia was still far behind her Western counterparts. The Marxists saw the nation's industrial development as validating the master's prediction.[30] If they had been more sensitive they would have realized that the Russian proletariat in the cities still maintained a bumpkin consciousness to a certain degree. To quantify this connection is hard to determine but figures are telling, for the city worker kept up close ties with their roots: eighteen percent returned to work in their villages, fifty-two percent channeled money back, and about seventy per cent still held onto their allotment lands. By the turn of the century the proletariat had grown to seven percent of the population.

The government's concern for the welfare of the men, women, and children who toiled for endless hours in the factories was minimal. Unions and strikes were not legal but work stoppages mounted. Despite a rise in wages over time, near starvation was widespread, abetted by the rising cost of necessities. Conditions in the workplace were unsanitary and hazardous and life in regimented factory barracks was appalling. As industry grew increasingly more subject to a variable world market and periodic depressions, the misery of proletarian lives was exacerbated.

Alexander III (1881-1894), the son of the assassinated tsar, made no pretense of liberalism.[31] The manifesto issued in April 1881 reaffirmed the principle of absolute autocracy. Four months later, the "Regulations on Measures for the Defense of the Governmental Order and of Public Safety" were promulgated. Initially a temporary decree designed to strengthen the powers of the state, it was to remain in force until 1917. Local and regional administrative initiative was curtailed, university rights were stripped, the franchise for municipal and village assemblies was narrowed, and censorship became more vigilant. The authorities were given broader powers including searches, fines, arrests, and exile. A state of siege by the government against all radical and liberal notions set in. Also among victims were minorities, particularly the Jews.

Holy Russia was not hospitable to Jews. Especially since the partitions of Poland in the late eighteenth century, Jews became the victims of official harassment. They were restricted to a ghetto life within the Pale of Settlement and subject to stringent laws, forced assimilation, discrimination in jobs and schooling and religious persecution by the general populace. Living in the secluded *shtetlekh*, they served the authorities as an object of obloquy for the release of social tensions.[32] The reign of Nicholas I inaugurated the first organized attempt to reshape the Jews. Children might be torn from their homes, forcibly conscripted into the army, marched across Russia, or even killed when resisting conversion. Herzen's description of these pitiful children is famous.[33]

The first twenty years of Alexander II's reign, when some restrictions were relaxed, were a time of respite, primarily for the Jewish middle and upper classes. Despite their continued plight, most Jews were loyal to the tsar. Many began to think of themselves more as Russians than as Jews. The prospect of pogroms, however, especially after the assassination of Alexander II in 1881, brought fear into the shtetlekh, of which hundreds dotted the Pale.[34] It was generally believed in government circles that radicalism was primarily the work of Jews and that the murder of the tsar was a

Semitic plot. Upon the accession of Alexander III in 1881, Russification, nationalism, and intolerance increased.

Many officials ignored the violence of the pogroms and allowed the circulation of bogus imperial proclamations sanctioning these activities. The purported suggestion of Konstantine P. Pobedonostsev, the Over-Procurator of the Holy Synod, that one-third of the Jews should be forced to emigrate, another third to embrace Christianity, and the remainder to die of starvation, caught the spirit of the repression.[35] The "Temporary Administrative Measures" of 1882, also known as the May Laws, increased restrictions. Other legislation followed over the years. Most Jews who had resided outside the Pale had to return. A tightening of restrictions on employment and education fostered a renewed religious ardor and a slowing of the assimilation process, which wealthier Jews had favored. Visions of equality faded from the thinking of the Jews.

At least one-third of the Jews emigrated.[36] Some had been radicalized from years of persecution or the breaking up of the family structure under the duress of poverty. On the whole the Jew who lived a secluded and traditional life was less apt to succumb to the appeal of revolution. Lacking legal parties, the Pale in face of persecution became open to left-wing ideologies. A small number, including Natanson, became Narodniks. Those who did, felt estranged from Jewish culture and, despite the prevalence of anti-Semitism within the peasantry, identified instead with the Russian people. Later on many more Jews turned to Marxism and anarchism. Most Jews, however, resented the Jewish rebels. Many Jews held prominent places in the radical movement and they also carried these ideas to the ghettos of London and the United States. Many of the terrorists, explains Philip Pomper, were Jews whom pent-up frustration drove to "suicidal extremism."[37]

In the reign of Nicholas II (1894-1918), the last of the Romanovs, the policy of inviolate "Orthodoxy, Autocracy, and Nationality" continued unabated. The pogroms became, according to one historian, "wholesale massacres."[38] Other nationalities and religious groups were also subject to this legalized brutality.

Since the heyday in the eighteenth century aristocratic life had been suffering from an increasing impoverishment. Many an illustrious family could claim only its name and title. They affected foreign styles (especially that of the French), spent more than what came in, were easily swayed by trends, and in general subject to a self-imposed inertia called *oblomovshchina* (from the main character of Ivan Goncharov's book *Oblomov*, 1859), and a refusal to adapt to new methods and ways, The Emancipation actually hastened the process of dessication. Despite efforts of the state to shore up the intemperance of its main support, by 1905 a third of the lands of the patrician classes had been sold and another third mortgaged to pay an alarming increase in insolvency and debt. Some progressive nobles did manage to adopt to the times.

The autocracy remained untouched. The Tsar-Liberator failed, like his two successors, to reconcile autocracy with modernity. In theory the Russian emperor was the most powerful monarch on the globe. In practice he was limited by his functionaries. The bureaucracy was inept, unimaginative, torpid, and corrupt. Selfless examples, among them Lenin's father, of service to the people and loyalty to the crown were in the minority. Many protocols, orders, and their execution got lost in the myriads of tiny offices, both on the imperial level and within the provinces. To the bureaucracy, the plight of the peasant meant little. Despite attempts at reform, the military too was crumbling from within. On the surface, however, command by members of the nobility gave it an Old World patina of panache.

The literature of Pushkin, Turgenev, Dostoevsky, Tolstoy and others provided a contribution to Russian society. Another came from the thousands of selfless individuals working in the *zemstvos*—the teachers, the veterinarians, the physicians, and the agricultural specialists who labored daily for the betterment of the peasant. Created in 1864, the zemstvos were local bodies of administration, and despite lack of funds and official curtailment of powers and scope, roads were built, swamps were drained, literacy increased, and health improved. Among these tireless energetic people, frustration at the ineptitude of the bureaucracy and the intransigence of the autocracy grew, breeding ideas of a liberal change.

This then was the late nineteenth-century Russia of Tolstoy—a backward land with a decaying nobility and a reactionary and insensitive government that stifled freedoms, repressed minorities, meanwhile sporadically and unsuccessfully trying by artificial industrialization to catch up with the West. Alcohol was the single most remunerative source of revenue for this tottering giant. The muffled beginnings of *pugachevshchina* (an outbreak of mass peasant riots) were just becoming audible. The intelligentsia was at spiritual war with the state while Tolstoy constituted virtually a third party, determined to save Russia from hatred, injustice, and the imminent chaos with a solution consonant with her history and people.[39]

Notes

1. See pages 6-7.
2. Tolstoy, *Voina i mir* [War and peace], *PSS*, 11: 266.
3. Alexander I. Herzen, *Byloe i dumy* [My past and thoughts], *SSH*, 8: 61. Five Decembrists were hanged and many others were exiled to Siberia. Their influence on subsequent radicals was enormous.

4. Peter A. Kropotkin, *Zapiski revoliutsionera* [Notes of a revolutionary] (Moscow: Izdatel'stvo "Mysl'," 1966), 143. Kropotkin (1842-1921) was a noted anarcho-communist theoretician whom Tolstoy admired to a certain extent. He advocated mutual aid and for the most part eschewed violent means to achieve a just society.

5. The first decree on censorship goes back to 1720 but it was the "Pig Iron Code" of 1826 during Nicholas I's reign that caused major problems for writers of all persuasions, especially the radicals, who did not agree with "Orthodoxy, Autocracy, and Nationality." Many authors, to conceal social and political criticism, became known for "Aesopian language," i.e., the use of various words, allusions, phrases, etc. to cover up their real intent.

6. M. Gershenzon, ed., *P. Ia. Chaadaev: Filosoficheskie pis'ma i apologiia sumashedshego* [P. I. Chaadaev: Philosophical letters and apology of a madman] (Moscow, 1913; reprint, Ann Arbor: Ardis, 1978), 9. This quotation is from P. Ia. Chaadaev's first letter in a series of eight "Letters on the Philosophy of History."

7. The Third Rome theory was first propounded in 1510 in a letter by Philotheus, an abbot from Pskov, to Tsar Basil III.

8. A. S. Khomiakov (no source given); quoted in Nicolas Berdyaev, *The Russian Idea* (New York: The Macmillan Co., 1948), 47.

9. This age-long aspiration resurfaced in the form of the soviets during the revolutions of 1905 and 1917. See page 34.

10. There are many fine books on the influence of European thought on the intelligentsia. For a primary source, see P. V. Annenkov's *The Extraordinary Decade: Literary Memoirs*, trans. Irwin R. Titunik (Ann Arbor: The University of Michigan Press), 1968. For secondary sources, the reader could begin with Franco Venturi, *Roots of Revolution: A History of the Populist and Socialist Movements in Nineteenth Century Russia*, trans. Francis Haskell (New York: Grosset & Dunlap, 1961) and Martin Malia, *Alexander Herzen and the Birth of Russian Socialism* (New York: Grosset & Dunlap, 1965).

11. Raznochintsy can be translated as "those of various ranks," or of an origin other than both the peasantry and the upper classes. They brought into the radical movement a more impetuous and materialistic outlook.

12. Transplanting Russian Populism to Western Europe, Bakunin (1814-1876) created the international anarchist movement

13. Michael A. Bakunin, "L'Empire knouto-Germanique et la révolution sociale" [The knouto-Germanic Empire and the social revolution], *Œuvres* [Works], ed. P.-V. Stock, vol. 3 (Paris: Tresse et Stock, 1895-1913), 51-52.

14. Ibid., 365.

15. Ibid., 194.

16. The wavering relations between Herzen, as representative of the "older" generation, and the "children" of the sixties have been amply illustrated elsewhere. At times, he supported tsarist reform. That did not suit the more impetuous younger radicals.

17. Herzen, "Ispolin prosypaetsia!" [The giant is awakening!], *SSH*, 15: 175.

18. The Emancipation of 1861 was the most important reform during the 1860s. Tsar Alexander II wanted to create a more favorable political, social, and

economic status for the peasants that would forestall revolutionary activity. This particular reform concerned itself with the distribution of the land to the former serfs. Historians have been debating its effectiveness and its contribution to revolution. There are many works on the Emancipation, its causes, implementation, and influence. Consult, for instance, Jerome Blum, *Lord and Peasant in Russia: From the Ninth to the Nineteenth Century* (Princeton: Princeton University Press, 1972), 536-620; Geroid T. Robinson, *Rural Russia Under the Old Regime: A History of the Landlord-Peasant World and a Prologue to the Peasant Revolution of 1917* (Berkeley: University of California Press, 1969); and an article by Terence Emmons, "The Peasant and the Emancipation," in *The Peasant in Nineteenth Century Russia*, ed. Wayne Vucinich (Stanford: Stanford University Press, 1968), 41-71.

19. This paragraph is a generalization. There were regional variations and differences between the status of the former state serfs and those owned by the nobles.

20. Nikolai G. Chernyshevskii, *Chto delat'?: Iz rasskazov o novykh liudiakh* [What is to be done?: Tales about new people], *PSSC*, 11: 327. For an explanation of this important book and its implications, see Francis B. Randall, *N. G. Chernyshevskii* (New York: Twayne Publishers, 1967), 104-130.

21. Chernyshevskii, "Chto delat'?" [What is to be done?], *PSSC*, 11: 210. For information pertaining to the influence of this book on Lenin, consult Derek Offord, *The Russian Revolutionary Movement in the 1880's* (Cambridge: Cambridge University Press, 1986), 149-152 and 155. *What Is To Be Done?* was written nine years before the first translations of Marx's writings—and Soviet scholars considered Chernyshevskii the first authentic native communist.

22. Ishutin, (no source given); quoted in Venturi, *Roots of Revolution*, 331.

23. Karl Marx, *Capital: A Critical Analysis of Capitalist Production*, vol. 1 (Moscow: Foreign Languages Publishing House, 1961), 15.

24. According to one Soviet writer, Chernyshevskii among others, philosophically advanced Russia "in the direction of Marxism" (M. Grigoryan, *N. G. Chernyshevsky's World Outlook* [Moscow: Foreign Languages Publishing House, 1954], 30).

25. Vera N. Figner, "Mark Andreevich Natanson," *Katorga i ssylka* [Hard labor and exile] 56 (1929): 141 and 142. Revolutionaries, including Lenin mourned Natanson's death in 1919. Venturi claims that Natanson symbolized the revolutionary of the times" more clearly than anyone" (Venturi, *Roots of Revolution*, 472).

26. According to one Soviet historian: "Having been assigned . . . in literature the name of the circle [Chaikovskii]—is an historical injustice. Chaikovskii never was the founder of it, nor the leader. . . . Several times Soviet historians made the attempt to [rename it] . . . but many years of tradition have won the upper hand" (V. N. Ginev, ed., *Revoliutsionery 1870-kh godov: vospominaniia uchastnikov narodnicheskogo dvizheniia v Peterburge* [Revolutionaries of the 1870s: remembrances of the participants of the narodnik movement in St. Petersburg] [Moscow: Lenizdat, 1986], 16). Kornilova-Moroz, a participant, adds great support to this statement, observing that at the end of 1870 [when Chaikovskii belonged to the Natanson circle]: "we knew nothing and had not yet talked about such a Chaikovskii circle" (A. I. Kornilova-Moroz, "Perovskaia i osnovanie

kruzhka chaikovtsev" [Perovskaia and the foundation of the Chaikovskii circle], *Katorga i ssylka* [Hard labor and exile] 22 [1926], 22).

27. Venturi. *Roots of Revolution*, 472.

28. According to one historian, "going to the people," was primarily a hopeless "children's crusade." A few thousand enthusiastic and starry-eyed students went into the poor countryside to convert the peasants to agrarian socialism and free them from the yoke of autocracy. Most of the students were rejected by the wary peasants and arrested (Daniel R. Brower, *Training the Nihilists: Education and Radicalism in Tsarist Russia* [Ithaca: Cornell University Press, 1975], 29-30). Brower claims that the idealization of the peasantry was more a "search for virtue" [than] "a study of actual conditions" (Ibid., 170). One Soviet historian asserts that the failure of "going to the people" was an important step in the passage from utopian socialism to scientific Marxism. The Narodniki, he writes, began to think that the realization of anarchism in its entirety in the near future was impossible, and they became more practical (I. K. Pantin, *Sotsialisticheskaia mysl' v Rossii: perekhod ot utopii k nauke* [Socialist thought in Russia: the transition from utopia to science] [Moscow: Izdatel'stvo politicheskoi literatury, 1973]: 269-270).

29. Sergei I. Witte (1849-1915) was minister of finance and then prime minister. He was instrumental in securing foreign loans and fostering railway expansion and industrialization. He negotiated a peace treaty with Japan (1905) and advocated the granting of a constitution and the Duma.

30. Marx thought that Russia, unlike the more advanced West, could skip the capitalist phase and achieve socialism because of the commune.

31. It was love for man that moved Tolstoy to write to Alexander III, asking for clemency, in the name of Jesus, for the assassins of the Tsar's father. K. P. Pobedonostsev, the Over-Procurator of the Holy Synod (the presiding official from 1880-1905), responded: "My Christ stands for strength and truth; He heals the weak; yours is a weakling who himself needs healing" (No source given; quoted in Adam Ulam, *In the Name of the People: Prophets and Conspirators in Prerevolutionary Russia* [New York: The Viking Press, 1977], 367). Pobedonostsev was also tutor to Alexander III. See his *Reflections of a Russian Statesman* (Ann Arbor: The University of Michigan Press, 1968). The Holy Synod was established in 1721 by Peter I to replace the Patriarchate. It was the highest governing body overseeing the Russian Orthodox Church, which in effect, became part of the state bureaucracy. Its existence ended in 1917.

32. *Shtetlekh*, a Yiddish word, is plural of *shtetl*. Shtetlekh were poor villages in eastern Europe prior to World War II. Consult Leo Rosten, *Hooray for Yiddish: A Book About English* (New York: Simon & Schuster, 1982), 308-310.

33. Herzen, *Byloe* [My past], *SSH*, 8: 232-233. William J. Fishman on page 6 in *Jewish Radicals: From Stetl to London Ghetto* (New York: Random House, 1974) writes: "In the many attempts at genocide prior to the holocaust, none were so manifestly depraved as this exercise in the moral and physical destruction of Jewish children."

34. Pogrom is Russian for massacre. A strict definition is an organized massacre for the extirpation of any people or class. The word appeared in English in 1881.

It was first exclusively applied to the Jews by English newspapers in 1905 (*The Compact Edition of the Oxford English Dictionary* [New York: Oxford University Press, 1971], s.v. "pogrom"). There had been countless organized pogroms in Europe for centuries, but the modern pogrom began in 1881. This new version was an outburst of popular violence, sometimes spontaneous and sometimes fueled by the tsarist government against the Jews. Plunder, burnings, torture, rape, and murder were its methods, whether in Russia or elsewhere.

35. This quotation has not been substantiated but it does reflect Pobedonostev's thinking. In a letter to Dostoevsky, dated August 14, 1879, Pobedonostsev writes: "Yids . . . have undermined everything. . . . They are at the root of the revolutionary socialist movement and of regicide . . . they have in their hands the financial markets, the people as a whole fall into financial slavery to them. . . ." (Quoted in Robert F. Byrnes, *Pobedonostev: His Life and Thought* [Bloomington: Indiana University Press, 1968], 205).

36. Between 1851 and 1914, 2,018,300 Jews migrated from Eastern Europe to the United States. Seventy-seven percent of them were from the Russian Empire (1,557,100). These figures can be found in Shaul Stampfer, "East European Migration to the United States," in *Migrations Across Time and Nations: Population Mobility in Historical Context*, eds. Ira A. Glazer and Luigi De Rosa (New York: Holmes & Meier, 1956), 228.

37. Philip Pomper, *The Russian Revolutionary Intelligentsia* (Arlington Heights, Ill: Harlan Davidson, 1970), 175.

38. Louis Greenberg, *The Jews in Russia: The Struggle for Emancipation*, vol. 2 (NewHaven: Yale U. Press, 1965), 47-54.

39. The following additional books and articles have been used in this essay. For complete citiations consult the bibliography. O. Aptekman, "Dve dorogie teni;" P. Avrich, *Russian Anarchists;* I. Berlin, *Russian Thinkers;* J. Billington, *Icon and the Axe;* V. Broido, *Apostles Into Terrorists;* D. Brower, *Training the Nihilists;* F. Copleston, *Philosophy in Russia;* S. Dubnow, *Jews in Russia and Poland* and *History of the Jews*, vol. 5; N. Dzhakupova, "Memuary kak istochnik dlia izucheniia revoliutsionerov-razochintsev;" R. Fillippov, "K otsenke programmnykh osnov 'Zemli i voli';" H. Frederic, *New Exodus;* N. Georgieva, "Sovetskaia istoriografiia studencheskogo dvizheniia v Rossii;" A. Gleason, *Young Russia;* H. Heilbronner, "Pale of Settlement;" I. Howe, *World of Our Fathers;* B. Itenberg, *Dvizhenie revoliutsionnogo narodnichestva* and "P. L. Lavrov i revoliutsionnoe podpol'e Rossii;" R. Johnson, "Mark Andreevich Natanson;" N. Laktionova, "Nekotorye osobennosti narodnicheskogo dvizheniia;" E. Lampert, *Sons Against Fathers;* N. Levin, *While Messiah Tarried;* G. Majeska, "Byzantine Influence on Russia;" J. Maynard, *Russia in Flux;* D. Offord, *Russian Revolutionary Movement;* P. Pascal, *Religion of the Russian People;* N. Pereira, *Thought and Teachings of N. G. Chernyshevskij;* M. Raeff, *Origins of the Russian Intelligentsia;* Z. Ralli, "Mikhail Aleksandrovich Bakunin;" O. Saiki, "Iz istorii 'Molodoi' partii narodnoi voli;" C. Timberlake, "Alexander II;" H. Tobias, "Bund;" D. Tschizewskij, *Russian Intellectual History;* R. Warth, "Nicholas II;" W. Weidle, *Russia: Absent and Present;* A. Yarmolinsky, *Road to Revolution;* and V. Zenkovsky, *History of Russian Philosophy.*

Chapter 2

The Influence of Henry George on Tolstoy

Ever since Tolstoy's young adulthood, a sensibility toward man's relation to nature and a distaste for the artificialities of urban society had grown in him.[1] *The Cossacks*, published in 1863, is his romanticized vision of a purer society amidst the Caucasus inhabited by mountaineers, people living in unison with nature who struggle against the incursions of an alien and artificial aristocratic society. Tolstoy, like other conscience-stricken members of the intelligentsia, was concerned with the exploited peasantry. Even prior to the 1861 Emancipation Tolstoy was preoccupied with the peasants on his estates. In *A Landlord's Morning*, issued in 1856, we meet for the first time the autobiographical Prince Nekhludov.[2] This *barin* has left the university to devote himself to bettering the peasants' lot. Tolstoy's plans for land reform failed. He established, however, a school for peasants where his progressive methods and writings were a success. To facilitate a fair land distribution provided by the Emancipation's provisions and to smooth relations between nobility and peasantry, Tolstoy served in the official capacity of "arbiter of peace." His fellow nobles were chagrined that Tolstoy at times sided with the peasantry; frustrated, he resigned.

Between 1863 and 1869 Tolstoy published *War and Peace*. Pierre Bezukhov's painful search for the meaning of existence can be seen as Tolstoy's own agonizing quest for the good. The peasant Platon Karatayev is the "unfathomable, rounded, eternal personification of the spirit of simplicity and truth."[3] The novel says that it is such common people, working in unison, who move history, not the emperors and other leaders; and that higher knowledge comes not from books, but from living plainly in harmony with nature, as a divine beneficence. Tolstoy's second most famous work, *Anna Karenina*, published in 1878, is more somber than *War and Peace*. Tragedy and psychological turmoil reflect Tolstoy's own growing doubts. Levin, like Bezukhov, eschews the superficialities of society and seeks a grander purpose in the harvest and the simple life of the peasant.

During a profound spiritual crisis in 1879 Tolstoy became depressed almost to the point of suicide. He adopted manual labor so as not to exploit others and became a vegetarian. His religious vision had become sensitized and shifted, although not so precipitously as many have believed, for most of the elements of his later philosophizing are present in his early writings. Morality and religion in the service of humanity became indistinguishable. In his *Confession* of 1880, he writes that the secret of existence is not to be found in

> the life of the parasites, but the life of the simple working people, the one that gives life . . . its meaning [is that] every man has come into this world by the will of God, and . . . every man can ruin or save his soul. The problem of man's life—is to save his soul according to God's word . . . he must renounce all the pleasures of life, must labor, be humble, endure. . . . The [Russian] people derives . . . its entire faith [from this] meaning [which is] close to my heart.[4]

Tolstoy was plagued by the separation between reason and faith, science and the masses. But it was the childlike faith of the people in their closeness to the soil that won his trust. The rationality of the savants is empty: innocent faith unlocks the mysteries and laws of life. In the pristine uncorrupted countryside, turning over the fresh earth, far from urban influences, technical progress, and institutional authority, there is goodness and peace, and the possibility of universal communal love and the renewal of spiritual and moral values.[5] For this idyllic vision Tolstoy's own Russia served as the model. In his view, the Russian peasant had a holy mission to be the foundation of a future utopia. This concept then became Tolstoy's *idée fixe*.

Fraternal amity, Tolstoy believed, can be achieved through an uncoerced individual moral transformation. Within each person dwells an infinite moral and a finite physical force. But a "terrible brake" resists these forces, "the love of self or rather the memory of self which produces powerlessness." The need is to "tear oneself away from this brake . . . [to] obtain omnipotence. . . . The best salvation from memory of self, the most conformable with the life common to all mankind, is salvation through love for others."[6] The "world is a huge temple in which light falls in the center. All people who love light strive towards it. . . . Unity is attained only . . . when [the searcher] seeks not unity, but the truth. . . . Seek the truth and you will find unity."[7] Unity will arrive with a spiritual revolution of the heart that reaches out from the self to humanity, all living creatures, the universe, and God.[8] If everyone "will believe in the spirit [that is] within him, then all will be joined together. Everyone will be himself, and everyone will be united."[9] Individual consciousness in a constant drive for self-perfection will become the basis of community.

Tolstoy looked to love as an earthly means of overcoming selfishness and the fear of death.[10] The renunciation of desire and of self, their replacement with love and self-perfection will create a transitional state between an earthly paradise and a spiritual eternity. Tolstoy believed that these basic truths embodied in his faith underlay all religions, but he thought Jesus' formulation of them to be the most cogent.[11] Tolstoy presents Jesus' teachings as a rational presentation of truths for liberation and a practical life. In essence, through his reinterpretation of the Gospels, especially the Sermon on the Mount, he concludes in *What I Believe* (1884) that the ultimate goal through love and nonresistance in the face of evil is to unite man with God the Father.[12] The individual must "open . . . what closed the source of living water—*the divine life, which is in us.*"[13] God is life in the here and now and the individual must not only never place his needs above his neighbor but must work for the good of all. To this end, Jesus' teachings were distilled into five commandments: avoid anger, do not commit adultery, eschew oaths, do not defend yourself by violence, and do not go to war. Following these desiderata should serve as basis for a transformation of the world for a just political ordering and an equitable economic system.

This new world must not be restrained by any human institutions, laws, or coercion. "[E]very faith praises itself as the one [true faith], but . . . all of them crawl around like blind puppies. . . ."[14] Counterproductive to the enhancement of happiness and progress of man, they were endemic in the use of force. "[O]f all the godless ideas and words there is no idea and word more godless, than that of a church." Tolstoy writes, "there is no idea, which has produced more evil, there is no idea more hostile to Christ's teaching, than the idea of a church."[15] The "sanctification of state authority by Christianity is blasphemy, it is the ruination of Christianity."[16] The foundation of governmental authority is physical violence, whether the ruler is an elected president or Genghis Khan.[17] States are like "a gang of thieves" and incompatible with God's commandments.[18] Tolstoy, in his pronouncement of an ethic of uncompromised love, was perhaps more than any other anarchist an opponent of chauvinism and all particularistic emotions that contribute to it and to mental slavery.[19] Thomas Masaryk, Czechoslovak President and scholar, writes in 1919 of Tolstoy's envisioning a "society to be the city of God in the strictest sense of the word. He means all men to be united in an invisible church. His failure to find perfection in society and himself led him to the conclusion that salvation is within you, and this amounts to little less than ethical and religious anarchism."[20]

Tolstoy as a concerned member of the aristocracy had access to the debates between the Slavophile and the Westerner that began in the 1840s and among the radicals later on, though he stood apart from them. In his own peculiar way as the decades progressed, many of the conflicting philosophical elements combined in his idealistic thinking with other streams of religious and metaphysical thought. After the Emancipation it was the Narodniki along with Marxists and other intellectuals who wrangled over those "cursed questions," often poring over foreign literature for answers to man's relationship to the universe and a just society. Radical economists and other writers staggered under the weight of dense and abstruse material in the "thick journals," which at times even passed the laxity of the imperial censors in this atmosphere of repression. Rebels avidly read, among many others, Proudhon, Marx, and Saint-Simon. The name Henry George was also familiar to the Russian intelligentsia as it grappled for a solution to the chronic and endemic poverty of the peasant. His ideas became the objects of a vigorous debate.[21]

The Russian Marxists assigned to the urban proletariat, even in predominately agrarian Russia, the central place in revolution. Marxists rejected any attempt to refashion society on an agricultural rather than an industrial basis.[22] Poorly received by the Marxists, George had among the Narodniki a generous reading. Their reverence for the Russian land and the people made them receptive to George's concept of the land as common property, redeemable from its monopolization by private ownership. Still, George, as a defender of capitalist and bourgeois property could obtain from the Populists at best an ambivalently friendly audience.

The eminent Marxist-turned-Populist economist M. I. Tugan-Baranovskii, in an article "Henry George and the Nationalization of Land" (1897), calls George's writings charming, enthusiastic, and eloquent. *Progress and Poverty* is the "first independent and original American response to the old problem which agitates the present-day civilized world—how to eliminate poverty and the raising of economic relations to the sphere of freedom, equality and brotherhood, which was proclaimed by the French Revolution as the basis of the modern social order."[23] But Tugan-Baranovskii dismisses as absurd the Georgist notion that land monopolization was the source of economic problems, or that since landowners were the real enemy labor and capital have to be natural allies. George's remedies such as rent confiscation deny class antagonisms and would favor the large industrialist. The essay labels George's ideal society a reformist "bourgeois utopia," inapplicable to Russia.[24]

A lengthy two-part article, "Relating to the Question of Poverty, Its Causes and Elimination (According to the Economic Theory of George)" by S. Iuzhakov, was published in *Notes of the Fatherland* in 1883. Iuzhakov finds in George both ill and good. A "basic failure" in George's arguments in his claim that land monopolization is the major factor in the lowering of wages and allowing the large landowners to appropriate everything for themselves.[25] His great merit lies in the active political interest he awakened in the United

States and England.[26] That same year *Russian Wealth* printed in Russian a lecture given by George. The editors praise George as a "rising star" whom "we consider not without value, although we do not share all his views."[27]

In the "Social Question (According to Henry George)," published two years later, M. M. Filippov critically examines George's political economy. He commends George for looking beyond mere illusory political freedoms: without economic freedom there is only "slavery to capital." George's great merit, as Filippov perceives it, lies in exposing a "sorrowful page within a sick foreign civilization." For the "worshippers" of the West in Russia are "charmed by the outer bright scenery which is infected with suffering, not seeing under its scintillating rags plague infestation and death spasms."[28] "V. V." in the *Northern Herald* in 1886 is more favorable. In "Henry George on Protectionism," he endorses George's belief in free trade, observing that tariffs and protectionism create monopolies, are counterproductive, and burden the working class.[29]

In 1892, L. Slonimskii's "Henry George and His Theory of Progress" appeared in the *Herald of Europe*, Slonimskii admires the eloquence and ingeniousness of George's arguments, but finds George optimistic in thinking that a landowner would voluntarily give up his holdings. He also questions George's reliance on a beneficent government serving society as a whole. "George wonderfully ascertains and analyzes the sickness, but the suggested means of cure would not even touch its essence."[30] In a piece in the *Northern Messenger* published the same year, Ivan Ianzhul discusses George's response to the Papal *Rerum Novarum* in "An Open Letter of Henry George to Pope Leo XIII." He considers George a "naive bourgeois" lacking in logic and theory and who purveys a "perfervid fantasy . . . [and] proposes a new Eden, a door to heaven."[31] The single tax would be class robbery and is incapable of providing proper funding for any government. Bad harvests would dot the land and economic crises would multiply. An article entitled "Henry George as Economist," by B. Efrusi, came out in *Russian Wealth* in 1898. Efrusi, here revealing one similarity between Marxists and Narodniki, rejects George's concept of harmony between capital and labor. The substitution of the single tax for all other taxes would slow down production, burden the poorer classes, ruin the small landowners, enrich the capitalists, and fail to provide adequate state funding. George's attempt "to solve the great problem of present society would end up as a complete failure."[32]

In his search for absolutes, a purer spirituality, and a solution to society's moral and economic problems, Tolstoy also scrutinized thinkers ranging over millenia and over the globe. The United States contributed: Tolstoy avidly read Henry David Thoreau, Walt Whitman, Edward Bellamy (the author of *Looking Backward, 2000-1887*, 1888), and the abolitionist William Lloyd Garrison. Henry George, however, most fired his imagination.

The first indication that Tolstoy knew George's work is in a letter of February 20, 1885, to his wife Sophia Andreyevna. While suffering from the flu in Moscow, he declares that he preferred reading George to doing his own writing.[33] Another letter to her on the 22nd reports:

> I read my George [*Progress and Poverty*]. Tell Sasha [A. M. Kuzminskii] that if he has time, he must read it through. It is an important book. This step is an important one on the road towards the common good, as the freeing of the peasant and liberation from private property in land. The views in this book present a theme which is an affirmation of people. It is necessary to read George, who has clearly and definitely presented this problem. It is impossible to equivocate after reading this. It places one either on one side or the other—my demands go much farther than his, but this step is one on the first rung of the ladder that I am climbing.[34]

Another letter of the same day informs Vladimir G. Chertkov, a close associate, that reading George had made Tolstoy "wiser."[35] The next day, having finished reading *Progress and Poverty*, Tolstoy thought it important that George's works be translated and he wanted to write to the American.

George's political economy became a lively topic of discussion.[36] On the 24th, Tolstoy wrote again to Chertkov:

> I was sick for a week but consumed by George's latest [*Social Problems*] and the first book *Progress and Poverty*, which produced a strong and joyous impression on me. When you have the time you must read it through . . . This book is wonderful, but it is beyond value, for it destroys all the cobwebs of Spencer-Mill political economy—it is like the pounding of water and acutely summons people to a moral consciousness of the cause and even defines the cause. There is weakness in it, as with anything created by man, but there is a genuine humanitarian thought and heart, not scientific trash. I would like to learn his address and write a letter. I see in him a brother, one of those who according to the teachings of the Books of the Apostles [have more] love [for people] than for his own soul.[37]

Still consumed by *Progress and Poverty* Tolstoy in a letter of February 26 advises Prince L. D. Urusov, an avid disciple, to read it. George is "a marvelous writer—a writer who will usher in an epoch."[38]

Tolstoy initially held certain misgivings about a government's applying George's tax project, and at times they would haunt him. *What Then Must We Do?* (1886), which grapples with the problem of poverty, warns that the state is coercive: "as long as there will be violence maintained by the bayonet, there will be no distribution of wealth among the people, and all the riches will go to the oppressors."[39] "As a striking illustration of this assertion," Tolstoy observes,

> Henry George's project . . . will serve. George proposes to recognize all the land as the property of the state, and therefore to substitute the land rent for all taxes . . . anyone who utilizes the land would have to pay to the state the value of its rent. What would be the result? . . . [L]and would belong to the state . . . there would be slavery. . . .
>
> After a bad harvest, the farmer's rent would be exacted from him by force because he could not pay it . . . and to maintain his land, he would have to enslave himself to the person with money. . . .
>
> As long as there is an armed man with the recognized right to kill another man, there will be an inequitable distribution of wealth, that is, slavery.[40]

Since Tolstoy was an international celebrity, his name was more than familiar to the American reading public. Henry George himself, in the pages of his weekly single tax newspaper, *The Standard*, acquainted his readership with the great Russian novelist. On March 26, 1887, George published an English translation of Tolstoy's short story *Ivan the Fool*, depicting a kingdom of love, honest toil, and nonresistance where "all the sensible [people had] departed" and "only fools remained. And no one had any money. They lived and labored and fed themselves and all good people."[41] The next year on January 28, an article entitled "Charity and Justice" graced the first page of *The Standard*. In the course of his pleas for social justice including a condemnation of welfare as inimical to the development of individual integrity, George cites the "eloquent words" of *What Then Must We Do?*[42] An item in *The Standard* for December 15, 1888 quotes W. T. Stead of the *Pall Mall Gazette* of London. Stead reports that Tolstoy was mesmerized with George's vision of a program of land nationalization imbued with spirituality. Tolstoy had explained to Stead that the peasants with whom he talked received George's ideas warmly. Tolstoy favored expropriation of the land without compensation and still preferred communalization to nationalization, which implied state authority.[43] "Of course, I do not hold with George about the taxation of the land. If you could get angels from heaven to administer the taxes from the land you might do justice and prevent mischief. I am against all taxation."[44] Yet despite these misgivings, Tolstoy thought that George "has indicated the . . . next step that must be taken. His ideas will spread—nay, they are spreading."[45] Rarely had the novelist been so taken by another person's thinking.

Meanwhile, in 1889 Tolstoy published the play *Fruits of Enlightenment*. This farce, which pokes fun at the nobility, depicts the gulf between them and the poor land-hungry peasantry. Four years later Tolstoy's *The*

Kingdom of God Is Within You appeared, his most important statement on nonviolence, passive resistance to evil, and the ill of war-mongering institutions. Tolstoy looks forward to the day of a spiritually perfected society.[46] *The Kingdom of God* condemns the inequity of land possession, especially by the few, for bringing starvation to the masses. The individual must renounce this crime, serve the Lord, and establish a union with all beings.[47] In the period following his psychological crisis, then, echoes of George's thought became even more manifest in Tolstoy's artistic and didactic writings.

At the beginning of the 1890s Tolstoy experienced much stress. Family disputes over his rejection of property and copyrights to his works, tsarist persecution of his followers, censorship, and an intense personal involvement with relief for a famine which was raging over Russia dispirited him greatly. During the early 1890s Tolstoy also reconsidered his hesitations about George. Early in 1894, the Berliner Bernhard Eulenstein, an ardent land reformer and devotee of George, reporting to "To our beloved Prophet, My dear Mr. George," asked of him: "Count Tolstoy—by the way—did you ever correspond with him? He is our man. He has been reading *Progress and Poverty* to his peasants."[48] Tolstoy felt a profound spiritual kinship, deepened by a further deliberation of George's works through his involvement in the translation of an article by George entitled "Equal Rights and General Rights."[49] There is no evidence of why Tolstoy's views shifted, but it probably was the famine with its great hardships and the inadequacy of society's response, along with his continuing search for a practical means of social and economic amelioration, that was transforming him into a wholehearted supporter of George. Writing *The Kingdom of God* no doubt intensified his response to the massive suffering of famine-stricken Russia. George's simple piety, which was similar in tone to Tolstoy's anarchist spirituality, also attracted him. This passage from George's "The Condition of Labor: An Open Letter to Pope Leo XIII," could have come from Tolstoy:

> Is it not clear that the division of men into classes rich and poor has invariably its origin in force and fraud; invariably involves violation of the moral law; and is really a division into those who get the profits of robbery and those who are robbed; those who hold in exclusive possession what God made for all, and those who are deprived of his bounty? Did not Christ in all his utterances and parables show that the gross difference between rich and poor is opposed to God's law?[50]

Now Tolstoy did not reject the single tax and its implementation as an intrusive governmental coercion. He could see it, like man's inward transformation and mutual love, as a way station to a perfected world—a brotherhood of love under the aegis of a living Father.[51] *Progress and Poverty* also insists that the functions of government will be greatly simplified and purified. And who shall measure the heights to which our civilzation may soar? . . . It is the Golden Age of which poets have sung and high-raised seers have told in metaphor! It is the glorious vision which has always haunted man with gleams of fitful splendor. . . . It is the culmination of Christianity—the City of God on earth . . . It is the reign of the Prince of Peace![52]

An entry of June 14 in Tolstoy's diary reports that he has just written "an exposition of . . . George's project."[53] Upon rereading George's *Perplexed Philosopher* soon afterwards, he exclaimed to a visitor: "How wonderful. I again became vividly aware of the sin of land possession. It's amazing how [people] do not see it. It would be necessary to write about this—to write a new *Uncle Tom's Cabin*."[54] V. F. Lazurskii, a tutor at Tolstoy's estate, Yasnaya Polyana, reports a conversation in which Tolstoy was in low spirits but quickly perked up at a discussion of his favorite theme, George's plan of land nationalizaton. "The possession of land as such," Tolstoy observes,

is illegitimate, like the possession of serfs. Whoever controls the source of food has also enthralled the poor. For me, it is now so obvious. . . . But how long will it take for this idea to enter into the general consciousness! I have lived twenty years [since the Emancipation of 1861] without realizing this. And here is Henry George, who for thirty years has clearly and simply explained everything.[55]

During this summer one of Tolstoy's daughters, Tatiana, became enraptured with Georgist philosophy. Moved by the poverty of the peasants on her estate, Ovsyannikovo, she took her father's advice to charge them a nominal rent for the land. The money was to go into a general fund for communal needs. Tolstoy gave a speech to the peasants explaining these arrangements.[56] All went well for a while. After a few years, however, the peasants stopped all payments and even engaged in land speculation.[57] This failure did not damper Tatiana's or Tolstoy's ardent belief in George.

In September, 1894, Tolstoy wrote this letter to Mrs. MacGahan thanking her for bringing him some of George's books. The Russian considers George's writings to be masterpieces and the golden key to a better world. Tolstoy likens George's mission to that of Moses, striving for the betterment of his people without seeing the "Promised Land."

I have a request for you, Varvara Nikolaevna: Convey my best thanks to Henry George for the feelings that prompted him to send me his books, as well as for the books themselves. I value very highly [both his sentiments and his works]. Some of those books—*The Perplexed Philosopher*—(an excellent book)—I hope to get its translation through the censor's office), *The Land Question,* and *Free Trade* were unknown to me before. I read these, and as I always do with Henry George's books, felt great admiration at the lucidity, brilliance, the masterly exposition and their conclusiveness, as well as a feeling of indignation against such people who do not understand his preachings or pass them over in silence. His ideas are formulated with such clearness and persuasiveness, that every man who sets out to reflect on these questions cannot help accepting his project as soon as he would understand it. And yet, although nearly a score of years has elapsed since he has come forward, nowhere have his ideas been put to a practical test—and that notwithstanding the fact that there are about seventy papers advocating Henry George's doctrines. I always felt greatly impressed at the Biblical account as to how Moses never saw the Promised Land to which he led his people. Not that it would be necessarily unavoidable for a man not to see the fruit of his labors, but that men— the best of men—work at the most important task in this world, not only without any expectation of any reward for it, but even without any hope of seeing the fulfillment of that to which they have devoted their life.

Henry George belongs to these people. He was the first to set a strong foundation for the building of the economic organization of the age to come, and mankind will forever remember his name with gratitude and respect. But will it be given to him to witness the fruits of his labors? I never despair. It seems to me that one must work so as to be ready to put one's ideas into effect. Were it even on the morrow, yet one must not lose heart were that delayed for another century.

Henry George has composed a multiplication table which is clear, undisputable, and comprehensible to anyone. . . . Now let the practical workers do their work. One thing is undoubted: that people who would make calculations cannot do so without having recourse to the multiplication table, are like those who would set to organize the social conditions of human life on more just conditions and will be unable to avoid having recourse to the projects of Henry George and would have to take it for their foundation. Tell him that I value him very highly and that I love him.[58]

In the early fall Tolstoy was assisting Chertkov in a presentation of the work ethic of T. M. Bondarev, a peasant sectarian writer, that people should labor for themselves without taking advantage of others: an idea akin to George's. "I am so pleased," Tolstoy says, "that your present work brings you joy for it [contains] a profound truth with the highest significance."[59] Tolstoy wrote to Ernest Crosby, an American disciple, on November 24,

> Henry George has sent me all his books. I know some of them, but some others, as the *Perplexed Philosopher* and others were new to

me. The more I know of him, the more I esteem him, and am astonished at the indifference of the civilized world to his work.

If the new Tsar [Nicholas II] would ask me what I would advise
him to do, I would say to him: use your autocratic power to abolish the
land property in Russia and to introduce the single tax system; and
then give up your power and [grant] the people a liberal constitution.

I write this to you, because I know that you are one of the co-
workers of H. George, and that you . . . [believe in] his ideas.

I wish you success in your work.[60]

In the meantime, Eulenstein was making arrangements for George
and Tolstoy to meet in Berlin in 1896 for an international land reform conference. At the beginning of 1896 Eulenstein wrote to George, "It seems to
be allmost [sic] certain, that Count Tolstoy will also give us the honor of his
presence."[61] Prior commitments during an election forced George to decline.[62] In a letter dated March 15 he expresses his delight that Tolstoy
sympathizes with his views and says that he wishes to see his Russian ad-
mirer on a later visit to Europe.[63] Tolstoy enthusiastically responded in
English:

> The reception of your letter gave me a great joy, for it is a long
> time that I know you and love you. Though the paths we go by are
> different, I do not think that we differ in the foundation of our thoughts.
>
> I was very glad to see you mention twice in your letter the life to
> come.
>
> There is nothing that widens so much the horizon, that gives
> such firm support or such a clear view of things as the consciousness
> that although it is but in this life that we have the possibility and the
> duty to act, nevertheless this is not the whole of life but that bit of it
> only which is open to our understanding.
>
> I shall wait with great impatience for the appearance of your
> new book, which will contain the so much needed criticism of the or-
> thodox political economy.[64] The reading of every one of your books
> makes clear to me things which were not so [evident] before and con-
> firms me more and more in the truth and practicality of your system.
> Still more do I rejoice at the thought that I may possibly see you. . . .[65]

Tolstoy in a diary entry for June 8, 1896 claims that "The economic
progress of mankind will be accomplished by three means: the abolition of
private property in land, [the establishment of an] inheritance tax, . . . and a
tax on fortunes."[66] During the summer of 1896 Jane Addams visited Tolstoy.
A letter from William Lloyd Garrison, Jr. to Henry George reports that she
"spent a day with Tolstoi last summer who spoke warmly of you. Said he
should break through his habit of non-travelling, hating to journey in a box,

as he calls a railroad car, and go to Berlin to see you. He expected you might be there according to rumors of your intended European trip."[67]

Tolstoy, the most famous disciple of George, was never to meet his beloved teacher. On the morning of October 29, 1897 during the New York City mayoral campaign, in which he was a candidate, George collapsed and died.[68] His untimely death was a blow to Tolstoy. "Yesterday," he laments in a letter to his wife

> Seryozha [Tolstoy's brother] told me that Henry George had died. No matter how . . . this could be said, his death struck me like the death of a very close friend. . . . One feels the loss of a real comrade and friend.[69]

Two months later, in a letter to Ernest Crosby, Tolstoy was still expressing his grief in intimate terms.

> The death of George was a loss of a near friend to me. I hope that his ideas will spread more after his death. That those ideas are not generally acknowledged is always a puzzle to me.[70]

Following Tolstoy's spiritual crisis many people had come to regard him as a "crackpot anarchist" espousing odd ideas, such as vegetarianism, nonresistance, and a doctrine of love. The death of his friend Henry George spurred him on to renewed endeavors. Tolstoy became the world's most noteworthy exponent of the American's ideology, which integrated his previously scattered commitments. Armed with his universal moral and religious beliefs harmoniously and gently forged with Georgist philosophy, he became the conscious of the world. It was a monumental effort to ground justice in a rational economics and spread enlightenment for the benefit of suffering people.

To this end, Tolstoy was instrumental in establishing in 1884 a publishing house, *Posrednik* [Intermediary]. Its goal was to spread to all corners of the Empire wholesome literature, including folk tales and legends for moral uplift, social betterment, and the sharing of love. Tolstoy wrote a number of them, which sold for about a penny a piece. Despite harassment by the censors, twenty million copies were distributed in the first nine years. The establishment in Britain of the Free Age Press in 1898 by Tolstoy's friend and collaborator Vladimir Chertkov was part of this campaign.

This propaganda of the heart was an important component of Tolstoy's spirtual conversion. The role of the artist took on a mission in service to humanity. He rejected art for art's sake: works of creativity had to have a morally uplifting purpose.[71] Accepted canons were challenged. Literature and art were to be a medium for the truth, for opposition to violence, for the encouragement of self-perfection, and conducive to a better life. Folk literature took on a spiritual meaning and was elevated to the universal; so-phisticated works Tolstoy dismissed. His rejection of his own past writings as well as the other great writers and his renunciation of copyright laws to his works after 1881 were congruent with his new beliefs. He tells us in *What is Art?* (1897), which he struggled on for a decade and a half, that the artist's duty is to "infect" feelings of love for God and humanity, emotions of joy and pity: those that are common to all men. Literature must be written in the clearest way possible to unite all people.

In an unpublished conclusion to *What is Art?* Tolstoy writes that not only art but science must be subsumed to this higher calling. In Tolstoy's thinking science *(nauka)* is the study of everything. The concept "science" has a broader meaning in Europe and in Russia than in English usage. It refers to any field of knowledge that utilizes empirical inquiry or rational intuition, which can include history and philosophy. Tolstoy finds the work of scientists laudable when they sweep the heavens with telescopes or seek the mysteries of nature in the microscope but condemns them for being tools of the privileged classes and perpetuating evil, and for ignoring the more important social issues such as, to take two examples, the ending of warfare and prostitution. The great teachers, such as Socrates and Confucius, are irrelevant to their ideals of modernity, power, and money. The main goal of science should expose people to the laws of life which will "infect" them with goodness. These precepts must be transferred from the consciousness to feeling, for science is also art.[72] Tolstoy declares that real science, since it should concern itself with the advance of society and not with the defense of the existing order, should make as an object of study the land question, and expose the immorality of private property in land.

> Such a scientific work has been around for a while. [Although it has been challenged by all orthodox science which defends the existing order] for more than thirty years Henry George's *Progress and Poverty* . . . has been deemed unscientific and orthodox political economy indicates that his thinking in this work is wrong and that private property in land is legitimate and rational.[73]

George's works are therefore to be considered a perfect blend of art and science. By World War I, all of George's works had been translated into Russian and most of these works were published by Posrednik. This feat was primarily accomplished by an avid Georgist, Sergei D. Nikolaev, a close friend of Tolstoy.[74] Whenever Nikolaev visited Yasnaya Polyana a lively conversation regarding the agrarian question and the applicability of Georgist ideas to Russia was sure to take place, especially about taxing away the large landowners.[75]

The literary giant was also the consummate rebel and iconoclast. His

running broadsides against the injustices of society inside Russia and beyond reached their climax in *Resurrection* (1899), his third major novel. He
battled not for the conquest of power but for man's soul and a perfected
world. He blasted the sources of oppression—the church, the government,
the prison and exile system, the military, prominent individuals (such as
Konstatine P. Pobedonostsev, the Over-Procurator of the Holy Synod, who
was portrayed as Toporov) and the upper classes with their exploitation of
the poor.[76] But much of the ammunition of this gunnery master fell upon
private landowning for its injustice, cruelty, and new form of effective enslavement. The idea for *Resurrection* first came to him from a friend in 1887.
Prince Nekhlyudov (as Tolstoy) reappears as the repentant noble who eschews his peers for the salvation of people. In a diary entry from 1895, Tolstoy,
wrestling with a fever, notes that "[I] didn't write during the day, and then
wrote in the evening again, and rather a lot, so that more than half has been
drafted. It's turning out strangely: Nekhlyudov must be a follower of Henry
George and this [should be] brought in. . . ."[77] Anguished in conscience
Nekhlyudov mused that:

> Everything seemed so clear to . . . [Nekhlyudov] now, that he
> could not stop wondering how it was that everybody did not see it, and
> that he himself had been so long in perceiving what was so clearly
> evident. The people were dying out; had got used to the dying-out
> process, and so had formed habits of life adapted to it: there was the
> great mortality among the children, the over-working of the women,
> and the under-feeding, especially of the aged. And so gradually had
> the people come to this condition that they did not realize the full
> horror of it, and did not complain, and we therefore considered their
> condition natural and proper. Now it seemed as clear as daylight that
> the chief cause of the people's deep poverty was one that they them-
> selves knew and always pointed out, i.e., that the land which alone
> could feed them had been taken from them by the landlords.
> And how evident it was that the children and aged died because
> they had no milk . . . because there was no pasture land, and no land to
> grow corn or make hay on. It was quite evident that all the misery of
> the people, or a least the greatest and direct cause of it, lay in the fact
> that the land which should feed them was not in their hands, but in
> those who, profiting by the ownership of the land, live by the work of
> these people. The land, so necessary to men that they die when de-
> prived of it, was tilled by these people on the verge of starvation, so
> that the corn might be sold abroad and the landowners might buy hats
> and canes, and carriages and bronzes. Nekhlyudov now understood
> this as clearly as he understood that horses when they have eaten all
> the grass in the enclosure where they are kept, must of necessity grow
> thin and starve unless they are placed in another one.

This was terrible, and must not go on. Some means must be found to remedy, or at least one must not take part in it. "And I will find them," he thought, as he walked up and down the path under the birch trees. "In scientific circles, government institutions, and in the papers, we talk about the causes of poverty among the people and the means of ameliorating their condition; but we do not talk of the only sure means which would certainly lighten their lot, namely, giving back the land to them, which they need so much.

Henry George's fundamental position recurred vividly to him. . . . "the earth cannot be any one's property; it cannot be bought or sold any more than water, air, or sunshine. All have an equal right to the advantages it gives to men."[78]

Inescapably a member of the countryfied patrician class, Tolstoy had preached to his peasants about morality, and of course, Georgist philosophy. Such episodes appear in his latest work. Nekhlyudov, who desires to relinquish his estates, speaks with his peasants "and began to explain Henry George's single-tax system":

"The earth is no man's; it is God's," he began.

"Just so; that it is,' several voices replied.

"The land is common to all. All have the same right to it. But there is good land and bad land, and every one would like to take the good land. What is one to do in order to get it justly divided? In this way: he who uses the good land must pay the [assessed] value of it to those who got none," Nekhyudov went on, answering his own question. "As it would be difficult to say who should pay to whom, and as money is needed for communal use, it should be arranged that he who uses the good land should pay the [assessed] value of that land to the commune for its needs. Then every one would share equally. If you want to use land, pay for it—more for the good land, less for the bad land. If you do not wish to use land, don't pay anything, and [let] those who use the land pay the taxes and the communal expenses for you."

"That's correct," said the oven-builder, raising his eyebrows. "He who has good land must pay more."

"Well, he had a head, that George!" said the imposing patriarch with the curly hair.

"If only the payment is according to our strength," said the tall man with the bass voice, evidently seeing what the plan led to.

"The payment should be not too high and not too low. If it is too high, it will not be paid and there will be a loss; and if it is too low, land will be bought and sold. There would be speculation in land," replied Nekhyudov. "Well, that is what I wished to arrange among you here," he went on.

"That is just, that is right; yes, that would do," said the peasants encouragingly, fully understanding.

"He had a head, this George," said the broad-shouldered old man with the curls. "See what he has invented."[79]

Tolstoy used the Russia of his time as a universal model of a virtuous society. The age-old local communal arrangement was to be retained in an administrative and judicial capacity without any national government—though without periodic repartition that had made for impoverishment and inefficiency with the system of small and sometimes difficult-to-reach scattered strips of land based on the natural inequalites of soil productiveness. Land would be owned in common, individuals having only the right of usage. Schemes based on pure sharing were deemed impractical, since two people could never contribute the same and not effort but laziness would be rewarded in an unbalanced community. George's system fit in neatly, for it provided the balance between man and society on the one hand, and on the other between God and man. The Georgist commune was to eventually develop into what Tolstoy envisioned as a mirror image of heaven on an earth with man and all creatures living in concord, and in the future, even without the cherished single tax.

Land itself, in its bounty and purity, was to be the nurturing ground for the growth of man as man, and man as a child of beneficent God. A life of communal harmony founded on the soil would promote morality, perfection, salvation, and freedom from all depravity and oppression. But though the land and the commune would foster personal virtue, that virtue was the primary force: from it the outer communal institutions would discover and sustain their pattern. Nekhyudov's search for forgiveness and perfection in universal absolutes thus carries a special meaning for us, for it gives an idea of Tolstoy's struggles with himself and suggests an introspective means of liberation for ourselves in service to others.

Readers around the world waited anxiously for the publication of this work. Russian censorship, although cutting *Resurrection* to pieces, could not stop smuggled copies from returning, let alone the numerous foreign translations (which were tailored according to national prejudices). Toporov's real life model Konstantin P. Pobedonostev had earlier written to Tsar Alexander III that

> It is impossible to conceal from oneself that in the last few years the intellectual stimulation under the influence of the works of Count Tolstoy has greatly strengthened and threatens to spread strange, perverted notions about faith, the Church, government, society. The direction is entirely negative, alien, not only to the Church, but to the national spirit. A kind of insanity has taken possession of people's minds.[80]

Imperial authorities were irate: Tolstoy increasingly became a symbol of resistance, virtually a second tsar. *Resurrection* was a major factor in Tolstoy's excommunication two years later. Georgists around the world were ecstatic with Tolstoy's new work and considered it an incredible condemnation of economic and social injustice, a renewed clarion call for their ideas, and the Russian their greatest living exponent. Passionate adulation appeared in their papers. One reviewer exclaimed that it

> will leave imperishable impressions. For it is a powerful, vivid, and inspiring book . . . It is . . . especially gratifying to single taxers to know that in this book their fundamental reform is given a prominent place, and that the great work *Progress and Poverty*, which Henry George gave to the world, forms one of the means instrumental in that moral and spiritual awaking, which comes to Tolstoy's hero, and which is pictured with magnificent uplifting power.[81]

Tolstoy's protests against the government contributed to his growing popularity, and demonstrations took place in his name. The first two years of the new century meanwhile brought an economic depression to Russia. Strikes broke out in the bustling cities, and the provinces were punctuated with riots. Tsarist repression, of course, did not help matters, nor did its foreign policy of incursions in the Far East. Pogroms continued to plague the Pale to the moral indignation of the world. Anarchist groups, the just-formed agrarian socialist Social Revolutionaries, and Marxist organizations of differing shades were becoming more aggressive. Assassination of reactionary government officials spread fear into the ministries and even the imperial family. Middle class liberals were growing angry.

Russia in 1902 was still suffering from economic depression and there had been a poor harvest the year before. The proletariat in the cities were out on the picket line in greater force and more often, and peasant revolts, having increased in number and in violence, would continue for the next few years. Burnings of estates, murders of landlords, and property seizure, was concentrated in the provinces of Poltava and Kharkov in 1902. Repression, the time-honored tsarist cure, aggravated popular anger. The military was called in to support the police; retaliation was brutal. Radicals responded with more assassinations of government officials. Soviet historians were to characterize this situation as "an intensification of the class struggle." Tolstoy himself feared a revolution that would engulf his homeland. To address the crisis he wrote numerous appeals including one to Tsar Nicholas II. Essays and pamphlets came to light in almost frantic-like succession. Much of this material during this period can be found in chapters three and four of this book. Letters during this period still attest to his adherence to the single tax as the only cure for the prevalent maladies. To the Canadian John Baker, Tolstoy writes that: "I was very glad to know that you are a warm partisan of Henry George. I am quite sure that in the long run he will conquer, and I will try to help in this as much as I can."[82]

Meanwhile, man took to flight at Kitty Hawk on the shores of the Atlantic; so did the Russian Imperial Eagle in the Far East on the shores of the Pacific. Its two heads received third degree burns from the Rising Sun of Japan. The poor peasant was forced into a war far from the village that was his only life. He didn't know why he was there. Neither, for that matter, did the court or the general staff. Nor did the leaders know how to fight. But the army fought doggedly through one defeat after another. The fall of the naval base at Port Arthur in late 1904 was followed six months later by the destruction at Tsushima of the tired Baltic Fleet, which had circumnavigated the globe. A day of national celebration for an upstart power became a source of pride and an inducement to Pearl Harbor.

The war that broke out in 1904 from a meddling Russia too weak to fend for herself in Europe was muddled by the tsar. With ancient precedents, it was meant to be a quick defeat of the pagans that would heighten prestige and direct the people's minds to glory, away from the unresolved domestic problems of starvation, onerous labor conditions, poverty, political repression, mental oppression, and land hunger. But the bungling of the war brought on increased burdens at home; nor could it stop social and economic forces and progressive thought. Peasant riots and strikes continued, and on January 9, 1905 revolution began.[83] On that Bloody Sunday, peaceful petitioners carrying icons and seeking help from the tsar were shot in the streets of St. Petersburg. For a year and a half strikes and peasant revolts increased in waves of massive rebellion. Many cities completely shut down. Sailors mutined, while professionals of all kinds and even civil servants protested. Soviets appeared for the first time seizing authority in the name of the people. In many instances, they would exist side-by-side with tsarist poltical organs. Twelve years later the Bolsheviks for show purposes would pervert these organs of democracy into a mockery of Russian spontaneity. The granting during a general strike of the October Manifesto, which increased liberties, and the convening of the First Duma in April 1906, prorogued very quickly, could not tame the fury.

Tolstoy's fears had become a monstrous reality. Not only were people suffering even more but now blood was pouring in the streets, the villages, and the battle lines. One month after Bloody Sunday Tolstoy, reflecting not only his contempt for liberal reform but his occasional hope for a Tsar-Savior, wrote:

> The crime committed in St. Petersburg is agonizing. It is truly hideous that the government ordered the murder of people, with the soldiers shooting their brethern, and [also] the unholy agitators who for their own nefarious ends led the simple people to their death. I do not blame the people, but I have no words sufficient to express my

disgust for those who misled them. The people are not revolutionary at heart. The townsfolk seek only peace to work under honest conditions—the country people desire only the use of the land. The creed of Thoreau and Henry George is ingrained in every Russian heart. But the Russian people have no desire for representative government—none. On the contrary, they wish for the continuance of the autocratic monarchy, which is their best safeguard against the nobility and the landed aristocracy.[84] In fact, the Tsar is the master of evey inch of the soil, and he could and should give it to the toilers. The people know the Tsar, and they believe he will do it. So they will not support the middle and noble classes in order to crystallize and make permanent the status quo through the granting of unimportant concessions. Consciously or unconsciously, the people know that the right way for them to goodness is not by arms and murder, but by spiritual enlightenment; [they] know that the only permissible or expedient action is passive resistance and a campaign of education.[85]

Tolstoy's scorned liberal improvements with greater freedoms, constitutional rights, and consultative or legislative assemblies on the grounds that they retarded spiritual growth, were war-mongering, were not commensurate with the real interests of the people, and they were a sham. His rejection of them and his good will toward Nicholas II were paradoxically consonant with his rejection of all legal authority. Liberal government would be perpetuating evil; the tsar, expressing the will of the whole people, could act at once, above and outside government: very much like a spiritually anointed regent of God. Progress could never be measured in these kind of democratic terms. Tolstoy's animosity to liberalism alienated many of his supporters. That admonition against alienation is still unheeded.

As early as April 1905 the anguished Tolstoy had observed in his diary that "I very much want to write an exposition of my beliefs as well as something about Henry George, whom I read in Nikolaev's edition and again I become elated. There have been moments recently when I've had a clear understanding of life such as I've never had before. It's as if a complex equation had been reduced to the most simple expression and solution."[86] Even during the turmoil that was engulfing his country he clung to his belief in Georgism. His Russia, now torn apart not only from the outside, but from the inside as well, impelled the seventy-six year old man to churn out more works than ever. Chapter five contains representative samples begging people to transform their inner selves, to work in harmony with one another, and to apply Georgist economics throughout Russia.

A letter in March 1906 extends to all property Tolstoy's injunction against ownership, which contradicts both George's convictions (that what we earn by the sweat of our brow is rightfully ours) and Tolstoy's remarks elsewhere:

. . . My relationship not only to land but to any private property is that no Christian should consider anything his. No force, therefore, should be used to defend his property, even when it is the product of his labor: more especially, he should not defend his land by arms, since everyone has identical rights [to it]. Twenty-five years ago, I came to the conclusion regarding this relationship between force and any kind of property.[87]

Biographers report that Tolstoy was agitated by all the violence and suffering during the revolution. Henry George's single tax was a topic of which he never tired. He considered it the only bridge to a better and more just life and that Russia was now in a position to proclaim to the world the need for universal land reform. "People talk and argue about Henry George's system," notes a diary entry for April. "It isn't the system which is valuable (although I neither know nor can imagine a better one), but what is valuable is that the system establishes a relationship to the land which is universal and identical for all people. Let them find a better one."[88]

Nicholas II as a statesman and ruler never played with a full deck, was surrounded by a court of gallooned jokers and a paper shuffling bureaucracy primarily composed of deuces and treys. Only rarely could he find a high card to deal out. When he did, he discarded it. Peter A. Stolypin was the last ace up the Romanov sleeve. Declaring martial law in most of the European provinces, he ruthlessly put down uprisings with executions and transportation. The "Stolypin neck tie" and "Stolypin car" entered popular vocabulary.[89] The new prime minister knew that the land problem was the key to pacification and a stable country. To address this issue he created the beginning of a new phase in Russian history. No longer holding faith in the repartitional commune as an economic, social, and political entity, he established the groundwork for the consolidation of land strips into unitary holdings. Private property in land was to be the central factor of his planning. The Law of November 9, 1906 contemplated the peasants' having their own stake in the country. But not all peasants were sufficiently aggressive to get land, nor was there enough to go around for everyone. So landlessness with a displaced peasantry would continue.

By 1915 only ten percent of the peasants with holdings had taken advantage of the law and the scattered strip system still predominated. Most attempts at the creation of individual holdings were vigorously opposed by members of a commune. The peasant population was still growing, subsisting on smaller plots, suffering from high direct taxes, and many indirect taxes along with increasing prices, primarily on necessities.

The cities were bursting with the excess population from the villages. From twelve million in 1897 (12.8% of the population) the urban areas in European Russia witnessed an increase to nineteen and a half (14.8% of the population) in 1914. The ranks of the proletariat in that same period had swelled to four and a quarter million from one and a half. Especially after their participation in the Revolution of 1905, they were subject to restrictive laws. The workers became more and more receptive to radical ideas but still maintained strong connections with the countryside.

The economic status of the nobility was still declining. Between 1897 and 1905 members of the old school lost twenty-one million *desiatinas*, and ten million more slipped away over the next ten years.[90] A third of the remaining land was heavily mortgaged and arrears continuously mounted.

Russia in the years before World War I, to be sure, was relatively prosperous and, on the surface, stable. The industrial base expanded, and despite the persistence of archaic agricultural methods and tools there were a number of good harvest years. The government's budget was balanced. Yet Russia was the world's greatest debtor nation. A gauge of her world position is that she was primarily an exporter of agricultural products and an importer of industrial commodities.

Stolypin easily brushed aside the Dumas, the first two dismissed quickly, the third being more pliable. So did Tolstoy, in his dismissal of the importation of Western ways. Many of his followers were disenchanted with his recalcitrance and failure to compromise. He lost many of them and his popularity took a beating. Still gravely concerned about the land question and the future of his Russia, on a number of occasions he conversed with members of the Duma to bring up the single tax for consideration as a basis for renewing the tired country, but to no avail.[91] In an interview of June 1907 with an American correspondant, Stephen Bonsal, Tolstoy expressed his chagrin with the new flirtation with democracy in its refusal to adopt Georgist land reform.

> Of course, as you must know, the vital phase of our situation in Russia entails the land question, and yet no man, much less a party, not those who say yes to confiscation any more than those that say nay, dares to approach it in frankness and sincerity. In this very Duma the agrarians of the Liberal groups stand convicted of bad faith or of ignorance. There is but one solution of the land question in Russia as well as elsewhere, which can be regarded as just and equitable and final, as far as anything can be final in this transitory world—it is, of course, the land laws as preached in their modern form by Henry George.
>
> But our wily agrarians[92] never mention this solution because it promises no class an advantage, and I take it as a recognized axiom in party politics that if you want to secure votes and get into office you have to promise a numerous class decidedly favorable treatment. As I understand it, the idea of the land confiscators would seem to be that those from whom the land is taken should still be compelled to pay the

taxes in the future, while those to whom the land is given should not be harassed by taxes, but live happily ever afterward in ease and plenty and without labor. Of course, this makes a better battle cry than the words of Henry George, and, of course, battle cries are necessary to success in party strife, while principles—well, they are better thrown overboard. Then, of course, George was an honest man, and the world rejected him! Our agrarians are not so honest, and they [will not allow themselves to] be rejected if they can help it.[93]

Friends and acquaintances still reported quite frequently his endless talk about the land problem, Stolypin's land law, and the single tax. His wife claimed that he talked about George incessantly. Every now and then Tolstoy would still have hesitations about the single tax but he was an inveterate questioner and reexaminer of everything.[94] In any event, he dismissed his temporary misgivings. People who held conversations with him report his continuing love of George, and his notations still refer to the American as "a great man" and take delight when people fight for the cause of the single tax.[95] Correspondence still abounds concerning Tolstoy's concern for the plight of his country and the relationship to the land question. The aging novelist emphatically states that: "The land is God's. It should not and cannot belong to anyone. All people have an equal right to it and the only concern is how to distribute it. . . . Genuine property is determined only by labor and people must work in harmony on the land."[96] Naturally, he also mailed Georgist literature to his correspondent. Elsewhere, he writes:

> The Russian people have always understood their relation to the earth, in spite of all the attempts the state forces to introduce among them a false understanding of landownership. According to the people's understanding, which is sensible, the land cannot be an object of ownership and all people should have an equal right to its use. So that this right will be the same for everyone, it is necessary that those who use the land should pay an equal amount of rent to the community at large.[97] This money should replace all those direct and indirect taxes which are now collected from everyone. I estimate that in Russia, if the lands were taxed even much lower than their values, the land tax would still be greater than all the [present] taxes put together. Thus, it would be in accordance with the ways of the farming people, [if they] were to pay a low rent for the land they used. Those who don't use it would also benefit from the lowering of the cost of consumer goods, which would come about from [the absence of] indirect taxes.[98]

August 28, 1908, was to be the eightieth birthday of Tolstoy. Letters poured in from around the world. Single tax newpapers called for demonstrations in honor of George's most noted exponent. A characteristic statement declared that he was "The great Russian whose slightest word is more potent than the thunder of the Czar's Cossacks . . . the most eminent of those who stand for the truth as it is in Henry George."[99]

The Australian single taxers, not to be outdone, sent a birthday greeting to Tolstoy declaring their reverence and love. He towers, they declared, over all kings and leaders, for he was the greatest living moral force and champion of the oppressed whose memory will always endure. "When we learned," the missive continues, "that you also had embraced the economic teaching of our dear, departed master, Henry George, our hearts gained new courage in the advocacy of the ideals for which we strive; new confidence in the coming of the Kingdom of Righteousness. . . ."[100] Tolstoy's response in English emotionally reaffirms his belief in the single tax, the evils of private property, and predicts its imminent realization. He claims that he not done enough for the mutual cause that binds Georgists all over the world.

> Your address has deeply touched me. To my regret, I have done too little for the cause so dear to you and me, which unites us. Of late I have been thinking more and more about it, and should I yet be afforded power for work, I will endeavor to express the teaching of Henry George—who has, as yet, been far from appreciated according to its merits—as clearly, as briefly, and as accessibly to the great mass of land workers as possible.
>
> The injustice and evil of property in land has long ago been recognized. More than a hundred years ago the great French thinker, Jean-Jacques Rousseau, had written:
>
> "The one who first fenced in a plot of land, and took upon himself to say, 'this land is mine,' and found people so simple-minded as to believe him, that man was the first founder of the social organization which now exists. From how many crimes, wars, murders, calamities, cruelties would mankind have been delivered had some man then uprooted the fences and filled up the ditches, saying, 'Beware, do not believe that deceiver; you will perish, if you forget that the land cannot belong to anyone, that its fruits belong to all?'"[101]
>
> The injustice of the seizure of the land as property has long ago been recognized by thinking people, but only since the teaching of Henry George has it become clear by what means it can be abolished. In our time the realization of this teaching has become especially necessary, not only in Russia—where the land problem is, unfortunately, being solved in a way most contrary to justice, to the people's consciousness, and to reason—but in all so-called civilized states. This problem, i.e., the abolition of property in land, everywhere at the present time demands its solution as insistently as half a century ago the problem of slavery demanded its solution in Russia and America.

Its solution is of the utmost necessity, because the supposed right of landed property now lies at the foundation, not only of economic misery, but also of political disorder, and above all, the depravation of people. The wealthy ruling classes, foreseeing the loss of the advantages of their position inevitable, are endeavoring by various false interpretations, justifications and palliatives, with all their power, to postpone as long as possible its solution. But the time comes for everything, and as fifty years ago the time came for the abolition of the supposed right of property over man, so the time has now come for the abolition of the supposed right of property in land, which entails appropriating other people's labor. Nothing can arrest the abolition of this dreadful means of oppressing the people. Yet some effort, and this great emancipation of the nations shall be accomplished. I, therefore, particularly sympathize with your cause, with the efforts you are exerting, and will be very glad if I shall be able to add my small exertions to yours.[102]

William Jennings Bryan had visited Tolstoy in late 1903. Bryan considered himself to be a disciple of the Russian, often mentioning his name in speeches. They got on to the point that Tolstoy broke his daily routine. When "the Great Commoner" ran for the presidency a third time in 1908 Tolstoy wrote to a Philadelphian:

In response to your letter of August 24 [1908], I can express very frankly the wish for Bryan's successful candidature for the United States presidency. From my point of view, since I do not recognize any kind of government, [for all are] based on force, I cannot justify the presidential function in a republic, but in as much as this capacity still exists, I am assuredly desirous that it should be fulfilled by people who are worthy of trust.

I speak of Mr. Bryan with great respect and feeling. I know that the principles on which he bases his [platform] are congruent with mine, in regard to our [mutual] sympathy for the workers, antimilitarism, and the recognition of the evils engendered by capitalism.

. . . I hope, that Mr. Bryan will be an advocate of land reform in the spirit of Henry George and his single tax system, the realization [of which] I consider at present to be totally essential [, a system] which every leading reformer should keep foremost in mind.[103]

Quite a bit of praise for a politician from the world's leading anarchist! The *Circle of Reading*, reworked after an absence of a few years, also appeared during this time. It was a compendium of quotations depicting various spiritual themes to be discussed for any given day for a year. Citations from the father of the single tax number an impressive thirty.[104] Tolstoy was still writing under the influence of his revered American philosopher,

George, as well as that of his beloved Jewish teacher, Jesus. A portrait of Henry George hung in a prominent place on a wall.

Much correspondence and many journal entries from Tolstoy's later years attest to his commitment to George along with his disgust at Stolypin's privatization of land. Anyone interested in the land question was sure to receive a parcel of Georgist literature. One letter of 1909, for instance, exclaims to a man who sent Tolstoy a copy of a book he wrote: "I am very much astonished to find that an American, discussing the land question, does not make any allusions to Henry George and his great theory, which alone completely solves the land question."[105] A lengthier epistle written in English, to a group of British single taxers, allies Georgist economics with the highest dictates of relgious consciousness.

> In Russia, where people have never recognized landed property, this infamous action [Law of Nov. 9] is particulary loathsome on the part of a stupid and coarse government which is endeavoring not only to retain the slaves in their servitude, but also by depraving the people to intensify their future slavery. I regard as stupid the action of our present government, because if it had put into practice Henry George's principle that land cannot become exclusive property—a principle always recognized by the great mass of the Russian peasantry— [it] would alone, more effectually than all the acts of state violence and cruelty, have pacified the people, and rendered impossible the revolution. The Russian government, however, has had recourse to a contrary measure by encouraging in every way the transference of the land from communal ownership to private individual ownership. In this I see the govenment's astounding stupidity. In those measures which the government uses to repress the people's disaffection, which naturally flows from their want in land, is manifested this astounding cruelty.

> Therefore the activity of the Single Tax League organized in England is especially gladdening.

> Henry George is especially to be appreciated by those who profess Christianity in its true sense, for not only the foundations of his teaching, but also his methods are truly Christian. As Jesus in his utterance, "Ye have heard that it was said: Thou shalt not kill, but I say unto you, Resist not evil," has pointed out that the commandment, *"Thou shalt not kill,"* never, absolutely in no case, can be broken, that neither may the pretext of retribution or of defence serve as a reason for the violation of this commandment; exactly so does Henry George point out that the commandment, *"Thou shalt not steal,"* can and should in no case be violated. As in the law of non-resistance to evil by violence, i.e., the prohibition of killing under any circumstances whatever, has been elucidated the injustice and harmfulness of the justification of violence under pretext of defence and common good, so also in Henry George's teaching on the equal rights of all to the

land, has been elucidated the injustice and harmfulness of the justification of robbery and theft under the pretext of either the exclusive right of some people to the land, or the depriving of those who labor of the produce of their labor in order to use it for social needs.

In this lies the essence of George's philosophy. However those, who need to do so, may endeavor to conceal this teaching, it is so clear and indisputable that it cannot but be recognized by mankind.

God help you. On your side are justice, reason, and love. On your side is God, and therefore you cannot but be successful. . . .[106]

A letter a few months later, in 1910, expresses Tolstoy's continued dissatisfaction with Stolypin's land reform and the inevitable results.

The dissolution of the commune and the strengthening of individual personal property plots is a very disgusting and criminal activity perpetuated by the government. I foresee three consequences of such an action: it will increase the number of homeless paupers, who will become money slaves to the rich; it will give the rich landowners the opportunity to look bravely into the eyes of the not-so-rich peasant owners and say "I have . . . three thousand desiatinas, and you have five and ten—you are the same kind of landowner as I am," and it will violate the high moral conviction of the Russian people. [Only] the product of labor can be property: not the land, which is "God's land."[107]

An essay that exists in English translation under the title "Tolstoy's Last Message," apparently written in 1910 or shortly before, is a short article recapping his position relating to Henry George's philosophy. Beginning on the sad note, "I now write because I am standing at the brink of the grave and cannot keep silent," he ends with words of victory.

As I pointed out in my introductory note to the Russian version of *Social Problems*,[108] Henry George's great idea, outlined so clearly and so thoroughly more than thirty years ago, remains to this day entirely unknown to the great majority. This is quite natural. Henry George's idea, which would change the entire life of nations in favor of the oppressed voiceless majority and to the detriment of the ruling minority, is so undeniably convincing, and above all so simple, that it is impossible not to understand it. It is therefore impossible not to make an effort to introduce it into practice. So the only means [usable] against this idea are to pervert it and to pass it in silence.

And this has been true of Henry George's theory for more than thirty years. It has been both perverted and passed by in silence, so that it has become difficult to induce people to attentively read his works and to think about it.

To my regret I have done too little for the cause which unites us. Of late I have been thinking more about it, and should I yet be afforded power for work, I will endeavor to express the teaching of Henry George as clearly, as briefly, and as accessibly as possible to the great mass of workers. . . .

The supposed rights in landed property are the foundation not only of economic misery but also of political disorder, and, above all, of the moral depravation of people.

The wealthy ruling classes, foreseeing as inevitable the loss of the advantages of their position, by various false interpretations, justifications, and palliatives are endeavoring with all their might to postpone its solution as long as possible.

But the time comes for everything. As it came for the abolition of man's property in man, so it has now arrived for the abolition of the supposed right of property in land, which involves the appropriation of other people's labor. The time for this is now so near at hand that nothing can halt the abolition of this dreadful means of oppresssing the people.

Yet with a little effort this great emancipation shall be accomplished for the nations.[109]

Tolstoy never got the chance to see the liberation of the world to which he had devoted his life, and he was spared the sight of Russia under the Bolsheviks. While fleeing by train from home he preached love, nonresistance, and of course Georgist philosophy to his fellow passengers. He never completed the journey. Taking sick, he died at a lonely train station on November 20, 1910. Georgists around the world mourned the death of their greatest advocate. A statement by English single taxers extolled Tolstoy as "the staunch, courageous and eloquent apostle of righteousness and justice, of peace on earth and good-will to all men."[110] A resolution passed in New York at the Fels Commission Conference declares that

> *Whereas*, the news having arrived of the death of Count Leo Tolstoy, we, the Single Taxers of America, desire to tender our sympathies to Countess Tolstoy; and
>
> *Whereas*, this foremost man of the world, whose teachings have made him famous in all lands, has repeatedly announced his belief in the doctrines of Henry George for which we stand, and which we are engaged in popularizing in the United States; therefore be it
>
> Resolved, that we deeply deplore the passing of the Russian Prophet, but our abiding hope is that the endorsement by this man on whose soul rested so much of
>> "The burden and the mystery
>> Of all this unintelligible world,"
> of those doctrines to which we are pledged, and his statement that he regarded Henry George as the greatest of Americans, may be the

means of drawing world-wide attention to the plan of industrial salvation to which he lent the weight of his splendid name.[111]

Henry George, Jr., present at this meeting, seconded the resolution. In his own commentary on the death of Tolstoy he could draw on his meeting with the novelist-student of his father:

> . . . The last words this great man addressed to me in parting at the time of my visit to him at Yasnaya Polyana were in relation to my father. He said we should never meet again in this life; that soon he would meet my father and he asked what message he should bear to my father. I gave him the message. I believe he is now with my father, and giving him that message, and glad tidings of the movement that both of them worked for in this world. . . . Within the last few hours the greatest spirit of the world has passed . . . his death is a new inspiration. For now all the contradictory things, the things not understandable, will fall away, and the majesty of this prophet of brotherhood and justice in our modern world will shine out. Great is Tolstoy; greater the truths he taught; and greater still will both become as the centuries roll on.[112]

Tolstoy had valiantly and single-handedly endeavored to stop the flow of events that he saw would lead to destruction in his Russia. He rejected a reality that never measured up to his dreams of a peaceful world, busy at the sowing and harvesting of crops, of happy children playing in the streets in a small village, of a life attuned to the endless change of seasons: a world without gloom, without war, and without suffering. It was to be so definable and so simple that it had to be the most complex thing to achieve. Georgist philosophy had transformed into a coherent system Tolstoy's earlier amorphous economic thinking. So caught up with Georgist thought did Tolstoy become that he even modified his strictures against the state as a viable means of effecting change. His philosophy contained one simple formula: God, Land, and Man. The basis for a harmonious society is the relationship among these three components. God created the land and mankind. It is therefore the duty of all people to live a simple natural life peacefully tilling the soil far away from the corrupting influence of cities: so concluded Tolstoy, ignoring that George celebrated the working of land and its resources into all the ingenious devices of a technically advanced society, the imprinting upon nature of human mind and energy at its most purposeful. It is also incumbent upon everyone, so Tolstoy stated in full accord with George, to develop a personal relationship with God. What holds together this union between God and Man is love: for Tolstoy, the last major exponent of the single tax, it was the ultimate principle inherent in George's philosophy. Much of Tolstoy's works and correspondence bespeak his love for George, as man, as altruist, and above all as a spiritual economic teacher. For a man of his temperament to call himself a student of anyone other than of divine precept is quite astonishing.[113]

Notes

1. A portion of this essay first appeared as "The Influence of Henry George's Philosophy on Lev Nikolaevich Tolstoy: The Period of Developing Economic Thought (1881-1897)" in *Pennsylvania History*, 63, 2 (Spring 1996), 233-252. This article would have been unthinkable without the kind assistance of Dr. William Pencak (editor of this journal) and the generous support of the Robert Schalkenbach Foundation, New York.
2. Prince Nekhlyudov will figure prominently in *Resurrection* over forty years later. See pages 30-32.
3. Tolstoy, *Voina i mir* [War and peace], *PSS*, 12: 50.
4. Tolstoy, *Ispoved* [Confession], *PSS*, 23: 47.
5. Tolstoy, *Mnogo li cheloveky zemli nuzhno?* [How much land does a man need?] of 1886 gives a wonderful portrayal of the vanity of materialism and avariciousness. *PSS*, 25: 67-78.
6. Tolstoy, "Otryvok dnevika 1857 goda; putevye zapiski po Shveitsarii" [Extract from the diary of 1857; travel notes through Switzerland], *PSS*, 5: 196.
7. Ibid., *PSS*, 50: 92.
8. Ibid., *PSS*, 51: 88.
9. Tolstoy, *Voskreseniia* [Resurrection], *PSS*, 32: 419.
10. Tolstoy, *Chem liodi zhivy?* [What men live by?], for instance, depicts the strength of love. *PSS*, 25: 7-25.
11. Though Tolstoy did not believe in the divinity of Jesus, he did use the term Christian to denote a follower of his ideas.
12. See *B Chem moia vera* [What I believe], *PSS*, 23: 304-465.
13. Tolstoy, *PSS*, 54: 39. Emphasis in original.
14. Tolstoy, *Voskreseniia* [Resurrection], *PSS*, 32: 418-419.
15. Ibid., *Tserkov' i gosudarstvo* [Church and state], *PSS*, 23: 477.
16. Ibid., *PSS*, 23: 479.
17. Ibid., *Tsarstvo bozh vnutri vas* [The kingdom of God is within you], *PSS*, 28: 131-132.
18. Ibid., *PSS*, 55: 10.
19. Ibid., *Khristianstvo i patriotizm* [Christianity and patriotism], *PSS*, 33: 65.
20. Thomas G. Masaryk, *The Spirit of Russia: Studies in History, Literature and Philosophy*, trans. Eden and Cedar Paul, vol. 3 (London: George Allen & Unwin, 1961), 183. Tolstoy, Lenin writes, "succeeded with remarkable force in conveying the moods of the broad masses who are oppressed by the . . . system, in depicting their condition and in expressing their spontaneous feelings of protest and indignation. . . . [He was a veritable] slap in the face of bourgeois liberalism . . . [and] his heritage which . . . departs from the past belongs to the

future. This heritage will prevail and the Russian proletariat can work with it" (Vladimir I. Lenin, "L. N. Tolstoi," *PSSL*, 20: 20 and 23). Even the contradictions in Tolstoy's writings reflect those of Russian life itself—though immature and hence incapable of understanding the proletarian struggle towards socialism, they were a correct protest against advancing capitalism, tsarist coercion, and the ruination of the peasantry ("Lev Tolstoi, kak zerkalo russkoi revoliutsii," [Lev Tolstoy, as a mirror of the Russian revolution], *PSSL*, 17: 209-210). Though Tolstoy lacked a Marxist understanding, from his work the proletariat will assuredly "learn to know its enemies better" ("Tolstoi i proletarskaia bor'ba" [Tolstoy and the proletarian struggle], *PSSL*, 20: 71).

21. For a synopsis of George's political economy, consult Volume I *(An Anthology of Henry George's Thought)* of *The Henry George Centennial Trilogy*.

22. Karl Marx regarded George with disdain. A letter to Friedrich Sorge describes George's thinking as a "cloven hoof (at the same time [an] ass's hoof)" for it is "theoretically . . . *total arrière* [retrograde]." It is "simply an attempt, trimmed with socialism, *to save capitalist rule* and indeed to *re-establish* it on *an even wider basis* than its present one . . . [George] has the repulsive presumption and arrogance that distinguish all such panacea-mongers" (Karl Marx to Friedrich Sorge, June 20, 1881, in Karl Marx and Friedrich Engels, *Letters to Americans: 1848-1895* [New York: International Publishers, 1969], 127 and 129). Emphases in original.

23. Ibid., 114.

24. Michael I. Tugan-Baranovskii, "Genri Dzhordzh i natsionalizatsiia zemli" [Henry George and the nationalization of land], *Novoe slovo* [New word] 6 (June 1897): 117 and 121-123, SB.

25. S. Iuzhakov, "K Voprosu o bednosti, eia prichinaxh i ustranenii" [On the question of poverty, its causes and elimination], *Otechestvenniya zapiski* [Notes of the fatherland] 266 (Jan. [?]1883): 133-134, SB.

26. Ibid., 267 (Feb. [?]1883): 452.

27. "Izuchenie politicheskoi ekonomii Genri Dzhordzha" [The Study of of Henry George's political economy], *Russkoe bogatstvo* [Russian wealth] 3 (1883): 609, SB. This speech was delivered at Berkeley on March 9, 1877. For more details see Barker, *Henry George*, 240-243.

28. M. M. Filippov, "Sotsial'nyi vopros (po Genri Dzhordzhu)" [The Social question according to Henry George], *Russkoe bogatstvo* [Russian wealth] 5-6 (May 1885): 316 and 319, SB.

29. V. V., "Genri Dzhordzh o protektsionizm" [Henry George on protectionism], *Severnyi vestnik* [Northern messenger] 12 (Dec.1886): 35, SB.

30. L. Slonimskii, "Genri Dzhordzh i ego teoriia progressa" [Henry George and his theory of progress], *Vestnik evropy* [Messenger of Europe] 4 (1889): 344, SB.

31. Ivan Ianzhul, "Otkrytoe pis'mo Genri Dzhordzha k pape L'vu XIII" [Open Letter of Henry George to Pope Leo XIII], *Severnyi vestnik* [Northern messenger] 1 (Jan. 1892): 283, SB. See 255-292.

32. B. O. Efrusi, "Genri Dzhordzh, kak ekonomist" [Henry George as economist], *Russkoe bogatstvo* [Russian wealth] 1 (Jan. 1898): 201, SB. See 179-202. Tolstoy

was aware of this debate. A number of his works had appeared in some of these journals.

33. Tolstoy to Sofia A. Tolstoy, Feb. 20, 1885, *PSS*, 83: 479.
34. Tolstoy to Sofia A. Tolstoy, Feb. 22, 1885, *PSS*, 83: 480-481.
35. Tolstoy to V. F. Chertkov, Feb. 22, 1885, *PSS*, 83: 482.
36. Tolstoy to V. F. Chertkov, Feb. 23, 1885, *PSS*, 83: 483.
37. Tolstoy to V. F. Chertkov, Feb. 24, 1885, *PSS*, 85: 144. Tolstoy read *Social Problems* before *Progress and Poverty*.
38. Tolstoy to Prince L. D. Urusov, Feb. 26[?], 1885, *PSS*, 63: 212. According to one of Tolstoy's Russian biographers, it was the last paragraph of the introduction to *Progress and Poverty* that produced "the strongest and most favorable impression," especially those lines in which George declares:

    I propose to beg no question, to shrink from no conclusion, but to follow truth wherever it may lead. Upon us is the responsibility of seeking the law, for in the very heart of our civilization today women faint and little children moan. . . . If the conclusions that we reach run counter to our prejudices, let us not flinch; if they challenge institutions that have long been deemed wise and natural, let us not turn back (See Gusev, *Tolstoi*, 387 and George *Progress and Poverty* [New York: Robert Schalkenbach Foundation, 1992], 13).

39. Tolstoy, *Tak chto zhe nam delat'?* [What then must we do?], *PSS*, 25: 290. Tolstoy condemns material concerns, the class structure, landownership, labor extortion, charity, and money but extols self-sufficiency.
40. Ibid. George was against land nationalization. His scheme would employ no force. Everyone, especially in time of need, would be provided with sustenance. In the event of a poor harvest the single tax would also be lessened and even eliminated.
41. *The Standard*, Mar. 26, 1887, GR. Another short fable by Tolstoy simply labeled by *The Standard* as "A Russian Folk Lore Story" appeared in 1892 (*The Standard*, Aug. 31, 1892, GR). The real title is *The Worker Emelian and the Empty Drum*.
42. *The Standard*, Jan. 28, 1888, GR. I have not been able to ascertain George's reactions to Tolstoy's condemnation of his ideas!
43. *The Standard*, Dec. 15, 1888, GR. In the August 13, 1890 issue of *The Standard* appears a short blurb entitled "Tolstoi's Opinion: Thomas Stevens' letter to the World."

    In the matter of landownership Tolstoi is a great admirer of the theories of Henry George. He considers George the greatest American citizen of the present time. He believes, however, in a system of communal, rather than a national ownership of the land. The ideal state of society is the simple, rural communes, in which every family would have the right to till soil enough for its own support. There would be no taxes and no government. The count believes that all forms of government are humbugs, and that the whole machinery of law and lawyers, court[s] and judges, is a bar-

barity, and an excuse for setting one man above another, and enabling the privileged few to rob the many (*The Standard*, Aug. 13, 1890, GR).

44. Ibid.

45. Ibid. In another article, entitled "Tolstoi at Home," James Creelman in Harper's Weekly reports that Tolstoy's "library is selected with catholic taste, and contains the works of every philosopher from Plato to Henry George" (*The Standard*, June 22, 1892, GR).

46. Tolstoy, *Tsarstvo bozh vnutri vas* [The kingdom of God is within you], *PSS*, 28: 1-293.

47. Ibid., *PSS*, 28: 266-267 and 291-293.

48. Bernhard Eulenstein to Henry George, Mar. 24, 1894, #4, HGP. Eulenstein was an ardent German Georgist.

49. See S. Rozanovoi, ed., *Lev Nikolaevich Tolstoi perepiska c Russkimi pisateliami* [L. N. Tolstoi, correspondence with Russian writers] (Moscow: Gosudartsvo izdatel'stvo khudozhestvennoe literatury, 1962), 661. In a letter to M. M. Lederle on October 25, 1891, Tolstoy rated the influence of books at various stages of his life. For the decade after fifty *Progress and Poverty* received a rating of "very large," but not "great." If reconsiderd three years later, I think, this work would move up a notch. See *PSS*, 66: 68.

50. Henry George, "Condition of Labor," in *The Land Question*, 83. Monopolization of land and the unjust distribution of wealth were just as much slavery as the owning of bodies (Ibid., 7 and 86-88 and George, *Progress and Poverty*, 339-340).

51. George, "Thou Shall Not Steal," in *Our Land and Land Policy*, The Complete Works of Henry George, vol. 8 (New York: Doubleday, Page & Co., 1904), 251-252 and "Thy Kingdom Come," in *Our Land*, 289-291.

52. George, *Progress*, 455-456 and 552.

53. Tolstoy, *PSS*, 52: 120. This writing was for T. M. Bondarev, who wrote in *Industry and Idleness* that everyone should labor for his own bread. In May Tolstoy wrote to his wife that the American Ernest Crosby, whom he had advised to assist the "remarkable George," had become an "energetic fighter for Georgist affairs" (P. Biriukov, *L. N. Tolstoi: Biografiia* [L. N. Tolstoy: Biography], vol. 3 [Moscow: Posrednik, 1913], 384).

54. Ibid., *PSS*, 52: 131. Mrs. MacGahan had brought an autographed copy of *A Perplexed Philosopher* inscribed with the words: "To Count Tolstoy with respect from Henry George" *(PSS*, 52: 362).

55. V. F. Lazurskii, *Dnevnik* [Diary], June 24 1894, in S. N. Golubova, et al, eds., *L. N. Tolstoi v vospominaniiakh sovremennikov*, vol. 2 (Moscow: Gosudartsvo izdatel'stvo khudozhestvennoe literatury, 1960), 10-11. This conversation refers to Ivan Ianzhul's condemnation of George in the January 1892 issue of the *Northern Messenger.* See page 21. George's first economic work entitled *Our Land and Land Policy* was published in 1871.

56. This speech was later used in *Resurrection* (T. L. Sukhotina-Tolstaia, *Vospominaniia* [Remembrances] [Moscow: Khudozhestvennoi literatury, 1976], 357). See pages 31-32 for an example. In a diary entry, Tolstoy had noted: "We

talked to Tanya about Ovsyannikov, and I very much want to arrange things
for her there so that the money from the land should go to serve the community [as recommended by] Henry George" (Tolstoy to M. L. Tolstaya, Aug. 30,
1894, *PSS*, 67: 211).

57. Sukhotina-Tolstaia, *Vospominaniia*, 357-360.

58. Tolstoy to an American Lady (Mrs. Barbara MacGahan), Sept. 22, 1894, in
Russia: Russian-American Monthly Magazine [New York], March 1950, 3-4, HGS.
This letter is to found in *PSS*, 67: 225-227. Written in English.

59. Tolstoy, *PSS*, 87: 301. In October Tolstoy was trying to obtain copies of
George's newspaper *The Standard*, although at this time he did know its name
(PSS, 87: 300).

60. Tolstoy to Ernest Crosby, Nov. 24, 1894, in R. F. Christian, ed., *Tolstoy's Letters,
1880-1910*, vol. 2 (New York: Charles Scribner's Sons, 1978), 512. Three books
were sent with the American journalist V. N. MacGahan: *Perplexed Philosopher,
The Irish Land Question*, and *Protection or Free Trade*. Economic progress was
unthinkable without an inheritance tax, a tax on the wealthy, and the application of Georgist ideas *(PSS*, 53: 97-98).

61. Bernhard Eulenstein to Henry George, Feb. 29, 1896, #6, HGP.

62. Barker, *Henry George*, 597-598.

63. Tolstoy, *PSS*, 69: 77. No copy of this letter could be found in *PSS*.

64. A reference to The Science of Political Economy. George's last work, which was in-
complete, was first published posthumously in 1898.

65. Tolstoy to Henry George, Apr. 8, 1896, in Agnes George de Mille, *Henry George:
Citizen of the World* (Chapel Hill: University of North Carolina Press, 1950),
219. Written in English. See also *PSS*, 69: 76-77. It is dated April 8, 1896. According to the editors of *PSS*, this letter was in response to a communication of
March 15, 1896, by George, who expressed his hope to visit Europe in the near
future and meet Tolstoy to converse about topics on which they have come to
the same conclusion from different points of view. This letter, however, was
not found in *PSS*. See note in *PSS*, 69: 77.

66. Tolstoy, *PSS*, 53: 98.

67. William Lloyd Garrison, Jr. to Henry George, Feb. 14, 1897, 3, #6, HGP. Three
years later in an address before the Rhode Island Single Taxers, Garrison, Jr.
delcared:

> Alas, that another historic conjunction was prevented by the death
> of our exemplar! The visitor at Yasnaia Poliana finds the works of
> Henry George in constant evidence and HIS NAME CHER-
> ISHED as a household word. On hearing of his proposed visit to
> the continent, Tolstoi, overcoming his repugnance to railroad
> travel, determined to make a journey to Berlin to meet and greet
> him. It was not to be. "I shall certainly see Tolstoy if I go to Eu-
> rope," said Mr. George, and doubtless in anticipation he counted
> on the pleasure of meeting his illustrious disciple, for from no lips
> have come more understanding and appreciation of the single tax
> and its exponent than from those of Tolstoi. How touching is the
> picture of the neighboring peasants gathering around their teacher

and brother to learn the gospel of equal opportunity and the right
to the use of the earth *(The National Single Taxer,* March 1899, HGS).

68. The *New York Journal,* in a journalistic hoax intended to take advantage of the
great outpouring of feeling for the deceased, reproduced Stead's article in the
Pall Mall Gazette, which had appeared in *The Standard* in November 1888. The
Journal claimed that it was Tolstoy's cabled response to a request for commentary on George. See page 23. An editorial in this newspaper declares that Tolstoy
has abandoned "the peculiar features of his own ideas of community ownership of land in favor or the single tax theory of Henry George. It is an extraordinary example of self-abnegation on one side and convincing power on the other."

69. Tolstoy to Sofia Tolstoy, Oct. 24, 1897, *PSS,* 84: 298.

70. Tolstoy to E. H. Crosby, Dec. 29, 1897, in *The Single Tax: A Journal Devoted to
the Cause of Taxing Land Values,* June 1898, 2, HGS. This letter was not found in
PSS.

71. *What is Art?* [Chto takoe isskusstvo?] argues that art must be accessible to everyone and must have a higher moral purpose *(PSS,* 30: 27-203).

72. Tolstoy, *What is Art?* [Chto takoe iskusstvo?], *PSS,* 30: 416-426.

73. Ibid., *PSS,* 30: 422.

74. Sergei D. Nikolaev (1861-1920) translated these Georgist works (with dates of
publication): *Progress and Poverty* (1896), *A Perplexed Philosopher* (1902), *Protecton
or Free Trade* (1903), *The Land Question* (1907), *Social Problems* (1907), as well as
many articles and speeches. In a diary entry for 1909 Tolstoy wrote that "Dear
Nikolaev came twice. What a wonderful worker he is in the Henry George
sense and what a good person in general" (May 19, 1909, *PSS,* 57: 70).

75. Alexandra Tolstoy, *The Tragedy of Tolstoy,* trans. Elena Varneck (New Haven:
Yale University Press, 1933), 169 and 172.

76. See page 11.

77. Tolstoy, May 26, 1895, *PSS,* 53: 33.

78. Tolstoy, *Resurrection,* trans. Louise Maude (New York: Dodd, Mead & Co., 1903),
248-249. See *Voskreseniia* [Resurrection], *PSS,* 32: 217-218. The entire novel
with variations is located in *PSS,* 32 and 33.

79. Ibid., 262-263. See *Voskreseniia* [Resurrection], *PSS,* 32: 230-231. In one of the
first variations of *Resurrection* Nekhlyudov marries Maslova and settles in Siberia. He also sends a petition to the tsar for establishing his domain on the
basis of Georgist economics (Biriukov, *L. N. Tolstoi,* 565). Tolstoy anticipated
his own action two years later. See pages 109-114.

80. As quoted in Ernest J. Simmons, *Tolstoy* (London: Routledge & Kegan Paul,
1973), 204. No source given.

81. Review, "The Novel of the Decade—'Resurrection,'" *National Single Taxer,*
May 1900, 18. On page 27 of this newspaper an advertisement ran by the
publisher Dodd, Mead & Co. exclaimed that "this great book appeals very
strongly to all admirers of Henry George, and his Single Tax Theories—as
Tolstoy is an ardent follower of the great Single Taxer."

82. Tolstoy to John Baker, Jan. 10, 1901, in *The Public,* May 4, 1901, HGS. This
letter was not found in *PSS.*

83. For more on the Revolution of 1905, see Sidney Harcave, *First Blood: The Rus-*

sian Revolution of 1905 (New York: The MacMillan Co., 1964) and Walter Sablinsky, *The Road to Bloody Sunday: Father Gapon and the St. Petersburg Massacre of 1905* (Princeton: Princeton University Press, 1976).

84. Here Tolstoy is looking to a strong monarch to be a protector of the people. For a short discussion of this departure from his anarchism, see page109.

85. Tolstoy, in *The Public*, Feb. 11, 1905, 711, HGS.

86. Diary Entry, Tolstoy, Apr. 16, 1905, *PSS*, 55: 134.

87. Tolstoy to Afanasii S. Marov, March 22, 1906, *PSS*, 76: 126-127.

88. Tolstoy, Apr. 2, 1906, *PSS*, 55: 216-217.

89. Stolypin, born in 1862, was assassinated in 1911 by a Socialist Revolutionary terrorist who was also a police agent.

90. A desiatina is equivalent to 2.7 acres.

91. A diary entry of Aug. 28, 1909 reports: "[I] invited Maklakov and spoke with him about raising the [land] question in the Duma. He said that he knows nothing about H[enry] G[eorge] and that the question will not only not take place but will provoke [passions] . . . He . . . is completely deaf to all the real necessary questions for the people . . . " *(PSS*, 57: 126-127). See also *PSS*, 78: 90.

92. Agrarian was a generic term for either a *pomeshchik* [gentry, landowner] in particular or any person with a large landholding.

93. Stephen Bonsal, "Tolstoy Prophesies the 'Fall of America,'" in *New York Times*, July 7, 1907. This article was not found in *PSS*. Bonsal visited Tolstoy on May 7, 1907. See note in *PSS*, 65: 565.

94. Tolstoy was even dismayed to find out that George was for the restriction of Chinese immigration (V. F. Bulgakov, *L. N. Tolstoi v poslednii god ego zhizn* [L. N. Tolstoy in the last year of his life] [Moscow: Khudozhestvennoi literatury, 1960], 322.

95. Tolstoy, *PSS*, 56: 253.

96. Tolstoy to [?] Rgotinov, Aug. 29, 1908, *PSS*, 78: 215.

97. Tolstoy slipped a little here. According to his and George's thinking people would pay a percentage ranging up to the full tax based on the assessed value of the land, which is determined by locality, quality, and amount of land.

98. Tolstoy to A. Shil'tsov, May 30, 1908, *PSS*, 78: 147-148.

99. "For a General Tolstoy Demonstration," *Single Tax Review*, (Mar.-Apr. 1908), 33-34, HGS. The next line of this quote reads: "'Greatest of Americans' is the title by which he designates him."

100. "A Birthday Address to Count Leo Tolstoy," *Progess*, July 1908, 3-4, HGS.

101. See Jean-Jacques Rousseau's 1754 work *Discours sur l'origine et les fondements de l'inégalité parmi les hommes* [Discourse on the origin and the causes of inequality among men] (Paris: Éditions Gallimard, Paris, 1965), 87.

102. Tolstoy to the Federation of Single Tax Leagues of Australia, Sept. 2, 1908, in *Progress*, Dec. 1, 1908, HGS. This letter can be found in *PSS*, 78: 221-222.

103. Tolstoy to "Raiersony Dzheningsy" [to Ryerson Jennings], Sept. 28(?), 1908, *PSS*, 78: 231.

104. Tolstoy, *Krug chteniia*, *PSS*, 41: 11-606 and 42: 7-553.

105. Tolstoy to S. A. Fishburn, May 5, 1909, *PSS*, 79: 183. Written in English.

106. Tolstoy to the English Henry George League, Feb. 27-Mar. 31, 1909, *PSS*, 79: 135-137.
107. Tolstoy to F. F. Bolabol'chenkov, Apr. 3, 1910, *PSS*, 81: 201. Other letters express the same concern. Tolstoy declares to N. Pestriakov on July 1, 1910, for instance, that "[T]he goal of the government in the Law of November 9 is tantamount to the destruction of the just and wise perception of the Russian people that the land cannot be the object of private property. . . . Perhaps the goal is to introduce a powerful and terrifying discord among the peasants by the government in order to weaken them" (*PSS*, 82: 66-67).
108. See pages 195-198.
109. Tolstoy, "Tolstoy's Last Message," trans. Joseph Edwards, in *The Commonweal*, Mar. 31, 1928, 8, HGS. Original in English and not found in *PSS*. It has been slightly edited for smoother reading.
110. "Leo Tolstoy," *Land Values*, Dec. 1910, 139, HGS.
111. "Tolstoy Resolutions in New York," *The Public*, Dec. 2, 1910, 1144, HGS.
112. Ibid., 1144-1145.
113. The following additional books and articles have been used in this essay. For complete citiations consult the bibliography. D. Anuchin, *Neskol'ko chasov;* V. D'iakov, "L. N. Tolstoi o zakonomernostiakh;" P. Dukes, *History of Russia;* A. Gol'denveizer, *Vblizi Tolstogo;* N. Gudzii, *Lev Tolstoi;* N. Gusev, *Dva goda* and *Lev Nikolaevich Tolstoi;* B. Kurbskii (G. S. Petrov), *Y L. N. Tolstogo*, in B. Lakshin, ed., *Interviu i besedy;* V. L'vov-Rogachevskii, *Ot usad'by k izbe;* D. Makovitskii, *Iasnopolianskie zapiski;* Maude, *Tolstoy and His Problems;* Molochnikov, *Tolstoi i o Tolstom;* G. Postypaev, in S. N. Golubova, et al, eds., *L. N. Tolstoi v vospominaniiakh;* G. T. Robinson, *Rural Russia;* N. Shubakov, *Y L. N. Tolstogo*, in B. Lakshin, ed., *Interviu i besedy;* Simmons, *Leo Tolstoy* and *Tolstoy's Writings;* Spence, *Tolstoy the Ascetic;* and H. Troyat, *Tolstoy*.

PART TWO—
THE WORKS OF
LEV NIKOLAEVICH TOLSTOY

Chapter 3

Twilight of the
New Century: 1894–1901

Letter to Bernhard Eulenstein[1]

Tolstoy's lengthy letter to Eulenstein, written in the spring of 1894, declares that George's ideas are practical and endowed with a singular religious spirit. George is then lauded as the originator and leader of a movement that will end the immorality of land slavery and usher in a new age of a higher consciousness. The promulgation of these truths is a sacred duty.

In response to your letter of March 23rd, it is with special pleasure that I hasten to communicate this to you:

I have been acquainted with Henry George since the appearance of his *Social Problems*. I read it through, and was struck by the correctness and excellence of its fundamental thought, which cannot be found in similar scientific literature. Clarity, straightforwardness and force of presentation, and an exceptional Christian spirit pervade the whole book. After reading it I turned to George's previous work, *Progress and Poverty*, and learned to appreciate still more the significance of his accomplishments.

You ask my opinion of Henry George's work, and of his single tax system. My opinion is this: mankind continually advances towards an enlightened consciousness, and towards the establishment of [better] modes of life corresponding to this changing consciousness. And therefore in every period of mankind's existence, there takes place on the one hand an awakening of consciousness, and on the other hand, a realization in life of this enlightenment.

At the end of the last century and the beginning of the present one there transpired in Christendom a process of enlightenment relating to the status of workers, who were subjected to various types of slavery, and another process which established new forms of life corresponding to this clearing of perceptions: the eradication of slavery, replaced by freely hired labor. At the present time people are coming to a new comprehension of land use and it seems to me that a realization in life of this consciousness should be approaching.

This enlightenment relates to the working out of land use, which is the major problem of our day. Henry George is the foremost spokesman and leader of the movement. He thus holds a great and paramount significance. With his wonderful books he has contributed to the awakening consciousness and a practical framework responding to this question.

If I remember correctly during the time when slavery was abolished, there is now occurring an identical repetition regarding the abolition of the revolting right of landownership. The governments and ruling classes, knowing that with land comes their advantages and authority, position in society, maintain an appearance of being preoccupied with the welfare of the people, so they establish workers' banks, inspections, income taxes, and even an eight hour work day, while diligently ignoring the land question. Even with the help of their obliging science [political economy], which could prove anything and is neccessary for them, they assert that the expropriation of land is useless, harmful, and impossible. The same thing is now happening that occurred with slavery. People at the beginning of this century and the end of the last one had felt that slavery was an awful and outrageous anachronism, but pseudo-religion and science proved that there was nothing wrong with it; that it was indispensable, or, at least, that its abolition would be premature. Now the same thing is taking place relating to property in land. Pseudo-religion and pseudo-sham science are similarly proving that there is nothing wrong with private property, and that there is no need to abolish it.

It should seem evident to every educated man of our time that the exclusive right to land by people who do not work on it prevents hundreds and thousands of impoverished families from having access to it. It is as evil and base as the possession of slaves. Nevertheless, we see quasi-educated and refined English, Austrian, Prussian, and Russian aristocrats use this cruel and base right, who are not only not ashamed, but proud of it. Religion blesses such possession, and the science of political economy proves that it is and should be for the greatest good of mankind. Henry George's merit is that he not only crushed all this sophism with which religion and science justify landed property but has brought the question to its final degree of clarity. Now it is impossible not to recognize the unlawfulness of landownership, which people have ignored. George was the first to present the solution to the question. He was the first to give a clear and unequivocal answer to the usual excuses made by the enemies of any progress, which they deem full of impractical and inapplicable dreams.

Henry George's system destroys these excuses by placing the question in such a fashion that by tomorrow committess could be appointed to examine and deliberate the solution, and then put it into law. In Russia, for instance, discussion about the buying up of land or taking it away without payment for its nationalization could begin tomorrow, and [would be confronted with] precisely the same various unexpected complications, but could be resolved [in a similar manner] as with serf emacipation thirty-three years ago. A clarification of how people's situations will change would be necesary to demonstrate its feasability (improvements in the the single tax system may be necessary, but the fundamental idea is realizable); and therefore they can only do what their reason dictates. It is only necessary that this idea should be propagated and explained in the same way that you are doing for it to become part of public opinion. It is a cause that I sympathize with wholeheartedly. I wish you success.

Letter to a Siberian Peasant[2]

In 1897, Tolstoy adumbrated to T. M. Bondarev an outline of George's ideas. This succinct description of the single tax plan explains that the land will belong to the whole nation, everyone paying to a benign state a share for the benefit of the public good without other burdensome taxes. Only people who put the land to use will have access to it. The exploitation of labor will surely end.

The plan of Henry George is as follows. The advantage and profit from the use of the land is not everywhere the same. Since the more fertile, convenient portions, adjoining populous districts, will always attract many who wish to possess them; and as the more these portions are better and more suitable, so they ought to be appraised according to their advantages—the better, dearer; the worse, cheaper; the worst, cheapest of all.

Where the land attracts only a few individuals, it should not be appraised at all, but left without payment to those who are willing to cultivate it by their own manual labor. According to such an assessment, convenient plow land in the province of Tula, for example, would be valued at about five or six rubles a desiatina; market-garden land near villages at ten rubles; the same, but liable to spring floods, fifteen rubles; and so on. In towns the assessment would be from 100 to 500 rubles a desiatina; and in Moscow and St. Petersburg, in busy places, and by the harbors of navigable rivers, several thousand or tens of thousands of rubles a desiatina.

When all the land in the country has been thus appraised Henry George proposes to pass a law declaring that all the land, from such a year and date, shall no longer belong to any separate individual, but to the whole country, to the whole nation. Everyone who possesses land thereafter must gradually pay to the state—that is, to the whole nation—the price at which it has been appraised.

This payment must be expended on all the public needs of the state, so that it will take the place of every kind of monetary imposition, both domestic and foreign, including customs.[3]

According to this plan, a landowner who presently possesses 2,000 desiatinas would continue to own them but would have to pay to the treasury in Tula between twelve and fifteen thousand rubles a year, since it includes the best land for agricultrual and building purposes. No large landowner would be able to bear the strain of such a payment, and he would be obliged to give up the land. Whereas our Tula peasant would have to pay about two rubles less for each desiatiana of the same ground than he does at present, there will always be available land around him which he can rent for five or six rubles. In addition, he will not only have no other taxes to pay but would receive all Russian and foreign articles which he needs duty free. In towns the owners of houses and factories can continue to possess this property, but will have to pay for the land they occupy, according to its assessment, into the common treasury.

The advantages of such a system will be:

1. That no one will be deprived of the possibility of using the land.

2. That idle men possessing land, and forcing others to work for them in return for the use of the land, will cease to exist.

3. That the land will be in the hands of those who work it and not of those who do not.

4. That the people, being able to work on the land, will cease to enslave themselves as laborers in factories and as servants in towns, and will then disperse throughout the country.

5. That there will no longer be any overseers and tax collectors in factories, stores, and customs houses, but only collectors for the land payment. It would be impossible to steal since it is the most easily collected tax.

6. (And chiefly). That those who do not labor will be freed from the sin of profiting by the labors of others (for which they are not often to be blamed, being educated in idleness from childhood, and not knowing how to work). [They will also be liberated] from the still greater sin of every kind of falsehood and excuse to shift the blame from themselves. That those who do labor will be delivered from the temptation and sin of envy, condemnation of others, and exasperation against those who do not work. Thus will disappear one of the causes of dissension between men.

From *The Slavery of Our Times*[4]

The *Slavery of Our Times* depicts the onerous conditions men have to endure to eke out a living both in the cities and in the fields and the system of organized violence which perpetuates this new form of serfdom. Tolstoy also condemns the indifference of society towards the suffering of the laborer; socialism with its proletarianization, piecemeal reforms, legislation, and unions; all governments including democracies; false amenities that entice the worker; taxation; peasant suffering due to land hunger; and a poltical economy for justifying poverty in service to the capitalists. The root of the evil is separation from the land. The people must reclaim a simpler life in the village. Refusal to participate in the government, in the military or in any form of violence; to pay taxes, to take advantage of another's toil: these negations are essential to a more moral life. Maude writes that the

> main intention and drift of the work is to show that progress in human well-being can only be achieved by relying more and more on reason and conscience and less and less on man-made laws; that we must be ready to sacrifice the material progress . . . rather than acquiesce in such injustice and inequality . . . and that we must more and more free ourselves from the taint of murder that clings to all robes of state.[5]

The search for an absolute truth amidst the clashing practical exigencies and moral demands of daily existence can make for any number of inner conflicts. Such was the case with Tolstoy along with other Russian radicals. An example occurred in *The Slavery of Our Times* which had first appeared fourteen years earlier in *What Then Must We Do?*, and in which he came out against George's economics.[6] In many earlier letters, and later in *Resurrection,* Tolstoy extolled the single tax as the transitional means towards his anarchism. To complicate matters, all his works subsequent to *The Slavery of Our Times* returned to his endorsement of George. So a few explanations are in order. Tolstoy was a consummate genius with an ego to match. To be a follower of anyone other than God the Father was unthinkable. It could also be that an element of New World dynamism in George's individualism, which would glorify men working in technical or scientific enterprises, went against Tolstoy's idealization of simple peasants. But more likely, it was Tolstoy's absolute rejection of any state authority, even a benign one with no police or administrative functions, that temporarily turned him against Georgist political economy. Whatever the reasons, Tolstoy the absolutist was termporarily unable to accomodate himself to George's ideas of social betterment. Pavel Axelrod, an eminent Marxist, records these observations by Tolstoy in conversation with one interlocutor.

> For a true Christian neither Henry George exists nor anything [else]. All his efforts are directed only towards what is in his power, that is towards himself, and at the same time there lives in him an unshakable conviction that there is no more worth-while activity for

the world than this work on himself. Henry George is a concession, a weakness. Not to kill people is good; not to kill people or animals or parasites is better. To live honorably with one's wife in marriage is good; to live chastely with her in marriage is still better; to live without a wife in complete chastity is still better. Similarly: some say that for the good of the people a gallows has to be put in every town; others say, "No, socialist planning is better"; and we say that Henry George is still better. But, I repeat, this is weakness . . .[7]

Tolstoy was the ultimate hard liner. But though he considered George's single tax a weakness, he could not come up with a better idea, for it was absolute in its simplicity, and universal in application, one he could not shake off for mechanistic economic ideals. What Tolstoy could not see at this time was that George's system looked not to a lesser but to a differing life of virtue, in which the worker would commit himself to the reshaping of nature for the betterment of society. For the restless industrial project that George embraced, more sophisticated administration would be necessary than any that Tolstoy wanted.

8. Slavery Exists Among Us.

If between the slaves and slaveowners of today it is difficult to draw as sharp a dividing line as that which separated the former slaves from their masters, and if among the slaves of today there are some who are only temporarily slaves and then become slaveowners, or some who, at one and the same time, are slaves and slaveowners, this blending of the two classes at their points of contact does not upset the fact that the people of our time are divided into slaves and slaveowners as definitely as, in spite of the twilight, each twenty-four hours is divided into day and night.

If the slaveowner of our times has no slave John, whom he can send to the cesspool to clear out his excrements, he has three rubles of which hundreds of Johns are in such need that the slaveowner of our times may choose anyone out of hundreds of Johns and be a benefactor to him by giving him the preference, and allowing him, rather than another, to climb down into the cesspool. . . .

Slavery exists in full vigor but we do not perceive it. . . . It is the same among us: people of our day consider the worker's position to be a natural, inevitable economic condition, and they do not call it slavery. . . .

The question of the slavery of our time is now exactly the same phase in which that of serfdom stood in Europe at the end of the eighteenth century, and as serfdom among us and slavery in America stood in the second quarter of the nineteenth century.

The slavery of todays' workers is just beginning to be admitted by advanced people in our society: the majority, however, are convinced that no slavery exists.

What leads to this present misunderstanding is that in Russia and America we have only recently abolished slavery. But in reality the abolition of serfdom and of slavery was only the abolition of an obsolete form of slavery. There was the substitution by a firmer form of slavery holding a greater number of people in bondage. The abolition of serfdom and of slavery was like what the Crimean Tartars did with their prisoners. They invented the method of slitting the soles of the prisoners' feet and sprinkling chopped-up bristles into the wounds. They then released them from their weights and chains. The abolition of serfdom in Russia and of slavery in America did not destroy its essence. It was done only when the bristles had formed sores on the soles, assuring that without chains or weights the prisoners would not run away, but would have to work. . . .

In Russia serfdom was abolished only when all the land had been appropriated. When land was granted to the peasants they were burdened with payments which replaced their former slavery. In Europe, taxes that kept the people in bondage were abolished only when the people had lost their land, had become unaccustomed to agricultrual work, and, having acquired town tastes, were quite dependent on the capitalists. Only then were the taxes on corn abolished in England. Germany and other countries are only now begining to abolish the taxes on the workers and to shift them on to the rich—only because the majority of the people are already in the hands of the capitalists. One form of slavery is not abolished until another has already replaced it. There are several forms. And if not one, then another and sometimes several together will enslave people wherever a small number of men have full power over the labor and the life of the majority: herein lies the main cause of the people's misery. Therefore the means to improve the workers' lives must consist in admitting that slavery exists, not in some figurative, metaphorical sense, but in the simplest and plainest sense. It is a slavery which keeps the majority of people in the power of the minority. [We must] find the causes of this enslavement and eliminate them.

9. What is Slavery?

In what does the slavery of our time consist? What are the forces that make some people the slaves of others? If we ask all the workers in the factories or in other places of employment and in the towns and villages in Russia, Europe, and America what has made them choose their mode of life, they will all reply that they had either no land on which they could or wished to live and work (that will be the reply of all the Russian workmen and of many Europeans), or they could pay direct and indirect taxes only by selling their labor. [Another response is that] they are tied to factory work, because they are ensnared by the more luxurious habits that they can only gratify by selling their labor and their liberty.

The two first causes, the lack of land and the taxes, drive men to compulsory labor, while the third, increased and unsatisfied needs, decoy and hold them.

We can imagine that the land may be freed from private proprietors by Henry George's plan, and that, therefore, the lack of land driving people into slavery may be eliminated. We can also imagine the direct abolition of taxes, or their transference from the poor to the rich, as is being done in some countries. Under the present economic organization, however, it is inconceivable that the multiplying luxurious habits among the rich (many of them harmful) would not, little by little, pass to the lower classes, as inevitably as water sinks into dry ground. In order to be able to satisfy these new perceived necessities, the workers will be ready to sell their freedom.

So that this third condition, though it is voluntary (and would seem that a man might resist the temptation) and though science does not acknowledge it to be the firmest and most irremovable cause of the workers' miserable enslavement, [proves to be the stubbornest].

Workmen living near rich people are always infected with new wants and obtain the means to satisfy them only by devoting their most intense labor. So that the workmen in England and America, who receive sometimes ten times as much as is necessary for subsistence, continue to be just as much slaves as they were before. . . .

All the workers are brought to their present state, and are kept in it, by these three causes . . . none can escape from . . . [the enslavement to those who control the taxes, the land, and the articles necessary to satisfy their wants]. The farmer who has no land, or not enough, will always fall into perpetual or temporary slavery to the landowner, so he can feed himself. Should he, in one way or other, obtain land enough for sustenance, direct or indirect taxes would again relegate him to slavery.

If, to escape from land slavery, he ceases to cultivate, and [is forced to] live on someone else's land, engages in a handicraft, and exchanges his wares for necessities, then there will be taxes on the one hand. On the other hand, competition, from a capitalist system that produces similar articles but with better implements of production, will compel him to go into temporary or perpetual slavery to the manufacturer. Although working for a capitalist, he might set up free relations, and not be obliged to sell his liberty, yet the new wants which he develops deprive him of any such possibility. So that, one way or another, the laborer is always in slavery to those who control the taxes, the land, and the articles necessary to satisfy his wants.

10. Laws Concerning Land, Taxes, and Property.

. . . Laws were formerly established enabling some people to own, buy and sell other people, and to make them work. But now people have passed laws so that men may not use land that belongs to someone else, must pay required taxes, and must not use articles considered to be the property of others, and so we have slavery in modern form.

11. Laws—the Cause of Slavery.

The slavery of our times results from three sets of laws: land, tax, and property laws. And therefore all the efforts of people who want to improve the laborers' lives inevitably, but unconsciously, are directed against them.

Some people have repealed burdensome taxes on the working classes, and have transferred them onto the rich. Others propose to abolish the right of private property in land, and attempts to do so are being made in New Zealand and in an American state (the limitation of landords' right in Ireland goes in the same direction).[8] A third set, the socialists, propose to communalize the means of production, to tax incomes and inheritances, and to limit the rights of capitalist employers. It would therefore seem that the legislative enactments which cause slavery are being repealed and we may therefore expect slavery to be abolished. But to be convinced that not only the practical but even the theoretical projects for the improvement of the workers' lives are merely replacing one slave-producing law with another establishing a newer form of slavery, we need only look more closely at the conditions these legislative enactments bring about. Thus, for instance, those who abolish taxes and duties on the poor first eliminate direct dues, and then transfer the burden of taxation from the poor to the rich. But by necessity they retain the laws permitting private property in land, the present means of production, and on other articles to which the entire burden of taxes is shifted. Though the workers are freed from taxes, maintaining the laws concerning land and property holds the workers in slavery to the landowners and the capitalists. Henry George and his partisans would abolish the laws allowing private property of land but propose new laws imposing an obligatory rent on the land. And this obligatory land rent will necessarily create a new form of slavery, because a man compelled to pay rent or the single tax may, at any failure of the crops or other misfortune, have to borrow money from a lender, and will again lapse into slavery.[9] Those who, like the socialists, who in theory would abolish the legislation of property in land and in the means of production, would not only retain tax legislation, but would inevitably introduce laws of compulsory labor—they would re-establish slavery in its primitive form.

In one way or another, then, all the realized and theoretical repeals of certain laws which maintain slavery in one form have always replaced it by new legislation creating slavery in another form.

What happens is something like what a jailer might do who shifted a prisoner's chains from the neck to the arms, and from the arms to the legs, or took them off and substituted bolts and bars. All the improvements taken place pertaining to the status of workers' have been of this kind.

The laws giving a master the right to compel his slaves to perform compulsory work were replaced by laws allowing the masters to own all the land. The laws permitting all the land to become the private property of the masters could be replaced by taxation law, but the control of the taxes would still be in their hands. The taxation laws may be replaced by others defending the right of private property in articles of use and in the means of production, or they may in turn be replaced, as is now proposed, by the enactment of compulsory labor.

So it is evident that the abolition of one form of legislation producing our present slavery (whether taxes or landowning or property in articles of use or in the means of production) will not destory slavery. It will only repeal one of its forms, which will immediately be replaced by a new one, as was the case with the abolition of chattel slavery and serfdom. Even the mutual elimination of all three groups of laws will not end slavery but create a new form, which is now already beginning to show itself. The freedom of labor will be shackled by legislation regulating the hours of work, age, and health, as well as by obligatory attendance at schools, by deductions for old age insurance or accidents, by measures of factory inspection, and so forth. All this is nothing but transitional legislation—it will pave the way for a new and as yet untried form of slavery.

It has become apparent that the essence of slavery lies not in those three basic types of legislation on which it now rests and not even in various legislative enactments. It is the very existence of legislation itself—the power certain people hold to decree laws profitable for themselves. As long as they have that power there will be slavery.

Formerly it was financially rewarding for people to have chattel slaves and so laws about slavery arose. Afterwards it became profitable to own land, to take taxes, and to keep acquired things, so they made laws to correspond. Now it is advantageous for people to maintain the existing direction and division of labor and they are devising such laws as will compel people to work under these conditions. Thus the fundamental cause of slavery is legislation: the power to make laws. . . .

12. The Essence of Legislation is Organized Violence.

. . . Many constitutions have been devised, begining with the English and the American and ending with the Japanese and the Turkish, and these people in these countries believe that all the laws are established by their own will. But everyone knows that not in despotic countries only, but also in the ones nominally most free (England, America, France, and others) the laws are made not by the will of everyone, but by those who have power, who always and everywhere are are the ones to profit: be they many, or few, or only one man. Everywhere and always the laws are enforced by the only means that has compelled some people to obey the will of others, that is, by blows, by deprivation of liberty, and by murder. There can be no other way.

And so the essence of legislature does not lie in Subject or Object, in rights, or in the idea of the dominion of the collective will of the people, or in other such indefinite and confused conceptions. Its essence is that people who wield organized violence have power to compel others to obey.

The exact and irrefutable definition of legislation, which is intelligible to everyone, is that: *laws are rules, made by people who govern by means of organized violence, for noncompliance with which the noncomplier is subjected to blows, to loss of liberty, or even to murder. . . .*

13. What are Governments? Is it Possible to Exist Without Governments?

The cause of the miserable condition of the workers is slavery. The cause of slavery is legislation. Legislation rests on organized violence.

It follows that an improvement in the condition of the people is possible only through the abolition of organized violence. . . .

[The state] is harmful and dangerous because its effect on all society's evils is not to lessen and correct, but rather to strengthen and confirm it, since it is justified, put in attractive forms, or secreted.

All that well-being of the people which we see in so-called well-governed states (ruled by violence) is but an appearance—a fiction. Everything that would disturb the external appearance of well-being (all the hungry people, the sick, the revoltingly vicious) are all hidden away where they cannot be seen. But the fact that we do not see them, does not show that they do not exist. On the contrary, the more they are hidden the more there will be of them, and the more cruel towards them will those be who are the cause of their condition. It is true that every interruption or stoppage of state action (especially organized violence) disturbs these external appearances of well-being in our life. But such a disturbance does not produce this disorder but rather brings to the surface what was hidden and makes possible its amendment. . . .

Until the end of the nineteenth century people thought that they could not live without governments. But life flows onward and its conditions and people's views change. And notwithstanding the efforts of governments to maintain people in that childish condition in which an injured man feels as if it were better for him to have someone to complain to, people (especially the laboring people, both in Europe and in Russia) are emerging from this juvenile state and are beginning to understand life's true conditions better. . . .

We see . . . that in the most diverse matters [including education, public administration, etc.] people can now arrange their own lives incomparably better than those who govern them. . . .

I have known people (Cossacks of the Oural), [for instance], who have lived without acknowledging private property in land. And there was such well-being and order in their commune as does not exist in society where landed property is defended by violence. And I now know communes that live without accepting an individual's right to private property. According to my recollection all the Russian peasantry have never accepted the idea of landed property. The defense of it by state violence does not abolish the struggle for landed property but, on the contrary, intensifies it, and in many cases causes it.

Were it not for the defense of landed property and its consequent rise in price, people would not be crowded into such narrow spaces but would scatter over the still numerous free lands over the globe. But as it is, a continual struggle goes on for it; a struggle with the arsenal that the government furnishes through its laws of landed property. And in this struggle it is not those who work on the land but always those who take part in state violence, who have the advantage.

It is the same with reference to anything produced by labor. Things really made by a man's own labor, and that he needs, are always protected by custom, by public opinion, by feelings of justice and mutuality, and they do not need to be protected by violence.

Tens of thousands of acres of forest lands, belonging to one proprietor (while thousands of people close by have no fuel) need protection by violence. So, too, do factories where several generations of workmen have been defrauded. Yet [there are always] hundreds of thousands of bushels of grain, belonging to one owner, who has held them back to sell them at triple the price in time of famine. But no man, however depraved (except a rich man or a government official) would take from his countryman living by his own labor the harvest he has raised, the cow he has bred (from which he gets milk for his children) or the tools of his livelihood. If even a man were found who did take from another articles the latter had made, such a man would rouse against himself such indignation from everyone living there, that he would scarcely find his action profitable. A man so immoral as to do it under such circumstances, would be sure to do it under the strictest system of property defense by violence. . . . If it has not quite been destroyed, it has considerably weakened people's innate consciousness of justice regarding the use of articles and has sapped the natural and innate right of property [of personal possessions], without which humanity could not exist. . . .

Either people are rational or irrational beings. If they are irrational beings, then they are all irrational, and then everything among them is decided by violence, and there is no reason why certain people should, and others should not, have a right to use violence. And in that case, state violence has no justification. But if men are rational beings, then their relations should be based on reason, and not on the violence of those who happen to have seized power. And in that case, again, state violence has no justification.

14. How Can Governments be Abolished?

Slavery results from laws, laws are made by governments [which are ogranized violence], and therefore people can be freed from slavery only by the abolition of governments. . . .

And thus the only means to destroy governments is not by force but through the exposure of [the fraud that governments embody]. . . . Robbers generally plunder the rich but a government generally steals from the poor and protects those rich men who assist in their crimes. . . .

Towards governments, as towards churches, it is impossible to feel otherwise than with veneration or aversion. Until a man has understood what a government is, and until he has understood what a church is, he cannot but feel a veneration for those institutions. As long as he is guided by them, his vanity makes it necessary for him to think that what guides him is something primal, great, and holy. But as soon as he understands that what guides him is not something primal and holy, but that it is a fraud carried out by unworthy people, who, under the pretense of guiding him, make use of him for their own personal ends, he cannot but feel aversion towards these people; and the more important the side of his life that has been guided, the more aversion will he feel. . . .

People must feel that their collaboration in the criminal activity of governments [such as the paying of taxes and serving in the military] . . . is harmful to oneself and to one's brothers, is also a participation in the crimes unceasingly committed by all of them. . . .

The age of veneration of governments, notwithstanding all the hypnotic influence they employ to maintain their position, is passing away. And it is time for people to understand that they are not only not necessary, but are harmful and immoral . . . .

And as soon as people clearly understand that, they will naturally cease to [collaborate in any manner whatsoever with governments]. . . . And as soon as a majority of people refuses to do these things, the fraud which enslaves them will be abolished.

Only in this way can people be freed from slavery.

Where Is The Way Out?[10]

Whereas *The Slavery of Our Times* negatively depicts Georgist economics, *Where is the Way Out* (1900) reverts to praise of the single tax as the only just and sensible solution to land monopolization and onerous taxation. A return to the land would rescue workers from the artificial habits developed in the cities and from taxes that necessitate slave bondage in the factories. Here Tolstoy's horror of proletarianization and its inherent revolutionary outcome reached its apogee. He condemns any form of government and its military arm, the defender of the state and the agent of sin. He urges a refusal to serve in the military, for then the state would collapse.

1. Born in the country, a boy grows up and works with his father, grandfather, and mother.

The field is harvested after it has been plowed, harrowed, and seeded by his father and himself and then cut with a sickle by his mother and the girl. The boy then witnesses the first sheaves which he himself help pulled down from the rick taken by his father not to his own house but beyond the garden to the threshing floor of the proprietor of the land. Driving past the manor with the squeaky wagon, which he and his father had themselves fastened with ropes, the boy sees on the balcony a finely-dressed lady. She is sitting near a shining samovar on a table, which is covered with dishes, pastry, and sweets.[11] On the other side of the road, in a cleared space, the owner's two boys are playing ball in embroidered shirts and shining boots.

One boy throws the ball over the wagon.

"Pick it up, boy!" he shouts.

"Pick it up, Vaska!" Vaska's father, while walking beside the wagon with reins in his hand, takes off his hat and cries out to his son.

"What is this?" thinks the boy. "I am worn out from work. They play and I have to pick up their ball."

But he picks up the ball. Without looking at the boy the young lord takes the ball in his white hand out from the sunburned black one and goes back to his game.

The father has walked on with the wagon. The boy catches up with him on a run, shuffling his tattered low boots in the dust of the road. They drive onto the manorial threshing floor which is full of wagons with sheaves. The busy steward in a linen frock coat which is wet from perspiration in the back, and with a rod in his hand, meets the boy's father, whom he scolds for not having driven to the right spot. His father makes excuses, walks as though fatigued, jerks the tired horse by the rein, and drives the wagon to the other side.

The boy goes up to his father and asks:

"Father, why do we take our rye to him? *We* harvested it?"

"Because the land is theirs," the father angrily answers.

"Who gave them the land?"

"Ask the steward. He will show you who. Do you see their rod?"

"Where will they put all this corn?"

"They will thresh it, and then they will sell it."

"And what will they do with the money?"

"They will buy those cakes that you saw on the table which we drove passed."

The boy grows silent and falls to musing. But he has no time for that. They are shouting to his father to move the wagon closer to the barn. The father climbs on the wagon and moves it. Loosening the ropes with difficulty, he then throws the sheaves into the mow, straining his rupture even more, while the boy holds the old mare to keep the flies away from her, as his father commands him to do (he has been driving her to pasture for two years). He thinks and thinks, and cannot understand why the land does not belong to those who work on it, but to those sons of the lord, who in embroidered shirts play ball, drink tea, and eat cakes.

The boy continues to think about it at work, and when he goes to bed, and when he pastures the horses. He can find no answer. All say it must be so and everyone [continues] to live in that manner.

And the boy grows up, he is married off, and children are born to him. His children ask the same question and he answers them in the same way that his father answered him. And living like [his father] in want, he works submissively for other idle people.

And so he and all around him live. Wherever one travels, so he hears from a pilgrim, it is the same. Everywhere peasants work above their strength for the idle. By overworking they get ruptures, asthma, consumption, take to drinking from grief, and die before their time. The women exhaust their last strength in cooking, attending to the cattle, washing for their men, and making their clothes. They also age before their time and waste away from overwork and untimely labor.

And everywhere those they work for furnish themselves with buggies, carriages, trotters, horses, build arbors, and play games. Day in and day out, from Easter to Easter, from morning until evening, they dress up, play, eat, and drink as if every one were the greatest holiday—this is not the case with the man who works for them.

2. Why is that so? The first answer which comes to the mind of the laboring farmer is that the land was taken from him and was given to those who do not work it. Although he and his family have to eat, the working peasant has either no land at all or so little of it that it will not support his family. Thus he must starve or else rent land which belongs to the idle and must even agree to their conditions.

It seems, at first glance, that there are peasants who have enough land and can support themselves.

But the real cause is that all or part of the peasants sell themselves into slavery. Why is that so? Because the peasants have to purchase plow-shares, scythes, horseshoes, building materials, kerosene, tea, sugar, liquor, rope, salt, matches, cottons, and tobacco. But the money which a peasant earns through the sale of his produce is always taken away by direct and indirect taxres, so the price of those necessary articles is raised. The majortiy of the peasants are thus unable to provide themselves with the needed money except by selling themselves into slavery to those who have funds.

Some of the peasants and their wives and daughters sell themselves [as laborers] in their locality while entire families do so a distance away in the cities and in the [imperial and provincial] capitals. They are taken on as lackeys, coachmen, nurses, wet-nurses, chambermaids, bath servants, wait-ers, and, above all, factory hands.

Having sold themselves into these urban occupations the country people grow unaccustomed to farm labor and a simple life. They get used to city food, dress, beverages, and through these habits insure their slavery even more.

Thus it is not merely the lack of land that causes the laborers to be the slaves of the rich. The cause can also be attributed to taxes, the raised price of commodities, and the adopted luxurious city habits by the [dispossesed] country workers.

The slavery began with the taking away of the land from the workers. But this slavery has been strengthened and confirmed when they lost their village skills through city luxury, which cannot be satisfied in any other way than by selling themselves to the rich. This slavery is growing and becom-ing more entrenched.

In the country people live on semi-starvation rations. Since they are enslaved to the landowners they labor constantly and are in want. In the cities and [especially] in the factories, the laborers live in slavery to the manufacturers. Generation after generation is physically and morally cor-rupted by the monotonous, tedious, unhealty work. The situation of both classes is getting worse and worse over the years. In the country the people are getting poorer while an ever growing number are going to the factories. In the cities the people are getting not poorer, but seemingly richer. At the same time they are becoming more incontinent and unable to do any other work than the kind they have become accustomed to—they are even more in the control of the manufacturers.

Thus the power of the landowners and the manufactures, of the rich in general, is getting stronger, while the condition of the laborers is getting worse. What, then, is the way out of this situation? Is there one?

3. Liberation from land slavery could be very easy. What is needed for this emancipation is only to recognize what is self-evident if people had not been deceived—that every man born has the right to earn his sustenance from the land, just as every man has a right to the air and the sun. Anyone who therefore does not till the soil himself does not have the right to regard it as his own or to keep others from working on it.

But the government will never allow this liberation from land slavery because the majority of its participants own some of it on which their enitre existence is based.

They are aware of this legal right so they try with all their might to maintain and defend it.

About thirty years ago Henry George proposed not only a rational but a very practical system for the emancipation of the land from private owner-ship. But neither in America or in England (in France it is not even spoken of) has this project been adopted. They have tried in every way to overturn it, but since it is impossible to be stifled, it is passed over in silence.

If this system has not been adopted in America and in England, there is still less hope that it will be done in monarchical countries, such as Ger-many, Austria, or Russia.

In Russia vast expanses of territory have been seized by private indi-viduals, including the tsar and the imperial family. So there is no hope that these men (feeling themselves as helpless without the legal right to the land as nestlings do without a nest), will refrain from fighting with all their strength and give it up. And so, as long as the power shall be on the side of the government, which is composed of proprietors, there will be no eman-cipation from landownership.

There will be even less of a chance for a liberation from taxes. The whole government, from the head of the state, the tsar, down to the last policeman, lives on them. And so tax abolition by the state would be as unthinkable as a man who takes from himself his only means of existence.

It is true that some governments seem to be trying to relieve their people from the tax burden by transferring them to incomes based on a graduated increase. But such a tax transference from a direct levy to the income cannot deceive the masses. The rich, who are composed of merchants, landowners, and capitalists with the increase of taxes will proportionally increase the price of the land and necessities, and will also lower wages. Thus the whole tax burden will again be shouldered by the laborers.

So that the laborers could be freed from the slavery of the capitalist ownership of implements of production, the educated have proposed numerous measures. For instance, the wages of the laborers are to increase all the time while their work hours would diminish. There is even [the proposal] that the implements of labor must pass from the capitalists' possession to those of the workers. They will then control the factories and will not be compelled to give up a part of their labor, so that they will earn necessities by their own hands. This method has been advocated in Europe, [especially] in England, France, and Germany for more than thirty years, but so far neither this means nor any other similar approach has been implemented.[12]

Labor unions and strikes have been established and the factory hands have been demanding fewer working hours and greater pay. But since the governments, who are united with the capitalists and will never allow the implements of production to be taken away, the crux of the problem remains the same.

Receiving better pay and doing less work, the laborers increase their needs and so remain in the same slavery to the capitalists.

Thus the slavery in which the working people find themselves cannot be destroyed so long as the governments protect landownership for the nonworkers, collect direct and indirect taxes, and defend the property of the capitalists.

4. The slavery of the working people is caused by governments. It would seen that their emancipation would naturally be effected with the establishment of new ones. The liberation from landownership, the abolition of taxes, and the transference of capital and the factories into their hands would then [seem to] be plausible.

There are men who recognize this means as possible and work towards this end. But fortunately such actions are now impossible since they are always connected with violence and murder. They are also immoral, ruinous, and self-defeating, as has been frequently repeated in history.

The time has long ago passed when the governments naively believed in their beneficent destiny for humanity and have not take any measures for securing themselves against rebellions (besides, there were no railways and no telegraphs then), and they were easily overthrown, as was the case in England in the 1640s, in France during the great Revolution [of 1789], and later in Germany in 1848. Since then there has been but one revolution, in 1871, and it transpired under exceptional conditions.[13] At present revolutions and the overthrow of governments are patently impossible, because authorities know their uselessness and harmfulness. Since no one believes in their sanctity, they are guided by nothing but a feeling of self-preservation. They make use of all the means at their command and are constantly on the lookout for anything which may impair or even shake their power.

Every contemporary government has an army of officials, which is connected by railways, telegraphs, and telephones. They have fortresses and prisons with all the most modern appliances. Photography, anthropometric measurements, mines, cannon, guns, and all the most perfect instruments of violence [are at their disposal]. The moment something new apperars [violence] is immediately applied for self-preservation. There is also an organization of espionage, a venal clergy, scholars, artists, and press. Above all else, every government has a body of officers who are corrupted by patriotism, bribery, and hypnotism. Millions of physcially sound but morally undeveloped children of twenty-one years of age become soldiers—they are rather a rabble of immoral hirelings stultified by discipline and ready to commit any crime on order.

And so it is now impossible to forcibly destroy an ever-vigilant government which possesses these means. No government will allow this to be done. And so long as there is a government, it will maintain landownership, the collection of the taxes, and the possession of capital, because the larger estate owners and the officials who receive their salaries from taxes, and the capitalists form the government. Every attempt of the laborers to possess the land will always end the same way—the soldiers will come to beat and drive away those who seized the land and return it to the owner. Every attempt not to pay taxes will end in the same fashion—the soldiers will take away the taxes due and beat those who refuse to pay. The same will happen to those who will attempt, not so much to seize the implements of production or the factory, but simply to institute a strike or to keep scabs from lowering the wages. The soldiers will come and disperse the participants, as has always occurred everywhere in Europe and in Russia. So long as the military is in the hands of the government, living on taxes and in league with the landowners and capitalists, the structure of society will always remain the same, so a revolution would be impossible.

5. And so there naturally arises the question: Who are these soldiers?

These soldiers are the same people whose land has been taken away, from whom the taxes are being collected, and who are in slavery to the capitalists.

Why do these soldiers act against their brothers?

They do so because they cannot do otherwise. By a long and complex process through education, religious instruction, and hypnotization they have been brought to an unreflective state of mind only capable of obeying. The government, having in its hands seized money, bribes all kinds of enlisted

leaders, who in turn teach soldiers, which deprives them of human consciousness. But above all, the government bribes the teachers and the clergy,
who have to use every effort for impressing adults and children that militarism (the preparation for murder), is not only useful for men but also good
and pleasing to God. And year after year, though they see that they are
enslaving the masses to the rich and the government, they still submissively engage in everything prescribed even though it is obviously a detriment to their brothers or could even kill their own parents.

The bribed officials, military teachers, and clergy prepare the soldiers
through stupefaction.

The soldiers, at the command of their superiors, threaten to deprive
liberty, inflict wounds and death, take the income from the land, take taxes,
and the income from the factories and trade for the benefit of the ruling
classes. But the ruling classes use part of this money for bribing the chiefs,
the military teachers, and the clergy.

6. Thus the circle is closed and there does not seem to be any way out.

The solution suggested by the revolutionists to use violence to over-
come violence, is obviously impossible. The governments, which are already in possession of a disciplined military, will never permit the formation
of another disciplined force. All attempts of the past century have shown
how vain they are. Nor is there a way out, as the socialists believe, by means
of forming great economic strength [in order] to successfully wage a fight
against a consolidated capitalist power. Never will the labor unions, which
may be in possession of few miserable millions, be able to fight against the
economic power of the multimillionaires, who are always supported by the
military. There is even less of a chance, as is proposed by other socialists, to
obtain a majority in the parliament.[14] Such a majority will not achieve anything, so long as the army is in control of the governments. The moment
the parliamentary decrees would oppose the interests of the ruling classes,
the government will prorogue such a body, as has been so frequently done
and will be done due to military presence.[15] The introduction of socialist
principles into the army will not accomplish anything. Military hypnotism
is so artfully applied that so long as the most free-thinking and rational
person is in it, he will always perform what is demanded. Thus revolution
or socialism offers no solution.[16]

If there is a way out, it is one which has not yet been used. It alone
would indubitably destroy the entire consolidated, artful, and long-estab-
lished governmental machine which enslaves the masses—men must refuse
to join the army, before being subjected to its stupefying and corrupting
influence of discipline.

This way out is the only one which is not only possible but is also obligatory and inevitable for everyone, because existing violence is based on three governmental actions—the robbery of the masses, the distribution of money to those who commit the robbery, and the drafting of the masses into the army.

A private individual cannot keep the government from practicing robbery through a drafted army, nor can he keep it from distributing the money collected to those who control the military and the soldiers' stultification. He can, however, keep men from entering the army, by [setting an example] by not joining it himself and by explaining to others the essence of the deception to which they would fall prey if they did.

Not only *can* every man do this—every man *must* do so. Everyone must do this because entrance into military service is a renunciation of every religion, no matter which one he may profess (all of them prohibit murder) and a renunciation of human dignity. It would be a voluntary entrance into slavery with the sole purpose of murder.

This [means] is the only possible and inevitable necessary solution to the enslavement of the working people by the ruling classes.

It entails not destroying violence by violence, seizing the implements of production or fighting the governments in the parliaments. Every man must recognize the truth for himself, practice it, and act in accordance with it. Humanity must universally recognize the truth that one must not kill his neighbor.

Let men only apply their energies, not to external phenomena, but to the causes of them and to their own lives—like wax before the fire all that power of violence and evil which now holds and torments people will melt.

Need It Be So?[17]

In the same year, the first of the century, as the previous selection *Need It Be So?* appeared. Here Tolstoy expresses the gross iniquities of class differences sanctioned by tradition. He questions the right of the rich to live in idle luxury while the poor starve and work themselves to death. He argues, as always, that man's hardships arise from the possession of the land. He also indicts the control of factories and the products of labor, as well the collection of taxes whether in an autocracy or a democracy. Laws, he contends, only safeguard stolen property. Again Tolstoy calls for an end to all violence, which protects the rich and perpetuates injustice. He condemns the military and its system of propaganda, which bestializes the poor conscript, in the most vehement terms. Finally he attacks the false Christianity perpetuated through the centuries by church and state, which sanctions the promulgation of hatred, enslavement, and murder.

1. Amidst fields there stands a foundry surrounded by a wall, with incessantly smoking chimneys, clattering chains, furnaces, a railway siding, and scattered little houses of the managers and laborers. In this foundry there are mines with passages two hundred feet underground, which are dark, narrow, damp, and constantly threaten [the miners] with death. The working people swarm like ants. They are at work mining the ore from morning until night, or from night until morning. Others in the darkness, bending over, take this ore or clay to the shaft and bring back empty cars, and again fill them, and so work for twelve or fourteen hours a day all week long.

Thus they work in the mines. In the foundry itself, some work at the furnace in oppressive heat, while others work at the melted ore and slag trough. There are engineers, stokers, smiths, brickmakers, carpenters who work in the shops. [Everyone here] also works the entire week from twelve to fourteen hours a day.

On Sunday all these men receive their wages, wash themselves, or sometimes even do not bother to, and go to the inns and saloons, which entice them since they surround the foundry. Early Monday morning they go back to work.

Near this same foundry peasants plow someone else's field with lean, worn-out horses. These peasants get up at dawn, unless they have passed the night in the pasture near a swamp, which is the only place where they can feed their horses. They then come home, harness the horses, and taking with them a slice of bread, go out to plow the landlord's field.

Other peasants are sitting by the road not far away from the foundry, and having made themselves a protective covering from matting are breaking rocks for its construction. The legs of these men are bruised, their hands are all calloused and their whole bodies are dirty. Not ony their faces, hair, and beards, but even their lungs are permeated with lime dust.

Taking a small unbroken stone from a heap, these men put it between the soles of their feet, which are covered with bast shoes and wrapped in rags, and strike it with a heavy mallet, until broken. When the stone has been broken, they take the smaller parts and strike them until these are broken fine—and again they take whole stones, and again. And thus these men work from the early summer dawn until night for fifteen or sixteen hours, resting only for two hours after dinner, and twice, at breakfast and at noon, fortifying themselves with bread and water.

And thus do these men work in the mines and the foundry, as do the plowmen, and the stonebreakers, from early youth until old age. And their wives and their mothers live similarly, who [also] work beyond their strength, suffering from diseases of the womb. And so live their fathers and their children who, poorly fed and poorly dressed, work from morning until evening, from childhood until old age, which is beyond their strength and ruins their health.

And past the foundry, past the stonebreakers, past the plowing peasants, and past the ragged men and women with their satchels who wander from place to place begging in the name of Christ, there races by a carriage with tinkling bells. It is drawn by four matched chestnut horses of good height, the worst of which is worth the whole farm of any of the peasants who are admiring the four-in-hand. In the carriage are seated two ladies, displaying brightly-colored parasols, ribbons, and hat feathers, each of which costs more than the horse with which the peasant plows his field. On the front seat sits an officer, shining in the sun with lace and buttons, and dressed in a freshly-laundered shirt, and on the box sits a ponderous coachman, in blue silk shirtsleeves with a velvet sleeveless coat. He came very near crushing some female pilgrims, and almost knocked a peasant in a dirty ore-soiled shirt from his empty cart, although it kept jolting along in the ditch.

"You see this?" says the coachman, showing his whip to the peasant, who was not quick enough in turning aside. With one hand the peasant pulls the rein and with the other timidly pulls his cap off his louse-infected head.

Back of the carriage, glinting in the sun with the nickle-plated parts of their machines, noiselessly race two men and one woman on bicycles. They laugh merrily as they overtake and frighten the wandering women, who make the sign of the cross.

On the sidepath of the highway pass a man on an English cob and a lady on an ambler. To say nothing of the cost of the horses and the saddles, the one black hat with the lilac veil is equivalent to two months' work of the stonebreakers. As much was paid for the fashionable English whip that could be earned in a week by that young lad (who is happy that he was hired to work underground in the mine). Jumping out of the way, [this boy could not help but] admire the sleek forms of the horses and riders, and the fat, imported, immense dog in an expensive collar, who is running behind them with a protruding tongue.

Not far from this company there is traveling in a cart a dressed-up, smiling maid with curls, wearing a white apron, and a fat, ruddy man with well-groomed side-whiskers, who is whispering something to her. In the cart may be seen a samovar, bundles wrapped in napkins, and an ice cream chest.

These are the servants of the people who are traveling in the carriage, on horseback, and on bicycles. Today nothing is out of the ordinary. They live in such a manner the entire summer, going out for pleasure almost every day, and at times, as now, taking with them tea, beverages, and sweets, so they can picnic, [always] in some new place.

These people comprise three families who are passing the summer in the country. One is the family of a proprietor, the owner of two thousand desiatinas of land, another that of an official who receives a salary of three thousand rubles, and the third (the wealthiest family) the children of a manufacturer.[18]

All these people are not in the least surprised or touched by the sight of all this poverty and hard labor which surrounds them. They think that this is the way everthing should be. They are interested, [however], in something quite different.

"No, that is impossible," says the lady on horseback, looking back at the dog, "I cannot see that!" and she stops the carriage. All talk together in French and laugh, and they put the dog into the carriage and set out, covering the stonebreakers and the itinerants with clouds of lime dust.[19]

And the carriage, the riders, the bicyclists have flashed by like beings from another world, while the people in the foundry, the stonebreakers, and the plowmen continue their hard monotonous work for somebody else. [All this labor] will end only with their death.

"Some people have a fine time!" they think, as they watch the travelers go by. And their painful existence appears even more so.

2. What is this? Have these laboring people done anything criminal at all to be punished in such a manner? Or is this the lot of all men? And have those who drove by in the carriages and on the bicycles done something particularly useful and important to be so rewarded? Not in the least! On the contrary, those who are working with such exertion are for the most part moral, continent, modest, and industrious people, while those who drove past are by and large corrupt, lustful, impudent, and idle people. This [situation] occurs because such a way of life is considered natural and normal [and is condoned by a] world of people who assert that they are professing Christ's commandment to love thy neighbor, or [think] that they are cultured or refined.

Such a life exists, not only in that corner of Tula Province, which I am very familiar with since I am frequently there,[20] but everywhere: not only in Russia (from St. Petersburg to Batum) but also in France (from Paris to Auvergne) and in Italy (from Rome to Palermo) and in Germany, in Spain, in America, in Australia, and even in India and China. Everywhere two or three people in a thousand live in such a way that, without doing anything for themselves, they consume in food and drink in one day what would support hundreds of people for a year. They wear clothes which cost thousands, live in palaces, where thousands of laboring people could find room, and spend on their whims even more thousands of rubles and millions of work days. [This injustice occurs] while others, getting neither enough sleep nor enough food, work beyond their strength, ruining their bodily and their spiritual health for these select few.

For one class of women, when they are about to bear children, they send for a midwife, a physician, and even sometimes for two physicians for one woman. Their layettes contain a hundred baby shirts and swaddling clothes with silk ribbons and they prepare little wagons that swing on springs. The other class of women, the vast majority, bear children in any chance place and manner, and without aid, swaddle them in rags, put them into bast cradles on straw, and are glad if they die.

The children of one class, while the other is lying in bed for nine days, are taken care of by the midwife, the nurse, and the wet nurse while the children of the other class are not taken care of. Since there is no one to do so, the mother herself gets up immediately after childbirth, makes the fires in the oven, milks the cow, and sometimes washes the clothes for herself, her husband, and her children. One class of children grows up among toys, amusements, and lessons while the other children at first crawl with their bared bellies over thresholds, become maim, are eaten up by pigs, and at the age five begin to work beyond their strength. The first are taught all the scientific wisdom of their time while the others learn vulgar curses and the most savage of superstitions. The well-off ones fall in love, carry on romantic affairs, and then marry, after they have experienced all the [sensual] pleasures, while the indigent are married off to those whom the parents choose, between the ages of sixteen and twenty years, for the purpose of receiving additional aid. The rich eat and drink the best and the most expensive things in the world, feeding their dogs on white bread and beef while the poor eat nothing but bread and *kvas*, nor do they get enough bread, and what they get is stale, so that they may not eat too much of it.[21] The [fortunate ones] change their fine underwear every day to avoid soiling while the [unlucky] who are constantly doing work for others, change their coarse, ragged, louse-infected underwear once in two weeks, or even do not change them and wear them until they fall to pieces. The rich sleep between clean sheets, on feather beds, while the poor sleep on the ground, covering themselves with their tattered caftans.

The prosperous drive out with well-fed horses, not to work, but simply for pleasure, while the lower classes labor hard with ill-fed horses, and walk, if they have to. The former wonder what to do to occupy their leisure time while the latter find no time to clean themselves, to wash, to take a rest, to say a word, or to visit their relatives. The well-off read four languages and amuse themselves daily with the greatest variety of things while the poor do not even know how to read but only know one amusement—drunkenness. The rich know everything and believe in nothing while the workers know nothing and believe any nonsense that they are told. When the well-off get sick, they travel from place to place in search of the best curative air, to say nothing of all kinds of waters, every kind of medical attention, cleanliness, and medicine, while the peasants lie down on the oven in a smoky hut, and with unwashed sores, stale bread, and with air infected by ten family members, calves and sheep, rot alive and die before their time.

Must it be so?

If there is a higher reason and a love which guides the world, if there is a God, He cannot have wished to see such divisiveness among men. [He could not desire] one class that does not know what to do with their surplus wealth and senselessly squander the fruit of the labors of others, while many grow sick working beyond their strength living an agonizing life and die before their time.

If there is a God, this [inequality] cannot and must not be so. But if there is no God, such a way of life, in which the majority of men must waste their lives, is still disadvantageous for everyone. It is from the simplest human point of view tasteless because for a small number who may enjoy an abundance, [it is a life] which corrupts and weighs heavily upon them.

3. Why, then, do men live thus?

It is natural for the rich, who are used to their wealth and do not see clearly that it does not bring happiness or maintains their status. But why does the vast majority, in whose hands is every power, assume that there is happiness in wealth, and continue to live in want and submit to the minority?

Indeed, why do all the vast majority who are strong in muscle, in artisanship, and in habits of work submit and give in to a handful of feeble people, pampered old men, and mainly women, who for the most part are not fit for anything?

Take a walk before the holidays or during bargain weeks along the business streets, say through the Moscow Passage. Ten or twelve passages, consisting of solid rows of magnificent shops with immense plate glass windows, are filled with all kinds of expensive wares. Exclusively feminine [in nature, there are] frills, dresses, laces, gems, footgear, house adornments, furs, and so forth. All these things cost millions and millions and they have been manufactured in establishments by laboring people [many of whom] ruin their lives over this work. And all these articles are superfluous, not only to the working people, but even to the wealthy men since they are either for feminine amusement or adornment. At both sides of the entrances stand porters in galloons and coachmen in expensive garments are on the boxes of well-appointed carriages, which are drawn by trotters that cost thousands. Millions of working days have been wasted on the production of the luxurious harnesses as well. Old and young working people, men and women, have devoted their entire lives to their production. And all these articles are in the power of a few hundred women. In expensive furs and hats of the latest fashion they saunter through these shops to make their purchases.

A few hundred women arbitrarily dispose of the labor of millions of working people, who [are forced to] work to support themselves and their families. On the whims of these women depend the fate and the lives of millions.

How did this happen?

Why do all these millions of strong people who have manufactured these articles submit to these women?

Now a lady in a velvet fur coat and a hat of the very latest fashion drives up with a span of trotters. Everything on her is the most expensive and latest fashion. A porter hurries to throw back the boot of her sleigh, and respectfully helps her out, by supporting her under her elbow. She walks down the Passage as though through her kingdom. She enters one of the shops, and buys five thousand rubles' worth of material for her drawing room, and, having given the order to send it up to her house, goes elsewhere. She is an evil, stupid, and not at all beautiful woman, who has not given birth to any children and has never done anything for anyone. Why, then, do the porter, the coachman, and the clerks fawn so servilely before her? And why have all those articles that thousands of workmen have labored on become her property? Because she has money, and the porter, the coachman, the clerks, and the workmen in the factory need money to support their families. Money has become the most convenient [means of purchase] for them and it can be earned only by menial work.

And why has this woman money? She has money because people who have been driven off the land and have forgotten how to do any other work are living in her husband's factory.[22] Since her husband gives his workmen only enough for their support, he can take the profit to the amount of several hundred thousands, and, not knowing what to do with it, gladly gives it to his wife, so she can spend it on any whim.

And here is another lady, in a still more luxurious carriage and garments, who is buying all kinds of expensive and useless things. Where does she get the money? She is the mistress of a wealthy landowner with twenty thousand desiatinas. This land was given to his ancestor by a harlot queen for his debauchery with her.[23] This wealthy man owns all the land around a colony of peasants, and lets it out to them at seventeen rubles per desiatina. The peasants pay this money because without the land they would starve. And this money is now in the hands of the mistress with which she buys things made by other peasants who have been driven off the land.

Yet another third rich woman, with her fiance and mother, is walking down the Passage. She is about to marry and is buying bronzes and expensive dishes. She has been given money by her father, a distinguished official who receives a salary of twelve thousand rubles. He gave his daughter a dowry of seven thousand rubles. This money was collected from import revenues and taxes taken from the peasants. These same taxes have forced the porter, who opens the door (he is a Kaluga peasant and his wife and children are left at home), and the coachman, who drove them (he is a Tula peasant), and hundreds, and thousands, and millions of men, who labor in their homes[24] or have been compelled to leave their homes to work in factories. They toil on articles consumed by ladies who receive money from the manufacturers, landowners, and officials who have [in turn] collected profits from the factories, the land, or taxes.

Thus millions of workmen have submitted to these women, because one man has taken possession of a factory, the land, or another has seized the taxes collected from them. It is this [injustice] that produced what I saw in the foundry.

The peasants plow someone else's fields because they have not enough land and the owner permits them to use his on condition that they work only for him. The stonebreakers break rocks because only by this means of work can they pay the demanded taxes. In the foundry and in the mines the people toil, because the earth from which the ore is extracted and the smelter do not belong to them.

All these working people onerously labor not for themselves, because the rich have taken possession of the land, collect the taxes, and own the factories.

4. Why does the idle person and not the one who works own the land? Why do a small number of men make use of the taxes collected from all men, and not those who pay them? Why are the factories owned not by those who built or work in them but by a minority who did not build or work in them?

The question why the nonworkers have seized the land from the workers is customarily answered by the fact that it was purchased or given to them for their merits. To the question of why one small set of men (the nonworking managers and their helpers) collect and use it at will for themselves the greater share of the wealth from the working people there is the usual answer: that the men who collect the money manage, defend, preserve order and decency. And to the question of why rich people of leisure own the workers' products and implements of labor the answer is that they or their ancestors earned them.

And all the landowners, servants of the government, merchants, and manufacturers are sincerely convinced that what they possess is quite just and that they have a right to it.

But neither land possession, nor the collection and use of the taxes, nor the possession of the products and implements of labor by the idle has any justification. Possession of land by nonworkers has no justification. It is like the water, the air, and the sunrays, since it is an indispensable condition of every man's life and cannot be the exclusive property of anyone. If the land and not the other elements has become a possession, it is not because it is not as indispensable and appropriable for people's existence but because it is impossible to deprive people of water, air, and sun, while it is the contrary with land.

Landownership originated through conquest, then some people have appropriated and then given or sold it. It has remained in spite of every effort at turning it into a [natural] right, still an act of violence by the strong and armed against the weak and defenseless.

Let a man who is working the land violate this imaginary right, let him plow the land which is considered to be the property of another, and there will soon appear police and then the military.[25] Soldiers will bayonet and shoot those who are trying to make use of their genuine right—to support themselves by farming. Thus, what is called the right of landownership is nothing but violence exerted against all those who are deprived of it. This right to the land is like the right to a road which robbers have seized and do not allow travelers to use without a ransom.

A still lesser semblance of justification is the right of the government to levy taxes by force. It is asserted that they are used for state defence against foreign enemies, for the establishment and support of domestic order, and for necessary public works.

In the first place, foreign enemies have long ago ceased to exist. Even according to the declarations of the governments themselves they all have assured their peoples that they wish for nothing but peace. The emperor of Germany wants peace, the French Repubic wants peace, England wants peace, and Russia also wants the same. Still more urgently do the Transvaalers and the Chinese want peace.[26] So against whom are we to defend ourselves?

In the second place, in order to surrender money for the establishment of domestic order and public works, it is necessary for those who are entrusted to establish a just order to do so and that the public works will actually be needed by society. However, as it has been always and everywhere been repeated, the taxpayers are not convinced of the fitness, or even of the honesty of those who maintain order. The taxpayers, moreover, consider the order itself to be bad and public works unnecessary, so it is evident that the only right to collect taxes is by violence.

I remember the words of a Russian peasant, who was religious and therefore truly liberal. Like Thoreau, he did not consider it just to pay taxes for things which ran counter to his conscience.[27] When he was asked to pay his share of the taxes, he asked what they were to be used for, saying, "If the taxes shall be used for a good thing, I will immediately give you not only what you demand, but even more; but if they shall be used for something bad, I cannot and will not give a kopeck of my own free will."[28]

Of course, they wasted no time with him. The officials broke down his locked gate, carried off his cow, and sold it for taxes. Thus, in reality there is but one genuine cause of taxes—the power which collects them. For those who do not pay willingly, the possibility of robbing them, even of beating and putting them in prison is very real.

The fact that in England, in France, in America, and in general in constitutional governments, the taxes are determined by a parliament, that is, by the supposed gathered representatives of the people, does not change the matter, because the elections are so arranged that they represent not the people but the politicians. If they were not [corrupt] to start with, as soon as they get into parliament they become so, and are more concerned with their personal ambition and the interests of the warring parties.

Just as groundless are the justifications based on the supposed right of ownership, which the idle claim to be the products of other people's labor.

This right of ownership, which is even called a sacred right, is generally justified on the ground that property is the result of continence and of a utilitarian industriousness.[29] But we need only analyze the origin of great fortunes to be convinced of the contrary.

Fortunes always originate either in violence (this is most common) or in nastiness, or in rascality on a large scale, or in chronic cheating, like that practiced by merchants. The more a man is moral, the more certain he is to be deprived of the fortune which he has, and the more he is immoral, the more certain he is to gain and retain a fortune. Popular wisdom says that one cannot earn stone palaces by honest toil—that labor gives one stooping shoulders and not wealth. Thus it was in times of old, and it is still more true of the present, that the distribution of wealth is transpiring in a most irregular manner. Though we may admit that in primitive society a more abstemious and industrious man will gain more than an incontinent man who does not work much, nothing of the kind is farther from the truth in our contemporary society. No matter how abstemious and industrious a laborer may be who must work on somebody else's land, must purchase articles at a price established for by others, and who works with other people's implements of labor, he will never acquire any wealth. But the most incontinent and idle of men (as we see in the case of thousands of individuals) who work in the government or where there are involved rich usurious men, who [are associated with] a factory, a house of prostitution, or the sale of liquor, will easily acquire a fortune.

The laws which are supposed to protect property are those which only protect the stolen property which is already in the hands of the rich.

They not only fail to protect the laborers, who have no property, except their labor, but even aid in robbing the poor of their labor.

We see an endless number of administrators, such as the tsar, his brothers, uncles, ministers, judges, and the clergy, who receive enormous salaries collected from the people, and do not even perform those easy duties which they have undertaken for this remuneration. And so, it would seem, these people steal the salary collected from the masses, which is the property of the masses, but no one condemns them.

But let a laborer make use of even a part of the money received by these people, or buy anything with it. He has then violated the sacred right of ownership and is either sentenced, imprisoned, or deported.

While the millionaire manufacturer promises to pay the laboring man a wage representing one ten-millionth part of his fortune, that is, almost nothing, the laborer puts himself under obligation because of his needs. [In exchange] he must furnish throughout the year with the exception of the holidays his daily twelve hour work, which is dangerous and harmful for his health. He thus sacrifices to the manufacturer the greater part of his life, perhaps his whole life, while the government protects property.

By these means the manufacturer, as is well known, year in and year out robs the laborer of the greater share of his earnings. It would seem to be obvious that the factory owner robs more than a greater part of his property, and so ought to be made responsible for it, however, the government considers such property as sacred. The worker who carries off two pounds of copper under his coat, a mere one-billionth part of the manufacturer's property, will be [most assuredly] punished.

Let the laborer try to take away from the rich a very small part of what was lawfully taken from him, as occurred during the anti-Semitic riots.[30] Let a starving man take a loaf of bread, which has recently occurred in Milan, while the rich sell at a high price taking advantage of the famine, or let a laborer by means of a strike endeavor to get back a small part of what was taken from him. Since everyone has violated the sacred right of property the government immediately dispatches its army to assist the landowner, the manufacturer, or the merchant. Thus the right on which the rich base their landownership and the right to levy taxes and possess the products of other people's labor has nothing in common with [true] justice for it is only based on violence.

5. If a farmer tries to plow the field necessary for sustenance, or refuses to pay any taxes, or tries to take unearned provisions of corn, or uses the implements of labor without which he cannot work, the army will use force to prevent him.

Thus the alienation from the land, the levying of taxes, the power of the capitalists form, not the cause, but the result of the wretched condition of the laborers. The fundamental reason why millions of laborers live and work at the will of the minority is not that the latter has seized the land, the implements of production, or has taken the taxes, but that it *can* do so since violence is [readily resorted to]—there exists an army at the beck and call ready to kill whoever transgress its will.

Whenever the peasants want to take possession of the idle man's land, or when they do not want to pay taxes, or when the strikers want to keep other laborers from taking their places, there appear the same taxpaying peasants and laborers, whose land has also been taken away, except that they wear uniforms and bear arms. But they compel their brothers (who are not in uniforms) to vacate the land, to pay taxes, or to break the strike.

When a man comes to understand this fact, at first he can hardly believe it, since it seems so strange.

The working people want to free themselves, but they compel themselves to submit to slavery.

Why do they do this?

Because the working people, who are drafted or hired into the army, are subjected to an artificial process of stupefaction and corruption. They can then only blindly obey their superiors no matter what they are compelled to do.

It is done in this way: a boy is born in the country or in the city. In all the continental countries, as soon as he reaches the age when his strength, agility, and flexibility have reached the highest point and while his spiritual forces are in a a very vague and indeterminate state (about twenty years) he is taken into the army. He is examined like a beast of burden, and when he is found to be able-bodied, is placed in a particular part of the army, and is made to solemnly swear that he will slavishly obey his superiors. He is then removed from all the former conditions of his life, is filled up with whiskey or beer, is dresed up in motley garments, and with other lads is locked up in barracks, where he lives in absolute idleness (that is, doing no useful or rational work). He is taught the most insipid military rules and names of objects, and the use of implements of murder, such as the sword, the bayonet, the rifle, and the cannon. Most importantly, he is taught not only blind but even mechanically reflex obedience to his superiors. It is done in the countries where there is military service. Where it does not exist, men specially appointed for the purpose seek out, for the most part, dissipated but strong men, who have fallen from the right way and who either do not wish or are unable to live by honest labor. They then fill them with liquor, bribe and enlist them in the army, and similarly shut them up in barracks subjected to the same discipline. The main problem of the superiors consists in bringing these men to a state like a frog which, when touched uncontrollably, jerks its leg. A good soldier is like this frog, in response to certain shouts of his superior, for he unconsciously makes the ordered motion. This [brainwashing] is obtained by commanding these unfortunate men, who are dressed in the same motley uniform, to walk, twist around, jump, for weeks, months, and years, at the sound of the drum and of music, all together as a body. Every failure to obey is punished with the most cruel punishments, even with death. With this, drunkennness, debauchery, idleness, vulgarity, murder are not only not prohibited but even encouraged. The soldiers are given whiskey, houses of prostitution are arranged, they are taught obscene songs, and instructed in murder. (Murder in this circle of men is considered such a good and praiseworthy matter that under certain conditions the officers are compelled to kill a friend. It is called a duel.) And so a meek and peaceful fellow, after having passed in such a school for about a year (before that time the soldier is not yet ready, since he still has some human qualities left in him), is turned into a senseless, cruel, powerful, and terrible instrument of violence in the hands of his superiors.

Whenever I walk past the palace in Moscow in the winter I see a young lad, the sentinel by the booth, who in his heavy sheepskin fur coat is standing or walking, plashing his enormous overshoes on the sidewalk, supporting on his shoulder a rifle of the latest fashion with sharpened bayonet. I always look into his eye and every time he turns his glance away form me I always think: "a year or two years ago he was a merry village lad, natural, good-natured, who would cheerfully have talked to me in his good Russian, while aware of his peasant dignity, telling me his whole history." Now he looks maliciously and gloomily at me, and to all my questions knows only how to say, "Yes, sir," and "Can't know, sir." If I would enter through the door where he is standing (I always feel like doing so) or would put my hand on his gun, he would without a minute's hesitation stick the bayonet through my abdomen, pull it out, wipe it off, and continue to walk, plashing with his overshoes on the asphalt, until the arrival of the relief with the corporal, who would whisper the watchword into his ear. And he is not the only one. In Moscow alone, I think, there are thousands of such lads, almost children, who are turned into armed machines. There are millions of them throughout Russia and in the whole world. These unthinking but strong and agile lads are picked up, corrupted, and bribed, and thanks to them, the world is held in subjection. All that is terrible. What is [even more] terrible is that bad, idle people, thanks to these deceived soldiers, are in possession of all those palaces and criminally acquired wealth, taken from the masses' labor. But most terrible is that they have to bestialize these simple, good fellows—they have partially succeeded.

Let those who own wealth defend it themselves. That would not be so disgusting. But what is [even more] reprehensible is that to rob the people and defend what has been stolen, they use those very ones whom they have robbed and corrupted in soul.

Thus the soldiers, taken from the laboring classes, use violence against their own brothers, because they have been molded by governments into an unconscious instrument of murder.

6. But if that is so, inadvertently there arises the questions: why do people become soldiers. Why do their fathers let them become soldiers?

They become soldiers and are subject to military discipline because they do not see its consequences. But having learned its results, why do they continue to subject themselves to this deception?

It occurs because they consider military service not only useful, but unquestionably honorable and good. And it is deemed so, because they have been subjected to that doctrine from childhood well into adult years.

And so the existence of the army is not a basic cause but only an effect. The fundamental reason is to be found in that doctrine which is inculcated in people that military service, which has for its purpose killing, is not ony sinless but also good, virtuous, and praiseworthy. Thus the origin of men's wretched condition lies even deeper than it initially seems to be.

At first it seems that the causes entail the seizure of the land by the few and the implements of labor have been taken over by the capitalists, while the government forcibly takes the taxes. But when you ask yourself why the working people cannot [better themselves] you will realize that there is an army which protects the land, collects the taxes from the laborers, and guards the factories with its expensive machines, all for the benefit of the rich. If you ask yourself why the working people who form the army, the [very same] people from whom everything necessary is taken, attack their fathers and brothers, you will realize that it arises from the drafting or enlisting of soldiers—for they are specially adapted and instructed to lose everything human and are turned into unconscious instruments of murder, ever submissive to their superiors. When, finally, you ask yourself why people, seeing such deception, continue to join the army or pay taxes for its support, you will see its cause lies in the doctrine, which is inculcated in all men—that miliary service is a good and praiseworthy and murder in war is innocent.

Thus the fundamental cause of everything is due to this inculcated doctrine of every person.

From this comes poverty, debauchery, hatreds, punishments, and murder.

What is this doctrine?

This doctrine is called Christian, and consists in [these tenets]: there is a God, who six thousand years ago created the world and the man Adam. Adam sinned, and God punished all men for this and then sent down to earth His son, just such a god as the Father, to have him crucified there! This very act serves as a universal redemption from their punishment for Adam's sin.

If people believe in this, they will be forgiven Adam's sin—if they do not, they will be cruelly punished. The verifiable proof used is that all this was revealed to [certain] men by that same God whose existence we have learned from the preachings of those very same men. To say nothing of the many variations in this fundamental doctrine of the different denominations, the general practical deduction from all of them is the same: that men must believe in what is preached to them and must obey the existing authorities.

It is this doctrine that forms the fundamental cause of the deception that considers miliary service to be useful and good. So men enter the army, and being turned into machines without a will [unconsciously] oppress themselves. If there are unbelievers among the deceived, they [are incapable of] not believing in anything else since they have no point of support and submit like the believers to the general current even though they see the deception.

And so, to destroy the evil from which men suffer, we need not the liberation of the land, or the abolition of the taxes, or the nationalization of the implements of production, or even the overthrow of the existing government. It can be effected only by the destruction of that false Christian doctrine in which our contemporary men are reared.

7. At first it seems strange to people who know the Gospel how it was possible for Christianity, which preaches a sonhood to God, a spiritual freedom, a brotherhood of men, the abolition of all violence, and a love for our neighbors, to have degenerated into a strange doctrine, still called Christian—for it now preaches blind obedience to the authorities and murder whenever demanded. But when you stop to think of the process by which Christianity has entered various countries you will realize that it could not have been otherwise.

The pagan sovereigns Constantine, Charlemagne, and Vladimir accepted Christianity swaddled in pagan forms.[31] When they had their nations baptized, it did not even occur to them that the teaching which they accepted would disrupt their regal power, the army, and the state itself—everything that could not be imagined by all those who were the first to introduce Christianity. Initially, the destructive force of Christianity was not at all perceptible. On the contrary, they thought that it would support their power. But the longer the Christian nations existed its essence became more evident and the more obvious became the danger with which it threatened the pagan order. The more this danger became obvious, the more carefully did the ruling classes try to subdue and, if possible, to put out the fire, which they had unconsciously introduced into the world. They used every possible means, such as the injunction against translating and reading the Gospels, the slaying of all those who pointed out the true meaning of the Christian teaching, the hypnotization of the masses through the solemnity and splendor of surroundings, and, above all, through shrewd and refined interpretations. To the degree that these means were used, Christianity changed more and more until it finally became a doctrine which had in itself nothing dangerous for the pagan order of things, and even justified it. There then appeared even Christian rulers, wealth, courts, punishments and even Christ-loving armies.

The ruling classes did the same thing to Christianity that physicians do to infectious diseases.

They worked out a culture of harmless and false Christianity. When inoculated it makes the real Christianity harmless. Inevitably, this ecclesiastic Christianity had either repelled sensible people since it presents itself as a horrible insipidity, or upon adoption, distanced them so far from true Christianity that they no longer see its real significance and could only regard it with hostility and fury.

It is out of a sense of self-preservation that this innocuous but false Christianity has permeated the ruling clases throughout the ages with which the masses have been contaminated. It forms a doctrine for which men calmly commit immoral acts, which are totally incompatible with the demands of conscience and are harmful to themselves and their neighbors. The most important result of its practical consequences is entering an army to commit murder.

The main harm of this innocuous, but speciuos Christianity is that it prescribes nothing and forbids nothing. All the ancient teachings (like the law of Moses and the law of Manu)[32] preach rules which demand or forbid certain acts, as in the Buddhist and the Islamic religions. The ecclesiastic [Christian] faith, however, gives no rules whatever except verbal confessions, the recognition of dogmas, fasts, holy sacraments, prayers (and for these even excuses have been invented for the rich) but only lies permitting everything, even [things] contrary to the lowest demands of morality. According to this ecclesiastic faith everything is allowed. Owning slaves (in Europe and in America the churches have been the defender of slavery) and the amassing of wealth from the labor of our oppressed brothers are permitted. It is not only allowed to be rich amidst Lazaruses who crawl under the tables of the feasting but it is even good and laudable to do so, especially if one-thousandth of their earnings is contributed to the churches and hospitals. The church gives its blessing to the forcible defense of our wealth against the needy, to the imprisonment of men in solitary cells, to chaining them up, to fastening them to wheelbarrows, and to executing them. It is allowed to commit debauchery during a whole youth, and then to call one such debauchery marriage (also allowed is divorce and to re-marry). It is also possible to kill, not only in self-defense but also in defense of one's apples, and as a punishment (punishment means instruction—to kill as an instruction!). And above all else, the church not only permits but even commands that it is right and laudable to kill in war by order of the authorities.

Thus the root of everything is in this false doctrine.

Let this false teaching be destroyed and there will be no army. If there is no army, all acts of violence will naturally be eliminated, as well as the oppression, the corruption, which nations now practice. But so long as men are brought up in the pseudo-Christian teaching which permits everything, including murder, the army will be in the hands of the minority. This small group will always make use of the military for the purpose of depriving the masses of the products of their labor and, what is still worse, contribute to their [moral] corruption—without this corruption it could not take advantage of the people.

8. The root of everyone's wretchedness is based on that false doctrine which is taught to them under the guise of Christianity.

And so it would seem to be obvious that the duty of every man who has freed himself from this religious deception and wishes to serve the masses must by words and deeds help the deceived men to free themselves from that artifice. In addition, the general duty of every moral man is to expose the lies and profess the truth. Those who wish to serve the masses cannot but help free their brothers from the [benighted] life which causes that unhappiness. And yet these same people who are free from the deception and have been educated at the expense of the working classes fail to see this for they are obliged to serve them.

"The religious teaching is not important," say these people. "It is a matter for each man's conscience. What is important and necessary is the political, social, and economic structure of society. All the efforts of men who wish to serve the masses should be directed here. But all the religious teachings are of no importance because like all superstitions they will disappear in time."

Thus speak the cultured people, and without indicting the religious deception in which the deceived masses [exist, they] wish to serve the masses by entering government service, such as the army, the clergy, or the parliament, and try through their administrative participation to improve the external forms of life. Others, like the revolutionaries, whose beliefs are also distant from the masses, engage in a struggle with the government, and try to take possession of the power by the same means of deception and violence that governments practice. Others again, like the socialists, establish labor unions, societies, and strikes, assuming that the masses' condition can be ameliorated, even though they still remain in the same error of superstition and ignorance generated by the false doctrine. But none of them hinder the dissemination of the false religion on which all evil is based. When the necessity for it arises, they even perform religious rites, which they consider to be false—they take oaths and take part in divine services and solemnities which stultify the masses, and do not interfere with instruction given to children in what is called religion, that very enslaving lie. This failure to comprehend the main cause of the evil (and the cultured people should help destroy this false doctrine more than any others), and to properly direct their deviated efforts from one of the main causes why our life (which is obviously false and pernicious for people) is persistently maintained, is done so in spite of its easily-recognized incongruity.

All the calamities of our world arise because the true Christian teaching, which corresponds to the demands of our time, is concealed from men while a false doctrine is preached.

If the men who want to serve God and their neighbors could comprehend that humanity is moved not just by animal demands, but by spiritual forces, [they could achieve effective change]. The main spiritual force which moves humanity is religion, which is the determining factor of the meaning of life. In other words, it distinguishes betwen good and evil, and between the important and the unimportant. If men only understood that, they would immediately see that the fundamental cause of the present calamities of humanity lie not in external material causes such as in political or in economic conditions. It is rather in the distortion of the verities of the Christian religion with the substitution of a collection of senseless, immoral insipidities and blasphemies, called the ecclesiastic faith, which considers the bad as good, and what is unimportant as important, and vice versa.

The best of the free people, who sincerely wish to serve the masses, must understand that it is impossible by any external measures to improve the condition of a man who considers it bad to eat meat on Friday and good to punish the guilty with death. They must learn that it is important to show proper respect for an image of the emperor, and unimportant to swear to do the will of other people and to commit murder. If they could only understand that no parliaments, strikes, unions, consumers' and producers' leagues, inventions, schools, universities, and academies, or revolution, can be of any essential value to people with a false religious world view, all the resources of the best people would naturally be directed upon the cause, and not to the effect—not directed to the actions of state, revolutions, or socialism, but to the arraignment of the false religious doctrine, and would strive for the establishment of the true teaching.

If men would only act in this manner then all the poltical, economic, and social questions would naturally solve themselves the way they should, and not as we foretell or prescribe.

All these questions will naturally not be immediately solved in accordance with our wishes, since we are accustomed to arrange the lives of others by focusing our attention only on external forms (precisely what all the goverments are doing). These problems, however, will certainly be addressed only if peoples' spiritual world view will be changed—they will be solved all the more quickly the more we apply our forces not to the effects but to the causes of the phenomena.

But we are told that the indictment of the false religion and the assertion of the true religion can be effected by slow means with a chance of success only in the distant future. Whether it be distant or slow, it is the only means, for without it all other means will be ineffective.

As I look at human society which runs contrary to reason and to feeling, I ask myself: "Need it be so?"

And the answer to which I come to is that it need not be so.

It need not be, it must not be, and it will not be.

But it will [change], not when men reconstruct their relations in one way or another but only when men stop believing in the lie in which they are brought up, and believe in the highest but [the most] clear, simple, and reasonable truth, which was revealed nineteen hundred years ago.

The Only Means[33]

The Only Means, published in 1901, lays at the feet of the working people, both in the factories and in the fields, all their sufferings and their exploitation by the state, capitalists, and landowners. To be free of these age-old burdens, they need only have faith in God and obey the golden rule of doing unto others as we would that others should do unto us, rather than the secular, scientific, and religious authorities who support injustice, poverty, and violence. Mutuality will corrode man-made institutions and superstitions, establish a harmonious world, and bring universal salvation.

"Therefore all things whatsoever ye would that men should do to you, do ye even so to them; for this is the law and the prophets" (Matt. 7:12).

1. There are more than one thousand million working people in the world. All the bread, all the commodities of this world, everything they and the rich live by, is made by them. But they live in constant need, ignorance, and slavery, and are scorned by those whom they dress, feed, provide for, and serve.

The land is taken away from them and considered the property of those who do not work on it; thus, to gain his sustenance, a laborer must do everything the landowners demand. And if the worker leaves the land and goes to work in the factories he falls into slavery to the rich, for whom he must work ten, twelve, and fourteen hours a day, doing somebody else's monotonous, tedious, and frequently injurious labor for his entire life. If he manages to provide for himself on the land or work for somebody else to feed himself, he will not be left alone. The authorities will compel him to pay special taxes for the military or put him into the army for three, four, or five years. If he wants to use the land without paying for it, or if he goes out on strike and wants to keep other laborers from taking his place, or refuses to pay the taxes, they will dispatch the army and force him to work and pay taxes as before.

Thus, the working people across the globe, live not like men, but like beasts of burden. For their entire lives they are compelled to do not what they need but what their oppressors want, receiving in return precisely as much food, clothing, and rest as they need in order to be able to work without cessation. That small minority which lords over the working people enjoys everything which the masses produce, and lives in idleness and mad luxury, thus uselessly and immorally wasting the labors of millions.

So live the majority of men everywhere, not only in Russia, but in France, in Germany, in England, in China, in India, and in Africa. Who is to blame for it? And how can it be corrected? Some say that those who are to blame do not work on the land, but own it, and that the land ought to be given back to the working people. Others say that the rich are to blame, who own the implements of labor and the factories, which should become the property of the working people. Others again say that the whole structure of life is to blame, and that it should be changed.

Is all this true?

2. Some five years ago, during the coronation of Nicholas II, the masses in Moscow were promised a free treat of wine, beer, and lunch. The masses moved toward the place where the food was distributed, and a crush ensued. Those in front were knocked off their feet by those who were behind them, and these, in their turn, were pushed by others still farther back, and all, without seeing what was going on in front, pushed and crushed one another. The feeble were knocked off their feet by the stronger, and then the strong people themselves, jammed in and suffocating, fell and were trampled upon by still others who were behind them who could not stop the motion. Thus several thousand people, old and young, men and women, were crushed to death.[34]

When all was over, people began to reflect as to who was to blame for it. Some said that the police were to blame; others pointed to the managers; others again named the tsar, for having contrived this stupid celebration. All, but themselves, were blamed. And yet it would seem clear that it was only those who were the first ones to get a handful of cakes and a beaker of wine, and without paying any attention to anyone else, had then rushed forward and pushed and crushed the others.

Does not the same happen with the working people? They are worn out, crushed, turned into slaves and they ruin their own lives and those of their brothers only for the sake of insignificant advantage. They complain of the landowners, the government, the manufacturers, and the army.

But the landowners use the land, the government collects the taxes, the manufacturers dispose of the workmen, and the army suppresses the strikes solely because the working people not only aid them but also collaborate with everything they complain about. If a landowner is able to use thousands of desiatinas of land without touching it himself, he does so only because the working people slave for him, and serve as his janitors, outriders, and clerks. In the same way the government collects the taxes from the working people. With an eye to a salary, which is collected from themselves, the workers become elders, tax collectors, policemen, custom house servants, border guards. In other words, they abet the government through the very activity they bemoan. Again the working people complain that the manufacturers lower the wages and make them labor longer hours; but this, too, is done only because they knock down one another's wages and, besides, hire themselves to the manufacturers as receivers, superintendents, janitors, and chief workmen. And for their masters' advantage they search, fine, and in every way oppress their brothers.

Finally the working people complain that when they want to take possession of the land which they consider their own, or do not pay the taxes, or arrange strikes, the army is sent out against them.

But the army consists of soldiers, and are composed of the same working people who, some from advantage, others from fear, enter military service and make a promise under oath which is contrary both to their consciences and to the divine law they recognize: that they will kill by order of the authorities.

Thus all the calamities of the working people are brought upon them by their own doing.

They need only stop aiding the rich and the government, and all their miseries will be destroyed by themselves.

Why, then, do they continue to do what ruins them?

3. Two thousand years ago people first became acquainted with God's law—that it is necessary to do unto others as we would have others treat us, or, as

it is expressed by the Chinese sage Confucius, "Do not do to others what you do not want that others should do to you."

This law is simple and comprehensible to every man, and obviously gives the greatest good accessible to men. And so it would seem that, as soon as men have learned this law, they should immediately carry it out to the best of their ability, and should use all their might to pass it on to younger generations and familiarize them with its realization.

Surely all people ought to have acted so long ago, for this law was almost simultaneously expressed by Confucius, by the Jewish sage Hillel, and by Christ.

The men of Christendom, it would seem, should particularly act in such a manner, once they recognize as the chief divine revelation that what the Gospel states directly is a code of life that contains the entire law and all the [knowledge] of the prophets, which are all the teachings men need.

Meanwhile almost two thousand years have passed, and men, far from executing this rule themselves and teaching it to their children, for the most part do not even know it, or, if they know it, consider it to be unnecessary or impracticable.

At first this seems strange, but when you consider how people lived before the discovery of this golden rule, and even how long they have lived that way and how incompatible it is with the life of more complicated humanity, you will begin to understand why this happened.

It is because men do not know that this law is for the good of all since everyone selfishly tried to obtain as much power over others as possible. Having seized such power, each man, to be able without molestation to enjoy it, was compelled in his turn to submit to those who were stronger than he, and to aid them. The stronger, in their turn, had to submit to others still stronger, and so on.

Thus, in those societies which did not know the law that we ought to treat others as we wish that others should treat us, a small number of men have always ruled all the rest.

And so it is comprehensible that when this law was revealed to men, the small number of rulers not only did not wish to accept this law, but did not want the people over whom they ruled to learn it.

The ruling people have always known fully well that their power is based on the fact, that those over whom they rule are constantly at war with one another, each trying to make the other submit.

And so they have always employed all the means at their command to conceal this golden rule from their subjects.

They do not conceal this law by denying it (which is, indeed, impossible, since the law is clear and simple) but they promulgate hundreds and thousands of other laws, presenting them as more important and obligatory than the golden rule.

Some of these people, the priests, preach hundreds of church dog-mas, rites, sacrificial ceremonies, prayers, which have nothing in common with the golden rule—giving them out as the most important laws of God, the nonperformance of which leads to eternal perdition.

Others, the rulers, accepting the doctrine invented by the priests and regarding it as law, establish governmental decrees on its basis which are directly opposed to mutuality, and under the threat of punishment demand that all men shall perform them.

Others again, the learned and the rich, who do not recognize God or any obligatory law, teach that there is only science and its laws. Since only the learned can reveal it and the rich can know it, and that, for all people to fare well, it is necessary to use schools, lectures, theaters, concerts, galler-ies, and assemblies to acquire their same idle life—then all that evil from which the working people suffer will come to an end of its own accord.

Neither of these deny the golden rule itself, but [piled on it] is such a mass of every kind of theological, governmental, and scientific law that amidst them that clear and all-acccessible law of God, the fulfillment of which liberates the majority of men from their sufferings, becomes imper-ceptible and even entirely disappears.

So the working people, who are crushed by the governments and by the rich, continue to ruin their lives and the lives of their brothers genera-tion after generation. Having recourse, for the sake of alleviating their con-dition, to the most complicated, cunning, and difficult of means, such as prayers, sacrificial ceremonies, the humble execution of governmental de-mands, unions, savings banks, assemblies, strikes, revolutions, they are de-nied recourse to the one means, the fulfillment of the law of God, which will certainly free them from all their calamities.

4. "But is it possible that in so simple and short an utterance, that men must act toward others as they wish that others should act to them, is contained the whole law of God and all the guidance of human life?" At least, those who are used to the intricacy and confusion of theological, governmental, and scientific considerations will ask this question.

Indeed, the golden rule is very brief and very simple, but it is this very brevity and simplicity that shows that it is true, indubitable, eternal, and good. It is a law of God, worked out over a millennium by the whole of humanity, and not the production of one man or of one circle of men, which calls itself the church, the state, or science.

The theological reflections about the fall of the first man, about his redemption, about the second advent, or the governmental and scientific disquisitions about parliaments, supreme power, the theory of punishment, of property, of values, the classification of the sciences, natural selection, and so forth may be very astute and profound: but these are never accessible to more than a small number of men. But the command to treat other people as we would have others treat us is accessible to all men, without distinction of race, faith, culture, or even age.

Besides, the theological, governmental, and scientific reflections which are regarded as the truth in one place and at one time are regarded as a lie elsewhere; but the golden rule is regarded as true wherever it is known, and never ceases to be the truth for those who have learned it.

But the main advantage and the chief difference between this law and all other ones is that all the theological, governmental, and scientific laws not only do not pacify people and create good, but frequently cause the greatest enmity and sufferings.

The golden rule, however, can produce nothing but concord and the good. The deductions from this law are infinitely beneficent and varied, defining all men's possible relations with one another. Men, having freed themselves from the deceptions which conceal this law, would recognize its majesty and work out all its applications to life. Then would appear that most important science, now absent, but available to everyone, which shows how on the basis of this golden rule all individual and social conflicts can be settled. If this [true] science were established and worked out, and if all adults and children were taught it, as they are now taught harmful superstitions and frequently useless or harmful sciences, all men's lives would be changed with all their grievous conditions.

5. The Bible tradition says that long before the golden rule about not doing to others what we do not want others to do to us God gave His law to men.

In this law was the commandment, "Thou shall not kill." It was for its time as significant and as fruitful as the later golden commandment, but it befell the same fate. Men did not directly reject it but, like the later commandment of mutuality, it was lost amidst other rules and precepts, which were recognized as equal or even superior to the law of the inviolability of human life. If there were but this one commandment, and Moses, according to tradition, had brought down on the tablets as the only law of God nothing but the few words, "Thou shall not kill," men should have recognized the obligation to fulfill this law, for which no other obligation could be substituted. And if men had recognized this law as the only law of God, and had carried it out strictly, as they now carry out the celebration of the Sabbath, the worship of the images, communion, the noneating of pork, and so forth, the whole of human life would have been changed. There would have been no possibility of war, or slavery, or the rich men's seizure of the land of the poor, or the private possession of the products of the labor of others, for all this is based only on the threat of murder.

[Life] would have been thus [improved] if the law, "Thou shall not kill," were recognized as the only law of God. But since people began to recognize as just as important the commandments about the Sabbath, about not pronouncing God's name, and other commandments, there naturally arose new decrees of the priests, which were recognized as of equal importance to the only and greatest law of God. "Thou shall not kill," which had changed the whole life of men, was drowned among them, and cases were found when it was possible to act quite contrary to it, so that even to this day it has not even received proper significance.

The same thing happened with the law about acting toward others as we would that others act toward us.

Thus the chief evil from which men suffer has for a long time been not that they do not know God's true law, but that the knowledge and the execution of it became inconvenient. Being unable to destroy or overthrow it, they invent "precept upon precept and rule upon rule," as Isaiah says, which become just as obligatory as or even more commanding than the true divine laws.[35] And so the only thing that is now needed for freeing men from their sufferings is that they should liberate themselves from all the theological, governmental, and scientific reflections which are proclaimed to be obligatory laws of life. Having freed themselves, they should naturally recognize as more binding upon them than all the other precepts, that true, eternal law which is already known to them and gives the greatest possible good in life not only to a few but to all men.

6. "But," some will say, "no matter how correct in itself may be the law about doing to others what we would that others should do to us, it cannot be applied to all cases in life. Let men recognize this law to be always binding, without any exceptions whatever, and they will be compelled to recognize as inadmissible the use of any violence. But without its use the individual cannot be made safe, property cannot be protected, the country cannot be defended, the existing order cannot be maintained."

God says to men: "So that you may always be well off everywhere, fulfill my golden rule."

But men who established a certain order in the year 1901 in Finland,[36] Germany, France, or Russia say: "Suppose we should fare worse, if we fulfilled the law given to us by God?"

We can accept a law which is made by an assembly of men, no matter how strange it may be and by what bad men. We are not afraid to fulfill it. But we are afraid to obey the law which is not only an agreement with reason and conscience, but is directly expressed in the book which we accept as God's revelation, as though saying: "Supposing something bad should result from it, or that it should lead to disorder?"

Is it not obvious that the men who speak so talk not of order, but of that disorder in which they live, for their own advantage?

In their opinion [social] order is a state in which they are able to feast on other people and disorder a state in which the people being devored wish that men should stop devoring them.

Such considerations show only that the men who belong to the small number of the ruling class feel, for the most part unconsciously, that the recognition and fulfillment of the law about doing unto others as we would that others should do unto us not only destroys their advantageous social position but also reveals all their immorality and cruelty. These people cannot reflect differently.

But for the working people, who are driven off the land, crushed under taxes, forced into convict-like labor in factories, changed into slave soldiers, who torture themselves and their brothers, the time has come to understand that only the belief in the law of God and its fulfillment will free them from their sufferings.

Disobedience to this golden rule and the ever-increasing calamities resulting from that disobedience forces them to [shun it]. It is time for the laboring people to understand that their only salvation lies in the fulfillment of the golden rule. Their lives will be improved in proportion to the increase in the number of men who act in a just manner.

These are not mere words, not abstract reflections, like the religious, governmental, socialistic, scientific theories, but an actual means of liberation.

The theological, governmental, and scientific reflections and promises proffer good to the working people, some in the world to come, and others in this world. But it is to be at such a distant future that the bones of those who live and suffer now will long ago have rotted. But the fulfillment of the golden rule would immediately and incontestably improve the condition of the working people.

Not all the working people see clearly that by laboring on the lands of the proprietors and in their factories they give the capitalists the chance of using the products of their brothers' toil, which violates the law of mutuality. Even if through want they did not have the strength to decline such work, and if only a few would refrain from such activity, the capitalists would be embarrased and the general condition of the working people would immediately improve. And abstaining from direct collaboration with the capitalists and the government as overseers, clerks, collectors of taxes, custom house servants, and so forth, labors that obviously are opposed to the law of mutuality, would improve the condition of the working people still more, even if everyone were not to abstain from such action. And refusal by the working people to take part in the army (which has murder for its aim) and which has lately been more frequently directed against the laborers—an act anathema to the golden rule of mutuality—would absolutely change their position for the better.

7. God's law is God's law not because, as the priests always assert of their laws, it was in a miraculous way enunciated by God Himself, but because it faultlessly and obviously points out to men that path which, if they travel on it, will certainly free them from their sufferings. It will also give them the greatest spiritual and physical good, not only for a chosen few but for all men without exception.

Such is the law of God about treating others as we would that others should treat us. It will show to people that by fulfilling it, they will certainly receive the inner, spiritual good—a consciousness in harmony with the will of God and with an increase of love in themselves and in others. At the same time their social life will receive the greatest good. By departing from it, they will certainly make their condition worse.

Indeed, it is obvious to every man who does not take part in wordly struggles but [simply] observes, that the people who fight among themselves act precisely like gamblers who give up their certain, though insignificant, property for the very doubtful possibility of its increase.

Whether a working man who underbids his companions or goes to work for the rich or enters military service will improve his condition is as doubtful whether the gamester will win in putting up his stake.

There can be thousands of happenstances by which his condition will remain such as it is, or even get worse. But it is unquestionable that his agreement to work for smaller wages or his readiness to serve the capitalists and the government will slightly worsen the condition of all the working people—and this is as unquestionable as that the gambler will certainly lose the stake which he risks.

For a man who does not take part in the struggle but observes life, it is obvious that as in games of chance, in lotteries, in the stock exchange, it is only the keepers of the gambling houses, of the lotteries, and of the brokers' offices who get rich. So also in life it is the governments, the rich and the oppressors in general who become richer—it is all the players who get ruined. All the working people who, in the hope of improving their situation, depart from the law of mutality, only make their own situation worse.

God's law is God's law because it defines man's position in the world, showing him the better things which he can do both spiritually and physically.

"Therefore take no thought," it says in the Gospel in explanation of this law, "saying, What shall we eat? or, What shall we drink? or, Wherewithal shall we be clothed? For your heavenly Father knoweth that ye have need of all these things. But seek ye first the kingdom of God, and His righteousness; and all these things shall be added unto you." And these are not mere words, but the explanation of man's true position in the world.

If men only do what God wants of them, and fulfill His law, God too will do for them everything which they need. Thus the golden rule of mutuality also refers to God. For Him to do to us what we would that He should do to us, we must do for Him what He wants us to do. What He wants us to do is to treat others as we would that others should treat us.

The only difference is this, that what He wants of us He needs not for Himself, but for us, giving us the highest accessible good.

8. The working people must purify themselves so that the governments and the rich will stop devoring them.

An itch develops only on a dirty body, and feeds on that body only so long as it is dirty. And so for the working people to free themselves from their wretchedness, there is but one means—to purify themselves. But to do so they must free themselves from the theological, governmental, and scientific superstitions, and believe in God and His law.

This [way] is the one means of salvation.

Take an educated laborer and a simple, unlettered working man. Both are full of indignation against the existing order of things. The educated working man does not believe in God or in His law, but knows Marx and Lassalle, and watches the activity of a Bebel or a Jaurès in the parliaments,[37] and delivers fine speeches about the injustice of the seizure of land, the implements of labor, against the hereditary transmission of property, and so forth.

The unlettered working man, though he does not know any theories and believes in the trinity, the redemption, and so forth, is also provoked against the landowners and capitalists, and considers the entire existing order to be wrong. But give a working man, either an educated or an uneducated one, the chance of improving his situation by producing some articles cheaper than others, though this may ruin tens, hundreds, thousands of his brothers, or the chance of taking with a rich man a place which gives him a big salary, or of buying land and himself starting an establishment with hired labor, and nine hundred and ninety-nine out of every thousand will do so without hesitation. He will often defend his agrarian rights or those of the employers with even more zeal than the landowners and capitalists who are to the manor born.

. But the participation [of such people] in murder, that is, in military service or in the taxes which are intended for the support of the army, is not only a morally bad act, but also very pernicious for their brothers and for themselves—that they contribute to the foundation of their slavery does not enter their heads. All either gladly pay their taxes for the army or themselves join it and consider such action to be quite natural.

Could such people have led to the formation of a society different from that which now exists?

The working people know the cause of their condition to be the greed and cruelty of the landowners, capitalists, and other despoilers; but all, or nearly all of them without faith in God and His law are just the same, even though they are smaller, or more unsuccessful landowners, capitalists, and despoilers.

A village lad, being in want of earnings, comes to the city, to a peasant of his own village, who is acting as coachman at the house of a rich merchant, and asks the coachman to find a place for him at lower wages than what is customary. Arriving the next morning he accidentally hears in the servants' room the complaints of the old man who has lost his place, and does not know what to do. The lad is sorry for the old man, and he refuses the job, because he does not want to do to another man what he does not want others to do to him. Or a peasant with a large family accepts the well-paid steward's job on the estate of a rich and strict landowner. The new steward feels that his family is now provided for. But upon beginning his duties, he has to mulct the peasants for permitting their horses to graze in their masters' fields, to catch the women who are collecting pieces of wood in their proprietor's forest, to lower the wages of the laborers, and to make them exert their last bit of strength in work. And the conscience of the steward who has taken this job does not permit him to do these things, and he gives up his place, and in spite of the reproaches and complaints of his family works elsewhere with less income. Or again, a soldier is brought with a squad against some rioting laborers and is commanded to shoot; he refuses to obey, and for this he suffers cruel torments. All these men act so because the evil which they do to others is visible to them, and their heart tells them outright that what they are doing is contrary to the golden law of God. When the working man knocks down the price of labor and does not see those to whom he does wrong, however, the evil which he causes his brothers is not diminished. And though a working man who goes over to the side of the masters does not see or feel the harm which he does as his own, it nonetheless remains.

The same is true of a man who enters military service and prepares himself to kill his brothers. If he does not yet see whom and how he is going to kill, and when he learns to shoot and to stab, he must understand some day that he will have to kill people. And so, for the working people to free themselves from their oppression and slavery, they must teach themselves a spiritual feeling, which forbids everything that worsens the general position of their brothers, even though it may not be perceptible. They must spiritually abstain, as people now do from eating pork or any other meat on fast days, from working on Sundays, and so forth, from working for capitalists, if they can get along at all without doing so, from offering to do work at less than the established wage, and above all else, from participation in state [-inspired] violence, whether in the police, customs house, or military service.

Only by such a spiritual response to such action can the working people be freed from their enslavement.

If a laborer is prepared from ambition or fear to agree to join the army as a murderer, without feeling the slightest compunction, or for the increase of his well being he is calmly prepared to deprive his needy brother of earnings, or for the sake of a salary [he is prepared] to go over to the side of the oppressors—he has no cause for complaint.

No matter what his condition may be, he creates [his future] himself and cannot be anything but an oppressed man or an oppressor.

Nor can it be different. So long as a man does not believe in God and His law, can he help but to desire to get for himself in his short life as much gain as possible, irrespective of the consequences this may have for others? And as soon as all men wish for themselves as much gain as possible, all men, no matter what order may be introduced, will form themselves into a cone, at the apex of which will be the rulers, and at the base the oppressed.

9. The Gospel says that Christ pities men for being exhausted and scattered, like sheep without a shepherd.

What would he feel and say now, if he not only saw men exhausted and scattered, but saw thousands of millions of men in the whole world, generation after generation, ruining themselves in beastly labor, in stupefaction, ignorance, vices, killing and tormenting one another: all this [sadness occurs] though the means of freedom from all these calamities was given two thousand years ago?

The key which unlocks the chain that fetters the working masses is placed near them, and they only need to pick it up to be free. But the laboring people have failed to do this. They either undertake nothing and surrender themselves to gloom, or lacerate their shoulders tugging at the unbreakable chain, in the hope of breaking it. Or, what is still worse, like a chained animal which rushes against him who wants to free it, they attack those who show them the key which can free them from bondage.

This key is the belief in God and His law.

Only when men reject those superstitions in which they are carefully reared, and will recognize that the golden rule about doing unto others as we would that others should do unto us is for our time the main law of God, such as they now believe in the celebration of the Sabbath, the observance of fasts, the necessity of divine services and communion, the fivefold prayers, or the fulfillment of an oath, and so forth—only then will the slavery and their wretched condition be destroyed.

And so without respect for the old habits and traditions and without fearing the external persecutions from church and state and the internal struggle with their relatives, the working people must first of all free themselves with boldness and determination from the false faith in which they are educated. The essence of the faith in God and of the law of mutuality which results from it must be made clearer to them and to others, especially children, and they must follow it to the best of their ability, though this may present a temporary discomfiture.

Such is the way working people must act.

But the ruling minority who, make use of the labors of the working people, have acquired all the advantages of culture and are clearly able to see the deceptions in which they are kept. If they truly wish to serve the working people, they must first of all try to free themselves from those religious and governmental deceptions in which they are entrapped by words and deeds. They must not support or strengthen these deceptions by their example, especially the major religious ones, which offer ineffective and even injurious medicines. They will not only not free the working people from their wretchedness, but even make their condition worse.

No one can tell whether this will ever be realized anywhere. One thing is certain: that this means can free a vast number of men—all the working people—from their humiliations and sufferings.

There is and there can be no other means.

Notes

1. Tolstoy to Bernhard Eulenstein, Apr. 27, 1894, in *The Single-Tax Courier,* June 21, 1894, 5, HGS. In Tolstoy's collected works it is to be found in *PSS,* 67: 103-105. As stated in note no. 43 in chapter two George did not believe in land nationalization. Tolstoy interpreted *Progress and Poverty* to mean that all land would become the common property of the community while an individual would have the right to use a particular plot without ownership.
2. Tolstoy to a Siberian Peasant, in Ethel Wedgwood, *Tolstoy on Land and Slavery: A Selection* (Land Values Publication Dept., 1909), 64-66. See pages 253-255 in the appendix for a similar short sketch penned in 1905.
3. Here Tolstoy accepts the state as a transitional form. See pages . . .
4. Tolstoy, *The Slavery of Our Times* (1900), trans. Aylmer Maude (1900; reprint, Joint Chapels, England: Briant Colour Printing, 1972), 30-35, 39-41, 43, 44, 45, 46, 47, 48, 49, 53, 54, and 55 *(Rabstvo nashego vremeni, PSS,* 34: 144-199). Selected sections of this pamphlet are presented.
5. Maude, *Tolstoy and His Problems,* 105-106.
6. See pages 22-23.

7. G.W. Spence,*Tolstoy the Ascetic* (New York: Barnes & Noble, 1968),121 (Conversation with [?] Nazhivin, quoted by Pavel Axelrod in *Tolstoy's Inner Tragedy*, vii). Maude on pages 203 to 204 in his *Tolstoy and His Problems*, writes:
   To free the land is the next great question [after slavery]. Henry George has directed attention to it; [not only has he] expressed himself with clearness, individuality, and persuasive force, but his practical scheme for dealing with the problem in a political society such as now exists, appears to Tolstoy to be workable and the best that has been proposed.

   We come upon what, at first sight, looks like a strange contradiction. Tolstoy disapproves of the use of violence between man and man. Not even an Emperor, or a Government elected by a majority, has a right to execute anybody or to imprison anybody. He is a peaceful anarchist. Yet he is delighted with Henry George, whose system presupposes the existence of a government enforcing the decisions of a majority on a possibly reluctant minority—and he would be glad to see the single-tax introduced in Russia.

   But the contradiction admits of explanation. It is as though a man in Quebec made up his mind to go as quickly as possible to Vancouver's Island and live there in the country. He meets another man who knows how best and most cheaply to get to Montreal. The first man joins the second man, and having convinced himself that Montreal is the next point he must make for on his way to Vancouver's Island, he feels a keen interest in his companion's preparations for the journey and heartily admires his skill in packing and arranging; though all the time his own aspirations are set on a country home on the Pacific coast, and he cares little for cities or railways.

   "The great majority of people still believe in governments and legality—then let them, at least, see that they get good laws" says Tolstoy [who could, at times, accept this level of consciousness].

8. Single taxers in New Zealand as well as Australia were able to get towns to adopt either the single tax or the two-rate tax. For more details see Geiger, *Philosophy of Henry George*, 385-398. Possibly a reference to the single tax campaigns either in Delaware or Colorado. See also Young, *The Single Tax Movement*, 147-152 and 156-159.

9. Tolstoy is here expressing the same reservations as in *What Then Must We Do?* See pages 22-23.

10. Tolstoy, *Where Is The Way Out?* (1900), in Weiner, *CWCT,* 23: 179-191 *(Gde vyod?, PSS,* 34: 206-2150.

11. A samovar is a traditional Russian urn for heating water to prepare tea. It literally means "self-boiling."

12. A reference to socialism.

13. Tolstoy refers to different times of unrest in these three countries. England of the 1640s witnessed the Puritan Revolution with Cromwell's Protectorate and

the execution of Charles I. The Bourbon monarchy ended with the French Revolution of 1789 and with the subsequent rise of Napoleon. In Germany, as in many places in Europe in 1848, there were a number of failed revolts of a liberal-nationalist tenor. The Paris Commune was an urban uprising which was brutally suppressed in 1871 after the defeat of Napoleon III by Prussia.

14. The revisionist socialists preferred legal means rather than revolution to achieve economic and social equity.

15. In 1900 Tolstoy anticipated the fate of the first two prorogued Dumas in 1906 and 1907.

16. Tolstoy's fears came true with the founding of the Red Army by Lev Trotsky.

17. Tolstoy, *Need It Be So?* (1900), in Leo Weiner, *CWCT,* 24: 195-224 *(Neuzheli eto tak nado?, PSS,* 34: 216-238).

18. When this pamphlet was written the gold ruble was worth approximately fifty cents.

19. It was common among the aristocracy or the rich to scorn their native Russian as too peasant-like and speak a foreign tongue, primarily French.

20. Yasnaya Polyana is located in the province of Tula.

21. Kvas is a mildly alcoholic drink made from different fermented cereals. Sometimes flavoring is added.

22. It was not uncommon that the workers lived in factory quarters.

23. Probably a reference to Catherine II, frequently called "the Great" (1729-1796), who was known for her promiscuity.

24. Individual artisanship or laboring for another at home was a common means of supplementing income for the peasant, especially during the winter season.

25. Throughout Russian history the military was regularly used in police action and the quelling of numerous types of domestic disturbances.

26. The first reference is to the Boer War (1899-1902) between Britain and the Orange Free State and the Transvaal, which subsequently became the Union of South Africa in 1910. The second reference is probably to the Boxer Rebellion (1899-1900) between the Chinese and the Western powers, including Japan.

27. Henry David Thoreau (1817-1862) was held in great respect by Tolstoy and wielded an enormous intellectual and spiritual influence on the Russian's thinking, especially with the practice of nonresistance.

28. A ruble is equivalent to one hundred kopecks.

29. Tolstoy never hid his disdain for utilitarian and liberal thinkers such as Jeremy Bentham (1748-1832) and John Stuart Mill (1806-1873). Utilitarianism is a system of ethics which claims that good actions are morally right and justified if they produce the greatest happiness and utility for the greatest number of people. Happiness can therefore be measured in economic terms. Liberalism developed among the commercial and industrial classes in their struggle with the monarchy, the church, and feudal landowners. It sought (albeit more restrictively than now) greater freedoms, representative government, and state protection of the individual. Economically it was associated with laissez-fairism and international free trade.

30. A reference to the pogroms, especially after the assassination of Alexander II

in 1881, that frequently plagued Jewish settlements of the Pale in the western section of the Russian Empire. See pages 10-11.

31. Constantine (274?-337), an emperor of Rome was baptized on his deathbed. Christianity first appeared in France in the 1st century A.D. and by 400 it predominated in the urban centers and among the aristocracy. The converson of royal power took place with Clovis in 496. Charlemagne (742-814), however, was crowned as the first emperor of the Holy Roman Empire in 800. Vladimir (956-1015) was the first Russian ruler to be baptized and made Christianity the official religion in 988. He was subsequently canonized.

32. In Hindu legend Manu was a divinely-inspired lawgiver. The Laws of Manu, which govern Brahmin life and ritual were compiled between 200 B.C. and 200 A.D.

33. Tolstoy, *The Only Means* (1901), in Weiner, CWCT, 23: 241-261 *(Edinstvennoe sredstvo, PSS,* 34: 254-269).

34. This tragic accident occurred in Moscow in 1896 during a coronation celebration for Nicholas II. At the time it was considered portentous for the new Tsar.

35. The biblical reference is to Isaiah 28: 10 and 13.

36. Finland was a Grand Duchy ceded by Sweden to Russia in 1809 and was accorded a high degree of latitude in domestic affairs until the early 1890s when freedoms were curbed. Independence was achieved in 1917.

37. As is well known, Karl Marx (1818-1883) was a major influential socialist thinker and social critic, whose theories have given birth to a multiplicity of interpretations. Ferdinand Lassalle (1825-1864) was a radical socialist thnker influential in Germany who emphasized the state and a workers' cooperative system. August Bebel (1840-1913) was a socialist and a founder of the German Social Democrat Party. Jean Jaurès (1859-1914) was a French socialist who advocted gradual and peaceful means to obtain economic justice.

Chapter 4

Murmurings of the First Groundswell: 1902

Letter to Tsar Nicholas Alexandrovich Romanov[1]

So fearful was Tolstoy of increased bloodshed in 1902 that he even wrote to Tsar Nicholas II. Here was a quirk in the Russian radical tradition—to fall back on an autocrat to effect egalitarian change, much as Alexander Herzen had done two generations earlier in imploring Alexander II to democratize society by sovereign will.[2] It was now "public enemy number one," Russia's unofficial tsar, who begged the emperor to end repression and all the abuses and by fiat to create a more just distribution of the land by implementing the Georgist economic system throughout Russia—to make her a happier land, secure peace, defuse the revolutionaries, and not only to preserve the monarchy but to make it a beacon of righteousness for the world.

Dear Brother:

I consider this form of address to be most appropriate because I address you in this letter not so much as a tsar but as a man—a brother—and furthermore because I am writing to you as if it were from the world beyond, since I expect to die very soon.

I do not want to die without telling you what I think of your present actions, of what they could be, and of what great good they could bring to millions of people and to yourself. If they continue in the same direction in which they are now going, they can bring to the people and yourself a great evil.

A third of Russia is in a state of emergency outside the law.[3] The army of police—open and secret—is constantly growing. Over and above the hundreds of thousands of criminals, the prisons, places of exile, and labor camps are overflowing with political prisoners and now workers are being added. The censorship has descended to nonsensical prohibitions, and [cannot even be compared to] the worst period of the [18]40s.[4] Religious persecutions have never been so frequent and cruel as they are now, and they are becoming even more so. The armed forces are concentrated everywhere in the cities and industrial centers and are sent out against the people with live cartridges. In many places there has already been bloodshed between brothers, and more cruel bloodshed is imminent everywhere.

And as a result of all this intense and cruel action on the part of the government, the people who work on the land (those hundred million peasants on whom the power of Russia is based) despite the excessive growth of the state budget or, more likely, because of this growth, have become more impoverished every year, so that famine has become a normal occurrence. And general discontent and hostility with the government among all classes have become just as normal.

There is one cause of all this and it is completely evident: that your aides assure you that by arresting any movement in people's lives they are assuring their well-being as well as your own peace and security. But it is far easier to halt a river's flow than stop mankind's continual progress as ordained by God. It is understandable that the people who benefit from the present order of things and in the depth of their souls say *après nous le deluge*[5] [would] assure you of [of the widsom of represssion]. But it is truly amazing that you, who are free and not lacking for anything, and a reasonable and good man, can believe them and follow their terrible advice. You thereby perpetrate much that is base for the sake of such an impracticable purpose as halting the eternal movement of mankind from evil to goodness, from darkness to light.

Surely you cannot fail to know that as long as we have been aware of human life, economic and social as well as religious and political [institutions], have constantly changed, progressing from harsh, cruel and unreasonable forms to more gentle, humane and reasonable ones.

Your advisers tell you that this is not true, that just as Orthodoxy and autocracy were once natural to the Russian people, so they will be natural to them to the end of time. Therefore, for the good of the Russian people it is necessary at all costs to maintain these two interconnected forms: religious belief and the political system. But this [view] is really a double falsehood. First, it is quite impossible to say that Orthodoxy, which was once natural to the Russian people, is now so. You can see from the reports of the Over-Procurator of the Synod[6] that the most spiritually developed people, despite all the disadvantages and dangers which they are subject to in renouncing Orthodoxy, are going over in greater numbers to the so-called sects. Second, if it is true that Orthodoxy is natural to the people, then there is no reason to so forcibly maintain this form of faith and to persecute so cruelly those who reject it.

As for autocracy—if it was natural to the Russian people when that people still believed that the tsar was an infallible God on earth and that he governed the people by himself, it is far from natural to them now that everyone knows, or as soon as they acquire a bit of education find out, that a good tsar is only *un heureux hasard*. Tsars can be and have been monsters and idiots, like Ivan IV or Paul,[7] and however good a tsar may be, he simply cannot govern 130 million people by himself, for they are governed by the tsar's closest advisers, who are more concerned about their own position than about the people's good. You will say: a tsar can select as his aides people who are disinterested and good. But a tsar cannot do this because he knows only a few dozen people who are close to him by accident or as a result of various intrigues, and they diligently fend away from him all those who might replace them. So the tsar chooses not from among those thousands of vital, energetic, genuinely enlightened, honest people who have the social cause at heart but only from among those about whom Beaumarchais said: [they] are *médiocre et rampant et on parvient à tout*.[8] And if many Russian people are prepared to obey the tsar, they cannot without a feeling of outrage obey people of their own circle whom they despise and so often govern in the name of the tsar.

You have probably been deceived about the people's love for autocracy and its representative, the tsar, by the crowds of people who everywhere in Moscow and in other cities where you appear run after you with shouts of "Hurrah!" Don't believe that this is an expression of devotion to you—they are crowds of inquisitive people who would run just the same after any unusual spectacle. Often these people whom you take to be expressing their love for you are nothing more than a crowd gathered together and organized by the police and obliged to represent themselves as your devoted people, as happened, for example, with your grandfather in Kharkov when the cathedral was full of people—all of them were policemen in disguise.[9]

If [only] you could, as I can, walk along the lines of peasants strung out behind the soldiers or along an entire railway line while the tsar passes by, and hear what these peasants were saying. The village elders and peasant policemen had rounded them up from neighboring villages. Waiting for several days in the cold and slush for the tsar to pass without reward and with (only) their bread, you would hear all along the line words totally incompatible with love for autocracy and its most genuine representatives of the people, the simple peasants. If some fifty years ago during the reign of Nicholas I the prestige of the tsar's authority was still high, during the past thirty years it has continually declined and it has recently fallen so low that no one from any class constrains himself any longer from boldly condemning not only the decrees of the government but also the tsar himself, even swearing and laughing at him.

Autocracy is an obsolete form of government which may suit the needs of a people somewhere in Central Africa, cut off from the whole world, but not the needs of the Russian people who are becoming more enlightened, which is now common throughout the whole world. And therefore the maintaining of this form of government and the Orthodoxy linked with it can only be effected as it is now, by means of every kind of violence. It is carried out by a state of emergency, administrative exile, executions, religious persecutions, the banning of books and newspapers, the perversion of education, and, in general, bad and cruel actions of every type.

Such have been the actions perpetuated during your reign up to now, starting with your reply to the Tver deputation which aroused the indignation of all Russian society by calling the most legitimate desires of the people "foolish daydreams."[10] All your decrees about Finland and the seizure of Chinese territories, your Hague Conference project[11] accompanied by the strengthening of administrative arbitrariness, your support of religious persecutions, your consent to the establishment of a monopoly on spirits, that is, government traffic in poison for the people, and finally your obstinacy in maintaining corporal punishment (despite all the representations made to you for the abolition of this senseless and entirely useless measure: humiliating to the Russian people), are actions which you could have avoided taking. You have set yourself, on the advice of your frivolous aides, an impossible goal—not only to halt the people's [desire for a just] life, but to return it to its former obsolete state.

The people can be oppressed by violent measures but they cannot be governed by them. The only means of effectively governing the people in our time is to put yourself at the head of their movement from evil to goodness, from darkness to light, and to lead them to the attainment of the goals nearest to it. In order to be able to do this, it is necessary to give the people the opportunity to express their wishes and needs, and to fulfill these needs, not of one class or estate but of the mass of the working people.

And these wishes which the Russian people will now express, if given the opportunity to do so, are in my opinion these:

Above all, the working people wish to be rid of those exclusive laws which place them in the status of pariahs who do not enjoy the rights of all other citizens. They want freedom of movement, instruction and profession of the religious faith natural to their spiritual needs; and most important, the whole one-hundred million people unanimously want freedom to use the land with the abolition of private ownership.

And this abolition of the private ownership of land is, in my opinion, the nearest goal. The Russian government must attain this in our time.

In every period of the life of mankind there is a step, appropriate to the time, which comes very close to realizing the best forms of life towards which mankind is striving. For Russia fifty years ago the abolition of slavery was such a step. Now such a step is the liberation of the working masses from the minority which wields power over them—what is called the labor question.

In Western Europe the attainment of this goal is considered possible by the transfer of the factories and workshops to the general use of the workers. Whether such a solution to the question is right or wrong, and whether it is attainable or not by the Western peoples—it is obviously not applicable to present day Russia. In Russia, where an enormous part of the population lives on the land and is totally dependent on large-scale land-owners, the liberation of the workers obviously cannot be achieved by the transfer of the factories and workshops to general use. For the Russian people such liberation can be achieved only by abolishing the private ownership of land and by recognizing it as common property—the very thing that has been their agelong heartfelt desire, for which they still look to the Russian government to put into effect.

I know that these ideas of mine will be taken by your advisers as the height of frivolity and impracticality on the part of a man who has no comprehension at all of the difficulties of governing a state, especially recognizing the land as the people's common property. But I know that [to ensure that no] more force and cruel violence will be perpetuated against the people, there is only one means of action: to attempt the attainment of a goal in advance of the people's wishes. Without waiting for the runaway cart to hit you on the knee, you must drive it yourself and be in the vanguard to obtain the best forms of a [just] life. For Russia such a goal can only be achieved by the abolition of the private ownership of land. Only then can the government be the leader of its people and effectively govern without making unworthy and forced concessions to the factory workers and students as it does now, and without fearing for its own existence.

Your advisers tell you that freeing the land from the [unnatural] rights of ownership is a fantasy and impracticable. In their opinion, to force 130 million people to cease living or manifesting signs of life, and to squeeze them back into the shell which they long ago outgrew, is not a fantasy and not only not impracticable, but the wisest and most practical course of action. But a little serious thinking is enough to reveal what really is impracticable (although it is now being attempted), and what is on the contrary not only practicable, but timely and necessary, although it has not yet begun.

I think that in our time the private ownership of land is just as obvious and as crying an injustice as serfdom was fifty years ago. I think that its abolition will place the Russian people on a high level of independence, well-being, and contentment. I also think that this measure will undoubtedly get rid of all the socialist and revolutionary agitation which is now flaring up among the workers and threatens the greatest danger both to the people and to the government.

But I may be mistaken. The solution of this question, in one way or another, can only be provided by the people themselves if they could only have an opportunity to express themselves.

The first business which now faces the government is to eliminate the oppression which prevents the people from expressing their wishes and needs. It is impossible to [improve] a man whose mouth we have gagged so that we cannot hear what he wants for his own good. Only by learning the wishes and needs of all people, or the majority of them, can anyone govern the people and do good.

Dear brother, you have only one life in this world, and you can agonizingly waste it on vain attempts to halt the movement of mankind, as ordained by God, from evil to goodness, from darkness to light. Or you can calmly and joyfully lead it in the service God and man, by carefully considering the wishes and needs of the people and by dedicating your life to their fulfillment.

However great your responsibility may be for your reign, with which you can do much good or much evil, your responsibility is much greater before God for your life here on which your eternal one depends, the life which God has given you so you can carry out His will. His will is not to do evil to people, but good.

Think about this, not in the presence of people, but in the presence of God, and do what God, that is, your conscience, tells you. And don't be troubled by the obstacles which you will encounter if you enter on a new life path. These obstacles will be eliminated of their own accord and you will not notice them, if only what you carry out is done not for human glory, but for your own soul, that is, for God.

Forgive me if I have unwittingly offended or angered you by what I have written in this letter. I was only guided by a desire for the good of the Russian people and for yourself. Whether I have accomplished this will be decided in the future, which I, in all probability, will not see. I have done what I considered my duty.

With sincere wishes for your true good,

Two Letters to
Grand Duke Nikolai Mikhailovich Romanov[12]

The tsar did not respond, but undaunted Tolstoy also corresponded with his cousin the Grand Duke Nikolai Mikhailovich. In this letter Tolstoy hoped to even abolish private property in land. According to the novelist, this action would realize the innermost yearnings of the peasantry and would salvage the autocracy from impending doom. What would have happened to Russia if this advice would have been heeded fifteen years later?

. . . I would still like to explain to you some of my thoughts . . . I hope that if you do not share my views you will understand me and look on my proposal not as the fruit of the fantasy of an impractical man in many ways—as I am sure I am regarded in government circles. It is as the result of a serious and continuous working out of ideas that I am persuaded that for the rescue of the autocracy from total ruin there is only one means: the adoption by the government of those foremost values toward which mankind strives and the carrying out of these goals of our people with the help of your authority. The foremost goal to which the Russian people have always striven, according to my convictions, is the liberation of the land from private ownership. On this subject there has been much written, but this question was worked out in a very basic form by Henry George in his large book *Progress and Poverty* and in the more concise *Social Problems*. This question, in my opinion, is as much in need of an urgent solution as were the issues of serfdom and slavery in the first half of the last century. Not only the means to a solution but even a clarification of the question has been blocked in our time, since the rich landowners of Europe and America, who are part of the government, have assiduously concealed it and they do not permit its access to state circles. Such a resolution of the problem is possible only through autocratic authority, and it is especially needed and important in Russia, since the larger part of the people are engaged in farming and the absence of land or the unequal distribution of it serves as the major hindrance [to their betterment]. Henry George's plan, which is called the Single Tax System, as you probably know, is very simple and could be easily carried out. All the land can be assessed according to the rent which it yields and this rent is paid by the users to the government and would compose all its revenue, replacing all other taxes.

What I can easily foresee, is that by the highest command a major foundation for the abolition of private property by gubernias can be introduced—through committees which will be entrusted with the rating of the land and other details. And so the Russian tsar who undertakes these measures would effect the greatest good not only for his people but for the entire world. Such a tsar would be secure from any socialist agitation and revolutionary intrigues. How steadfast he would feel, relying on the best people of his nation and on the masses, who would expect from him the realization of their cherished and very legitimate wishes: the right of each man to feed himself from the land, a gift from God not to a few, but to all the people without exclusion.

Such are my beliefs, but what I have written may be very possibly mistaken and there are other progressive aspirations to be achieved, which mankind deires. They should become the goals of the government. Perhaps it cannot be otherwise that the government will continue with the present system by supporting the most obsolete ways. It must rather set an example for the nation, showing goals which will impart a genuine good. It would also endure longer. . . .

This member of the royal family replied in telling and surprising fashion.

As for the means proposed [the single tax] in your letter of April 5th for saving the autocracy and improving the sad situation in which our country finds itself, please don't be hurt if I say that you are too great an idealist. You believe that we can do something in Russia that people do not even speak of in Europe or America. Every peasant is devoted to his little domain, and, if I understand you correctly, you would nationalize all the land, whose revenue would return to the State, or in other words, to the Treasury. I think that even if this method received the consent of the owning classess—that is to say, the proprietors of every kind—it would encounter the most violent opposition from the peasants. Furthermore, to realize this grandiose idea we would need a formidable emperor like Peter the Great, as well as collaborators of a very different type from those who surround Nicholas II. We should have to reform and revivify institutions whose supremacy runs back through the centuries. . . .

My conclusion, therefore, is that your idea is as farreaching and sympathetic as it is impractical. Clearly, we are living in a terrible period that demands immediate practical reforms; but where to begin? "That is the question." We are vexed with the question of public instruction and the teaching personnel, with the labor problem, the incompetent bureaucracy, the general passion for profit, excessive militarism, depraved morals, and so on, and in the face of all these you propose raising the agrarian question again. You run the danger of being the only soldier on the field, because even those who share your ideas will hesitate when it becomes necessary to pass from theory into practice. Our society seems to me so thoroughly rotten that convalescence is only possble by a united and gradual effort on the part of the different government departments.

To my mind, the autocracy can only be saved if its responsibilities toward a people of one hundred and thirty millions are limited and if the number of ministries is increased. One explanation for our evil condition is that it is extremely old. In the course of the nineteenth century life and the exigencies of life marched forward, but our institutions scarcely budged. Only when all of them have been reformed shall we be able to think of the complicated question you raise, and then perhaps men will be found who are capable of realizing this magnificent idea.[13]

Frustrated, Tolstoy again picked up his pen to write yet another missive. He did not appreciate being considered an impractical fool and reiterates the importance of adopting the Georgist single tax and the incompetance of Russian officialdom. In this response, the novelist wrote that

I received your long and interesting letter the other day. I was very pleased to get it but certain opinions have induced me to speak my mind with things with which I disagree that are particularly dear to me.

First of all, in calling me a great idealist on the basis of the project I am suggesting, you are essentially doing what all the emperor's advisers who are acquainted with my thinking are bound to do and that is to regard me as a fool who doesn't understand what he's talking about. The attitude of the majority of people towards me, even those who are well disposed, reminds me of a passage from one of Dickens' novels, *Hard Times*; I think, where a clever and serious man, a mechanic, is introduced who has made a remarkable discovery but precisely because he is a very remarkable inventor he is considered by his jolly, good-natured friend to be a person who understands nothing about life and needs watching like a child in case he should do a lot of very stupid things. His words, if he talks about anything outside his own specialty, are received by this good-natured friend with a condescending smile at the naiveté of a person who knows nothing in life except his inventions. The funny side of the situation is that the good-natured friend didn't draw the simple inference that if the mechanic had made important discoveries, he was obviously clever, and therefore wouldn't discuss, and particularly assert, something he didn't know and hadn't thought about.

I feel all the awkwardness and immodesty of this comparison, but I can't refrain from making it, so truly does it show all the falseness of society's attitude in general to the opinions of people who are distinguished in some way from someone else. This attitude is the more widespread because it absolves people from heeding the meaning of what such people say. "He's a poet, a mechanic, an idealist," and so there's no point in trying to understand the meaning of what he says. That's the reason why there is such a strange opinion. Even the habit exists of appointing to posts which require the greatest gifts and intelligence all sorts of Ivanovs, Petrovs, Zengers, Plehves, and the like,[14] whose only virtue is that they are no different from other people. That's the first point. The second point is that it seems to me—and I regret it very much—that you haven't read and are not familiar with the gist of George's system. The peasant class not only will not oppose the realization of this project but will welcome it as the realization of the wish of many generations of their own class.

The core of the project is that land rent, that is, the excess value of land as compared with land of the lowest yield, and depending not on man's labor but on the nature or the location of the land, is used for taxes i.e., for common needs. The only effect of this project is that if you own a certain amount of land in Borzhomi and I in the Tula province, nobody can take that land away from me, and I am only obliged to pay a rent for it which is always lower than its yield. I don't know about Borzhomi, but in the Krapiva district of the Tula province the land rent will be about five rubles [per desiatina], while the charge for renting the land now is about ten rubles, and so the owner of 1,000 desiatinas will be obliged to pay the treasury 5,000 rubles and if he is unable to do so, which will probably be the case with nine out of ten landowners, he will give up the land. The peasants, who now pay ten rubles each to rent it, will obviously be glad to grab it up for five rubles each and will hold it from generation to generation. So the great mass of the peasantry cannot help but sympathize with this project and will always be in favor of it.

That, in rough outline, is the essence of Henry George's project. That's the second point. The third point is that the failure of this measure to achieve enactment in Europe or America not only doesn't prove that it can't be effected in Russia, but on the contrary demonstrates that it is only in Russia that it can be done, thanks to the autocracy. Landowners in Europe and America who make up the greater part of the government due to their own interests will never tolerate the freeing of land from private ownership. But even there a movement in this direction is detectable, while in Australia and New Zealand this measure is already being realized.[15] Apart from that, this reform is particularly important now for an agricultural Russia, though Witte, Kovalevsky, Medeleyev and others earnestly wish to direct her on to the path of capitalism.[16]

That's the third point. Now the fourth point. You write that "for the realization of this grandiose idea, a tsar-hero like Peter the Great[17] would be needed, and different collaborators from those whom Nicholas II could have at his disposal." But I think that no particular heroism is needed for its realization, far less the drunken and debauched heroism of Peter the Great. Needed only is the reasonable and honest fulfillment of the tsar's duty, in this case most particularly profitable for the tsar himself, that is, for the autocracy, and it seems to me that Nicholas II with the kind heart, that everyone speaks of, could carry it out entirely, if only he understood its absolute importance for himself and especially for all his people. As for collaborators: of course the implementation of this measure is unthinkable with those bureaucratic corpses, who are al l the more dead the higher they

are up the hierarchical ladder, so all that company such as the Pobedo-
nostsevs, Vannovskys and Chertkovs will have to be removed.[18] But Russia
contains many participators who are capable and honest and eager to do a
real job which they will love. That's the fourth point.

As for what you say about the need for reforms in all branches of the
administration, the pernicious nature of the bureaucracy, the universal passion for profit, all sorts of "Panamas,"[19] excessive militarism, the dissolute-
ness of morals—all these things will automatically be eliminated from the
government as soon as unprincipled people, seeking only their own ad-
vancement and profit, are thrown out of it, and people are summoned to
the great cause who love it. And so I don't agree with you that the possibility of saving the autocracy lies in various patching-up jobs such as creating
ministerial responsibility, or the reforming and revitalizing the highest institutions like the Council of State, the ministries and so on.[20] On the contrary, I think that this illusion of putting things right by sewing new patches
on old rags is the most pernicious of illusions, giving support to our impossible system. Any such reformation without the introduction of a higher
idea in the name of which the people can work with inspiration and self-
sacrifice will only be *bonnet blanc et blanc bonnet*.[21] Generally speaking, the
carrying out of my idea which seems so unrealizable to you, is incomparably
more possible than what people are now doing by supporting an obsolete
monarchy without any higher idea, but only autocracy for the sake of autocracy.

When I speak about carrying out such a measure by means of the
force of authority, I am not speaking from my own point of view. I consider
any force, even though it seems to us beneficial, to be contrary to the Christian teaching which I profess. Rather, it is from the point of view of people
wishing to defend an autocracy which is obsolete and pernicious for the
autocrat as well as for the people, and to give it the best possible justification.

Forgive me for writing to you at such length about matters over which
we can hardly agree, but your letter, touching on problems which are very
dear to me and have occupied my thoughts for a long time, has roused me
to speak my mind. Goodbye; I wish you all the best and thank you once
again for carrying out my request. I am not writing to you in my own hand,
for I have recently had a relapse, not of pneumonia as the physicians say,
but of malaria, and I am very weak again.

To The Working People[22]

No longer hopeful of improvement from above, but still undaunted, Tolstoy
kept writing and writing, warning of impending cataclysm. In the fall of
1902 he published *To the Working People*. In this article Tolstoy insists that

violence in the city or in the countryside never solves but magnifies suffering and injustice. He takes aim at socialism as ungodly, dependant on the state, and perverse in relying on the proletariat in a predominately agricultural country. Only access to the land will liberate the people from every form of slavery, including bondage to the machine and the tempatations of luxuries. Large landowners must turn over their holdings to the people as a common possession and only to those who till the soil. Immoral private ownership of land forms the keystone of all governments and perpetuates injustice and starvation. Men must not join the military, tend or rent the holdings of putative owners, nor own land themselves. When enough people adopt such measures, the state will recognize the sinfulness of landowner-ship and decree it illegal or it will melt away on its own. And the most practical and just solution is George's single tax for it comports with the ways of a godly life and can be universally applied.

"And ye shall know the truth, and the truth shall make you free" (John 8:32).

I have but little time left to live, and before I die I should like to tell you, the working people, what I have been thinking regarding your oppressed condition and about those means which will help free you.

Maybe some of my reflecting (and I have been thinking much about it) will do you some good.

I naturally turn to the Russian workers, with whom I have been living and know better than any other ones in the world. I hope that my remarks will also not be useless to the latter.

1. Everyone who has eyes and a heart sees that you, the working men, are obliged to pass your lives in want and in unnecessary hard labor while idle people enjoy the fruits of your work—that you are the slaves of these men and should not be so.

But how can this be corrected?

The first, simplest, and most natural and oldest means for people is to forcibly take from those who immorally enjoy and live by your labor. Since remote antiquity the slaves in Rome and the peasants in the Middle Ages in Germany and in France have used such methods. Thus they have frequently acted in Russia since the times of Stenka Razin and Pugachev.[23] Even now the Russian laborers are at times engaged in such actions.

This means lends itself the most easily to working men. Not only does it never attain its end but always and assuredly worsens their condition. It was possible in ancient times, when the power of the government was not as so strong as it is now, to hope for the success of such uprisings.

Now, however, when in the hands of the government (which always protects those who don't work) are immense sums of money, railways, telegraphs, police, gendarmerie, and the army. All such attempts end, as did the
recent uprisings in the districts of Poltava and Kharkov, in the torture and
execution of the rioters while the power of the idle over the workers is
made more apparent.[23]

By trying to oppose violence by violence, to take away what is withheld
from you, you the working men are like one bound with ropes trying to free
himself, by tuggging at the ropes: only the knots are tightened which fetter him.

2. It has now become obvious that rioting does not attain its purpose—it not
only does not improve the working mens' lot but instead makes it worse.
And recently, men who desire, or at least say that they desire, the good of
the working masses have discovered a new teaching for their liberation.
After being deprived of the land the working people will become hired
laborers, which according to this teaching is to occur as inevitably as the
sunset. They will then establish unions, societies, demonstrations, and
choose their partisans for parliament. Their lives will constantly improve
and finally they will appropriate all the works, factories, the implements of
labor, as well as the land, and then everyone will be absolutely free and
prosperous. Although these propositions are full of obscurities, arbitrariness, contradictions, and simple absurdities, they have of late been disseminated more widely.

This doctrine is accepted not only in those countries where the majority of the population has fallen away from agricultural labor for several
generations, but also where most of the working men have not yet thought
of abandoning the land.

It would seem that a doctrine which requires the transition of the
agricultural laborer from the customary, healthy, and joyous life of farming
to the unhealthy, somber, and pernicious conditions of monotonous, stulti-
fying work, from that independence which the village worker feels in satisfying nearly all his needs to the complete slavish dependence of the factory
workman to his master, should not have any success in countries where the
laborers still live by the land. But the preaching of this modern doctrine
called socialism, even in such countries as Russia, where ninety-eight per
cent of the laboring population lives by agriculture, is gladly accepted by
those two per cent of the working men far removed from the village.

This [blindness occurs] because, when the working man abandons
farming, he involuntarily submits to those temptations of urban and factory
life. Their justification is found only in the socialist doctrine which considers the increase of necessities a sign of man's improvement.

Such working men, who have filled themselves with fragments of the socialist doctrine and propaganda, preach it with especial fervor to their fellow laborers, considering themselves, in consequence of those needs which they have developed, to be far more advanced than the coarse peasants. Fortunately, there are still very few such working men in Russia. The farmers who constitute the vast majority of Russian laborers have never heard anything about the socialist doctrine. If these laborers would ever hear of it, it would be not responsive to their real needs but regarded as entirely alien.

All those socialist methods used by the factory hands which employ unions, demonstrations, and parliamentary elections to try to lighten their enslaved condition offer no temptation for free agricultural laborers.

If the agricultural workers need anything, it is not a raise in wages, not a diminution of work hours, nor general funds, and so forth, but only one thing—the land. Everywhere they have too little of it to support themselves and their families. Nowhere is this one necessity for the peasants mentioned in the socialist doctrine.

3. All sensible Russian laborers understand that land, free land, is the only means for liberation from slavery and improvement.

[The following] is what a Russian peasant Stundist writes to a friend regarding [man's natural rights to the land]:[25]

> If a revolution is to be started while the land remains private proerty, then, of course, it is not worth while to start it. For example, our brothers who live in Rumania, tell us that nearly all the land is in the hands of the proprietors. So what use is this parliament to the masses? In this body, they say, there is only a struggle of one party against another taking place, but the masses are still terribly enslaved to the proprietors. The latter have [built] huts upon their lands. Half of the land is generally leased to the peasants and, as a rule only for one year. When a peasant has worked the land well, the proprietor himself sows this plot the next year, and allots another plot to the peasant. After these poor wretches have lived for a few years on the proprietor's land, they still remain in his debt. The government then takes their last possessions for taxes, such as their horse, cow, wagon, plow, clothes, bed, or utensils and sells them all at a low price. Then the poor wretch picks up his starving family and goes to another proprietor, who seems to be kinder. This one gives him oxen, a plow, seeds, and so forth. But after he has lived here for a short time, the same story is repeated. Then he goes to a third proprietor, and so forth. Then the proprietors who do their own sowing hire laborers during the harvest. It is their custom to pay wages after the work is completed and only a few of them ever pay their hands. The majority of them hold back half the pay, if [they give anything] at all. And there is no way of getting justice. So there you have a constitution! There you have a parliament! The land is the first indispensable condition that the masses

must struggle for. The factories, it seems to me, will naturally pass over into the hands of the working men. When the peasants get land, they will work on it and live freely by their labor. Then many will refuse to work in the factories and consequently there will be less competition. Then the wages will rise, and they will be able to organize their circles and funds, and to compete with their masters. Then the latter will find it disadvantageous to own factories and will enter into agreements with the working men. Land is the chief object of the struggle. This fact ought to be explained to the laborers. Even if an increase in wages would be obtained it would be only on a temporary basis for their assuagement. Then again the conditions of life will change: instead of one dissatisfied man ten others shall be waiting to take his place. How can they then ask for an increase in wages?

Though the information given in this letter concerning the state of affairs in Rumania is not quite accurate and even though these oppressive conditions do not exist in other countries, the essence of the matter is expressed with unusual clearness in this letter—that the primary condition for improved conditions of the working men is free land.

4. Land is the major object of the struggle! so writes this unlearned peasant. But the learned socialists say that it should be the factories. Only after they have taken possession of them will they possess the land. Men need land but the socialist prophets predict that to till it they must first of all abandon it, and then obtain it again by a complex process which includes useless factories. This demand for the possession of factories in order to get access to the land is meaningless for the peasants. It recalls the methods used by certain usurers. You ask such a usurer for a thousand rubles in cash, for you need only the money, but he tells you: "I cannot give just the one thousand rubles; take five thousand from me, four thousand of which will be in the form of a few tons of soap, a few bolts of silk stuffs, and so forth (things which you do not need), and then I shall be able to give you the needed one thousand rubles in money."

The socialists have similarly but quite irregularly decided that the land is exactly like an implement of labor. They propose to the laborers who are suffering only from lack of land that they should flee the land and take over the factories which produce cannon, guns, soap, mirrors, ribbons, and all kinds of articles of luxury. Only after these laborers have quickly and rapidly learned to produce these things and have become unfit to work the land should they then return to the village.

5. It seems strange to see a working man who has abandoned a life in the country amidst the freedom of the fields, meadows, and woods, and ten years later (even sometimes after several generations) rejoices when he

receives from his master a little house with a twenty-foot garden in which he can plant a dozen cucumbers and two sunflowers in the infected air— but such joy is comprehensible.

The possibility of living or gaining sustenance from the land by means of one's own labor, has always been and always will be one of the more important conditions for a happy and independent human life. This fact has always been known to everyone, so they have always striven and will never stop striving like a fish for the water, for at least a semblancé of such a life.

But the socialist doctrine preaches that for man's happiness such a life in which nearly all daily wants are satisfied by means of agricultural labor amidst plants and animals is not needed. [A life] in infected industrial centers with ever-increasing demands, which can be gratified only by means of senseless factory labor [is preferred]. And the working men who are enmeshed in their factory [and urban-induced] temptations believe this. They expend all their efforts in a miserable struggle with the capitalists, merely for the sake of hours of labor and additional pennies, thinking that this activity is very important. The only important task, however, those land-displaced working men should do is to [concentrate] all their forces to return to a life [in harmony with] Nature. "But," say the socialists, "even if it were true that a life amidst Nature is better than in a factory, there are now so many workers who have abandoned agricultural ways so long ago, that a return to the land would be impossible. It is impossible because such a transition will diminish manufacturing products, which form the country's wealth. Besides, even if this were not so, there is not enough free land for the settlement and sustenance of every factory worker."

It is not true that this land resettlement will sap the country's wealth, for a life on the farm does not exclude the possibility of participation, for a part of the time, in manufacturing at home or even in factories. Although this resettlement would cause the rapidly-produced manufacture of useless and injurous articles to be lessened and the present overproduction of necessities to end, the amount of corn, vegetables, fruit, and domestic animals will increase, and general wealth will grow.

But that argument is untrue that there will not be enough land for the settlement and sustenance of all the factory workers. In most countries, including England and Belgium, the land which belongs to the great proprietors would be [more than] sufficient (to say nothing of Russia, where the land held by the great estate owners would suffice for all the Russian factory laborers, [and even] the whole of Europe). Cultivation could then be carried out to such a stage of perfection by present technology or even to that degree of perfection achieved thousands of years ago in China.[26]

Let those who are interested in this question read Kropotkin's books, *La conquête du pain* [The conquest of bread], *Fields, Factories, and Workshops,* and the very good book published by Posrednik, Popov's *The Corn Garden*.[27] They will then see how many times the productiveness of agriculture may still be increased by intensive cultivation and even how a greatly-increased population could be fed from the same plot of ground. The improved methods of cultivation could certainly be effected by small proprietors. [This transformation could be achieved] if they were not compelled, as they now are, to give all their income to the large landowners, who have no incentive to increase its productivity since they derive a great income from those who rent it.

They say that there will not be enough free land for all the working people, and so it is not worth while to worry the landowners who withhold it.

This reasoning is like what an owner of a house would say of a crowd standing in a cold storm in front of his unoccupied house, who ask him for shelter: "These people must not be let in, since most of them cannot be accommodated. Let in those who beg for it, and then we shall see, from the way they settle themselves, whether all or only a some of them can be situated. And even if all of them cannot be lodged, why should I not admit those who can find room?"

The same is true of the land. Give to those who ask for the land which has been kept back from the working men, and then we shall see whether it is sufficient or not.

Besides, the argument about the insufficiency of land for the present factory workers is essentially incorrect. If the factory laborers now live on bought bread, there is no reason why, instead of buying the grain which others produce, they should not themselves work the cereal lands, no matter whether they are found in India, Argentina, Australia, or Siberia.

All the arguments why the factory workmen should not and could not go back to the land have no foundation whatsoever. On the contrary, it is clear that such a change would not only be not injurious to the common welfare, but would even increase it. Those chronic famines in India, Russia, and other places where the irregularity of the present land distribution has most blatantly appeared would certainly be eliminated.

It is true that where the manufacturing industry is particularly developed, as in England, Belgium, and a few states in America, the life of the working people has been so corrupted that a return to the land would be very difficult. But the problems engendered would by no means exclude the possibility of realizing such a change. For this return to be effected it is first of all necessary for the working people to understand that it would be indispensable for their good. They should also find the means to do so, instead of accepting (as the socialist doctrine now teaches) that their factory slavery is an eternal and immutable condition, which can be only alleviated but never destroyed.

Even the working men who have left the land and live by factory labor do not need unions, societies, strikes, childish processions with flags on the first of May, and so forth. What is necessary is only to find the means to free themselves from factory slavery and to settle on the land, which was seized by the idle landowners, the main impediment. It this that they should demand of their rulers. They will be insisting not on something that does not belong to them but on restitution of their most unquestionable and inalienable right. A right to live on the land and get sustenance from it without permission from anyone else is inherent to every animal.

It is this goal that the parliamentary representatives of the working men should struggle for and the workers' press should preach. The working men in the factories should thus prepare themselves.

Such is the case for the workers who have left the land. But for the majority of the Russian laborers, ninety-eight percent of whom still live on the land, the only question is—how they can improve their condition without abandoning their land and surrendering to the temptations of city life?

For [a solution] one thing is needed—to turn over to the workers the land now held by the large estate owners.

Talk in Russia with any peasant you meet, who is working in a town, and ask why he is not faring well, and he will invariably answer the same thing: "I have no land, nothing to apply my hands with."

And here, in Russia, where the whole nation raises an unabated cry because of land insufficiency, men who think that they are serving the masses preach not about the means for returning their seized land, but about the methods of struggle in the factories with the capitalists.

"But should *all* men live in the country and engage in agricultural pursuits?" people will say who are so accustomed to the present unnatural life [that a rural existence will seem] rather strange and impractcal. But why should not *all* men live and toil in the country? If people, however, have such strange tastes and would prefer factory slavery to the country, nothing will stop them. What is important is that every man should have a chance to live like a human. When we say that it is desirable that every man should have a family, we say that not every man should get married and have children, but that we do not approve of a society which would deny him the opportunity.

6. Even during the time of serfdom, the peasants used to say to their masters, "We are yours, but the land is ours."[28] Here they recognized that no matter how immoral and cruel was the possession of one man by another, the right of a idle man to own land was even more immoral and cruel. It is true that of late a few of the Russian peasants, imitating the landowners, have begun to buy and to speculate in land. Since its ownership is legal they are no longer afraid that it will be taken away. Only a few frivolous

peasants, [however], blinded by greed, act in such a manner. The majority, that is, all the real Russian peasants, firmly believe that the land cannot and must not be the property of those who do not work it. Although the land is confiscated from the workers by these idlers, the time will come when it will [in turn] be taken away from them and become, as it ought to be, commonly held. And these Russian peasant beliefs are quite correct. The time has come when the injustice, irrationality, and cruelty of landownership by idlers has become as obvious as that of serf ownership was fifty years ago. Because the other methods of oppression have been destroyed, or the number of people has increased, or men have become more enlightened, all (both those who own and those deprived of the land) now see clearly what they did not see before. [On the one hand there] exist peasants who have worked all their lives and have not enough grain, because they have no ground on which to sow it, there are those who do not have milk for the children and the old, because they have no pasture, and there are those who do not have a piece of timber with which to mend a rotten hut to keep it warm. [On the other hand there] is the neighboring idle landowner who lives on an immense estate, feeding milk to his puppies, building arbors and stables with plate glass windows, raising sheep, establishing forests and parks on tens of thousands of desiatinas, and spending in food in a week what would keep a famished neighboring village alive for a whole year. And [they see that] such a social structure should not exist. The injustice, irrationality, and cruelty of such a state of affairs now startles everybody, in the same fashion as men were by serfdom. And as soon as the immorality, senselessness, and the horrors of any system becomes evident, it will in one way or another end. Thus ended serfdom, and so property in land will very soon cease to exist.

7. Property in land must inevitably be destroyed, because the injustice, irrationality, and cruelty of this institution have become too obvious. The only question is how it will be eliminated. Serfdom and slavery, not only in Russia but also in all other countries as well, had been abolished by order of the governments. And it would seem that landownership could be similarly eradicated. But it is not likely that such an order can or will ever be promulgated by the state.

All governments are composed of men who live by other people's labor, and it is landownership more than anything else which makes it possible to lead such a life. It is not just the rulers and the large estate proprietors alone who will not permit this abolition. Men who have nothing in common with the government or with landownership, such as officials, artists, scholars, and merchants who serve the rich, instinctively feel that it is advantageous to be connected with this institution. They always defend it, and attack everything of less consequence.

A striking illustration of such a relation to the men of wealthy classes may be found in the altered views of the famous Herbert Spencer concerning landownership. So long as Spencer was a young beginner who had no ties with the rich and the rulers, he looked upon the question of landownership just like every man who is not fettered by any preconceived notions must regard it—it was deemed unjust and rejected in the most radical manner. But decades passed, and from an unknown man Spencer became a famous writer who established relations with the rulers and the great estate proprietors. He modified his views on landownership to such an extent that he tried to destroy all those editions in which he had so forcibly expressed his former ideas about its immorality.[29]

Thus the majority of well-to-do people feel instinctively, if not consciously, that their advantageous position depends on landownership. [It occurs] because the parliaments in their alleged concern for the good of the masses propose, discuss, and adopt the most varied measures which are to [slightly] improve their lot, but not the indispensable one which alone would really help—the abolition of landownership.

Thus, to solve the question about landownership, it is first of all necessary to destroy the entrenched silence by conscious consensus. So it is in those countries where part of the power is in the parliaments. But in Russia, where the entire power is [theoretically] in the hands of the tsar the abolition of landownership is far less possible. It is so because in Russia power is only nominally in the hands of the tsar, for in reality it is in the hands of a few hundred men, relatives and near friends of him, who compel him to do what they please. All these men own immense tracts of land and they will never allow the tsar, even if he should wish to do so, to free it. No matter how hard it was for the tsar who liberated the peasants to compel his retainers to give up the right of serfdom, he was able to do so, because they knew that they would [otherwise] lose their last chance of the living that they had been accustomed to.[30]

Thus it is abolutely impossible to expect land emancipation from the Russian government or from the tsar.[31]

It is impossible by means of violence to take away the land which is retained by its proprietors, because the power has always been and will always be on the side of those who have already seized authority. It is quite senseless to wait for the emancipation of the land in the manner proposed by the socialists, that is, to be prepared to give up a good life for the very worst in expectation of a brighter future.

Every rational man sees that this method would not only not emancipate but would make the working men even more the slaves of their masters. It would also prepare them for a future slavery to the managers of the new order.[32] It is still more senseless to wait for the abolition of landownership from a representative government or from the tsar.[33] The Russian peasants have been waiting for it for the last two reigns, but all the retainers of the tsar and the tsar himself own immense tracts of land. Though they pretend to be interested in the welfare of the peasants, they never will give them the one necessary thing—the land—for they know that they will be deprived of their advantageous position and idle life.

What, then, are the working men to do in order to free themselves from this oppression?

8. At first it seems that nothing can be done since the working men are so fettered that it is impossible to free themselves. But that is only speculative. They need only ponder on the causes of their enslavement to see instead of riots, socialism, and the vain hopes in government, in Russia and in the tsar, that they have always had a means of liberation which no one and nothing can interfere with.

Indeed, there is but one cause for the wretched condition of the working men—it is this, that proprietors own the land. But what is it that gives them the means to own it?

If working men seize the land, troops are dispatched who will disperse, beat, and kill them and then return it to the landowners. Now these troops are composed of you, the working men. Thus you yourselves, the working men, by becoming soldiers and obeying the military authorities, make it possible for the proprietors to own their land, which ought to belong to you. (I have written many times that a Christian cannot be a soldier or promise to use weapons to kill and I have also shown what the Gospel preaches in a pamphlet, *The Soldiers' Momento*, among others.)[34]

Besides making it possible for the proprietors to own the land (which should belong to you), through your participation in the army you also allow them to rent the very soil you work on. You, the laborers, need only stop doing this, and landownership will become not only useless and impossible for the proprietors but the land will be held in common. No matter how much the proprietors may try to substitute machines for laborers or in lieu of farming to introduce cattle-raising and forestry, they will never be able to get along without strong hands—all of them will then willy-nilly give up their lands.

Thus the means for freeing the working men from your enslavement entails the development of an awareness that landownership [is immoral]. You must not take part, either as soldiers, who confiscate land from the workers, or as laborers or tenants on the owners' property.

9. "But the nonparticipation, both in the army and in farming work on or renting from the proprietors' lands, would be effective," I shall be told, "only in case all the working people of the world strike and refuse to take

part in these crimes. It has never been and never can be the case. Even if some of the working men should abstain from the army and from working or renting land, other laborers, many of them of other nationalities, will not find such a restraint necessary, and the proprietors' status will not be impaired. Thus the working people who refuse to take part in landownership will be deprived of their advantages, without alleviating the anyone's condition." This retort is quite just, if it is a question of a strike. But what I propose is not a strike: only that the working people refuse to take part in the military (which exercises violence against their brothers) and in working or renting the proprietors' lands. [They must refuse] not because participation is unprofitable and produces their enslavement, but because it is [morally] bad, just like murder, theft, and robbery. Any decent man must abstain. That participation in the immorality of landownership is bad there can be no doubt, if the working men would only ponder on the total picture. To support the proprietors' landownership causes the privations and sufferings of thousands of people. Old men and children, are insufficiently fed, and work beyond their strength, die before their time because they do not have land.

If such are the consequences of landownership by the proprietors (and it is obvious to anyone) it is also clear that every man must eschew it, for abetting it is an evil. Hundreds of millions of men who consider usury, debauchery, violence against the weak, theft, murder, and many other things to be evil abstain from them without the picket line. The working men ought to do the same regarding landownership. They see its immorality and consider it a bad, cruel business. So why do they support it?. . .

10. Thus I propose not a strike but a clearer awareness of the criminality and the sinfulness of abetting landownership, and the abstention from such activity. It is true that such a refusal would not immediately unite all interested people on one issue and cannot give those results, defined in advance, which are obtained by a successful strike. On the other hand, such a refusal elicits a much more lasting and continuous movement. The artificial joining of men which arises at a strike comes to an end the moment its aim is attained. The consensus, however, from a concordant activity creates an identical consciousness which constantly grows stronger, attracting greater numbers. So it is when the abstention from supporting landownership is not through the awareness that this participation is sinful. It is possible that when the working men will understand this immorality, not all of them but only a small part [at first] will abstain from working or renting the proprietors' lands. But they will abstain not because of [prior] agreement, which has only a local and temporary significance, but from a timeless moral consciousness which is equally binding for all men. It will be natural for them

to constantly increase in numbers since the immorality of landownership and its consequences will be made more manifest.

It is absolutely impossible to foresee what changes in society will be generated when it is realized that landownership is bad. There is no doubt that these reforms will take place and will be the more significant because the [resultant] state of mind will be more prevalent. These changes will entail a refusal on the part of some people to work for or rent from proprietors, and the latter no longer finding landownership to be profitable, will either enter into advantageous arrangements with the former or entirely give up their holdings. It is also possible that the working men who are in the army will more frequently refuse to take part in acts of violence against their brothers (the farmers), and the government will be compelled to abandon protection of the proprietors' lands so they will freed.

Finally, having come to see the inevitableness of land emancipation, it may be possible that the government will find it necessary to forestall the working men's victory by lending it an aspect of legality and will abolish landownership.

The changes brought by this heightened awareness which can and must take place regarding landownership may be quite varied, and it is difficult to foresee precisely what character they will be, but one thing is unquestionable—that not one sincere effort of a man to act in a godly fashion or in accordance with his conscience will be lost.

"What can I do alone against all this?" people frequently ask, when they are confronted with a decision the majority does not countenance. To these people it seems that for a successful outcome *everyone* must be involved, or at least *many*. But there must be many participants for a bad thing [to be successful]. For a good thing it is enough that there is only one person, because God is always with him. And whomever God is with, sooner or later all men join.

In any case, all the improvements for the working men will only take place because they will themselves act more in conformity with God's will, more in accordance with their conscience, and in a more moral manner than they have acted before.

11. Working men have tried to free themselves by violence or riots but they have not attained their goal. They have attempted by socialist activity through unions, strikes, demonstrations, and parliamentary elections, but all these methods can only temporarily alleviate the slave-like convict labor—it [not only] does not free them but even confirms this slavery.

Working men have tried to free themselves individually by supporting illegitimate landownership which they themselves have condemned. If the condition of a few is improved for a brief time by participating in this evil their lot will only get worse. What permanently improves the condition of men (not of one man but of the society of men) is an activity which is in conformity with the rule that we should do unto others as we wish that others should do unto us. None of the three means which they have employed so far have been in conformity with it.

Riots and violence against proprietors are inconsistent with this golden rule. Not one man who takes part in the riots would like to have taken from him what he considers to be his own, especially since such a seizure is also generally accompanied by cruel acts of violence.

Also inconsistent with this golden rule is all kinds of socialism. By making class strife its basis, it provokes hostile feelings in the working men toward the masters and the nonworkers in general. Strikes are also incompatible with this rule, for they frequently use violence against those native or foreign working men who wish to take their places.

Similarly inconsistent with the law about doing unto others what we wish that others should do unto us, and even outright immoral, is the doctrine which promises the transference of all the implements of labor and the factories into the full possession of the workers. Every factory is the product of the labor not only of many working men of the present (those who have built the plant and have prepared the material for its construction) but also of a vast number of former generations, without whose work no factory could exist. There is absolutely no possibility of figuring out the role of all men in the working of a manufacturing plant. So according to the doctrine of the socialists, every factory, like the land, should be the common possession of all the people. But there is this one difference: landownership can be immediately abolished without waiting for the socialization of all the implements of labor. A factory, [on the other hand], can only become the legal possession of the people when the unrealizable socialist fancy regarding the socialization of all the implements of labor shall be achieved and not, as is proposed by the majority of working [revolutionary] socialists, when they shall have seized the factories for themselves. A master has no right whatever to own a factory, but just as little right have the working men to any factory as long as the unrealizable socialization of the implements of labor is not an accomplished fact.

For this reason I say that a doctrine which promises to the working men the seizure of those factories in which they work, prior to the socialization of all the implements of labor, as is generally proposed, is a doctrine which is not only contrary to the golden rule but is even downright immoral.

Similarly inconsistent with this rule is the working men's support of landownership, be it by means of violence on the part of soldiers, laborers or tenants. Such a support for a time improves the condition of those people who engage in them. They, [however], certainly make the lot of other working men worse.

Thus none of the means which the working men have heretofore used for the purpose of their liberation—direct violence, socialist activity, and the acts of separate individuals (who for the sake of self-advantge maintain the illicitness of landownership) have attained their purpose. They have all been inconsistent with the commandment to do unto others as we would that others should do unto us.

What will free the working men from their slavery is not even an action, but the mere abstinence from sin for it would be just, moral, and in conformity with God's will.

12. "But wait!" I shall be told. No matter how convinced a man may be of the immorality of landownership, if he is a soldier it would be difficult to refrain from marching orders or to work for the proprietors if he must feed his starving children. Or how can a peasant abstain from renting the proprietor's land when he has only half a desiatina per soul and knows that he cannot support his family?[35] It is true that this is very hard but one meets the same difficulties trying to abstain from anything not good. And yet, for the most part, men abstain from the bad. Here self-restraint is less difficult than in most harmful acts but the injury from the participation in the seizure of lands is more blatant than any other activity. I am not speaking of the refusal to participate in the army when the troops are sent out against the peasants. Such a refusal, to be sure, takes more than ordinary courage and a readiness to sacrifice. Not everybody is able to do so and these cases are rare. But it takes much less effort and sacrifice not to work or rent the proprietors' lands. If all working men fully comprehended this there would be fewer people ready to do so. Millions of people live without having any need of the proprietors' lands since they are at home or away engaged in some trade. Nor do those millions of peasants feel any need for the proprietors' lands, even though there is difficulty when they leave home, go to new places, and obtain all the land they wish. For the most part they do not suffer but even grow rich. Other thousands live without having any need of working or renting any proprietors' lands. Many such people live a Christian life, one not for themselves but of sharing for others, such as many Christian communes in Russia or the Dukhobors do.[36]

There can be want only in a society which lives according to the animal law of struggle, but among Christian societies there should be no [deprivation]. As soon as men would divide among themselves what they have and everyone always has what he needs there will still be much left. When the people who heard Christ's sermon grew faint with hunger, upon learning that some of them had provisions he commanded that all should sit down in a circle. Those who had provisions should give them to their neighbors on one side and having satisfied the hunger of these, to hand them to others farther away. When the whole circle was made all had their hunger appeased and there was still much left over.[37]

In a society which acts similarly there can be no want. People will not need to work for the proprietors or rent their lands. Thus deprivation cannot always be a sufficient reason for doing what is harmful to your brothers.

If working people abet proprietors they do so only because most of them have not understood the sinfulness of their acts or the total evil which they are perpetuating on their brothers and to themselves. The more of these kind of men there will be and the more clearly they understand the significance of their participation in landownership, the more the power of the idle over the workers will destroy itself.

13. The only sure and indubitable means for improving the working mens' conditions which is consistent with God's will is through land emancipation. This means can be attained not only by refusing to join the army but also by abstaining from working for and renting from proprietors. But it is not enough to be aware of this: you must also know how to manage and to distribute the freed land among the workers.

Most of you generally think that all that is necessary is to take the land away from the idle. But that is not so. It is easy to say: "Take the land away from the idle and give it to those who work it." But how is this to be done without violating [moral] justice and without giving the rich another chance to accumulate great tracts of territory [and increase their control over] the workers? Some of you think that each individual worker or society should work the land as is now done among the Cossacks. It is possible only where there are few people and much land of the same quality.[37] But where there are more people than the land can support and it is of varying quality, it is necessary to find a different means for the exploitation of the soil. To divide the land according to the number of men? But if this is done it will also come into the hands of those who do not know how to work it, and these nonworkers will rent or sell it to rich purchasers, and there will again appear idle people who own large tracts of land. To prohibit the nonworkers to sell or let the land? But then the land which belongs to a man who does not wish or is unable to work it will lie unused. Besides, in dividing up the land according to the number of men, how is it to be estimated according to its quality? There is black loam, fruitful land, and there is sandy, swampy, sterile land. There is also land in the cities, which brings in one thousand and even more rubles from each desiatina and there is the backwoods which does not generate any income. How, then, is the land to be distributed in such a way that without any debates, quarrels, or civil wars the idle who have been taking advantage of others will not get any land? Men have been busy discussing these questions for a long time. For the proper distribution of land among the workers many projects have been proposed.

For instance, there are the so-called communist projects for the reconstruction of society in which the land is regarded a common possession and is worked by all men in common. I am also acquainted with projects such as that of the eighteenth-century Englishman William Ogilvie.[39] Ogilvie says that since every man is born into this world, each person has the complete right to exist and to live by what the earth produces. This right cannot be limited by regarding great tracts of land as private property. Everyone thus has the free right to own such a plot of land as falls to his share. But if a person owns a greater extent of land than falls to his share, exploiting those plots to which all men who have also a right to them make no claim, the owner should then pay to the government a tax for this possession.

Another Englishman, Thomas Spence, a few years later solved the land question by recognizing the land as the property of parishes which could dispose of it as they pleased.[40] In this way the private possession of separate individuals was completely abolished.

A wonderful illustration of Spence's view concerning landownership occurred to him in 1788 at Haydon Bridge. He calls it a "Sylvan Joke."

> While I was in the wood alone by myself agathering nuts, the forester popped through the bushes upon me, and, asking me what I did there, I replied, "Gathering nuts."
>
> "Gathering nuts!" said he, "and dare you say so?"
>
> "Yes," said I, "why not? Would you question a monkey or a squirrel about such a business? And am I to be treated as an inferior to one of these creatures, or have I a less right? But who are you," continued I, "that thus take it upon you to interrupt me?"
>
> "I'll let you know that," said he, "when I lay you fast for trespassing here."
>
> "Indeed," answered I, "but how can I trespass here where no man ever planted or cultivated; for these nuts are the spontaneous gift of Nature, ordained alike for the sustenance of man and beast that choose to gather them, and, therefore, they are common."
>
> "I tell you," said he, "this wood is not common. It belongs to the Duke of Portland."
>
> "Oh! My service to the Duke of Portland," said I. "Nature knows no more of him than of me. Therefore, as in Nature's storehouse, the rule is 'first come first served,' so the Duke of Portand must look sharp if he wants any nuts."

Spence, in conclusion, declared that if he were called upon to defend a country in which he durst not pluck a nut, he would throw down his musket, saying, "Let such as the Duke of Portland, who claim the country, fight for it!"

The question was similarly solved by the famous author Thomas Paine in his *Age of Reason* and *Rights of Man*.[41] Recognizing land as a common possession, he proposed to abolish the right of landownership by separate individuals. The possession of land is not to be inherited and whatever land is private property will revert at the death of the owner to the nation's possession.

Patrick Edward Dove, in our century, was the next man after Thomas Paine to write about this subject.[42] Dove's theory states that the value of the land comes from two sources—the property of the land itself and the work put into it. The value of the land as a result of work exerted should be the possession of private indivduals. The value of the land which is contingent on its character, however, should be the possession of the whole nation and never to separate individuals.

Such is also the project of the Japanese Land Reclamation Society which posits that every man has the right to own as much land as is apportioned to him on condition of paying an established tax.[43] Therfore he has the right to demand a portion of the land which is the equal to that of any other person. But the best, most just, and most easily applicable plan, in my opinion, is Henry George's single tax.

14. I consider Henry George's proposal the fairest, most beneficent, and, above all, most adaptable of those that I am familiar with. On a small scale it can be projected in the following manner: let's say in some locality the entire land belongs to two proprietors, one very rich who is living abroad, and the other, not so well off who is living and farming at home. There are also a hundred peasants who own small tracts. In this locality there are also a few dozen landless men who work and live in rented houses, such as artisans, traders, and officials. Let us assume that all the inhabitants of this locality, having come to the conclusion that the entire land should be held in common, decided to apply [George's] idea.

What shall they do?

It is impossible to take the land away from those who own it and to allow anybody to use the land as he likes since there will be several candidates for the same tract. Dissension would also be endless. It would be inconvenient for everyone to unite into one cooperative society and to plow, mow, and harvest in common. Then to divide it up [would also be a problem] because some have plows, horses, carts, while others do not have them, and, besides, some of the inhabitants do not know how to till the land nor have the strength to do so. It is also very difficult to divide the land into separate holdings by quality according to the number of people and then to equalize them for everyone. If the entire land is divided up into small plots by differences in quality, so that each one should get a plot of the best, of mediocre, and of bad land, and one of field, of mowing, and of woodland, there will be too many such tiny plots.[44]

Besides, such a division is dangerous, because those who do not wish to work or who are in great need of money will sell their land to the rich and large estate proprietors will reappear.

And so the inhabitants of the locality decide to leave the land in the hands of those who now own it, but oblige each owner to pay into the common treasury an amount of money which corresponds to the income which the owners derive from the land they use (according to the valuation of the land; based on its quality and location and not by the labor put into it). And they would decide that this money would be divided into equal parts. Such a collection of money from all the landowners and its equal distribution among the inhabitants would be troublesome. Since all the inhabitants pay money for common needs, such as schools, churches, fire departments, shepherds, mending of roads, and so forth, and the money for public purposes is always insufficient, the inhabitants of the locality decide, instead of collecting the income from the land and distributing it to all and again collecting a part of it for taxes, to use the proceeds for these common necessities. Having established society in this manner the inhabitants would demand from the proprietors a fixed payment for their land and from the peasants who own small holdings. Nothing, however, would be demanded from the few dozen landless men and they will be permitted to freely use all the amenities supported from the land income.

The single land tax makes it unprofitable for the absentee proprietor, who produces little on his land, to continue holding it and so he will give it up. But the other proprietor, who is a good farmer, gives up only a part of his land, and retains only that part of it on which he can cultivate and produce more than what is demanded from him.

But those peasants who own small tracts and those who have none, but wish to support themselves by farming, would be given the land abandoned by the proprietors. With such a system all the land would pass into the hands of the inhabitants of this locality who want to live and work on the soil. The local public institutions would improve since more money is obtained for the general needs than before. More importantly, this transference of landed property would take place without any disputes, quarrels, interference, or violence, but by the voluntary abandonment of the land by those who do not know how to cultivate it profitably.

Such is how Henry George's system can be realized in an individual locality or even for all mankind. It is just and beneficent and, above all, can be easily applied in all societies everywhere no matter what type of agricultural methods prevail.

For this reason I consider this system to be the best. It is my opinion and may be faulty. But you, the working men, when the time comes, should discuss among yourselves the different projects and choose the one you consider the best. The reason I have explained them in detail is that you already understand the complete injustice, great difficulties, and complexities of landownership. A fair land distribution should not fall into thoughtless errors—for a struggle with those who seize the land would make your status worse in the new order than at present.

15. I shall briefly repeat the gist of what I wanted to say to you. I advise you, the working men, first to understand clearly what it is you need, and not to struggle for what is absolutely unnecessary. You need only one thing—free land on which to live and support yourselves.

Secondly, you must understand clearly how you may be able to obtain the land you need. You can do this, not by rioting (God forbid!), not by demonstrations, or strikes, or socialist deputies in parliaments, but only through nonparticipation in what you yourselves consider to be evil—do not support immoral landownership, either by military violence, or by working or renting the proprietors' lands.

Thirdly, I advise you to consider in advance how you will distribute the land when it becomes free.

To properly understand this you must not think that the land abandoned by the proprietors will become your property. If the use of the land is to be regularly and without bias apportioned among all men, the ownership of land, even though it would be only one square *sazhen*,[45] would not be acknowledged by anyone. Only by recognizing that the land is as much a common possession as the sun and air will you establish just land ownership among all men, according to any of the [proposed] existing systems or by a new one chosen in common.

Fourth, and this is most important, I advise you, for the purpose of obtaining everything you need, not to expend your energies on a struggle with the ruling classes by revolts, revolutions, or socialist propaganda but only by your own [efforts] so that you may live better.

People fare badly only because they themselves live badly. And there is no more injurious thought than that the causes of their wretchedness lies not in themselves but in external conditions. When men think that the evil they experience is due to external conditions and they direct their efforts to change them they will find that the evil will be increased. Their focus should be directed to their inner selves and their lifestyles. They must search for the causes of that evil from which they suffer in order to destroy it.

"Seek ye the kingdom of God and His righteousness and all these things shall come unto you." It is the fundamental law of human life. If you live badly, contrary to God's law, none of your efforts will give you the well-being you seek. If you live morally well, in accordance with God's will and [even though] you would make no efforts for the attainment of this well-being it will naturally come to everyone by itself and in a way that could never be imagined.

It seems so natural and simple to open the door, for on the other side is the good we seek, but behind us stands a crowd that is pressing and jamming us against this portal. The more stubbornly we try to open the door, the less hope there is to go through it. The door, [nevertheless, beckons and] opens towards us.

Thus, to obtain the good, a man must not concern himself about the change of external conditions, but only about changing himself. One must stop doing what is evil and do that what is good. All the doors which lead men to the true good will then open only outwardly.

We say that the working people are enslaved by the government and by the rich but who are these men who are part of the state and the wealthy classes? Are they heroes, each of whom can vanquish tens and hundreds of working people? Or are there many of them while there are but few working men? Or are these men, the rulers and the wealthy, the only ones who know how to produce everything necessary the people need? None of these things are true. These men are no heroes, but weak helpless people, and they are not only not numerous but even hundreds of times fewer than the laborers. And not they but the workers produce everything men live by— they are incapable of doing anything, unwilling to do it, and only devour what is produced by the toiling masses. Why, then, does this small band of feeble and idle men rule over millions of working men? There is but one answer—it is because the lives of the working men are guided by the same rules and laws which guide their oppressors. If the laborers toil and do not exploit the poor and the feeble as do the nonworking rulers and the wealthy, it is not because they consider this bad, but because they cannot do it as well as the rulers who are more agile and cunning. The leaders and the rich rule the working people only because the latter wish to lord over their own fellows in exactly the same fashion. Since the toilers live by the same standards they are unable to successfully rebel against their oppressors. No matter how intolerable it is for the working man to be oppressed by the rulers and the rich he knows in his heart that he himself would act similarly toward his brothers, even in small ways. The laboring classes have fettered themselves by their desire to enslave one another and so the shrewd people who have already got them in their power find it easy to do likewise. The working people must not be enslavers exactly like the rulers and the rich, who are concerned only about exploiting their neighbor's want for the purpose of establishing their own well-being. They should live fraternally, thinking of one another's [welfare] and mutually offering aid, then no one could control them. And so to free themselves from the oppression in which they are held, the toiling people have but one means—to free themselves from those principles by which their lives are guided. They will then stop serving mammon and begin serving God.

The pretended friends of the people tell you, and some of you even say to yourselves, that the present order must be changed. You think that you must take possession of the implements of labor and the land or that you must overthrow the present government and establish a new one. Since you believe this, you hope and work for the attainment of these goals. But let us assume that you establish a new state and that you take possession of all the factories, works, and the land. Why do you assume that the people who will form the new government will be guided by new principles different from those which guide them now? They will not only retain but also strengthen their power. For self gain they will extract as much from people as possible. Why do you assume that the people who will be in charge of the factories or of the land (men cannot manage all institutions [in common]), having the same views as those have now, will not find the means to seize the lion's share, leaving to the humble and meek only what is indispensable? I shall be told: "It will be so arranged that it will be impossible to do otherwise." But see how well all was arranged by God or by Nature so that all who live on the earth will have the right to its ownership—and yet people have been cunning enough to violate this divine arrangement. And those who are guided only by their personal welfare will discover thousands of means for distorting the human order. No modifications of externalities will ever improve society. And so my fourth and most important advice to you working men is that you must not condemn others or your oppressors but should direct your attention to your own lives and your inner selves.

Do you think that it is justified and useful to forcibly take away and appropriate what has been taken from you or that the teachings of erring men about the class struggle are moral and that it is practical to acquire other peoples' implements of labor? Do you you think that by serving as soldiers, you are obliged to obey the authorities, who compel you to perpetuate violence, and not to obey God? Do you think that by supporting the lawlessness of landownership by work or rental, you are not doing anything wrong? [No, all of this is untrue, for] your condition will become even worse and you will for ever remain slaves.

You must understand that for your true happiness you need only live a brotherly life which is in accordance with God's law by doing unto others what you wish should be done to you. [If you do], then to the degree that you comprehend and live by it, the goodness that you wished for will be reciprocated in like measure and your slavery will be destroyed. "Ye shall know the truth and the truth shall make you free."

From *The Light That Shines Through the Darkness*[46]

Tolstoy concerned himself in the 1880s with the unfinished play *The Light that Shines Through the Darkness* and worked on it periodically, the last time in late 1902.[47] In this one of the most poignant of autobiographies, Tolstoy depicts himself as Saryntsov, conscience-grieved at landownership that brings suffering to the peasants but at odds with his wife who insists that the property is needed for the welfare of the family. Saryntsov eventually deeds over the estate to his wife, a compromise that torments him. Tolstoy's self-depiction could be unmerciful: he must have suffered grievously articulating thoughtful rebuttals to his own views. The glaring differences between the rich and the poor, the Church which sanctions robbery of all kinds, and other social ills also came under fire.

Nicholas: (to Boris) "All those men are half-starved, many of them ill or old, living on bread and water. Look at that old man. He suffers from rupture. He works from four in the morning until ten at night, and is barely alive. And now, is it possible, [that even] when we once understand this, we go on living quietly and calling ourselves Christians? Can we call ourselves anything short of beasts?"

Boris: "But what are we to do?"

Nicholas: "Not to be a party to evil. Not to possess land. Not to feed on the toil of the peasants. How this can be managed I do not know. The thing is, or at least so it was with me, that I lived and did not understand that I was a son of God and that we were all sons of God and all brothers. But when I came to understand that, when I saw that everyone has equal claims on life, my whole being was changed. I cannot explain it very well to you, I can only say that before I was blind, just as my family still are, while now that my eyes are opened I cannot help seeing. And now that I can see it I cannot go on living as before. But, of course, for the present we must do as best we can. . . ."

Father Gerasim: "Do you not wish for a blessing?"

Nicholas: "No, I do not."

Father Gerasim: "I am Gerasim Feodorovich. Pleased to meet you. (Footman brings refreshments and wine.) It is fine weather, and very favorable for harvesting."

Nicholas: "I understand you have come on the invitation of Alexandra Ivanovna to convince me of my errors, and to lead me into the right way. If that is the case, do not let us beat about the bush. Let us come to the point. I do not deny that I disagree with the teaching of the [Russian Orthodox] Church. I used to believe in it but I have ceased to do so. Nevertheless, I long with my whole soul to be in harmony with the truth, and if you can show it to me, I will accept it without hesitation."

Father Gerasim: "How can you say you do not believe the teaching of the Church? What are we to believe if not the Church?"

Nicholas: "God, and His law, given to us in the Gospel."

Father Gerasim: "The Church instructs us in that very law."

Nicholas: "If that were so, I would believe the Church. But the Church teaches the very opposite."

Father Gerasim: "The Chruch cannot teach the opposite, for it is founded by our Lord. It is said, 'I give you the power, and the Gates of Hell shall not prevail against it.'"

Nicholas: "That refers to something quite different. But, supposing Christ did found a church, how do I know that it is *your* Church?"

Father Gerasim: "Because it is said, 'Where two or three are gathered together in My name. . . .'"

Nicholas: "That does not apply either, and does not prove anything."

Father Gerasim: "How can you renounce the Church, when the Church alone possesses grace?"

Nicholas: "I did not renounce the Church until I was totally convinced that it supports all that is contrary to Christianity."

Father Gerasim: "The Church cannot err, because she alone possesses the truth. Those who leave her will err. The Church is sacred."

Nicholas: "But I have told you I do not admit that, because the Gospel says, 'Ye shall know them by their fruits.' And I perceive that the Church gives her sanction to oath-taking, murder, and executions."

Father Gerasim: "The Church admits and consecrates the powers instituted by God."

(During the conversation Liuba, Lisa, Stephen, Tonia, and Boris enter one by one, who sit or stand and listen).

Nicholas: "I know that not only killing but anger is forbidden by the Gospel. And the Church gives its blessing to the army. The Gospel says, 'Do not swear,' and the Church administers oaths. The Gospel says. . . ."

Father Gerasim: "Excuse me—when Pilate said, 'I ask you in the name of the living God,' Christ accepted the oath, and said, 'Yes, that I am.'"

Nicholas: "Oh, what are you saying? That is simply ridiculous!"

Father Gerasim: "That is why the Church does not permit individuals to interpret the Gospel. She would perserve men from error, and she cares for them as a mother for her children. She gives them an interpretation befitting the powers of their mind. No! Allow me to finish. The Church does not give her children a burden heavier than they can bear. She requires only that they fulfill the commandments. Love, do not kill, do not steal, do not commit adultery."

Nicholas: "Yes. Do not kill me, do not steal from me what I have stolen. We have robbed the people, stolen their land, and then we have instituted the law against stealing. And the Church sanctions it all."

Father Gerasim: "That is all a snare, mere spiritual pride speaking in you. You want to show off your intellect."

Nicholas: "Not at all! I merely ask you how, according to the law of

Christ, am I to behave now, when I have recognized the sin of robbing the people and appropriating their land? What must I do? Go on holding my land, exploiting the labor of the starving peasants, just for *this?* (He points to the servant who is bringing in lunch and wine.) Or am I to give back the land to those whom my ancestors have robbed?"

Father Gerasim: "You must act as a son of the Church should act. You have a family, children, and must bring them up as befits their station."

Nicholas: "Why must I?"

Father Gerasim: "Because God has placed you in that station. And if you want to do charitable acts, then perform them by giving away part of your fortune, and by visiting the poor."

Nicholas: "Then why was it said that the rich man could not enter the kingdom of heaven?"

Father Gerasim: "It was said, [only] if he desired to be perfect."

Nicholas: "But I do want to be perfect. It is said in the Gospel, 'Be ye perfect, even as your Father in heaven is perfect.'"

Father Gerasim: "But you must understand to what it applies."

Nicholas: "That is exactly what I am trying to understand, and all that was said in the Sermon on the Mount is simple and clear."

Father Gerasim: "It is all spiritual pride."

Nicholas: "Why pride, if it is said that what is hidden from the wise shall be revealed to babes?"

Father Gerasim: "It will be revealed to the humble, not to the proud."

Nicholas: "But who is proud? Is it I, who think that I am like the rest, and therefore must live like the rest? I must live by my labor, and in the same poverty as all my brothers. Or is it they who consider themselves apart from the rest, as the priests who think they know the whole truth, and cannot err, and interpret the words of Christ to suit themselves?"

Father Gerasim: (offended) "I beg your pardon, Nicholas Ivanovich, I have not come to argue about who is right. I did not come to be lectured. I complied with the wish of Alexandra Ivanovna, and came to have a talk. But you appear to know everything better than I; the conversation had better cease. But I beseech you for the last time, in the name of God, to reconsider the matter. You are terribly wrong, and will lose your own soul."

Notes

1. Tolstoy to Tsar Nicholas II, Jan.16, 1902, in David Redfearn, *Tolstoy: Principles for a New World Order* (London: Shepheard-Walwyn, 1992), 171-177 *(PSS, 73:* 184-191). This letter was translated by R. F. Christian. See pages 252-253 in the appendix for a translation of a rough draft.

2. For more on Herzen see page 6.
3. Martial law ("Regulations on Measures for the Defense of the Governmental Order and of Public Safety") was declared in 1881 by Alexander III after the assassination of his father and lasted until 1917. See page 10.
4. A reference to the strict censorship policies under Nicholas I. See page 4.
5. In French "After us the storm." A remark purportedly made by Madame Pompadour, a close associate of Louis XV. "*Après moi le déluge*" has often been attributed to this king.
6. For more information on the Holy Synod see page 15 note no. 31.
7. Tsar Ivan IV (1530-1584) "the Terrible," a contemporary of Henry VIII, had seven wives. He was known for excessive brutality, cruelty, and deranged behavior. Tsar Paul I (1754-1801) was the son of Catherine the Great. His oppressive rule, eccentricity, suspicious nature, and domestic and foreign policies created a great amount of discontent among the nobility. He was assassinated with the knowledge of his son Alexander I.
8. From the play, *The Marriage of Figaro*, written by Pierre Augustin Caron de Beaumorchais (1732-1799) in 1778. It created quite a stir, when presented on the stage in 1784, for its irreverent treatment of the privileged classes.
9. Apparently another example in a different form of a recurring phenomenon in Russian history known as a "Potemkin village." On a state visit to a just-conquered province Catherine the Great was regaled by her lover Prince Grigorii A. Potemkin (1739-1791) with fake towns to make her think that they had been populated with settlers.
10. When Nicholas II ascended the throne in 1894 a petition was sent to him from members of the zemstvo of Tver asking for greater freedoms and reforms. In a famous response, the new tsar, desirous of maintaining autocracy inviolate, referred to them as senseless.
11. Nicholas II had abrogated the autonomy of Finland. See page 108 note no. 36. He pursued a reckless course in China by seizing territory and wringing railway concessions, which contributed to the Russo-Japanese War. This Tsar also initiated the first peace conference at the Hague for arms limitations but his motives have come under suspicion. Tolstoy had condemned all peace gatherings as futile for he argued that genuine harmony could only come about when all weapons and armies are banned.
12. 1) Tolstoy to Grand Duke Nikolai Mikhailovich, April 5, 1902 *(PSS,* 73: 228-230). Translated from *La Revue Mondiale,* Feb. 1, 1928. 2) Tolstoy to Grand Duke Nikolai Mikhailovich, April 25-May 1, 1902, in Redfearn, *Tolstoy,* 178-181 *(PSS,* 73: 236-240). Translated by R. F. Christian.
13. Grand Duke Nikolai Mikhailovich to Tolstoy, April 15, 1902, "Tolstoi and the Grand Duke Nicholas: A Revealing Correspondence," in *Land & Liberty,* June 1928, 120-121, HGS. Reprinted from *The Living Age* (Boston), Apr. 1, 1928. Grand Duke Nikolai Mikhailovich was an outstanding historian of Russia. He was executed by the Bolsheviks in 1918.
14. Nikolai I. Ivanov (1851-1919) was a noted military commander. Grigorii W. Zenger (1853-1919) was a Minister of Education who advocated strict conservative policies. Viacheslav K. Plehve (1846-1904) was chief of gendarmes and

minister of the interior. He wielded great power, used repressive measures against those who challenged the status quo, and was assassinated in 1904.

15. See page 106 note no. 7 for more information about Australia and New Zealand.

16. See page 9 for more information about Witte.

17. Peter the Great had been the symbol of Russia's destiny among the intelligentsia for his role of introducing Western ways. See page . . .

18. For Pobedonostsev see page 15 note no. 31. Peter S. Vannovskii (1822-1904) was a general, Minister of War, and Minister of Education who was noted for conservative policies.

19. Another negative reference to Theodore Roosevelt. The American's dubious dealings in Central America regarding the Panama Canal was but one reason for Tolstoy's aversion.

20. The Imperial Russian government from time to time had undergone various reorganizational shufflings to cope with changing circumstances or at the whim of a tsar. The Senate, for instance, established by Peter the Great, had different functions, internal organizations, and degree of authority.

21. French for "six of one and half-a-dozen of the other."

22. Tolstoy, *To The Working People* (1902), in Weiner, *CWCT,* 24:131-169 *(K rabochemy narody, PSS,* 35: 121-156).

23. Stenka Razin (d.1671) and Emilian Pugachev (1726-1775) were two of the most famous insurrectionary leaders who led large uprisings against the Russian government. Both movements were ruthlessly suppressed.

24. Possibly a reference to two well-known urban labor disturbances. Poltava was an industrial city with an active radical movement. Kharkov in 1900 witnessed a large May Day demonstration by railway workers with many arrests. Such incidents were growing with frequency around Russia. I think, however, that Tolstoy is probably discussing agrarian uprisings. There was a growing unrest in the countryside beginning in 1899. All this activity was no doubt related since the proletariat still retained much of a peasant consciousness and close ties with the village. Such an incendiary background most assuredly served as a catalyst for the Revolution of 1905. See page 33.

25. A Stundist was a general name for various Protestant religious sectarians. They were composed mostly of Orthodox Ukrainians who adopted different Protestant practices, including charitable acts, mutual aid, and economic cooperatives. After 1894 they were officially declared harmful but toleration was granted in 1905. Tolstoy aided them during times of persecution.

26. Here Tolstoy has made a rare departure and has grudgingly accepted modern technical advances to a certain degree.

27. For Kropotkin see page 13 note no. 4.

28. Reference to the years prior to the Emancipation issued by Alexander II in 1861.

29. Tolstoy had read Henry George's *A Perplexed Philosopher* (published in 1892), which was a response to the volte face in a new edition of Spencer's *Social Statics* of that same year. All mention of the injustice of land holding was deleted from the Englishman's original 1850 version.

30. A reference to Tsar Alexander II.

31. Tolstoy, at times, thought differently. See pages 109-114 earlier in this chapter for his letter to the tsar.
32. Bolshevik revolutionary horrors fulfilled this prophecy.
33. Here Tolstoy is anticipating the liberal Provisional Government (of 1917) which collapsed, in part, due to its failure to satisfy the peasants' demand to obtain land from the estates. See pages . . .
34. *The Soldiers' Momento* (1901) condemned military service. See *Soldatskaia pamiatka, PSS,* 34: 280-283.
35. A peasant was known as a soul.
36. See page 221 note no. 57.
37. The reference is to Matthew 15: 32-38.
38. The Cossacks were prized for their horsemanship and loyalty to the imperial crown after they were finally pacified. In exchange for their military services they held a singular and prosperous position in Russia. They constituted a separate legal class with a high degree of freedom including local self government and privileged land holdings. There were, however, poorer strata of Cossacks.
39. William Ogilvie (1736-1819) was an early English advocate of the single tax who wrote *An Essay on the Right of Property in Land with Respect to its Foundation in the Law of Nature.* See *An Anthology of Single Land Tax Thought,* (Vol. III of *The Henry George Centennial Trilogy* in preparation).
40. Thomas Spence (1750-1814) was another English promoter of the single tax and was the author of *The Meridian Sun of Liberty, or the Whole Rights of Man Displayed and Most Accurately Defined* (entitled earlier as *The Real Rights fo Man*). See *An Anthology of Single Land Tax Thought,* (Vol. III of *The Henry George Centennial Trilogy* in preparation).
41. It was Thomas Paine's (1737-1809) pamphlet *Agrarian Justice* which specifically touched upon the single tax and the land problem. See *An Anthology of Single Land Tax Thought,* (Vol. III of *The Henry George Centennial Trilogy* in preparation).
42. Patrick Edward Dove (1815-1873) was yet another English theoretician of the single tax and the author of *The Theory of Human Progression.* See *An Anthology of Single Land Tax Thought,* (Vol. III of *The Henry George Centennial Trilogy* in preparation).
43. From 1846 until the 1980s about five million acres of wasteland were reclaimed in Japan (from 9.08 to 14.08 million acres) for agricultural purposes and after 1900 for industrial uses.
44. A reference to the inefficient repartitional commune, which stymied Russian agriculture. See pages 7 and 36.
45. One desiatina is equivalent to 2400 square sazhens. One sazhen is a little over 1 1/3 yard in length.
46. Tolstoy, *Light that Shines Through the Darkness* (1896-1902), in *Father Segius and Other Stories and Plays,* trans. Aylmer Maude (1911; reprint, Freeport, N.Y.: Books for Libraries Press, 1970), 186-187 and 201-208 *(I svet vo t'me svetit, PSS,* 31: 113-184). See pages 251-252 in the appendix for a translation of a first draft not used.
47. See Simmons, *Tolstoy's Writings,* 180-183 for more details.

Chapter 5

In the Eye of the Storm: 1905–1906

Regarding the Social Movement in Russia[1]

In *Regarding the Social Movement* Tolstoy describes his anguish over the the sad events known as Bloody Sunday. The Imperial Russian government is lambasted for its cruelty. He also expresses misgivings about not only the efficacy of democratic institutions to represent people but condemns their involvement in imperialism and warfare. Tolstoy, for a solution, calls for the end of all states and private property in land. The moral vacuity of his generation is exposed and calls for a closer relationship to God. Finally, a quoted letter laments that even in the midst of suffering people fail to draw together and are alienated.

Two months ago I received a paid reply telegram of one hundred words from a North American newspaper, which asked me what I thought about the significance, goals, and probable consequences of the agrarian question. Since I have a very definite opinion, which does not conform with that of the majority, I consider it necessay to express it.

I responded thusly:

> The goal of the zemstvo agitation is for the limitation of despotism and the establishment of a republican government.[2] Whether the leaders of the unrest will achieve their goals or only prolong the social disorder, the real result will be a delay in genuine social betterment, which can be achieved only by the spiritual and moral perfection of each person. Political unrest makes for the pernicious illusion that changes of outer forms will better society and it usually forestalls real progress, as can be seen in all the constitutional states, such as France, England, and America.

The contents of the telegram were not fully or exactly printed in the

Moscow Gazette, and as a consequence I began to receive letters reproaching me, along with requests from American, English, and French newspapers that I explain what I think of the events now transpiring in Russia. I did not want to respond to either one or the other, but after the heinous St. Petersburg crime[3] and the complex feelings of indignation, fear, exasperation, and hatred which this evil evoked, I consider it my responsibility to express in great detail and definiteness, what was briefly asked of me in those one hundred words to the American newspaper. What I have to say is that many people need help to free themselves from the feelings of blame, shame, irritation, hatred, and the desire for strugggle and gain, as well as the consciousness of their helplessness. Most Russians must now attempt to channel their energy to their inner spiritual activity, which alone brings genuine good both to people and to society. In these complicated times this is all the more necessary.

Here is what I think about the events taking place:

Not only the Russian but any government I consider to be by tradition and custom as an overly-complicated institution consecrated to perfecting, by force with impunity, the most horrible crimes, murders, robberies, drunkenness, stupidities, depravaties, and exploitation of the people by the rich and the rulers. I suggest therefore that all the exertions of people who wish to better the community should be directed to freeing themselves from the government, which is primarily an evil, and whose hatred for it is now becoming more evident. In my opinion, this goal can be achieved only *by one single means: by an inner spiritual perfection of each individual.*

The higher people are in their spiritual-moral relations, the better will be the social relations; then there will be less state coercion and less evil for it to create. On the other hand, the lower in spiritual-moral relations of people in a given society, the stronger and more evil the government will be.

The evil which people suffer from the pernicious deeds of the government is always a function of the spiritual and moral composition of society, no matter what form this society has adopted.

Several people who now participate in the Russian government, which is an especially cruel, coarse, stupid, and lying one, see the evil. They think this is so because it is not set up as it should be, such as on the model of other existing governments (the same institutions that with total impunity perpetuate all types of crimes against their peoples). Everyone in authority imagines that a change in outer forms can change the essence.

Such activity I consider *inexpedient, irrational, incorrect, and harmful,* since people assert rights to themselves that they do not have.

I consider such activity inexpedient. The struggle by force and outer forms (and not by spiritual power alone), coupled with the vanity of a handful of people in a powerful government who have in their control millions of armed disciplined men and billions in money, is ludicrous. It is foolish, for those who have the possibility of success and pitiable from the point of view of those unhappy easily-swayed types who will perish in this unequal struggle.

I consider this activity irrational because those people who concede this very impossibility [of success], are those very ones who are struggling with the present government, and the status of the people cannot be bettered.

The present force-wielding government exists as such only because the society over which it rules consists of morally weak people led by ambitious, selfish, and proud men, unrestrained by conscience, who by all means attempt to seize and hold onto their authority. The rest, out of fear, ambition and vanity, or stultification, abet and submit to the leaders. No matter what form in which these people combine, from among them the very same force-wielding government always emerges.

I consider these actions to be incorrect because the people in Russia who are now struggling against the government (the liberal zemstvoists, physicians, lawyers, writers, students, revolutionaries, and the several thousands who are alienated from the people, and the propagandized workers, who call and consider themselves representatives of the people) do not have the right to this calling. These groups demand from the government in the name of the people freedom of the press, freedom of conscience, freedom of meeting, separation of church and state, the eight-hour work day, representation, and so forth.

They agitate for the masses, the one-hundred million peasants, because they believe that these are their demands, but the peasants will be at a loss to respond because freedom of the press, meetings, separation of church and state, even the eight-hour work day do not interest most of them.

They do not need anything of this, but they do need something else: they have waited and wished for it, and never stop thinking and speaking about it, while there is no liberal speech which carries one word about it and the revolutionary social program hardly mentions it in passing. They crave for one thing: the liberation of the land from property rights and its communalization. [They want a future] in which the land will not be taken away from them, their children will not have to go to the factories, and if they do, they will establish their own hours and prices.

[The reformers] say: give freedom and the people will be able to express their demands. This [liberal recourse] is not true. In England, France, and America there is full freedom of the press, but neither the parliaments nor the press talk about the liberation of the land. The question of the general right of all the people to the land is pushed further into the background.

And the liberal and revolutionary reformers, who compose programs [in the name] of people's demands, do not have the right to consider themselves representatives of the people: they represent only themselves, the people for them are only an ephemeral banner.

So, in my opinion, all this struggling with the government is foolish, irrational and incorrect: it is harmful because it diverts people from that single work—the moral perfecting of each individual which is the only means to those goals to which people aspire.

[Reformers] say: "One does not hinder the other." But this is wrong. It is impossible to do these two things at the same time: it is impossible to perfect yourself morally and to participate in political activity, which involves intrigues, cunning, struggles, exasperation and leads to murder. Political activity not only does not contribute to the emancipation of people from state force but on the other hand, makes people more incapable of that single activity which will free them.

So long as people are incapable of standing up against the temptations of fear, stultification, pride, ambition, and vanity, which enslave some and deprave others, they will always commit violence and deceit. The only way to prevent this [from happening] is for everyone to achieve moral power over himself. People can create this [inner strength] from the depths of their soul and they desire to attain this force but it can only be achieved by effort.

To explain this power and its relation to the world and how to inculcate it in people and foster it on the basis of the eternal law of doing to others what you would want them to do to you [is of the utmost importance]. We must suppress in ourselves those fears which force us to submit to others' authority, we must not be either master or slave, not dissimulate, not lie out of fear or for advantage, not shirk the demands of the higher law of our conscience—and all this demands effort. To imagine to oneself, the establishment of certain [perfected] forms by some mystical path will lead people, including myself, to any kind of justice or virtue [is absurd]. The attainment of this [perfection] cannot be done by the power of thought [alone] in spite of any [machinations] of a certain party, [which claims] that it takes place by itself without any effort.

For people to achieve this [goal], they must themselves be assured that it can be done. And there is a [purported] theory by which it can be shown that without effort people can attain the fruits of power. The theory is very similar to the one according to which we pray for our perfection through the atonement of sin by the blood of Christ or through a blessing which will be transmuted by [ritual] secrets. As a psychological illusion, [thinking of this sort] is the basis of that amazing notion that society is improvable by means of changing the outer foms which have produced such horrible poverty and most of all stymie mankind's genuine progress.

People are conscious that there is something bad in their lives and that it is necessary to improve. To better themselves people can only do what is in their power. In order to better themselves, it is necessary most of all to recognize that they have shortcomings, [especially since] they don't want to admit it to themselves. All their attention is turned not to what is always in their power—to themselves, but to those outer conditions which are not in their power. These changes can improve the condition of people as little as the shaking up wine and pouring it into another vessel to change its quality. What [really] follows is the idle, the vain (which make us look at other people's faults), and the evil (socially damaging belief that it is legitimate to kill) depravity.

"Let us rebuild institutions and society will benefit." It would be good if the welfare of mankind could be so easily achieved. Whoever is [truly] happy must be so [for other reasons than the shuffling of institutions], for the lives of mankind do not change from the alterations of outer forms, but only from the internal work of each man by himself. Anyone whose life is subject to control by other people will be very unhappy. Any power to change the outer forms, while their real condition remains unchanged, only depraves and belittles the life of those who (as with all political representatives, kings, ministers, presidents, members of parliaments, any type of revolutionary, and liberals) revert to this pernicious mistake.

Superficially judgmental and frivolous people, who were especially agitated by the fraticidal fight which took place the other day in St. Petersburg with all the accompanying events, think that the main reason for these evil deeds lies in the despotism of the Russian government. They think that if the autocratic monarchical form would be changed to a constitutional or republican type, such events would not be repeated.

But surely the major disaster (if seen in all its significance), from which the Russian people now suffer, is not the St. Petersburg events, but [the actions] by those scores of immoral people, who have undertaken a thoughtless, shameful, and cruel war. This war has already killed and crippled hundreds of thousands of Russian men and threatens to annihilate and maim still more. It has been ruining people, and in the form of debts and taxes will make for a still greater burden on the labor of future generations. It will also deprave people and destroy their souls. What transpired in St. Petersburg on January 9th is nothing in comparison with what took place in the Far East. In one day there was killed and wounded a hundred times more men than were killed on that day in the capital. And not only did the death of them out there fail to make society indignant, like the murdering in St. Petersburg, but people were indifferent, and some even regarded it sympathetically, so that fresher thousands of men will be sent there for the same thoughtless and aimless destruction.

This disaster is terrible. And therefore, if you have already considered the misfortunes of the Russian people, then [you will see that] the major disaster is this war, whereas the St. Petersburg events have only incidentally and circumstantially accompanied the larger disaster. The only way of avoiding these disasters is to find the means to avoid [the root causes of] both of them. A change from a despotic to a constitutional or a republican form of rule will not rescue Russia from either disaster. All constitutional governments are exactly the same as the Russian one, for they refuse to reject senseless war: the number of people with authority who take it into their heads to send their men off to fratricidal warfare [has merely increased]. The Abyssinian War, the Boer War, the Spanish War with Cuba and the Philippines, war in China and Tibet, and the wars with the African peoples— all of them are carried out by constitutional and republican governments.[4] All these governments are exactly the same when they find it necessary to suppress by armed force those uprisings and demonstrations of the people's will which they consider a violation of a particular law.

When a government, even if it is constitutional, is an organized force-wielding authority that people can possess by one means or another there always occur in one or another form (like the events now taking place in Russia) wars and the suppression of uprisings.

Such is the significance of the events which are taking place in St. Petersburg. It is not quite what the superficial people are thinking about, that these events have displayed the perniciousness of the despotic Russian government and it is therefore necessary to attempt to change it to a constitutional one. The significance is more far reaching. Though the actions of an especially stupid and coarse Russian government are more apparent to us rather than those of the more respectable ones, the evil and the hatred by every government compels submission, even if it is by the will of a majority.

In England, America, France, and Germany the perniciousness of governments is so masked that the people of these nations, while pointing to the events in Russia, naively claim that what is going on in Russia goes on only in Russia, and that they have complete freedom and do not need any improvement. They are, however, in the most helpless condition of slaves— the slavery of slaves who do not understand that they are slaves, and take pride in their status of slaves.

The status of us Russians is more onerous [in our being subject] to a far coarser force, but better since we have a greater ability to perceive its actions.

The relations, status, and mood of the Russian people, of the Europeans, and in particular the Americans, are totally like those of the two people who entered into the temple, as described in the Gospel of St. Luke.[5]

Engaging in this activity, any force-wielding government in essence becomes a hateful and greater evil. As with us in Russia, and as with all people who are enslaved by governments, we should not change one form of government for another for they must all be abolished.

My opinion of the events now taking place in Russia is that the Russian government, like any other, is a horrible, inhumane, and powerful robber, which acts perniciously like all the other existing ones: American, French, Japanese, and English. It is therefore incumbent upon all rational people with all their might to get rid of any government, including the Russian.

To get rid of a government, it is not necessary for people to struggle with the outer means at their disposal (laughably insignificant in comparison with the means the government [can muster]). It is only necessary not to participate or to support it. Then it will be destroyed.

In order not to participate or support governments necessitates freedom from those weaknesses by which people fall into their snare and make themselves either their slaves or their participants.

For that freedom, a man must establish a relationship to the All, to God, and live by the higher law, which flows out from this relationship, and to become a spiritual and moral man.

People see and feel more clearly the evil of the government—as now we the Russian people do with the very evident and painful evil of the stupid, cruel, and lying Russian state, which has already murdered hundreds of thousands, destroyed and depraved millions and has already begun to provoke us to murder one another. We should exert ourselves more to establish a clear and resolved spiritual consciousness and to more firmly employ the law of God which results from this consciousness. This law does not demand (from us) reforms from the existing government, or the establishment of a social structure which according to our limited view guarantees the general good, but demands from ourselves a single reform: a moral perfection, the liberation from all those weaknesses and vices which make us slaves to and participants of government crimes.

I finished this article but was undecided whether to publish it, when I received a remarkable unsigned letter:

Here is what the letter says:

> I am not equal to the task of figuring out what day it is.
>
> When someone begins talking about the workers, I begin to hate it, and I become physically sick.
>
> There were piles of bodies of women and children, dripping with blood, and driven off by cabs. How frightful is *this* ? Terrible were the soldiers with their customary unthinking kind of faces, as they slipped on the ice and waited for the command to shoot at someone. Terrible also was the public with its customarily curious faces. Even the most decent people came in order to see for themselves or to hear from others about that something "horrible"—the bodies which were dripping with blood and cut to pieces, and so forth. Perhaps there is something stranger than these soldiers, who were *their usual selves*, and these kind people who wanted something out of the ordinary, so their nerves could shiver from something terrible.
>
> Such people do not seem greatly frightened; they appear *not to understand*, to be undisturbed in their *normality*, even though there will be murder and everywhere the pavement drenched in blood in an hour. [To discover] that *there is no kind of tie* between people—that is the frightening thing.

Over there is someone in a grey coat and another in a black over-coat from the same village. Yet you cannot understand any of it: why those in grey coats joke about the frost and look tranquilly at the black ones passing them by, when they know that each has in his cartridge belt ten shots, and that in an hour or two all of them will be spent. And the black ones look at them, just exactly as this should be. One reads about this *alienation* in books, one speaks [of them] and yet do[es] not feel how strange this is. For the moment, all this [activity] of these days surrounds one [,] and everything else ceases to exist for a time. And there is *only* [the following]: the grey coats, black overcoats and the elegant fur coats and everyone participates *as one*, but everyone does so *differently*. No one is astonished, and not one of them knows why some shoot, others fall, and a third looks on. At other times there is the same frightful and incomprehensible life, while life is taken by command without any enmity or hatred, but during these days every-thing remaining has stopped for a time, and there remains only this fear. This sense of a chasm, not crossing it, although you are quite near, is intolerable.

Five times I have tried to write you, but have thrown my letter away, and finally I am writing, because to be silent day after day is unbearable. Everyone talks about helping the workers. But the horror is not their situation. It is not the workers who need help, but those who shoot and trample on people, and those who, the other day, walked around and stared at the broken glass, the street lights, the trails of bullets, and did not see the congealed blood on the sidewalk and scraped it off with their feet.

Yes, the whole problem is that people are alienated and there is no tie between them. The entire matter is that one should remove what alienates people and repleace it with what unites them. The alien-ation of the individual comes from *every* force-wielding government and they are united by one thing—by [an inner] relationship to God and a striving towards Him. God is the same for everyone, and the relationship that all people have to God should make everybody one.

Whether people want to recognize this or not, all of us are faced with the same ideal of a higher perfectioning, and only the striving toward it will destroy alienation and bring us closer to one another.

The Great Iniquity[6]

Fear of the land hunger and the continued injustice of private property fueling violence compelled him to write this out-and-out Georgist appeal. Since land is the basis of all social questions we must have equal rights to its use. Man must also continue to develop a deep spiritual realtionship with

God so that he can work in harmony on the soil. Reflecting the Slavophile sensibility that had traveled far beyond the reactionary right, Tolstoy declares that it is the Russian people who are to be the first to plant the seeds of Georgism, setting an example for the rest of the world. The essay first appeared in the *London Times* on August 1, 1905 and was greeted by single taxers over the world. J. H. Dillard wrote that:

> Of all living men, he whose words command most attention is Leo Tolstoy; of all publications, that which reaches the widest circle of readers is the *London Times*. That these two great forces should be combined to aid in spreading before the world the doctrine for which Henry George wrought and died—and in so few years after his death—that this should come to pass, is more than George himself, with all his faith, hope and optimism, could fairly dream of.
>
> The extraordinary letter on the land question, entitled "A Great Iniquity," which Count Tolstoy published in the *Times* of August 1st, will, more than any event since Henry George's death, draw the attention of thinking men, the world over, to the supreme importance of the land question.[7]

Russia is passing through an important period destined to have tremendous results.

The nearness and inevitability of the approaching revolution is, as usual, felt most keenly by those classes of society whose lives and energies are not expended on physical labor and can therefore participate in politics. These people include the gentry, merchants, officials, physicians, technicians, professors, teachers, artists, students, and lawyers (belonging for the most part to the so-called urban intelligentsia). They are now directing this movement and devote their energies to the replacement of the existing political order, which one or another party considers the best means for securing the liberty and welfare of the Russian people.[8]

These people continually suffer all sorts of restrictions and coercion by the government, such as arbitrary exile, imprisonment, prohibition of meetings, strikes, trade unions, and censorship of books and newspapers, as well as suppression of the rights of subject nationalities.[9] They are also living a life quite estranged from that of the majority of the agricultural Russian people. They naturally regard the restrictions imposed on them as the major evil from which the nation is suffering and liberation from them as the most important thing.

So think the liberals and the Social Democrats (Marxists), who hope that popular representation will enable them to utilize the power of the state to establish a new social order in accord with their theories. So also think the revolutionaries, who intend to replace the present government and to establish laws securing the greatest freedom and welfare for every-one.[10]

The idea has taken root among our intelligentsia, that the present work for Russia [entails] the introduction of political forms established in Europe and America, which are supposed to ensure the liberty and welfare of all citizens. Yet you need only free yourself for a while from this [delu-sion] and simply consider what is morally wrong in our life. You must see clearly that the main evil from which the Russian people most cruelly and unceasingly suffer (an evil of which they are keenly conscious and continu-ally complain) cannot be removed by any of these foreign political reforms. That fundamental evil from which the Russians suffer in common with Europeans and Americans is that the majority of the people are deprived of the indubitable and natural right to the use of the land. It is only necessary to understand the criminality and wickedness of this deprivation to realize that until this atrocity (which is constantly committed by the landowner) has ceased, no political reforms will insure freedom and welfare. On the contrary, only the emancipation of the masses from the present land-slavery can render political reform a real expression of the people's will, and not a plaything or tool in the hands of politicians.

That is the thought I wish to communicate in this article to those who, at the present crucial moment, sincerely wish to serve not their per-sonal aims but the true welfare of the Russian people.

1. The other day I was walking on the high road to Tula. It was the Saturday before Palm Sunday. Peasants were driving to market in carts with calves, hens, horses, and cows (some of the cows in such poor condition that they were being taken in carts). A wrinkled old woman was leading a lean and wretched cow. I knew her, and asked why she was taking the animal to market.

"She has no milk," said the old woman. "I must sell her and buy one that has. I dare say I shall have to pay an additional ten rubles but we had to spend eighteen rubles on flour, and we have only one breadwinner. I live with my daughter-in-law and four grandchildren. My son is a house porter in town."

"Why doesn't your son live at home."

"There's nothing for him to do. What land have we? Barely enough for kvas."

A lean and sallow peasant tramped by, his trousers spattered with mine clay.

"What business is taking you to town?" I asked him.

"I want to buy a horse. It's time to begin plowing and I haven't got one. But they say horses are dear!"

"How much do you want to give?"

"As much as I have."

"And how much is that?"

"I've scraped together fifteen rubles."

"What can you buy nowadays for fifteen rubles? Barely a hide!" put in another peasant. "Whose mine do you work in?" he added, looking at the man's trousers stretched at the knees and smeared with red clay.

"Komarovs'—Ivan Komarov's"

"How is it you've earned so little?"

"I worked on half-shares. He took half."

"How much did you earn?" I asked.

"I got two rubles a week, or even less. But what's to be done? We hadn't enough grain to last till Christmas. There isn't even enough to buy necessities."

A little farther on a young peasant was taking a sleek, well-fed horse to be sold.

"A good horse!" I said.

"You might look for a better but you wouldn't find one," he said, taking me for a buyer. "Good for plowing or driving."

"Then why are you selling him?"

"I can't use it. I have only two allotments of land and can work them with only one horse. I kept two through the winter but I'm sorry I did. The cattle have eaten up everything and we need money for rent."

"Who is your landlord?"

"Maria Ivanovna—thanks to her for letting us have some land, otherwise we might just as well have hung ourselves."

"How much do you pay her?"

"She fleeces us for fourteen rubles. But where else can we go? We have to rent it."

A woman drove up with a little boy wearing a small cap. She knew me and got down and offered him for service. The boy was just a mite with quick intelligent eyes. "He looks small but he can do anything," she said.

"But why do you want to hire out such a little fellow?"

"Why sir, at least it'll be one less to feed. I have four besides myself and only one allotment of land. God knows we've nothing to eat. They ask for bread and I have nothing to give them."

Everyone with whom one talks complains of want, and all alike everywhere harken back to the cause of it all. They do not have enough bread and that is so because of their lack of land.

These were casual encounters on the road; but wherever one travels in the peasant world throughout Russia one sees the horrors of want and suffering obviously caused by the deprivation of land. Half the Russian peasantry live so poorly that the question for them is not how to improve their lot but simply how to keep themselves and their families alive—and all because they are short of land.

Go throughout all Russia and ask the working people why their life is hard, and what they want, and all of them with one voice will name one and the same thing, which they all unceasingly desire, expect, and hope for.

And they cannot help thinking that apart from the main problem (the insufficiency of land to maintain themselves) most of them also feel themselves to be slaves to the gentry, landowners, and merchants, whose [large] estates surround their meager allotments. They are constantly suffering fines, blows, and humiliations, either because they have taken a sack of grass or an armful of wood (without which they cannot live) or because a horse has strayed on the landowner's field.

Once on the high road I began talking with a blind peasant beggar. Recognizing me by my conversation to be a literate man who reads the papers but not taking me for one of the gentry, he suddenly stopped and gravely asked: "Well, is there any rumor?"

"What about?" I asked.

"Why, about the gentry's land."

When I said that I had heard nothing, the blind man shook his head and did not ask me anything more.

I recently said to one of my former pupils, a prosperous, steady, intelligent, and literate peasant: "Well, are they talking about the land?"

"It's true the people are talking about it," he replied.

"And what do you think about it yourself?"

"Well, it will probably come over to us," he said.

In spite of what is transpiring,[11] this question alone is the most riveting and important for all the people. And they believe, and cannot but help believing that it will "come over."

It is plain to them that a growing agricultural population cannot continue to exist when people are allowed only a small parcel of land while all the parasites crawl around and feast on them.

2. "What is man?" says Henry George in one of his speeches.

> In the first place he is an animal, a land animal who cannot live without land. All that man produces comes from the land; all productive labor, in the final analysis, consists in working on the land or materials drawn from the land, into such forms as fit them for the satisfaction of human wants and desires. Why, man's very body is drawn from the land. Children of the soil, we come from the land, and to the land we must return. Take away from man all that belongs to the land, and what have you but a dismembered spirit? Therefore, he who holds the

land on which and from which another man must live, is that man's master; and the man is his slave. The man who holds the land on which I must live can command me to life or to death just as absolutely as though I were his chattel. Talk about abolishing slavery—we have not abolished slavery—we have only abolished one rude form of it, chattel slavery. There is a deeper and a more insidious form, a more cursed form yet before us to abolish, in this industrial slavery that makes man a virtual slave, while taunting him and mocking him with the name of freedom.[12]

"Did you ever think," says Henry George in another part of the same speech,

> of the utter absurdity and strangeness of the fact that, all over the civilized world, the working classes are the poor classes? . . . Think for a moment how it would strike a rational being who had never been on the earth before, if such an intelligence could come down, and you were to explain to him how we live on earth, how houses, and food and clothing, and all the many things we need, are all produced by work, would he not think that the working people would be the people who lived in the fine houses and had most of everything that work produces? Yet, whether you took him to London or Paris or New York, or even to Burlington, he would find that those called working people were the people who lived in the poorest houses.[13]

The same thing, I would add, occurs to a still greater extent in the country[side]. Idle people live in luxurious palaces, in large and handsome dwellings, while the workers live in the poorest houses.

> All this is strange—just think of it. We naturally despise poverty; and it is reasonable that we should. . . . Nature gives to labor, and to labor alone; there must be human work before any article of wealth can be produced; and, in a natural state of things, the man who toiled honestly and well would be the rich man, and he who did not work would be poor. We have so reversed the order of nature that we are accustomed to think of a workingman as a poor man. . . . The primary cause of this is that we compel those who work to pay others for permission to do so. You buy a coat, a horse, a house; there you are paying the seller for labor exerted, for something that he has produced, or that he has got from the man who did produce it; but when you pay a man for land, what are you paying him for? You are paying for something that no man has produced; you pay him for something that was here before man was, or for a value that was created, not by him individually, but by the community of which you are a part.[14]

That is why he who has seized the land and possesses it is rich, whereas he who works on it or with its products is poor.

We talk about overproduction. How can there be such a thing as overproduction while people want? All these things that are said to be overproduced are desired by many people. Why do they not get them?

They do not get them because they have not the means to buy them; not that they do not want them. Why have they not the means to buy them? They earn too little. When great masses of men have to work for an average of $1.40 a day in America and for fifty kopecks in Russia, it is no wonder that great quantities of goods cannot be sold.

Now why is it that men have to work for such low wages? Because, if they were to demand higher wages, there are plenty of unemployed men ready to step into their places. It is this mass of unemployed men who compel that fierce competition that drives wages down to the point of bare subsistence. Why is it that there are men who cannot get employment? Did you ever think what a strange thing it is that men cannot find employment? Adam had no difficulty in finding employment; neither did Robinson Crusoe; the finding of employment was the last thing that troubled them.

If men cannot find an employer, why can they not employ themselves? Simply because they are shut out from the element on which human labor can alone be exerted. Men are compelled to compete with each other for the wages of an employer, because they have been robbed of the natural opportunities of employing themselves; because they cannot find a piece of God's world on which to work without paying some other human creature for the privilege.

Men pray to the Almighty to relieve poverty. But poverty comes not from God's laws—it is blasphemy of the worst kind to say that; it comes from man's injustice to his fellows. Supposing the Almighty were to hear the prayer, how could He carry out the request, so long as His laws are what they are? Consider—the Almighty gives us nothing of the things that constitute wealth; He merely gives us the raw material which must be utilized by man to produce wealth. Does He not give us enough of that now? How could He relieve poverty even if He were to give us more? Supposing, in answer to these prayers, He were to increase the power of the sun, or the virtues of the soil? Supposing He were to make plants more prolific, or animals to produce after their kind more abundantly? Who would get the benefit of it? Take a country where land is completely monopolized, as it is in most of the civilized countries—who would get the benefit of it? Simply, the landowners. And even if God, in answer to prayer, were to send down out the heavens those things that men require, who would get the benefit?

In the Old Testament we are told that when the Israelites journeyed through the desert, they were hungered, and that God sent down out of the heavens—manna. There was enough for all of them, and they all took it and were relieved. But, supposing that desert had been held as private property, as the soil of Great Britain is held, as the soil even of our new states is being held; supposing that one of the Israelites had a square mile, and another one had twenty square miles, and another one had a hundred square miles, and the great majority of the Israelites did not have enough to set the soles of their feet upon, which they could call their own—what would become of the manna? What good would it have done to the majority? Not a whit. Though God had sent down manna enough for all, that manna would have been the property of the landholders; they would have employed some of the others, perhaps, to gather it up in heaps for them, and would have sold it to their hungry brethren. Consider it; this purchase and sale of manna might have gone on until the majority of the Israelites had given up all they had, even to the clothes off their backs. What then? Well, then they would not have had anything left with which to buy manna, and the consequence would have been that while they went hungry the manna would have lain in great heaps, and the landowners would have been complaining of the overproduction of manna. There would have been a great harvest of manna and hungry people, just precisely the phenomena that we see today.

I do not mean to say that, even after you had set right this fundamental injustice, there would not be many things to do; but this I do mean to say, that our treatment of land lies at the bottom of all social questions. This I do mean to say, that, do what you please, reform as you may, you never can get rid of widespread poverty so long as the element on which, and from which, all men must live is made the private property of some men. It is utterly impossible. Reform government—get taxes down to the minimum— build railroads; institute co-operative stores; divide profits, if you choose, between employers and employed—and what will be the result? The result will be that land will increase in value—that will be the result—that and nothing else. Experience shows this. Do not all improvements simply increase the value of land—the price that some must pay others for the privilege of living?[15]

Let me add that we constantly see the same thing in Russia. All the landowners complain that their estates are unprofitable and are run at a loss but the price of land is continually rising. It cannot but rise. For the population it is a matter of life and death.

And so the people give all they can, not only their labor but even their lives to land which is being withheld from them.

3. There used to be cannibalism, human sacrifices, religious prostitution and the killing of weak children. There used to be also blood vengeance and the slaughter of whole populations, judicial tortures, quarterings, burnings at the stake, the lash, has disappeared within our own memory, the *spitzruten*[16] and also slavery.

But our outliving those dreadful customs and institutions does not prove the nonexistence among us of ones which have become as abhorrent to enlightened reason and conscience as those horrible memories which were abolished in the past. The path of mankind towards perfection is endless, and at every moment of history there are superstitions, deceptions, and pernicious outmoded institutions which give us problems which should be suppressed. There are also others that are like the mists of a distant future. Capital punishment and punishment in general, prostitution, meat eating, militarism, and war are great problems—but the most prevalent and urgent problem of all is that land is held as private property.

People have never been able to quickly free themselves from the omnipresent injustices that have been recognized by the more sensitive people as harmful. Liberation has come in jerks, with stoppages and backlashes and then again by fresh leaps towards freedom, comparable to the pangs of birth. As was the case with the recent abolition of serfdom, so it is now with the abolition of land as private property.

Thousands of years ago prophets and sages pointed out the evil and injustice of landowning, and so have progressive thinkers of Europe more frequently. Activists in the French Revolution did this succinctly.[17] Subsequently, the increase of population and the seizure of free land by the rich, as well as the spread of education with a decrease in the harshness of manners, has made that injustice so obvious that progressive people and even very ordinary people cannot help but see it. But men, especially those who profit by landowning (both the owners themselves and others whose interests are bound up with that institution) are so accustomed to this order and have profited by it so long that they often do not see its injustice. They use every possible means to hide the truth from themselves and others. The truth, [however], is continually appearing more clearly, but they try to distort it, suppress it, or snuff it out, and if they cannot succeed they will try to hush it up.

A very striking example is the fate of the remarkable man who died at the end of the last century—Henry George[18]—who devoted his immense mental powers to elucidate the injustice and cruelty of the institution of landowning and to teach others the means to rectify it even under the present forms of government. He did this through books, articles, and speeches with such extraordinary force and lucidity that no unprejudiced person reading them could fail to agree with his arguments: [to awaken to the fact] that all reforms would be useless until this fundamental injustice was abolished, and that the means he proposes for its abolition are reasonable, just, and practical.

But what has happened? Henry George's works first appeared in English and spread rapidly throughout the Anglo-Saxon world and [it was unthinkable that] their high quality could not fail to be appreciated. Although it seemed as if the truth must prevail and come to fruition, it very soon appeared that in England (and even in Ireland where the crying injustice of private property in land was very manifest) the majority of the most influential and educated people were opposed to his teaching. Radicals like Parnell, who had at first sympathized with Henry George's projects, soon recanted, regarding political reform as more important.[19] In England all the aristocrats were opposed to it, among others the famous Toynbee, Gladstone, and Herbert Spencer.[20] This latter [person], after having at first expounded in *Social Statics*, the injustice of private property in land, later on withdrew that opinion and bought up the first edition to expunge all that he had said about it.

At Oxford when Henry George was lecturing, the students organized a hostile demonstration, and the Roman Catholic party regarded his teaching as sinful, immoral, dangerous, and contrary to Christ's teaching.[21] The orthodox science of political economy rose up against Henry George's teaching in the same way. Learned professors from the height of their superiority refuted it without understanding it, chiefly because it did not recognize the fundamental principles of their pseudo-science. The socialists were also inimical, considering the most important problem of the period to be not the land question but the total elimination of [all] private property. The main method used to oppose Henry George was, however, the one always employed against irrefutable and self-evident truths. Henry George's teaching is still being deliberately ignored. This method of hushing it up was practiced so successfully that Labouchere, a British Member of Parliament, could say publicly and without contradiction that he "was not such a visionary as Henry George, and did not propose to take the land from the landlords in order to rent it out again, but only demanded the imposition of a tax on the value of the land."[22] That is, while attributing to Henry George what he could not possibly have said, Labouchere corrected that fantasy by putting forward Henry George's actual proposal.

Thanks to the collective efforts of all those interested in defending the institution of private property in land, the teaching of Henry George (irrefutably convincing in its simplicity and lucidity) remains almost unknown, and as years go by attracts far less attention.

Here and there in Scotland, Portugal, or New Zealand, he is remembered, and among hundreds of scientists one is found who knows and defends his teaching. But in England and the United States the number of his adherents have dwindled more and more; in France his teaching is almost unknown; in Germany it is preached in a very small circle; and everywhere it is stifled by the noisy doctrine of socialism. So that among the majority of supposedly educated people it is known only by name.

4. People who argue with Henry George's teaching simply do not know it. (There is no other way when a man becomes acquainted with it but to agree.)

If Henry George is sometimes referred to, people either attribute to him what he hasn't said or reassert what he has refuted. They also contradict him simply because he does not conform to the pedantic, arbitrary, and supeficial principles of the so-called irrefutable political economy.

Experience in our time has made the truth so manifest that land cannot be private property. The best ways to maintain the present order in which its rights are preserved are either not to think about it, or to ignore the truth, or to become absorbed in other activities. And that is what is being done in contemporary Christendom.

The politicians of Europe and America busy themselves with all sorts of things for people's welfare, such as tariffs, colonies, income taxes, military and naval budgets, socialist assemblies, unions and syndicates, the election of presidents, diplomatic relations—everything except the one way without which there cannot be any true improvement—the reestablishment of the violated right of all men to use the land. And this transpires even though the politicians of Christendom feel in their souls that while they are expending their energies there is still industrial and military strife, but the only result will be the general exhaustion of the nations. Wanting only to forget themselves, they blindly yield to the demands of the moment and continue to whirl around in an enchanted circle from which there is no escape.

Strange as it may seem this temporary blindness of the politicians as well as the workers of Europe and the United States can be explained by the fact that all of them have already gone so far down the wrong path that most of them have been separated from the land (or as in the United States have never lived on it) and obtain their living in factories or as hired agricultural laborers. It is therefore understandable that to these politicians, catering to the demands of the majority, the chief means of improving the people would seem to be by tariffs, trusts, and colonies. But in Russia (where eighty percent of the nation is agricultural, and the people ask only one thing, the opportunity to be given land) it should be evident that something else is needed.

The people of Europe and the United States are in a position similar to that of a man who has already traveled far down a road which at first seemed the right one, but is afraid to recognize his mistake although the farther he goes the farther he is from his goal. But Russia is still standing at the crossroads, and can still, as the wise saying has it, "ask her way while yet on the road."

And what are those Russians doing who wish, or at least say they wish, to create a good life for the people?

They imitate Europe and America in everything they do.

In order to arrange a better life for people they concern themselves about freedom of the press, religious toleration, freedom for trade unions, tariffs, conditional punishments, the separation of church from state, cooperative associations, the future socialization of the implements of labor, and above all representative government as is the case in European countries and America. But such a government has never been and will never be conducive for the solution of the land problem, which alone will resolve all difficulties. If Russian politicians do speak about land abuses, which for some reason they call "the agrarian question" (possibly imagining that this stupid phraseology will conceal the substance of the matter), they do not suggest that private property in land is an evil that should be abolished. They merely propose various patching-ups and palliatives to cover up and avoid awareness of this essential, ancient, cruel, obvious, and crying injustice. It will, nevertheless, be abolished not only in Russia but throughout the entire world.

In Russia, where a hundred million people constantly suffer from the greed of private landowners, the conduct of those who pretend to seek everywhere (except where it lies) for the means of improving the people is astounding. It reminds me of what takes place on stage when the spectators can see perfectly the man who has hidden himself, and the actors can also see him but pretend not to, since they purposely divert each other's attention and look at everything except what is important for them.

5. People have driven into an enclosure a herd of dairy cows which had been providing sustenance. The cows have eaten up and trampled down the forage in the enclosure, they are famished and have chewed each other's tails. They are lowing and struggling to flee back to the pasture lands. But the people have surrounded the enclosure with fields of mint, dye-yielding plants, and tobacco plantations. They have cultivated flowers, and laid out a race course, a park, and lawn tennis courts and they will not let the cows out lest they should spoil these things. But the cows bellow and grow thin and people begin to fear that they will not have any more milk. So they devise various means of improving the cows' condition. They build awnings over them, they have them rubbed down with wet brushes, they gild their horns, and alter the hours of milking. They fret over the supervision and doctoring of the old and sick cows so they invent new and improved methods of milking and plant some kind of extraordinarily nutritious grass. They argue about these and many other matters, but do not (and cannot without disturbing all the surroundings of the enclosure) do the one simple thing necessary for the cows as well as for themselves—take down the fence and set the cows free, as was meant by Nature, in the abundant pastures that surround them.

People who act in this way behave unreasonably but there is an explanation for their conduct: they are reluctant to sacrifice the things with which they have surrounded the enclosure. But what can be said of those who have planted nothing around their enclosure but (imitating those who keep in their cows because of what they have planted around the enclosure) also keep their cows penned in, and claim that they do it for the cows' welfare?

But that is just what the Russians (whether for or against the government) do, who try to establish all kinds of European institutions for the people who are constantly suffering from land deprivation, and forget and deny the main thing, the one thing the Russian people require—the freeing of the land from private ownership and the establishment of equal rights to it for everyone.

It is understandable that the European parasites who do not draw their subsistence either directly or indirectly from the labor of their own English, French, or German working men, those whose bread is produced by colonial workers in exchange for factory products, do not see the labor and sufferings of the workers who feed and support them. So they devise a future socialist organization for which they are supposedly preparing mankind, and with untroubled conscience amuse themselves in the meanwhile by electoral campaigns, party struggles, parliamentary debates, the establishment and overthrow of ministries, and various other pastimes which they call science and art.

The real people who feed these European parasites are the laborers they do not see in India, Africa, Australia, and to some extent Russia. But this is not so for us Russians. We have no colonies where slaves we never see provide food for us in exchange for our manufactures. Our breadwinners, hungry and suffering, are always before our eyes, and we cannot transfer to distant colonies the burden of our unjust life so that invisible slaves should feed us.

Our sins are always before us. . . .

And here (instead of learning, listening, and solving the needs of those who support us), under the pretence of serving them we, their parasites, prepare a future socialist organization in the European manner. And yet we profess to help the very people from whom we are squeezing the last drop of strength.

We try to abolish book censorship, to get rid of arbitrary banishment, to establish primary and agricultural schools, to build more hospitals, to abolish passports, to cancel tax arrears, to establish strict factory inspection and compensation for injured workers. [We also attempt] to survey the land, to provide assistance through the Peasant Bank[23] for land purchases, and much else for the welfare of the people.

Once we realize the unceasing sufferings of millions of people: the dying of old men, women, and children from want, as well as [the high] mortality from overwork and insufficient food—once we realize the enslavement, the humiliations, all the useless expenditure of strength, and the perversion, and the horrors which arise from the lack of land—it becomes quite evident that all such measures which are propounded by the pseudo-defenders of the people would (even if they were realized) amount to an insignificant drop in the sea.

But not only do the men concerned with people's welfare of the people keep the hundred million workers in perpetual slavery, while devising insignificant changes that are unimportant both in quality and in quantity, but many of these men (and the most advanced of them) want to see these sufferings intensified more. So they drive the people to the necessity (leaving in their wake millions of victims who will perish from want and depravity) of exchanging their accustomed happy agricultural life for the [so-called] improved factory life.

The Russian people, because of their agricultural background, the love of this life, and their Christian character, and also because, almost alone among European nations, they still wish to remain farmers, have been providentially placed by historic conditions in the forefront of mankind's most progressive movement, the labor question.

Yet these Russian people have been invited by their fancied representatives and leaders to follow on the heels of the decadent and entangled European nations and America to pervert themselves by renouncing their calling.

Astonishing as is the poverty of thought of those men who do not think with their own minds but slavishly repeat what is said by their European models, the hardness of their hearts and their cruelty is still more amazing.

6. "Woe unto you, scribes and Pharisees, hypocrites! for ye are like unto whitened sepulchres, which outwardly appear beautiful, but inwardly are full of dead men's bones and of all [kinds of] uncleanliness. Even so ye also outwardly appear righteous unto men, but inwardly ye are full of hypocrisy and iniquity" (Matt. 23: 27-8).

There was a time when in the name of the true faith and of God, men were destroyed, tortured, executed, and slaughtered by tens and hundreds of thousands. And now from the height of our superiority we look down on the men who did those things.

But we are wrong. Such people exist among us; the difference is only that the men of old did these things in the name of God, while those who perpetuate similar evil among us now do it in the name of "the people." Among those men of old there were some who were insanely and confidently convinced that they knew the truth, these were hypocrites making careers for themselves under pretence of serving God while the masses unreasonably followed the most skillful and bold. So now those who do evil in the name of the people are composed of hypocritical men insanely and confidently convinced that they alone know what is right. Much evil was done in their time by the self-proclaimed servants of God, thanks to the teaching called theology. But if the servants of the people have done less evil by a teaching called scientific, that is only because they have not yet had sufficient time, although their conscience is already burdened by poisoning the people and [with the pouring of] rivers of blood.[24]

The features of both these groups are alike.

First, there is the dissolute and depraved life of the majority of these servants of God and the people. (In their opinion, their dignity as chief servants frees them from any necessity to restrain their conduct.)

The second feature is the utter lack of interest, attention, or love for that which they desire to serve. God has been and is merely a banner for those servants. In reality they did not love Him or seek communion with Him, and neither knew Him nor even wished to know Him. So it is also with the many servants of the people. The "People" have been only a banner, and far from loving the masses or seeking a communion with them they not only do not know them, but in the depths of their souls regard them with contempt, aversion, and fear.

The third feature is that while the servants of God and the people were engaged [in such machinations], they not only disagreed among themselves as to the means of service, but regarded as false and pernicious the activity of all who did not agree with them, and called for its forcible suppression. In the former case, came burnings at the stake, inquistions, and massacres; and in the latter, executions, imprisonments, revolutions, and assassinations.

And finally, the main and most characteristic feature of both is their complete indifference and absolute ignorance to what is proclaimed and demanded by the One they [claim to] serve. God, whom they have been serving so zealously, has directly and clearly expressed in what they recognize as a Divine revelation that He is to be [paid homage] only by men loving their neighbors and doing to others as they wish others to do to them. But they have not recognized this as the means of serving God. They have demanded something quite different, which they themselves have invented and announced as the word of God. The servants of the people do just the same. They do not recognize at all what the people clearly express and desire. They choose to serve them by what the people not only do not ask of them but [of which they] have no conception whatsoever. They serve them by means they have invented, and not by the one thing for which the masses unceasingly seek.

7. Of all the essential changes in the forms of social life there is one that is the most universally fruitful, without which no single step forward can be accomplished. The necessity for this change is obvious to every man who is

free from preconceived theories and it is the concern not only of Russia but of the whole world. All the present sufferings of mankind are connected with it. We in Russia are fortunate since the great majority of our people live by agricultural labor and do not recognize private property in land, but ceaselessly desire and demand the abolition of that ancient abuse.

But no one sees this or wants to see it.

What is the cause of this perversion?

Why do good, kind, intelligent men, of whom many can be found among the liberals, the socialists, the revolutionaries, and even among government officials—why do these men, who desire the people's welfare, do not see the one thing they are in need of and unceasingly strive for, and without which they constantly suffer? Why are they rather concerned with various schemes which cannot contribute to the people's welfare [and do not receive] their consent?

All the activity of these servants of the people (both governmental and anti-governmental) resembles that of a man who, wishing to help a horse that has got stuck in a bog, sits in the cart and shifts the load from place to place, imagining he is helping matters.

Why is this?

The answer to why the people, who might live well and happily, but are living badly and miserably, is the same for all inquiries.

It is because these men (both governmental and anti-governmental) who attempt to improve the people's welfare lack religion. Without religion, men cannot live a reasonable life. Still less can they know what is good and what is bad, what is necessary and what is unnecessary. That alone is why the men of our time in general, and the Russian intelligentsia in particular (who are completely bereft of spiritual consciousness and proudly announce that fact), so perversely misunderstand people's lives and demands. They claim for the masses many different things but not the one thing they need.

Without religion it is impossible to genuinely love men, and without love it is impossible to know what and how much they need. Only those who are not religious and therefore do not truly love, can devise trifling and unimportant improvements without seeing the main evil from which the people suffer, and which is also caused by those very attempts. Only such people can preach more or less cleverly devised abstract theories concerning the people's future happiness and not see their present sufferings which call for immediate alleviation. It is as if someone who has deprived a hungry man of food should give him advice (and that of a very doubtful character) as to how to get food in the future without considering it necessary to share with him the food he has taken from him.

Fortunately the great and beneficent movements of humanity are accomplished not by parasites feeding on the people's marrow (whatever they may call themselves: government officials, revolutionaries, or liberals) but by religious men, that is, by serious, simple, industrious people, who live not for their own profit, vanity, or ambition, but for the fulfillment of God's calling.

Such men, and only such men, can move mankind forward by their quiet but resolute activity. They do not try to distinguish themselves in the eyes of others by devising this or that improvement (such improvements can be innumerable and are all insignificant if the main problem is left untouched) but they try to live in accord with God and their conscience. They thereby naturally come across the most obvious infringement of God's law and seek the means of deliverance, not only for themselves but for others.

A few days ago an acquaintance of mine, a physician, was waiting for a train in the third-class waiting room of a large railway station and was reading a paper, when a peasant sitting by him asked about the news. There was an article about the "agrarian" conference. The physician translated the ridiculous word "agrarian" into Russian, and when the peasant understood that the matter concerned the land, he asked him to read the article. The physician began to read and other peasants moved forward. A group collected. Some pressed on the backs of others and some sat on the floor but the faces of all wore a look of solemn concentration. When the reading was over an old man at the back sighed deeply. He certainly had not understood anything of the confused jargon in which the article was written (which even men who could themselves talk that jargon could not readily understand) but he did understand that the matter concerned the great and longstanding sin from which he and his ancestors have been suffering. But he also understood that those who were committing this sin were beginning to be conscious of it. He mentally turned to God and crossed himself. And in that movement of his hand there was more meaning and content than in all the prattle that now fills the columns of our papers. He understood, as all the people do, that the seizure of the land by those who do not work on it is a great sin. While he and his brethren have suffered physically, those who have been committing this sin endlessly suffer spiritually. [He knew] that this sin like every sin (like serfdom within his own memory) must inevitably come to an end. He knew and felt this, and therefore could not but turn to God at the thought of an imminent solution.

8. "Great social reforms," says Mazzini, "always have and always will result only from great religious movements."

Such a religious movement now awaits the Russian people—the entire Russian people, the workers without soil to farm, the landowners (large, medium, and small), and also all the hundreds of thousands of men who, though they do not possess land, occupy advantageous positions thanks to the compulsory labor of the disinherited.

The religious movement now due among the Russian people consists in eradicating the great sin that has for so long tormented and divided people not only in Russia but throughout the world.

That sin cannot be remedied by political reforms or socialist systems planned for the future or by a revolution. Still less can it be cured by philanthropic contributions or government organizations for the purchase and distribution of land among the peasants.

Such palliative measures only divert attention from the essence of the problem and thus hinder its solution. No artificial sacrifices are necessary nor undue concerns about the people. What is needed is simple: that all who are committing this sin should be conscious of it and desire to free themselves from it.

It is only necessary that the undeniable truth which the best of the people have always known—that the land cannot be anyone's exclusive property, and that to refuse access to it to those who are in need of it is a sin—should be recognized by all men. It should be shameful to possess land to profit by the labor of men who are forced to work merely because they are refused their legitimate right to it.

What happened in regard to serfdom (when the landholding gentry became ashamed of it, when the government became ashamed to maintain those unjust and cruel laws, and when it became evident to the peasants themselves that a wrong for which there was no justification was being done to them) should come about in regard to property in land. And this is necessary not for any one class, however numerous, but for all classes, and not merely for all classes and all men of any one country, but for all mankind.

9. Henry George wrote that:

> Social reform is not to be secured by noise and shouting, by complaints and denunciation, by the formation of parties or the making of revolutions, but by the awakening of thought and the progress of ideas. Until there be correct thought there cannot be right action, and when there is correct thought right action *will* follow. . . .
>
> The great work of the present for every man and every organization of men who would improve social conditions is the work of education—the propagation of ideas. It is only as it aids this that anything else can avail. And in this work everyone who can think may aid—first by forming clear ideas himself and then by endeavoring to arouse the thought of those with whom he comes in contact.[25]

That is quite right, but to serve that great cause there must be something else besides thought—a religious feeling, that feeling in consequence of which the serf owners of the last century acknowledged that they were in the wrong, and sought the means (in spite of personal losses and even ruin) to free themselves from the guilt that oppressed them.

If the great work of freeing the land is to be accomplished, that same feeling must arise among people of the possessing classes and to such an extent that people will be ready to sacrifice everything, just simply to liberate themselves from this living sin.

To talk in various assemblies and committees about improving the people who still possess and trade hundreds, thousands, and tens of thousands of desiatinas and who benefit and live luxuriously thanks to the oppression of the people (without being willing to sacrifice one's own exceptional advantages obtained from that injustice) is not only foolish. It is also both harmful and horrid and is condemned by common sense, honesty, and Christianity.

It is not necessary to devise cunning means of improving the position of men who are deprived of their legitimate right to the land. What is needed is that those who deprive them of it should understand the sin they commit and cease to participate in it whatever the cost. Only such moral activity by every man will contribute to the solution of the problems now confronting humanity.

The emancipation of the serfs in Russia was accomplished not by Alexander II, but by those men who undertood the sin of serfdom and tried to liberate themselves from it regardless of their personal advantage. It was effected chiefly by Novikov, Radishchev, and the Decembrists.[24] They were men who (without causing others to suffer) were ready to suffer themselves and did suffer for the sake of loyalty to what they felt to be the truth.

The same should also occur regarding the emancipation of the land. And I believe there are men living today who will accomplish that great work which now confronts not only the Russian people but the whole world.

The land question in our time has reached such a stage of maturity as legalized serfdom had reached fifty years ago. Exactly the same thing is being repeated. People then sought the means of remedying the general uneasiness and dissatisfaction that society felt, and all sorts of external, governmental means were applied. But nothing helped or could help while the ripening question of personal slavery remained unsolved. Similarly, now no external measures will help until the pregnant question of landownership is settled.

Just as measures are now proposed for adding parcels to the peasants' land, and for the Peasant Bank to aid them for land purchases, and so on, so palliative measures were then proposed and enacted, such as: the so-called "inventories," rules restricting work for the proprietor to three days a week, and much else.[25] As now the landowners talk about the injustice of ending immoral landownership, so they then talked of the wrongfulness of depriving the masters of their serfs. Just as the Church then justified serfdom, so now science (which has taken the place of the Church) justifies property in land. Then the serf owners, more or less realizing their sin, endeavored to mitigate it in various ways without freeing the slaves, and allowed serfs to pay ransom to escape compulsory work, or to lessen the labor demanded. Now the more sensitive landowners, feeling their guilt, try to redeem themselves by renting their land to the peasantry on easier terms, by selling it through the Land Banks, or by establishing schools, ridiculous amusement houses, magic lanterns, and theaters.

And the indifference of the government is also the same. But then the question was not solved by those who devised ingenious methods for the improvement of the serfs. [It was solved] by those who acknowledged the urgent necessity for a solution and did not postpone it to the future. They did not anticipate special difficulties, but tried to end the evil at once. They did not concede that there could be circumstances in which an acknowledged wrong would continue, or took some course which appeared best under the existing conditions. So it is now with the land question.

That question will be solved not by men who try to mitigate the evil, or devise remedies for the people, or postpone the task, but by those who understand that however much a wrong may be mitigated, it remains a wrong—it is senseless to devise improvements for a man whom we are torturing.

The land question can be solved [only] by that method worked out by Henry George. He did it so thoroughly that even under the existing state organizations and compulsory taxation it is impossible to reach any more practical, just, and peaceful decision. Henry George said:

> To beat down and cover up the truth that I have tried tonight to make clear to you, selfishness will call on ignorance. But it has in it the germinative force of truth, and the times are ripe for it. . . .
> The ground is plowed; the seed is set; the good tree will grow. So little now; only the eye of faith can see it.[26]

And I think Henry George is right, for the elimination of the sin of landownership will be near. The movement he started was the last birth pang, and the birth itself is imminent—that of the liberation of men from the sufferings that they have borne so long. I also think (and I should like to contribute to this in however small a degree) that the removal of this great and universal sin will usher in a new era in the history of mankind and awaits our Russian people predestined by its spiritual and economic character for this momentous task. I think that the Russian people should not be proletarianized like the peoples of Europe and America, but should, on the contrary, solve the land question at home through the abolition of private landownership. They should also show other people the path to a sane, free, and happy life (without industrial, factory, and capitalist slavery and violence). In this lies its great and historic mission.

I should like to think that we Russian parasites should be condemned, because we have existed by the sweat of people's labor: that we must understand our sin and (without personal advantage) try to correct it, [if only] for the sake of the truth.

"Tolstoy on Land Ownership"[27]

"Tolstoy on Land Ownership," which came out in *The Evening Bulletin* of Philadelphia in 1905, is a translation, in part, of a short essay, "The Project of Henry George." It is a succinct synopsis of Tolstoy's interpretation of Georgism. The fruits of our labor belong to us, Tolstoy insists, and should not be taxed. But no one can own land, and ground rent of each plot according to its value will be the best way putting it to common use. Much government and other vices will be eliminated, and the production of wealth will increase. The single tax will most assuredly create conditions for the improvement of mankind. It is the most sane and practical method that has universal validity.

A number of suggestions have been made as to how to divide all the land among the workers in the most just manner. Of all these [plans] only the one made by the late Henry George appears to me to be practical.

The property right Henry George wrote in his books about the single tax, is founded not on human laws but on the laws of God. It is undeniable and absolute, and everyone who violates it, be it an individual or a nation, commits a theft.

A man who catches a fish, who plants a tree, builds a house, constructs a machine, sews a dress or paints a picture, becomes the owner of the results of his exertions—he has the right to give them away, to sell them or to leave them to his heirs. Since the land was not been created by us, and only serves as the temporary residence of changing generations of human beings, it is clear that nobody can own the exclusive right to its possession, and that the rights of all men to it are equal and inalienable.

The right to own land is limited by the equal rights of all others, and this imposes upon its temporary possessor the duty to remunerate society for the valuable privilege given him to use the land in his possession [use].

When we impose a tax upon houses, crops, or money in any form, we take from members of society something which by right belongs to them: we violate the property right and commit a theft in the name of the law. When we impose a tax upon land we take from members of society something which does not belong to them [singly], but to society [as a whole] and which cannot be given to individuals except at a detriment to others.

We thus violate the laws of justice when we place a tax on labor or the fruits of labor, and we also violate them if we do not levy a tax on land.

Let us therefore, decide to stop levying all taxes except the tax on the value of land, regardless of the building erected or the improvements made on it but only on the value which natural or social conditions give to it.

If we place the single tax on land the results will be the following:

1. The [single] tax will relieve us of the whole army of officials necessary to collect the present taxes, which will diminish the cost of government, while at the same time making it more honest. It will rid us of all the taxes which lead to lying, to perjury, and to frauds of all kinds. All land is visible, and cannot be hidden, and its value is fixed easier than that of any other property, and the single tax can be determined at less expense and less danger to public morals.

2. It will increase the production of wealth to a great extent, doing away with the discouraging tax upon labor and thrift, and it will make the land more accessible to those who want to work or improve it. The proprietors, who do not work themselves, but speculate in its increasing value, will find it difficult to keep such expensive property. The tax on labor, on the other hand, leads to the accumulation of immense fortunes in a few hands, and the increasing poverty of the masses. This unjust division of wealth on one side leads to the creation of one class of people who are idle and corrupt, because they are too rich, and the creation of another class of people who are too poor, and thus doubly delays the production of [genuine] wealth. This unjust division of wealth will create terrible millionaires on the one hand, and on the other vagrants, beggars, thieves, gamblers, and social parasites of various kinds. It will necessitate an enormous expense for officials to watch them, such as policemen, judges, prisons, and other means which society uses in self-defense.

The single tax is a remedy for all these evils.

I do not mean to say that this tax will transform human nature, for that is not within the power of man, but it will create conditions under which it will grow better instead of worse, as under the present conditions. It will make possible an increase of wealth, for which it would be difficult to form a [definite] idea. It will make undeserved poverty impossible. It will do away with the demoralizing struggle for a living. It will make it possible for men to be honest, just, reasonable, and noble, if they desire to be so. It will prepare the soil for the coming of the epoch of justice, abundance, peace, and happiness, which Christ [preached to] his disciples.

Let us suppose that in a certain place all the land belongs to two owners. One is very rich, who lives far away, and another is not rich, who lives and works at home And there are also a hundred small peasants owning a few desiatinas each. In addition, there are some scores of people who own no land, such as mechanics, merchants, and officials.

Now let us suppose that the people of that community, having arrived at the conclusion that the land is common property, decide to dispose of it according to their new conviction.

What would they do? Take all the land away from those who own it, and give everybody the right to take what he desires? That could not be done, because there would be several people who would want the same ground, and this would lead to endless quarrels. To form one society and work all things in common would be difficult, because some have carts, wagons, horses, and cattle, while others have none. Besides, some people do not know how to till the soil, or are not strong enough.

To divide all the land in equal parts, according to its [quality] and allow one part to each is very difficult, and would also be impractical, because the lazy and poor would lease their property to the rich for money, and they would soon be in possession of it all again.

The inhabitants of the community, therefore, decide to leave the land in the possession of those who used it, and to order each one to pay into the community treasury money equivalent to the revenue which had been decided on its appraised value. It is to based not according to the work or the improvements made on it, but according to its quality and location. And this money is to be divided equally among all.

It would be difficult to take this money from all those who held the land, and then divide it equally among all the members of the community. Since these people do have to pay for public needs, such as schools, fire departments, roads, etc. and because this funding was always needed, they decided to use all the money derived from those who had the use of the land, for public needs.

Having made this arrangement, the members of the community would levy the tax for the use of land on the two large owners, and also on the peasants with small allotments, but no tax at all would be imposed on those who held no land.

This plan would cause the one landowner who lived far away, and who derived little income from his property, to realize that it did not pay to hold on to the land taxed in such a fashion, so he would give it up. The other large landowner gave up part of it, and kept only that part which produced more than the amount of the tax.

Those of the peasants who held small properties, and who had plenty of men, and not enough land, as well as some of those who held no land at all, but who desired to make a living by working the land, could take up the land surrendered by its former owners.

After that, all the members of the community could make a living from the land. All the land would pass into the hands of or remained with those who loved to work it, and who can make it produce the most. The public institutions would flourish and the wealth of the community increased, for there was more money than before for public needs. But the most important fact is that this change in the use of the land would take place without any discussion, quarrel, or discord, but rather by the voluntary surrender by those who did not derive any profit from it.

Such is the project of Henry George, which if realized here, would make Russia wealthy and happy, and which is practicable all over the world.

The Three Lies[28]

This variation of the unpublished *The Three Lies* condemns taxation, the military, and most of all the denial to the people of access to the soil. These three sins create all the physical and spiritual evil in the world. The only escape for us is to submit to God and not to other people, whether rulers or revolutionaries. Tolstoy advises refusal to obey man-made laws, pay taxes, or join the military. By such means, along with the adoption of the single tax, the world can be remade.

"He who wields a sword shall perish by the sword" (Matt. 26:52).
"Blessed are the meek, for they shall inherit the earth" (Psalm 37:11).

There are three great lies—the military, taxes, and the separation of people from the land. All people suffer from them both physically and spiritually.

The first lie is the military. This lie is the largest and most harmful for the physical and spiritual good of the people.

A man lives, labors, and supports his family and suddenly the government, about which he knows nothing, starts a war. Money is collected for unnecessary military affairs, while he is torn away from his own work and sent off to murder—to kill others or to be killed. Worst of all, . . . the people who declare war destroys his home life and forces him to pay taxes for this evil. So as long as there is a military, a man can never be tranquil or assured that all his labors will not vanish for nought or that he will not be sent to murder. Such is the physical evil of soldiering. But the evil to the soul is still greater. Man preaches the Christian law of brotherly love. Then suddenly it is declared that his Christian command is to murder his brethern. Therefore men must choose one of the two: God's or man's law. But people in their weakness will entirely give up God's evangelical law to love their neighbor, and live with no divine law, but only man's, which the authorities have contrived and written. This [sad state constitutes] the great and main evil of the military.

The second lie is duties and direct taxes, based on so much per soul [person], on goods and all kinds of transactions and even on travel from place to place. So it is impossible for the working man to take a step or buy anything without having a part of his earnings taken away by people who use them as they want to. And this lie is also harmful for the physical and spiritual good of the people. The individual from whom the authorities take the taxes, no matter how much he works, can never know what will remain for him, for they can always designate new taxes, and the more he works, the more will be taken away. This lie [also] injures the souls of those who collect and use the taxes. They dispose of them as they please. The larger part goes to satisfy their own greed, ambition, and vanity. That corrupts them, since they do not work for what they have but are in control of someone else's property and they [also] corrupt all of the *pomeshchiks*.[29] They are either bureaucrats who distribute others' money, or they are envious of the bureaucrats and turn bitter or attempt with their unearned wealth to move up [the ladder] socially. Such is the desperation of people created by this lie.

The third lie, no less than the second one, creates much physical and spiritual evil. It is this: some people seize the land, and make out of it an object of all kinds of buying, selling, giving, and mortgaging.

That the pretended right to do this is a lie has become very evident to thousands. What was formerly hidden is now visible. People have multiplied and the rich have seized the best land. If the rich buy all the land and if they would live and feed themselves from the land the inhabitants will have to place themselves in slavery. As the people grow more impoverished, all this becomes especially evident to those who remain on the land and to those who leave the land and live in the cities working in factories or as servants.

This lie is more harmful to the body and spirit of the people than the other two. The physical harm affects the people who live without or with little land or live in poverty in the villages without wholesome food. They fade away or die out, or live wretched and unhealthy lives in cities, where they become feeble and cease to reproduce. The spiritual evil is that people who are deprived of the land become spiteful towards the rich who have seized it. Sensing this lie, they struggle and contrive deceitful excuses [for their existence] and hate those against whom in their turn sin. And people without land who go to the city, serving the rich, become unaccustomed to the [artificial] life and become depraved.

From these three evils—the military, taxes, and seizure of the land—comes all the evil in the world. How can we escape from them?

We now have an insurrection going on in Russia. And those who revolt say that if the autocracy would be eliminated, all woes will be cured. A republic must be built, so that all the people will elect the government themselves, and then the nation itself will learn how it can organize every-thing in general, so say the studies [that the radical reformers have carried out]. Everyone will equally work and equally divide the factories. It is true that reformers disagree among themselves. Some say that it is necessary to leave things as they are. Others say that it is necessary to retain the tsar but only if he is advised in all matters by a Duma, while others say that a tsar is not necessary, [and in his place] a single-elected Duma with a president will rule. A third group says that it is necessary for this Duma not only to rule in all social matters but to organize economic life in general, with facto-ries and lands held in common. These people agree between themselves not on how to arrange things but only on one thing: that it is necessary that a government should rule. Such people, who would rule others, devise and write laws and [and insist that] people must fulfill them.

But what these reformers want would not eliminate all the great sins from which people suffer. They would not be abolished merely because some people audaciously take into their hands the rule over others and establish man-made laws that others will feel obliged to obey *in toto*.

Those who rule would compel the people who obey to do things in the interest of the rulers but harmful for the ruled. From this comes the military, taxes, and land seizures. And this happens everywhere where there are rulers who demand the universal fulfillment of their laws. And it is the same everywhere where there is a single autocratic tsar or sultan, or a re-publican government where there rule not one, but many. There is the same military by levy or hire [across the globe], and everywhere there are unnecessary and harmful wars, and the rulers send to battle those who obey. [Such is what] occurred in Russia in the Japanese War, and England in the Boer War, and the American Republic against Spain in the Philippines. Where ever people are in authority, they always think of their own advan-tages and glory, and not the people's. An [alleged] blessing for the indoctri-nated is that there will be a sharing in the power. They collect the taxes with no concern for the people's needs and support lands for the rich on the notion that what is good for the rich is necessary for the people.

So how do we free ourselves from these three lies?

Escape is possible only by one way: we must submit ourselves to God and not to people.

If people would only believe in this, then all three lies will disappear of their own accord.

And for these lies to vanish, everyone, including the Russians during these present troublesome times, must not undertake or carry out anything [harmful]: neither revolts nor strikes. They will therefore avoid enslaving themselves. You must submit to God and not to people, whether those who still consider themselves part of the government or those who want to over-throw it on the morrow.

To reach our goals, we must declare the nonobedience to any kind of man-made authority, but must live the way we should live—not each one of us separately, but in mutual peace. Everyone must work for everyone else, agreeing on economic affairs by discussion in community gatherings, obeying only those to whom we willingly consent, and not to participate in such state matters as the military, taxes, police, and courts.

If we refuse to go off as soldiers or to pay taxes, then the government will be destroyed by itself, the same government which levies military forces, starts wars, extorts taxes from people's labor and supports land seizures. If the government would be eliminated, then the people in every village and in every village could easily arrange things so that there would be no military, wars, taxes or duties, and land would be accessible to everyone.

To render the military and warfare superfluous, people must establish a good and just life without taxes and restrictive lands. No one will make war upon such a nation but will endeavor to study these people who live freely without sin. If some cruel invaders were to set out to conquer such people, take property, their land, and their many advantages, or worse, make them submit, the conquered would of course endure all kinds of offenses. But it would be better to endure those kinds of evil oppression imposed by fate, rather than fight them. The worst of all is to do what is being done now—to suffer because, you [involuntarily] submit to that authority which torments you. It is necessary to endure, to bear up to evil, and neither fight evil nor submit to it.

So people can free themselves from the first evil, they must stop submitting to the military and arrange a good and just life, which will provide common access to land without taxes. There is a long-standing means, which people have already proposed many times in France, England, and America, and has been introduced in several localities where there is common land— all the money required for community affairs that is now collected through taxes and duties would be taken from the land and go to all the people for their general needs. This method has been proposed for a long time, but it has not been clear how to apply it. Recently an American writer by the name of Henry George has worked out this matter in every possible way. If we would apply it to all our [economic, social, and political] affairs, it could be adapted as easily to a small society as to a larger one.

The End of the Age[30]

Another pamphlet, *The End of the Age*, predicts that the false Christianity that has reigned for so long will be replaced by a genuine Christianity ushering in a period of justice and equality. This phenomenon has manifested itself most poignantly in Russia. The Japanese victory in 1905 is an object lesson in the sham of official, militaristic Christianity. What is needed is liberation from coercion, the total abstinence from violence, and a rational cooperation based on love. The people of Russia have preserved the spirit closest to this pure religion. Along with the war, the deprivation of land has brought Russia to her present crisis. Land slavery is the cruelest form of oppression, for it is the most impersonal form of subjugation—the slave of all, rather than of one. The denial of land forces a man to struggle with other men. Private property is therefore a deceit. So is any government, be it democratic, autocratic, or socialist. All are based on violence. Men must live according to the dictates of higher laws. The true meaning of the revolution engulfing Russia and then eventually mankind will be the elimination of man-made power and the establishment of a simple communal and godly agricultural life bereft of any authority and the madness of technology. Because of the great suffering of her people it is Russia that will be the standard bearer of a real revolution of the spirit.

The distortion of Jesus' teaching through the rejection of the commandment of nonresistance has brought Christian nations to [a state of] mutual enmity [with many] calamities. There is an increasing slavery and people of Christendom are beginning to feel this weight. This is the fundamental reason for the approaching revolution. There are two causes: the insanity of the growing militarism of the Christian world as manifested in the Japanese war[31] and the increasing distress and dissatisfaction of the working people, because they are deprived of their legitimate and natural right to use the land. . . .

[Since] the working people are deprived of their right to the land misery continually increases as does their exasperation with those who exploit their labor. This cause is especially noticeable in Russia because the majority of the working people still live by farming. The increase of the population and the insufficiency of land now force the Russian people either to abandon their accustomed farming life (in which alone they see the possibility of realizing the Christian commonwealth) or else to cease to obey the government. [It is the state] which supports the landowners, who have taken away the land.

It is generally thought that the cruelest slavery is personal slavery: when one man can do anything he likes to another, including torture, mutilation, [or even] killing him. But what we do not even call slavery—denying access to the land—is merely thought to be an unjust economic institution.

But this view is quite false.

What Joseph did with the Egyptians, what all conquerors have done with the vanquished nations, what men are now doing to others by preventing the use of the land is the most dreadful and cruel slavery. The personal slave is the slave of one but the man deprived of this right is the slave of all. Even this is not the principal calamity of the land slave. However cruel the owner of the personal slave might have been, keeping in mind his own advantage and his wish not to lose the slave [logic dictated that] he should not force him to work incessantly, did not torture him, or did not starve him. Whereas the man deprived of the land is always obliged to work beyond his strength, to suffer, to starve, and can never for one minute be completely provided for, [he is not] set free from the arbitrary will of men, and especially from those who are evil and avaricious. Yet even this is not the major calamity of the land slave. His principal affliction is that he cannot live a moral life. [Since he is] not living by labor on the land and not struggling with nature, he is inevitably obliged to do so with men, to endeavor to take by force or cunning from them that which they have acquired from the land and from the labor of another.

Land slavery is not, as is thought even by those who recognize deprivation of land as slavery, one of the remaining forms of enslavement but rather it is the radical and fundamental slavery, from which has been growing personal slavery. Personal slavery is merely one of the particular cases of exploitation by land slavery. The emancipation of men from personal slavery without their liberation from land slavery is not an emancipation, but merely the cessation of one form of exploitation. In many cases, as it was in Russia (when the serfs were freed with but a small portion of land), it is a deceit which can only for a time conceal from the slaves their true position.

During the days of serfdom the Russian people had always understood this, saying "We are yours, but the land is ours," and during [the time of] emancipation they unceasingly and unanimously demanded and expected land liberation. During the emancipation from serfdom the people were cajoled and little land was given them, and for a time [these demands] subsided. An increase of population, however, presented to them in the clearest and most definite form the question of land insufficiency.

During serfdom people used the land as much as was necessary for their existence. The government and the landowners took charge of distributing it to the increasing population, and so the the essential injustice of land seizure by private individuals was not perceived. But as soon as serfdom was abolished the government and the landowners ceased to concern themselves with farming, and I shall not say welfare, but the chance of [a tolerable] existence [for the peasants] was also abolished. The quantity of land which they might possess was once and for all determined without the possiblity of increase, and the people saw more clearly that it was impossible to live in such a manner. They waited for the government to rescind the laws which had deprived them of the land. They waited ten, twenty, thirty, and forty years but more of the land had been seized by private land-owners. People thus had the choice of starving, ceasing to multiply, or alto-gether abandoning rural life and forming generations of navvies, weavers, or locksmiths. Half a century passed, their position became worse, and it reached such a [sorry] state of existence [that the conditions] they regarded as necessary for a Christian life began to fall to pieces. And the government not only did not give them land but gave it to its minions. The state inti-mated to the people that they need never hope for land emancipation; meanwhile using the European models, it established an industrial life (with labor inspection, [for instance, as a sop]) which the people regarded as bad and sinful.

Keeping Russian people away from their legitimate right to the land is the principal cause of their calamitous position. The same cause is the basis of the misery and discontent of the working people in Europe and America. The difference is only this: since the seizure of the land from the European peoples was effected by recognizing the lawfulness of landed property and it took place long ago, so many new relations have covered up this injustice that people do not see the true cause of their position. They search for it everywhere else, such as in the absence of markets, in tariffs, in unfair taxation, in capitalism, in everything except the withholding of the land. To the Russian people the radical injustice (not having yet been to-tally perpetrated) is readily seen.

The Russian people living on the land clearly see what others wish to do with them, and they cannot reconcile themselves to it.

Senseless and ruinous armaments and wars, and the withholding from the people of their common right to the land—these, in my opinion, are the causes of the revolution impending over the whole of Christendom. And this revolution is now beginning only in Russia, because nowhere else has the Christian view of life been preserved in such strength and purity, and nowhere else has an agricultural life been maintained for the majority of the people. . . .

In order to free themselves from all the evils which now oppress them, the working men should, without strife, without coercion, cease to obey the authorities. . . .

But how and in what way can men of the Christian world live if there will not be any states?

The answer to this question lies in those very qualities of the Russian people and to the fact, I think, that the impending revolution must begin and must happen in Russia rather than in other countries.

The absence of governmental power in Russia has never prevented the social organization of agricultural communes. On the contrary, the inter-vention of state power has always hindered the intrinsic organization natural

to the Russians. The Russian people, like the majority of agricultural nations, naturally combine like bees in a hive into definite social relations
which completely satisfy the demands of their common life. Wherever the
Russians settle without government intervention they have always established a noncoercive order, founded upon mutual agreement, with communal possession of the land, thus fulfilling the demands of a peaceful social
life. . . . They live without needing a government, but merely suffering its
existence. The state has never been a necessity—always a burden.

The absence of government (which maintains by force the land which
is in the hands of the nonlaboring owners) can only contribute to that communal agricultural life which the Russian people regard as a necessary condition for a good existence. If that power which maintains private property
in land is abolished and will be freed, everyone will have an equal right to it.

The Russian people, when government is abolished, therefore need
not invent any new forms of mutual life with which to replace the former
one. Such forms have always been natural to them and have satisfied their
social demands.

These forms are a communal and egalitarian organization for all the
members of the mir,[32] which entails a cooperative system in industrial undertakings and common possession of the land. . . .

The cessation of obedience to governments must bring men to a farming life, and in its turn will enduce a communal organization most natural to
the conditions of life in small communities.

It is very probable that these communities will not exist in isolation,
but by reason of economic, racial, or religious connections, will enter into
new and free mutual combinations, completely different from the former
state order founded upon violence. . . .

The liberation of men from obedience to government, and from the
belief in the artificial combinations of states and of a [patriotic] fatherland,
must therefore lead them to the most natural, joyous, and moral life in a
farming community, subject only to their regulations, mutually realizable
by everyone, and not founded on coercion.

An Appeal to the Russians[33]

An Appeal to Russians: to the Government, the Revolutionists, and the People, issued in 1906, was Tolstoy's attempt to speak directly to all the contending
parties in the revolution. The old sage begs the government officials to
confess their sins and wipe out the injustice of private property in land.
Thereupon the peasants will again be supporters of the state and all opposition will vanish. Tolstoy tells the revolutionists that they represent only

themselves, not the people, to whom their ideas are alien. Tolstoy admonishes the people not to support either state officials or the radicals, for both groups in espousing violence are evil. The *Appeal* repeats Tolstoy's call for a communal life in the country with common property in land.

1. To the Government.

[By government I mean those people who avail themselves of established authority and who can change the existing laws and implement new ones. In Russia these people have been the tsar, his ministers, and his nearest advisers.]

The acknowledged basis of all governmental authority is solely to promote the people's welfare over whom power is exerted.

But what are you who now govern Russia, doing? You are fighting the revolutionaries with manoeuvres and cunning such as they employ against you; and, worst of all, with cruelty even greater than theirs.[34] But of the two contending parties the conqueror is not always the more shifty, cunning, cruel, or harsh, but is the one that is closer to the goal toward which humanity is advancing.

Whether the revolutionaries rightly or wrongly define their goal, they certainly desire a new order of life, while your only desire is to maintain yourselves in your established, profitable position. Therefore, you will be unable to resist the revolution, with your banner of Autocracy, even though it contains constitutional amendments, a perverted Christianity called Orthodoxy with a renovated Patriarchate,[34] and all sorts of mystical interpretations. All that is dead and cannot be revived. Your salvation lies not in elected Dumas and still less in rifle shots, cannons, and executions. It lies in the confession of your sin against the people while trying to divest yourself of it to redeem yourself while you have the time. You must set before the people ideals of equity, goodness, and truth, more lofty and more just than those your opponents advocate. Place such an ideal before the people (not to save yourselves) with a serious and honest attempt to do so and not only you will be saved but you will save Russia from those ills which afflict and threaten her.

Nor need you invent this ideal—it is the age-long belief of all the Russians: the restoration to everyone, not just to the peasants, but to the entire people, of their natural and just right to the land.

To men unaccustomed to think on their own this ideal seems unrealizable. It is not just a repetition of what has been effected in Europe and America for it has not been realized anywhere. It is the true and realizable ideal of our day, which, before it is effected in other countries, should be now accomplished in Russia. Wipe out your sins by a good deed; while you still have the power, strive to destroy the ancient, crying, cruel injustice of private property in land, from which the entire agricultural population suffers so acutely and grievously, and you will have the support of all the best people—the so-called "intellectuals." You will have on your side all true constitutionalists, who cannot but see that, before calling on the people to choose representatives, they must be freed from the land-slavery. The socialists, too, will have to admit that they are with you, for their goal, the nationalization of the tools of labor, is attainable only by the nationalization of the major tool, the land. The revolutionists, too, will be on your side, for the revolution which you will be accomplishing by freeing the land from private ownership is one of the major points in their program. On your side, above all, will be the entire one-hundred million farming peasantry, the genuine Russian people. Those in the government should do what you must do, and, while there is yet time, inaugurate a genuine reform for the people; and in place of the feeling of fear and anger which you now encounter, you will experience the joy of close union with these hundred millions. You will also know the love and gratitude of this kindly folk, who will not remember your sins, but will love you for the good you do them, as they now love him and those, who freed them from slavery.[36] Remember that you are not [in essence] tsars, ministers, senators, and governors, but men; and, in place of grief, despair and terror, you will find the joy of forgiveness and of love.

For this good to be realized, you must work not in a superficial manner, for the sake of [personal] safety, but sincerely, seriously, and with the entire strength of your soul. Then you will see what eager, reasonable, and harmonious activity will come about in the best circles of society, bringing to the front the best men of all classes, and rendering ineffective the entire power of those who now disturb Russia. Do this, and all those terrible, brutal elements of revenge, anger, avarice, vanity, ambition, and above all, ignorance which now infect, agitate, and torment Russia (and of which you are guilty) will disappear.

Yes, only two courses are now open to you, men of the government: a fratricidal slaughter, and all the horrors of a revolution resulting in your inevitable and disgraceful destruction, or the peaceful fulfillment of the ancient and just demands of the entire people. You will not only show other Christian nations that the injustice from which men have suffered so cruelly for so long can be abolished but demonstrate the means to do so.

Whether the form of government by which you hold power has or has not outlived its day, so long as you still hold power, you should use it not to multiply the evil you have already done and the hatred you have already provoked. Rather, you should use it to accomplish a great and good deed not for your nation alone but for all mankind. If this government has outlived its day, let the last act it effects be one not of falsehood and cruelty but of goodness and truth.

2. To the Revolutionaries.

[By revolutionaries I mean those people (beginning with the most peaceful constitutionalists and extending to the most militant radicals) who wish to replace the present state authority.]

You, revolutionaries of all types and denominations, consider the present government harmful, and in various ways organize assemblies (allowed or prohibited bv the government), formulate projects, print articles, make speeches, establish unions, strikes and demonstrations. And finally (as a natural and inevitable basis and consequence of these activities) by murders, executions, and armed insurrections you strive to replace the existing authority.

Though all of you are at variance among yourselves regarding the nature of this new authority, yet the means your groups use do not stop short of crimes including murders, bomb explosions, executions, or civil war.

You have no words strong enough to express your condemnation and contempt for those official personages who struggle against you. It should not be forgotten that all the cruel acts that the members of the government have committed in their struggle with you are justified in their eyes. From the tsar to the lowest policeman, they have been educated in undying respect for the established order hallowed by age and tradition, and feel fully convinced when defending it that they are doing what millions of people demand of them. So that the moral responsibility for their cruel actions does not rest on them alone but is shared by many people. You, on the other hand, the people in all sorts of professions outside the government, such as: physicians, teachers, engineers, students, professors, journalists, women students, railwaymen, laborers, lawyers, merchants, and landowners, have not been recognized or appealed to anyone but yourselves. You have suddenly become acutely aware of the precise social order needed by Russia, and in the name of this future society (which each of you defines in his own way) take upon yourselves the whole responsibility for these very terrible acts you have committed; and you throw bombs, destroy, murder, and execute.

Thousands have been killed—all Russians have been reduced to despair, have become embittered and brutalized. And what is this all for? It is done because a small group of people, hardly one ten-thousandth of the nation, have decided what is needed for the very best organization of the Russian Empire. [Some want] to continue the Duma, similar to the one that just met,[37] while others say that what is needed is a Duma elected by universal, secret, and equal ballot. A third party says that what is needed is a republic, and yet a fourth party declares that an ordinary republic is not needed, but a socialist one. And for the sake of all this you provoke a civil war!

You say that you do it for the people's good and that your main goal is their welfare. But the one-hundred million people for whom you do it do not ask it of you and do not want all these things which you, by such evil means, try to effect. The masses do not need you at all but have always regarded and cannot but regard you as useless and burdensome grubs who, in one way or another, consume the fruits of their labor. You must clearly realize and understand the life of these millions of Russian peasants, who alone constitute the Russian nation. All you professors, factory hands, physicians, engineers, journalists, students, landowners, women students, veterinarians, merchants, lawyers and railwaymen, the very people so concerned about their welfare, are all harmful parasites on that body, sucking its sap and rotting on it, by injecting it with your corruption.

You must keenly imagine these millions who patiently labor and support your unnatural lives on their shoulders living under your reforms, and you will see that these are foreign to them. They have other tasks and see more profoundly the goal before them. They express the awareness of their destiny, not in newspaper articles, but through their entire existence.

But no, you cannot understand this. You are firmly convinced that this coarse people has no roots of its own and that it will be a great blessing if you would enlighten them with the latest article you have read. By doing this you will make them as pitiful, helpless, and perverted as yourselves.

You say you want a just organization but in fact you can live only under an irregular and unjust one. Should a really equitable one be established with no place for those who live on the labor of others, all you landlords, merchants, physicians, professors, and lawyers, as well as factory hands, manufacturers, workshop owners, engineers, teachers, government officials, and producers of cannon, tobacco, spirits, looking glasses, and velvet would starve to death.

What *you* need is not a really just order of life: for nothing would be more dangerous for you than a society in which everyone had to do useful work.

You must cease to deceive yourselves: consider well the place you hold among the Russian people and what you are doing, and it will be clear to you that your struggle with the government is a battle between two harmful parasites on a healthy body. Speak, therefore, of your own interests but do not speak for the people. Do not lie about them but leave them in peace. Fight the government, if you cannot refrain, but know that you are fighting for yourselves, not for the people, and that your struggle is not only ignoble or bad, but is very stupid, harmful and above all, very immoral.

Your activity, you say, attempts to foster better general conditions for the people. But if their lives are to be improved it is necessary for people themselves to be better. This [fact] is as true as that to warm a vessel of water all the drops in it must be heated. People should concentrate more on their inner life. But outside events, especially strife, always diverts men's minds from the inner consciousness. Through the perverting of people, the level of general morality is always and eveywhere inevitably lowered as we now see most strikingly in Russia. The most unethical part of society thus rises to the top more frequently. An immoral public opinion is thus formed which not only permits but even condones crime, robbery, debauchery, and even murder. Thus a vicious circle is set up: the evil elements of society, provoked by the social struggle and who are seriously engaged into public activity, correspond to the low level of their morality and attract even more horrible elements. Morality is lowered more and the most unethical of men— the Dantons, Marats, Napoleons, Talleyrands, Bismarcks—become the heroes of the day.[38] So that participation in public activity and strife is not only not an exalted, useful, and good thing (as it is customarily supposed and said to be by those who are engaged in this struggle) but on the contrary, is a most unquestionably stupid, harmful, and immoral affair.

Reflect on this, especially you, young people, who are not yet immersed in the sticky mud of political activity. Shake off from yourselves the terrible hypnotism you are under and free yourselves from the lie of this pseudo-service to the people, in the name of which you consider that everything is permitted. Above all, think of the highest qualities of your soul, demanding neither equal and secret voting, nor armed insurrections, nor legislative assemblies, nor any similar stupidities and cruelties, but that you should live only decent and true lives.

What is necessary for your good and sincere life, first of all, is not to deceive yourselves by yielding to the petty passions of vanity, ambition, envy and bravado, or the desire to find an outlet for your spare energy, or to improve your own position, or [the conviction] that you can serve the people. No; what is necessary is to examine yourselves and to endeavor to correct your own failings and become better men. If you wish to think of public life, think first of your sins against the people. Try to use as little of their labor as possible, and if you cannot help the peasantry, try at least not to mislead and confuse them, committing terrible crimes by deceiving and provoking them to robberies and insurrections, which always end in suffering and even greater enslavement.

The complex and difficult circumstances amid which we live in Russia demand of you, especially at the present time, not newspaper articles, or speeches in assemblies, or shootings in the streets, or the (often dishonest) incitement of the peasants while you yourselves evade responsibility. [What is necessary is] a frank and strict relation to yourselves and your lives, which alone are in your power—their improvement is the sole means by which you can better the people.

3. To the People.

[By the people I mean the whole Russian people but especially the toiling farming peasants, who by their labor support the lives of everyone else.]

You, the Russian laborers, mostly [comprised of] the farming peasants, now find yourselves in an especially difficult position. However hard it was for you to live with a scarcity of land, with heavy taxes and duties, and wars (created by the government), you have done so until recently, believing that it was impossible [to exist] without a tsar to rule, so you humbly submitted to the government.

However badly the tsarist government ruled, you have humbly submitted to it since it was the only one. But now, it has come about that a part of the people has rebelled and ceased to obey the tsarist government. In many places instead of one government there are two, each of them demanding obedience.[39] You can no longer humbly submit to the powers that be, without considering whether either government rules you well or ill; you have to choose between them. What are you to do? Not those tens of thousands of workmen who bustle about in the towns, but you, the great and genuine one-hundred million peasants?

The old government of the tsar says to you: "Do not listen to the rebels; they promise much and will deceive you. Remain true to me and I will satisfy all your wants."

The rebels say: "Do not believe the tsar's government, which has always tormented you and will continue to do so. Join and help us and we will arrange a government for you like that of the freest countries. Then you will choose your own rulers, you will be able to govern yourselves, and right all your wrongs."

What are you to do?

Support the old government? But, as you know, the old government has promised to lighten your burdens for a long time, but instead of doing so, has only increased your greatest evils: landlessness, taxes, and conscription.

Join the rebels? They promise to arrange an elected government such as exists in the freest countries for you. But wherever they exist, in the countries that have most freedom, in the French and American republics for instance, the major ills of the people have not been remedied. As among us, and to an even greater degree, the land is in the hands of the rich. The people are laden with taxes and duties, the armies are maintained and wars declared when those in power desire it, without the consultation of the people. Our new government, moreover, is not yet established, and we do not know what it will be like.

Not only is it not to your advantage to support either government but you cannot do it conscientiously before God. To defend the old government means to do what was done recently in Odessa, Sevastopol, Kiev, Riga, the Caucasus, and Moscow—to capture, kill, hang, burn alive, execute, and shoot children and women in the streets. But to join the revolutionaries is to do the same thing: to kill people, throw bombs, burn, rob, fight the soldiers with executions and hangings.

Therefore, laboring Christian people: the tsar's government now calls on you to fight against your brothers, and the revolutionaries call on you to do the same—[but] not for your own benefit alone but before God and your consciences, you must refrain from *joining either the old or the new government, and take no part in the unChristian doings of either one.*

And not to take part in the doings of the old government means not to serve as soldiers, guards, constables, and town or country police. [It also means] not to serve in any government institutions and offices, county councils [zemstvos], assemblies, or Dumas. Not to take part in the doings of the revolutionaries means not to participate in meetings, unions, and strikes, not to burn or wreck people's houses, and not to join any armed rebellion.

Two governments hostile to each other now rule you, and they both summon you to take part in cruel, unChristian deeds. What can you do but reject all governments?

People say that it is difficult and even impossible to live without a government. But you Russian workmen (especially the peasants) know that when you live a peaceful work-filled country life in the villages, cultivating the land on terms of equality, and deciding your public affairs in the commune (mir), you have absolutely no need for one.

The government needs you but you Russian peasants do not need a government. And, therefore, during the present difficult circumstances, when it is equally bad to join either government, it is reasonable and beneficial for you, the Russian peasants, not to obey either one.

But if this is valid for the agricultural laborers, what should the more numerous factory workers do, [especially in] in the many lands which are regulated by governments?

They should do the same as the village workers: *They must not obey any government* and should devote all their energies to return to an agricultural life.

Only let the city workmen as well as the villagers cease to obey or serve the government, and, with the abolition of its power, the slavish conditions in which you live will vanish, since they are maintained only by organized violence. And the violence the government employs is supplied by yourselves. It is that power alone which places duties on imported or exported goods and collects taxes on articles made in the country. It alone makes the laws which maintain the monopolies and the right of private property in land. Only that power which controls the army, which you yourselves supply, holds you in continual subjection to the rich.

When you, the city workers as well as villagers, cease to obey the government, it will no longer be necessary for the former to accept whatever conditions the owners of the factories dictate. You yourselves will then give them your conditions, or the both of you can start your own cooperative (*artel*)[40] manufacture necessities, and having freed the land you will resume a natural farming life.

"But if we Russian folk will begin at once to live like that, not obeying the government, there will be no Russia," say those who think that the existence of the Russian Empire is necessary for the union of many different nations and is important, great, and useful.

In reality, this combination of many different nations, called Russia, not only is not important for you, Russian working men, but is a major source of your miseries.

They oppress you with taxes and duties, as they did your forefathers who accumulated vast debts which you have to pay.[41] They conscript you as soldiers and send you to different ends of the earth to fight people with whom you have nothing to do (and who have nothing to do with you). All this is done only to maintain an empire, a forcible combination of Poland, the Caucasus, Finland, Central Asia, Manchuria, and other lands and peoples. Aside from all your ills [more] come from this union called Russia, and when you obey the government you become involved in this great sin. So that Russia should exist as it does now, the Poles, Finns, Letts, Georgians, Tartars, Armenians, and others have to be held in subjection. And to do this it is necessary to forbid them to live as they wish, and if they disobey this order, they have to be punished and killed. Why should you take part in these evil deeds when you yourselves suffer from them? Let those who have need of such a Russia, dominating Poland, Georgia, Finland, and other lands—let them arrange it if they can. But for you, working people, this is not necessary at all. What you need is something quite different. You need only enough land, which cannot be taken by force, [you need not] be obliged to send your sons off to the military, and above all not to be compelled to do evil deeds. And these evils will cease, if you would only refuse to obey the orders of the government—demands which ruin and destroy both your bodies and your souls.

"But without a government, where people live in separate communities, how are all major public undertakings to be arranged? How will the means of communication, railways, telegraphs, steamers, the post, the higher educational establishments, the libraries, and trade be managed?"

People are so accustomed to see the state control all public affairs, that it seems to them that the work itself is done by it, and that without it, it is impossible to organize high schools, ways of communication, post offices, libraries, or commercial relations. But this is not true. The largest public affairs, not only national but international, are arranged by private individuals without governmental assistance. In this way all kinds of international, postal, academic, commercial, and industrial alliances are operated. Not only do governments not aid these voluntarily organized associations but when they take part in them they always hinder them.

"But if you do not obey the government, and do not pay taxes or supply soldiers, foreign nations will come and conquer you," add those who wish to rule over you. Do not believe it. You must live only by acknowledging that the land should be common property, by not being soldiers, not paying taxes (except what you voluntarily give for public works), and peacefully settling your disagreements through your village communes. Other nations, seeing your good life, will not come and conquer you. Or, if they do come, upon learning about your good life they will adopt it and, instead of fighting you, will unite with you. For all the nations, including yourselves, have been suffering from governments, strife in war, trade, industry, class, and differing parties. Among all Christian nations an inward transformation is occuring, the major goal being the emancipation from governments. This [movement] is particularly difficult for nations in which the majority have abandoned the agricultural life and live in towns employing the labor of others in industry. Among such nations liberation is being prepared by socialism. But for you Russian laborers, living mainly a farming life, and supplying your own needs, this liberation would be particularly easy. Government for you has long ceased to be a necessity or even a convenience and is a great and thankless burden and misfortune.

The government, only the government, by its power deprives you of land. Only it collects from you the taxes and duties from most of your labor. It alone deprives you of the labor of your sons, conscripting them into the military to be killed.

But a government is not an essential condition of human life, which will exist as long as mankind lasts, like the cultivation of the soil, marriage, the family, or human intercourse. A state is a human institution and, like all of them, is set up when it is needed and abolished when it becomes unnecessary.

In former times, human sacrifices, the worship of idols, divinations, tortures, slavery, and many other things were instituted. But they were all abolished when people became enlightened: they became superfluous burdens and evils. So also will it be with governments. They were instituted when nations were savage, cruel, and coarse. Nearly all the governments took their laws from the heathen Romans. Down to the present day they have remained as coarse as they were in the days before Christianity, with their requisitions, soldiers, prisons, and executions. But the people, becoming enlightened, have less need of them, and now most of the Christian peoples have arrived at the stage where [they think that] government only hinders [any progress].

The shell is necessary for the egg until the bird is hatched. But when the bird is ready, the shell is but a hindrance. So it is with governments. Most of Christendom feels this. But it is more acutely felt by the Russian farming populace.

"Government is necessary, we cannot live without a government," men say, and they are especially convinced of this now, when there are mass disturbances. But who are these men who are so concerned for its preservation? They are the very men who live on the labor of the people, and, conscious of their sin, fear its exposure, and hope that the government (being bound to them by unity of interest) will protect their wrongdoing by force. For these men, the state is very necessary, but not for you, the peasantry. For you the government has always been nothing but a burden. And now that it has by its evil rule provoked riots, and since there are two rival governments, it has become a blatant misfortune and a great sin, which you must repudiate for your bodily needs and spiritual welfare.

Whether you, laboring Russian people, free yourselves at once from obedience to any state, or whether you will yet have to suffer and endure at the hands of members of the old or of the new one (or possibly at the hands of foreign ones) you have now no other course but to cease to obey and live without them.

You, country laborers as well as the town workers, may at first have to suffer at the hands of the old as well as of the new governments for your disobedience, and also from disagreements among yourselves. But all the problems that may come from them are as nothing compared to the ills and sufferings you now endure and will yet have to endure from the government, if (obeying one or other government) you are drawn into the present murders, executions, and civil strife. They will continue for a long time by the contending states, unless you refuse to abet them.

You must not yield to what is demanded of you by this or that government: to support the old government and enter the struggle against the revolutionaries, serving in the army, or police, or joining the "Black-gang" mobs;[42] or support the revolutionaries, take part in strikes, the destruction of property, armed risings, or any unions, elections, or Dumas. Besides burdening your souls with many sins, with much suffering, before long another government (even though you may have promoted its triumph) will refasten the deadly noose of slavery in which you have lived.

Do not submit or obey, either to the one or to the other, and you will rid yourselves of your miseries and will be free.

From the difficult times now taking place, you, the Russian working people, have but one way of escape—by refusing to obey any force-wielding authority and to humbly and meekly endure violence and refuse to participate in it.

This way is simple and easy and will undoubtedly lead to a better life. But to act in such a manner you must submit to the rule of God and to His law. "He that endureth to the end will be saved": your salvation is in your own hands.

Preface to the Russian Edition
of Henry George's *Social Problems*[43]

In Tolstoy's "Preface to the Russian Edition of Henry George's *Social Problems*," translated by his friend S. D. Nikolaev, he regrets the neglect of George's political economy. The time has arrived for the adoption of the single tax, he says, for Russia's present turmoil primarily stems from outmoded property relationships and the denial to the people of use of the land. George's ideas are exactly in accord with the mind and spirit of the Russian peasants.

In one of the last chapters of this book, Henry George writes:

> To those who have never studied the subject, it will seem ridiculous to propose as the greatest and most far-reaching of all reforms a mere fiscal change. But whoever has followed the train of thought through which in the preceding chapters I have endeavored to lead, will see that in this simple proposition is involved the greatest of social revolutions—a revolution compared with which that which destroyed the ancient monarchy in France, or that which destroyed chattel slavery in our Southern States, were as nothing.[44]

Such is the great significance of the revolution proposed by Henry George, which up to this time people have neither understood nor recognized. The main reason is that his thought has been either distorted or ignored. Most people view Henry George's ideology as one of the systems for change in private property, which is often understood as a nationalization of the land in the socialistic sense. People who imagine themselves to be scholars tendentiously object to his thought. They easily dismiss it on alleged facts, or [on the supposition] that George never said it; or as evidence against him, they assert as irrefutable in their own opinion the essential conditions which have been refuted by Georgist fundamentals. Ignorant people, society people, landowners, and well-off people in general, who are completely unaware of Henry George or have an adverse reaction to him only have a foggy notion that he somehow wants to take land away from the present owners, and being conservative in nature and out of anxiety for their self-preservation, easily reject his ideas. [They will say:] "I know! I know! To tax the land on those landowners, already burdened with taxes, would be paying an additional land tax." Or. "I know! I know! So that the landowner is forced to pay more taxes, he must sell the best part of his land."

And for over thirty years it has been evident that a thorough and fundamental exposition of this great ideal has remained completely unknown to the great majority of people.

It could not be otherwise. George's economic thought, which will revolutionize the whole order of people's lives for the benefit of the oppressed voiceless majority to the detriment of the ruling minority, is so convincingly irrefutable and on the whole so simple that it is impossible not to understand it. This [practical solution] cannot but help make people put it into effect and therefore the only ways of combatting it are by distortion or by hushing it up. Both of these means have for over thirty years been successfully used against George's theories, so that it is difficult to induce people to read his works. It is true that in England, Canada, the United States, Australia, and Germany, a very few fine people subscribe to single tax periodicals. Among most thinking people, however, his thought continues to remain unknown, and the indifference to it has perhaps increased. Society deals with those ideas which threaten its peace as bees do with harmful worms that they are powerless to destroy. Bees coat their hive with a paste, so that the worms, although not destroyed, are prevented from further incursion to do damage. So the people of European societies deal with ideas harmful to its order, or rather habitual disorder, in this case with the ideas of George and his followers. "And its light shineth in darkness; and the darkness comprehended it not." A genuinely fruitful idea cannot be annihilated. So neither will it be smothered, for it will survive through all traversity, it will outlive all those muddled, simple, and pedantic ideas and words which attempt to choke it, and sooner or later, the truth will burn through the veils which have hidden it, and will shine forth throughout the whole world—such [will be the case with] George's philosophy.

And it seems to me that now is the right time in Russia. Right now a revolution is taking place. The cause of it is from denying to all the people, the real people, their own land. Now is the time, for the vast majority of the Russian people who have always [instinctively] lived according to the basic ideas of George—that the land is the common property of everyone and that taxes can be levied only on it—not on people's labor.

Henry George states that the transferral of all taxes to land rent cannot but make the most important social arrangements conform to natural laws. He also says that the land rent value should be used for the benefit of the entire society. It is just as natural for the whole community to adopt this means as it is natural for people to walk on their feet instead of their hands.

And the Russian peasants have not only shared this idea but have always tried to implement it when administrative powers have not hindered.

The statistician Orlov in the 1870s wrote the following about the peasants' relationship to the land:

> The peasant world does not understand and does not differentiate those diverse types of taxation, which are so familiar to tax officials. All the different taxes, duties, *volost*[45] and village tax levies which are taken from their community are done so through the mir's apportionment in one general assessed sum among the members of the obshchina by the number of the aforementioned paying souls [peasants]. A paying soul, in the peasant understanding of the term, fades into his part of the mir's land allotment. A paying soul is therefore unthinkable without the land. The soul, moreover, is in fact a particular plot of the mir's land and corresponds to a part of the mir's payment. If one householder responds to the question about the number of souls that two souls can be counted, another one will say that he has three souls: that merely means that the first householder possesses two plots of land, and the second one has three parcels of mir land. The mir's lands are definitely connected to everything in the community according to the payments of the taxpayers, whatever name designates them and whatever institution they are intended for.

In this short excerpt, the essential relationship of the Russian people to the land and to their taxes is described—exactly in the same fashion that Henry George teaches. These relations are not in reality an arrangement that is simply some division of the land, as is usually thought to be contained in George's writings, but guarantees for every man the full inviolability of the fruit of his labor, and the full opportunity for all people to use the land with all its advantages. Such is the world view of the Russian people on labor and on their rights to the land. And it is therefore understandable why the majority of Europeans whose entire established order and advantages the realization of Georgist practices would destroy should refer hostilely to his political economy and try to hush it up. We have, however, in

Russia a population more than ninety percent of which are engaged in farming. This theory would then be the only conscious expression of her people; the entire population will always recognize it. The present structure of society requires us to be especially receptive, be keenly open to its applicability, and complete the great movement for justice so falsely and criminally directed by the revolution.

Of all the wonderful books, speeches, and articles by Henry George, this book is without a doubt the best, for its brevity, clarity, strictly logical exposition, irrefutability of scientific argument, beauty of language, and sincere and profound love for truth, goodness, and people, which permeates it.

From *The Meaning of the Russian Revolution*[46]

The *Meaning of the Russian Revolution* was Tolstoy's largest work to describe the essence and plight of his country in time of internal disorder. Although autocracy was a rotten edifice he also feared that Russia would import alien ideas. Democratic governments, he says, are an illusion, offering a façade of freedom while they foster immorality, corruption and injustice, perpetuate private property and land slavery, and wage war. Since Western governments are based in industrialism they have to seek other markets, which has led to colonialism and enslavement of other peoples. Again, Tolstoy calls on the people to return to the land and lead a simple life conducting themselves humbly by nonresistance to evil. In a rare departure, Tolstoy says that we must retain whatever genuine goods modern technology has to offer; reject the luxuries of the rich and the weapons of the powerful. We must not submit to the laws of man or forms of power, or pay taxes, or abet the military, or take advantage of another's work. Deliverance from injustice and human laws entails the acceptance of a divine law. Since the Russian people are more Eastern in outlook, have retained a purer spirituality and have an innate reverance for the brotherhood of all men, they must and will make the wise choice.

A revolution is taking place in Russia. All the world is following it with eager attention, trying to foresee what its outcome will be for the Russian people.

Prediction may be interesting and important for outside spectators watching the Russian Revolution, but for us Russians, who are living and shaping it, the chief interest lies not in guessing what is going to happen, but in defining as clearly and firmly as possible what we must do in these immensely important, terrible, and dangerous times.

Every revolution is a change of a people's relation towards power.
Such a change is now taking place in Russia, and we, the entire Russian people, are accomplishing it.

To know how we can and should change our relation towards power, we must therefore understand its nature: what it consists of, how it arose, and how best to deal with it.

1. . . . The cause of any economic condition always has been (and could not be otherwise) through the oppression of some men by others. Economic conditions are a *result* of violence, and cannot therefore be the *cause* of human relations. Evil men (the Cains) who have loved idleness and were covetous of others have always attacked the good men (the Abels, the tillers of the soil), and by killing or threatening to kill them profited by their toil. Instead of fighting their oppressors, the good, gentle, and industrious people considered it best to submit. They did so, in part, because they did not wish to fight, or because they could not do so without interrupting their work of feeding themselves and their neighbors. Through this oppression of the good by the evil and not by any economic conditions, all existing human societies have been based and built.

2. From the most ancient times and among every nation, the relations of the rulers to the ruled have been based on violence. But this relation, like everything else in the world has been continually changing. It changes because the more secure their power becomes and the longer it lasts, the more do those in power (the leisured classes) grow depraved, unreasonable, and cruel, and the more injurious to their subjects do their demands become. [This relation also changes] because as they grow more depraved their subjects see more clearly the harm and folly of submitting to such distorted power.

3. . . . The Russian people are now confronted by the dreadful choice of continuing like the Eastern nations, to submit to their unreasonable and depraved governments in spite of all the misery they have inflicted; or, as all Western nations have done, realizing the evil of the existing governments, try to overturn them by force and establish new ones.

4. The majority of the Russian nonlaboring classes are quite convinced that the Russian people can do nothing better than follow the path the Western nations have been treading during this crisis: to fight the power, limit it, and place it more in the hands of the entire nation.

Is this opinion right, and is such action good?

Have the Western nations, traveling for centuries along that path, attained what they have striven for? Have they freed themselves from these evils?

The Western peoples, like all others, began by submitting to the power which demanded their obedience rather than fighting. But that power, in the persons of the Charleses (the Great and the Fifth) the Philips, Louis, and Henry the Eighth,[47] have become more depraved and have reached such a state that they could no longer endure it. At different times, the European nations revolted and fought against their rulers. This struggle took place in different forms at different periods but always found expression in the same ways: in civil wars, robberies, murders, and executions. Though it ended with the fall of the old power, a new one just as oppresive was put in its place. It too was upset, and was replaced by yet another one, which by the same unalterable nature of power became in due course as harmful as its predecessors. Thus, for instance, in France there were eleven changes of power within eighty years: the Bourbons, the Convention, the Directory, Bonaparte, the Empire, again the Bourbons, a Republic, Louis Philippe, again a Republic, again a Bonaparte, and again a Republic.[48] The substitution of new powers for old ones took place among other nations as well, though not so rapidly as in France. These changes did not improve the condition of the people in most cases. They could only conclude that the misery they suffered depended not on the people at the helm but on the power that the few exercised over the many. And therefore the people tried to render the power harmless by limiting it. And such limitations were introduced in several countries by elected chambers of representatives.

But the men who limited the arbitrariness of the rulers and formed the assemblies, having become themselves possessors of power, naturally succumbed to the depraving influence which accompanies it, the very same thing that autocrats had done. These men, becoming sharers in power even though not individually perpetrating jointly or separately the same kind of evil, became as great a burden on the people as the despots. Then, to limit the arbitrariness of power still more, monarchical power was abolished altogether in some countries, and a government was established chosen by the entire nation. In this way republics were instituted in France, America, and Switzerland and the referendum and the initiative were introduced, giving every member of the community the possibility of interfering and participating in legislation.

But the only effect of all these measures was that the citizens of these states, who were collaborating more in power, and being more diverted from serious occupations, grew more depraved. The calamities from which the people suffered remain, however, exactly the same under constitutional, monarchical, or republican governments, with or without referenda.

Nor could it be otherwise, for the idea of limiting power by the participation of all who are subject to it is not only unsound at the very core but self-contradictory.

For one man with the aid of his helpers to rule over all is unjust, and in all likelihood will be harmful to the people.

The same will be the case if the the minority rules over the majority. But the power of the majority over the minority would also fail to secure a just rule; for we have no reason to believe that the majority in a government is wiser than a nonparticipatory minority.

To extend the participation in government to all, as might be done by a still greater extension of the referendum and the initiative, would only mean that everyone would be fighting everyone else.

That a man should have a power over his fellows founded on violence is evil at its source—no arrangement that promotes man to do violence to man can make evil cease to be evil.

So among all nations, however they are ruled, whether by the most despotic or the most democratic governments, the major and fundamental calamities from which the people suffer remain the same: the same ever-increasing enormous budgets, the same animosity towards their neighbors, necessitating military preparations and armies; the same taxes; the same state and private monopolies; the same depriving the people of the right to use the land (which is given to private owners); the same enslaving of subject races; the same constant threatenings of war; and the same wars, which destroy the lives of men and undermine their morality.

5. It is true that the representative governments of Western Europe and America (constitutional monarchies as well as republics) have uprooted some of the external abuses practiced by the wielders of power. They have made it impossible for them to be such monsters as were the different Louis's, Charleses, Henrys, and Johns.[49] (In a representative government, [however], not only is it possible that power will be seized by cunning, immoral, and artful mediocrities, of whom many prime ministers and presidents [will serve as examples], but their structure is such that only that kind of person can obtain power.) It is true that representative governments have abolished such abuses as the *lettres de cachet*,[50] removed restrictions on the press, stopped religious persecutions, submitted the taxation of the people to discussion by their reprsentatives, made the actions of the government public and subject to criticism. They have facilitated the rapid development of all sorts of technical improvements providing greater comforts for rich citizens, and increased their military power. The nations which have representative government have doubtless become more powerful industrially, commercially and militarily than despotically-governed nations, and the lives of their leisured classes have certainly become more secure, comfortable, agreeable,

and aesthetic than they used to be. But is the life of the majority of the people in those countries more secure, freer, or most importantly, more reasonable and moral?

I think not.

Under the despotic power of one man, the number of people who come under the corrupting influence of power and live on the labor of others is limited, and consists of the despot's close friends, assistants, servants, flatterers, and helpers. The infection of depravity is focused in his court, from where it radiates in all directions.

Where power is limited, where many people take part in it, the number of centers of infection is augmented, for everyone who shares power has his friends, helpers, servants, flatterers, and relations.

Where there is universal suffrage, these centers of infection are even more diffused. Every voter becomes the object of flattery and bribery. The character of power itself is also changed. In place of power founded on direct violence, we get a monetary power, also founded on violence but indirectly through a complicated diffusion.

Under representative governments, instead of one or a few centers of depravity, there are a large number of them. There springs up a large class of people living idly on others' labor, the class called the "bourgeoisie;" they are protected by violence and set up for themselves comfortable lives, free from hard work.

Arranging an easy, pleasant, idle life not for a monarch and his court but for thousands of little kinglets, requires many embellishments and amusements. Whenever power passes from a despotic to a representative government, inventions appear, facilitating the supply of objects that add to the pleasure and safety of the wealthy classes.

To produce all these objects, an ever-increasing number of working men are drawn away from farming and their energy is devoted to the production of pleasing trifles for the rich, or even to some extent by the workers. So there develops a class of urban workers who are completely dependent on the wealthy. The longer the power of representative government endures, the larger grow the number of these people, and their condition worsens. In the United States, out of a population of seventy million, one-seventh are laborers, and the relations between them and the well-to-do are the same [wherever there is industry, be it] in England, Belgium, or France. In these countries there is an ever-increasing number of men exchanging for the labor of producing the objects of luxury, for that of primary necessity. It clearly follows that such a trend of affairs must result in the greater overburdening of that diminishing number of people who have to support the luxurious lives of the ever-growing number of the idle. Assuredly, such a way of life cannot continue.

What is transpiring is similar to the condition of a man whose body increases in weight while the legs grow thinner and weaker. When the support has disappeared, the body will have to collapse.

6. The Western nations, like all others, had to submit to the power of conquerors only to avoid the worry and sin of warfare. But when that power bore too heavily upon them, they began to fight it, even though they still continued to submit, which was regarded as a necessity. At first only a small part of the nation shared in the fight; then, when the struggle of that small part proved ineffectual, an ever greater number entered into the conflict. It ended with the majority of the people (not freeing themselves from the worry and sin of fighting), sharing in the wielding of power: the very thing they had wished to avoid when they first acquiesced to it. The inevitable result was the increase of the depraving infuence that comes from power, affecting not only a small number of people, as had been the case under a single ruler, but every member of the community. (Steps are now also being taken to subject women to it.)[51]

Representative government and universal suffrage cause every possessor of a fraction of power to be exposed to all its evils: bribery, flattery, vanity, self-conceit, idleness, and, above all, immoral participation in deeds of violence. Every member of [any] parliament is exposed to all these temptations to a greater degree. Every deputy always begins his career of power by befooling people and making promises he knows he will not keep; and when sitting in the House he takes part in making laws that are enforced by violence. It is the same with all senators and presidents. Similar corruption prevails in the election of a president. In the United States this election costs millions to those financiers who know that the [newly-] elected man will support certain advantageous monopolies or import duties, which will enable them to recoup its costs a hundredfold.

And this corruption is accompanied by [all kinds of] phenomena, such as: the avoidance of hard work and the enjoyment of pleasures at the expense of others; interests and cares, which have become inaccessible to a man engaged in work, which relates to the general business of the state; the spread of a lying and inflammatory press; and, above all, [the creation of] animosity among nations, classes, and men. [All these problems] have grown precipitously. The struggle of all mankind against their fellows has become so habitual a state of things that science, engaged in supporting all this nastiness, has decided that the struggle and enmity of all against all is a necessary, unavoidable and beneficent condition of human life.[52]

That peace which [once] seemed the greatest of blessings the ancients saluted each other with the words "Peace be unto you!" has now virtually disappeared from Western peoples.[53] By the aid of men of science, people have tried to assure themselves that not peace, but the conflict of all against all, ensures man's highest destiny.

And among the Western nations, an unceasing industrial, commerical, and military strife is continually waged; a war of state against state, class against class, labor against capital, party against party, and man against man.

Nor is this everything. The main result of this collaboration of men in power is that they have been further drawn away from actual work on the land. They are therefore more involved in different ways of exploiting the labor of others because they are deprived of their independence and forced to lead immoral lives. Having neither the desire nor the habit of living by farming their own lands, the Western nations were forced to obtain their means of subsistence from other countries. They could do this only in two ways: by fraud, that is, by exchanging things for the most part unnecessary or corrupting others with alcohol, opium, weapons, for the foodstuffs indispensable to them; or by violence, that is, robbing the people of Asia and Africa wherever they saw an opportunity of doing so with impunity.

Such is the state of affairs with Germany, Austria, Italy, France, the United States, and especially Great Britain, which is held up as an example for the imitation and envy of other nations. Almost all the people of these countries, having become conscious participators in deeds of violence, devote their strength to government activities, industry, and commerce, which are aimed at primarily satisfying the demands of the rich for luxuries. They also subjugate (partly by direct force and partly by money) the farmers both of their own and of foreign countries, who have to provide them with necessities.

Such people form a majority in some nations. In others they are still only a minority, but the percentage of men living on the labor of others is growing uncontrollably and very rapidly to the detriment of those who are still engaged in sensible agricultural work. A majority of the people of Western Europe are already (the United States is not yet, but is being irresistibly drawn towards it) incapable of subsisting by work on their own land. They are obliged in one way or another, by force or fraud, to take the necessaries of life from other peoples who still labor.

The primary result is that trade, aiming chiefly at satisfying the demands of the rich (including the government), directs most of its energies not to improving [natural, individual] farming but [to the increasing use of] machines that till large tracts of land (of which the people have been deprived). [In addition there are other superfluites, such as:] the manufacture of women's finery, the building of luxurious palaces, the production of sweetmeats, toys, motor cars, tobacco, wines, delicacies, medicines, enormous quantities of printed matter, guns, rifles, powder, unnecessary railways, and so forth.

And since there is no end to men's caprices when they are ministered to not by their own labor but by that of others, industry becomes more

diverted to the production of the most unnecessary, stupid, depraving products, and increasingly draws people from sensible work. No end can be
foreseen to these inventions for the amusement of idle people, especially if
it is stupider and more depraving, including the replacement of animals or
legs by motors, or railways that go up mountains, or armored cars with quick-
firing guns. And their inventors and possessors are [no doubt] particularly
pleased and proud.

7. The longer representative government lasted and the more it spread, the
more did the Western nations abandon agriculture and devote their energies to the manufacture of luxuries for the wealthy classes, to enable them
to fight one another, and to debauch the undepraved. Thus, in England,
which has had representative government the longest, less than one-seventh of the adult male population are now employed in agriculture. In Germany it is forty-five percent, in France one-half, and a similar number in
other nations. At the present, even if these countries could be freed from
the calamity of proletarianization, they could not support themselves independently of other lands. None of these nations are able to subsist by their
own toil. Just as the workers are dependent on the well-to-do classes, so
these countries are completely dependent on other ones, such as India,
Russia, and Australia, which can support themselves and are able to sell
them their surplus. England can support herself from the land less than a
fifth of her population, and Germany, less than half, as is the case with
France and with other countires—their condition of dependency on the
food supplies from abroad is growing yearly.

In order to exist, these nations must have recourse to the deceptions and
violence called in their langauge "acquiring markets" and "colonial policy."
They try to throw farther their nets of enslavement to all ends of the earth,
to catch those who are still leading rational lives. Vying with one another,
they expand their armaments and more cunningly, and under various pre-
texts, seize the land from the farmers, and force them to supply food.

Until now they have been able to do this. But the limit to the acquisition of markets, to the deception of buyers, to the sale of unnecessary and
injurious articles, and to the enslavement of distant nations is already apparent. The peoples of distant lands are themselves becoming depraved:
they are learning to make for themselves all those articles which the Western nations have supplied them, and above all, the not very cunning science of armaments, and they are becoming as cruel as their teachers.

The end of such immoral existence is already in sight. The people of
the Western nations see this coming, and feeling unable to stop, comfort
themselves (as people half-aware that they are ruining their lives always
do) by self-deception and blind faith; and such blind faith is spreading more

widely among the majority of them. This faith is a belief that those inventions and improvements for increasing the comforts of the wealthy classes and for fighting (that is, slaughtering) which the enslaved masses for several generations have been forced to produce are something very important and almost holy. It is called in the language of those who uphold such a mode of life, "culture," or even more grandly, "civilization."

As every creed has a science of its own, so this faith in "civilization" has a science: sociology. Its one aim is to justify the false and desperate position in which Western people now find themselves. The object of this science is to prove that all these sorts of foolish and nasty stupefying inventions, such as—ironclads, telegraphs, nitroglycerin bombs, photographs, electric railways, and others designed for the comfort and protection of the idle are not only good but sacred and predetermined by supreme unalterble laws. The depravity they call "civilization," then, must be a necessary condition of human life, which all mankind must inevitably adopt.

And this faith is just as blind as any other faith, and just as unshakable and self-assured.

Any other position may be disputed and argued about; but "civilization" (meaning those inventions, the follies, and nastiness which we produce and our different lifestyles) is an indubitable blessing, beyond all discussion. Everything that disturbs faith in civilization is a lie [and conversely] everything that supports it is the sacred truth.

This faith and its attendant science cause the Westen nations not to wish to see or to acknowledge that the ruinous path they are following will lead to inevitable destruction. The so-called "most advanced" among them cheer themselves with the thought that without abandoning this path they can attain not destruction but the highest bliss. They assure themselves that through further violence (which has brought them to their present ruinous condition), there will somehow or other appear men, now striving to obtain the greatest material, animal welfare for themselves (influenced by socialist doctrines), who will wield power without being depraved by it. [They envision that] an order will be established in which people accustomed to a greedy, selfish struggle for their own profit will suddenly grow self-sacrificing, all working together for the common good and sharing alike.

But this creed, having no reasonable foundation, has of late lost more credibility among thinking people. It is held only by the laboring masses, whose eyes it diverts from the miseries of the present, giving them some sort of hope of a blissful future.

Such is the common faith of the majority of the Western nations, which is drawing them towards destruction. And this tendency is so strong that the voices of the wise among them, such as Rousseau, Lamennais, Carlyle, Ruskin, Channing, Garrison, Emerson, Herzen, and Edward Carpenter, have left no trace in the consciousness of those who are rushing towards this annihilation, since they do not wish to see and admit it.[54]

European politicians, who are delighted that one more nation should join them in their desperate plight, now invite the Russian people to travel this path of destruction. And frivolous Russians urge us to follow this road, since they consider it much easier to slavishly imitate what the Western nations did centuries ago (before they knew where it would lead), rather than thinking with their own heads. . . .

9. What, then is the Russian nation to do?

The natural and simple answer is to follow neither path.

To submit neither to the government which brought it to its present wretched state nor, imitating the West, to set up a representative, coercive state, which have led those nations to a yet worse condition.

The simplest and most natural answer is peculiarly suited to the Russian people, especially during the present crisis.

It is indeed amazing that a peasant husbandman of Tula, Saratov, Vologda, or Kharkov province who suffers all sorts of misery because of his submission to the government, such as taxation, law courts, deprivation of land, and conscription, should up till now, have contradicted the demands of his own conscience by submitting and even aiding his own enslavement. He has done this [in two ways. The first is] by paying taxes without knowing how they would be spent. [The second is] by allowing his sons, who are so painfully reared and so necessary as workers, to be soldiers, knowing still less why they are sent off to suffer and die.

It would be even stranger if such peasants (living their peaceful, independent life without any need of a violent and unnecessary government, who wish to be rid of their burdens), instead of simply ceasing to submit to it were to employ the same violence from which they suffer and replace it by a new force-wielding power, as the French and English peasants did.[56]

Why!, the Russian peasant population need only cease to obey any kind of force-wielding government and refuse to participate in it; immediately taxes, military service, and all official oppression, as well as the misery from private property in land would end on their own accord. All these misfortunes would cease because there would be no one to inflict them.

The historic, economic, and religious conditions of the Russian nation place it in exceptionally favorable circumstances for acting in this manner.

In the first place it has reached the point at which a change of its old relations towards the existing power has become inevitable. After witnessing the wrongs of the path traveled by the Western nations (with whom it has long been in the closest contact), Russia can now fully perceive this.

Power in the West has completed its circle. The Western peoples, like all others, at first accepted a force-wielding power in order to escape from the struggles, cares, and sins of power. When that power became corrupt and burdensome, they tried to lighten its weight by limiting it, that is, by participating in it. This [phenomenon] has spread more widely affecting more people in the sharing of power. The majority of the people (who at first submitted to power to avoid strife and to escape from participation with it) have had finally to take part both in [the very same] strife and power, and have suffered its inevitable accompaniment—corruption.

It has become quite clear that the pretended limitation of power only means changing those in control, increasing their number, and thereby accelerating depravity, discord, and anger among men. (The power remains as it was: that of a minority of the worse men over a majority of the better.) It has also become plain that with an increase of those in power people have been taken away from natural labor on the land. [They have been forced to engage in] factory work for the production (and overproduction) of unnecessary and harmful things, and have obliged the majority of Western nations to base their lives on the deception and enslavement of others.

That all this has become quite obvious in the Western nations is beneficial to the Russian people, who have now reached the juncture when they must change their relation towards power.

The Russian people, if they were to follow the way the Western nations have walked, would be like a traveler who took a path on which those who went before him had lost their way and the most far-seeing of them were already [retracing their steps].

[It is also to the advantage of the Russian people] that they are changing their relation towards power, while all the Western nations have more or less abandoned agriculture. The immense majority of the Russians are still engaged in a farming life, which they love and prize so much that most of them when torn from it are always ready to return to it at the first opportunity.

This [trait] is of special value for Russians trying to free themselves from the evils of power, for an agricultural life [is conducive to] the least need of government. This kind of life gives a government fewer opportunities of interference. I know some village communes which emigrated to the Far East and settled in places where the frontier between China and Russia was not clearly defined, and lived there in prosperity, disregarding all governments, until they were discovered by Russian officials.

Townsmen generally regard farming as one of the lowliest occupations to which people can devote themselves. Yet the enormous majority of the population of the whole world are engaged in agriculture, and on it depends the existence of the rest of humanity. In reality, the human race are farmers. All the rest (ministers, locksmiths, professors, carpenters, artists, tailors, scientists, physicians, generals, and soldiers) are but the servants or parasites of the farmer. Agriculture, besides being the most moral, healthy, joyful and necessary occupation, is also the highest of human activities, and alone gives men true independence.

The enormous majority of Russians are still engaged in very natural, moral, and independent agricultural pursuits. This [reason] is the second, most important circumstance which makes it possible for the Russian people (now that they are faced with the necessity of changing their relations towards power), to alter and free themelves from this evil by simply ceasing to submit to any kind of government.

Both these conditions [beneficial to Russia] are external.

The third condition, an inner one, is [based on] the spiritual—that the inner consciousness of every Russian is a singular characteristic (according to the evidence of history and the observation of foreigners who have been especially [aware] of this fact) .

In Western Europe, the Gospels printed in Latin were inaccessible to the people until the time of the Reformation, and have remained until now inaccessible to the entire Roman Catholic world. The refined methods which the Papacy employs have also hidden true Christianity. The concentration in these [Western] nations on practical questions is another reason why the essence of Christianity (not only among Roman Catholics but also among Lutherans, and even more in the Anglican Church), has long ceased to be a faith directing people's lives and replaced by external forms. Among the higher classess there is indifference and even the rejection of all religion. For the vast majority of Russians (perhaps because the Gospels became accessible to them as early as the tenth century, or because of the coarse stupidity and clumsiness of the Russo-Greek Church in hiding the true meaning of its religion, or because of some peculiar trait in the Russian character, and because of agricultural pursuits), however, Christian teaching in its practical application has never ceased to be the major guide of life.

From the earliest times until now, the Christian understanding of life has manifested itself among the Russian people in the most diverse characteristics, peculiar to them. It shows itself in their acknowledgement of the brotherhood and equality of all men, of whatever race or nationality, in their complete religious toleration, in their refraining from condemning criminals but regarding them instead as unfortunate, in the custom of begging one another's forgiveness on certain days, and even in the habitual use of a form of the word "forgive" when taking leave of anybody. It can also be seen in the habit not merely of charity towards beggars, but even of respect for them, in the perfect readiness (sometimes coarsely shown) for self-sacrifice for anything believed to be religious truth, which even today leads individuals to burn themselves to death, or castrate themselves, and even (as in a recent case) bury themselves alive.[56]

The same Christian outlook has always appeared in the relation of the Russian people towards those in power. The people have always preferred submitting to power rather than sharing it. They have considered the position of [all] rulers to be sinful and repugnant. This Christian relation of the Russian people towards those in power is the most important factor which makes it now possible for them to continue their customary farming life, and avoid participating in either the old power or in the struggle between the old and the new.

Such are the three conditions (different from those of the Western nations) in which the Russian people now find themselves. These factors, it would seem, ought to induce them to choose the simplest way out of the difficulty, that is, by not submitting to any force-wielding power. Yet the Russian people have not chosen the natural way, but waver between governmental and revolutionary violence, and have begun (through their worst representatives) to take part in this strife. They thus seem to be preparing for a journey along the Western road to destruction.

Why is this so? . . .

11. We often read about the causes of the restless condition of Christendom now threatened by many dangers. And we also frequently hear discussions about the terrible position in which the distorted and partially brutalized Russian people are found. The most varied explanations are put forward, yet all the reasons can be reduced to one. Men have *forgotten God*, that is to say, their relations to the Infinite Source of Life, and the meaning of existence engendered by those relations: to be fulfilled for the soul's sake, by the law given by this Divine Source. It has been forgotten, because some people rule over men by threats of murder; and others have consented to submit or to participate in their rule. These men have denied God and exchanged His law for human law.

Having discarded their relation to the Infinite, the majority of men in spite of all the subtlety of their mental achievements live on the lowest level of consciousness, where they are guided only by animal passions and by the hypnotism of the herd.

That [deadened mental state] is the cause of all their calamities.

There is therefore but one escape from the miseries with which people torment themselves: it lies in reestablishing a consciousness of their dependence on God, and regaining a reasonable and free relation with themselves and others.

It is this conscious submission to God, with the consequent abandonment of the sin of power and [all its relations], that all suffering nations must now face.

All men dimly feel the necessity of ceasing to submit to human power and of returning to the laws of God but the Russians are now keenly aware of this. And in this vague consciousness of reestablishing their obedience to the law of God and ceasing to obey human power lies the essence of the movement now taking place in Russia.

What is happening in Russia is not, as many people suppose, a rebellion of the people against their government in order to replace it but a much greater and more important event. What now moves them is a vague recognition of the wrongness and unreasonableness of all violence, and the realization that life should be based not on coercion but on sensible and free agreement.

Whether the Russian nation will accomplish the great work now before it, that is, the task of liberating men from human power, or whether, following the Western path, it will lose its opportunity and leave it to another happier Eastern race, the leadership in the great humanitarian work is crucial.[57] There is no doubt that all nations are now becoming more conscious of changing this violent, insane, and wicked life for one that shall be free, rational, and good. And what already is in men's consciousness will inevitably be realized in life. For the will of God must be realized.

12. "But is social life possible without power? Without power men would be continually robbing and killing one another," say those who believe only in human law. People of this sort are sincerely convinced that men refrain from crime and lead orderly lives only because of laws, courts of justice, police, officials, and armies; without state power society would be unthinkable. Men corrupted by power fancy that since the government punishes some crimes, it is this action that prevents further criminal action. But this [deluded reasoning] does not at all prove that the existence of law courts, police, armies, prisons, and death penalties restrains men from all the crimes they might commit. That the number of illegal offenses committed does not at all depend on state punitive action is clearly proven. When society is in a certain mood nothing can prevent the most daring and cruel acts which imperil the safety of the community, which has been the case in every revolution and which is now strikingly apparent in Russia.

The reason is that the majority of men (all the laboring people) abstain from crimes and live good lives, not because there are police, armies, and executions, but because there is a moral perception (common to most of mankind), established by their common religious understanding and by the education, customs, and public opinion, founded on that understanding.

This moral consciousness alone, expressed in public opinion, keeps men from crimes, in towns and especially in villages, where most of the people live.

I repeat that I know many examples of Russian farming communities emigrating to the Far East which have prospered for several decades. These communes governed themselves unknown to the government. When state agents discovered them, they began to experience new calamities and developed an inclination towards criminal acts.

Not only does the action of governments not deter men from crimes; it increases them by always disturbing and lowering moral standards. This [fact] cannot be otherwise. Everywhere there is a government, its very nature [automatically replaces] the highest, eternal, religious law (written not in books but in men's hearts and universally binding) with its own unjust man-made laws, the object of which is neither justice nor the common good, but domestic and foreign expediency.

All the present unjust laws of every government entail: maintaining the exclusive right of a minority to the land, which is the common possession of all; giving some men a right over the labor of others; compelling men to pay money for murder, or to go to war; establishing monopolies for the sale of stupefying intoxicants, or forbidding the free exchange of produce across a frontier; and countenancing the execution of men for actions which are not so much immoral, as disadvantageous to those in power.

All these laws, and the exaction of their fulfillment by threats of violence, the public executions to uphold these laws, and above all the forcing of men to take part in wars with habitual military exaltation, inevitably lowers people's moral and social consciousness.

Such governmental actions not only do not uphold morality but have a depraving effect on people.

It could never enter the head of any ordinary scoundrel to commit all those horrors: the stake, the Inquisition, torture, raids, quarterings, hangings, solitary confinements, war murders, the plundering of nations, and so forth. All governments are still ostentatiously committing them. All the horrors of Stenka Razin, Pugachev and other rebels were but the end products and feeble imitations of the horrors perpetrated by the Johns, Peters, and Birons.[58] If (which is very doubtful) the actions of a government do deter some dozens of men from crime, hundreds of thousands of other wrongful acts are committed solely because they are educated in them by state injustice and cruelty.

Legislators, merchants, and industrialists who live in towns and share power may still believe in its beneficial results but farmers cannot but know that a government causes them all kinds of suffering, has always been useless and only corrupts those who come under its influence.

So that to try to prove to men that they cannot live without a government, and that the injury the thieves among them may do is greater than the material and spiritual injury which it incessantly does by oppressing and corrupting them, is as strange as to try to convince slaves that it is more profitable for them to be enslaved than to be free. In the days of slavery, despite the obvious wretchedness, the slaveowners created a belief that it was good for slaves to be slaves, and that they would be worse off if they were free (sometimes the slaves themselves became hypnotized and believed this). At present the government and the people who profit, argue that although it robs and depraves, it is necessary for well-being, and men yield to this suggestion.

Men have to continue to believe in all this [fabrication] since they reject the law of God and put their faith in human law. Absence of human law for them means the absence of all law; and for those who recognize no law, this is terrible and they do not wish to be deprived of it.

This disbelief in the law of God is the cause of a curious phenomenon. As soon as men begin to speak of establishing a society without that human law all the theoretical anarchists (clever and learned men from Bakunin and Proudhon to Reclus, Max Stirner and Kropotkin) attempt to prove with indisputable correctness and justice the unreasonableness and harmfulness of power and fall into indefiniteness, verbosity, rhetoric, and unfounded and fantastic hypotheses.[59]

This [reasoning occurs] because none of these theoretical anarchists accept that natural law of God common to all men. Without the obedience of men to one and the same law society cannot exist.

Deliverance from human law is possible on condition only of acknowledging a common divine law.

13. "But if a primitive agricultural society, like the Russian, can live without government," will be the reply, "what are those millions to do who have given up farming and are living an urban industrial life? We cannot all cultivate the land."

"The only thing any man can be is a farmer," is the correct answer by Henry George.[60]

"But if everybody now returned to a farming life," it will again be said, "the civilization mankind has attained would be destroyed and that would be a terrible misfortune and an evil. . . . "

. . . It is said that if men would cease to obey governments and would farm, all industrial progress will be lost, which would be bad. But there is no reason to suppose that such industries and achievements as are useful to mankind, without enslaving men, would be destroyed. The endless number of unnecessary, stupid and harmful things, which a considerable portion of humanity now produces and with which the idle people who invent all these things justify their immoral lives, would cease. That does not mean that all that mankind has worked out for its welfare would be destroyed. On the contrary, the elimination of everything that is maintained by coercion would promote an intensified production of all those useful and necessary technical improvements which, without turning men into machines and spoiling their lives, may ease the the farmers' labor and even make life more pleasant.

The difference will be only that when men are liberated from power and return to farming, the objects produced by art and industry will no longer aim at amusing the rich, satisfying idle curiosity, or preparing for slaughter. [Neither will there be] the preservation of useless and harmful [lives] at the expense of useful lives or the producing of machines by which a small number of workmen can fashion a great number of things or cultivate a large tract of land. They will aim at increasing the productiveness of those laborers who cultivate their own land and help to better them without taking it away or interfering with their freedom. . . .

16. Why should we suppose that people, who should be guided by God, will always remain under the strange delusion that only human laws (mutable, accidental, unjust, and local) are important and binding, and not the one, eternal, just universal law of God? Why should we think that man's teachers will always be preaching that there is no such law and that the only laws that exist pertain to a particular religious ritual for each nation and sect, or to the so-called scientifc and imaginary laws of sociology (which do not bind men to anything) or civil laws, established and changed by men? Such an error is possible only for a time. Why should we suppose that people with whom the one and the same divine law written in their hearts, which creates a joyful moral social life, and revealed in the teachings of the Brahmins, Buddha, Lao-Tse, Confucius, and Christ will not partake of it? [Why believe that] they will always follow that wicked and pitiful tangle of church, scientific, and state teachings which diverts their attention from the one thing needful, and directs it towards the useless, for it fails to instruct how each man should live?

Why should we think that men will continue to torment themselves, by trying to rule over others, or with hatred and envy submitting to the rulers and themselves seeking to become rulers? Why should we think that the progress men pride themselves on will always be based on population increase and the preservation of life, and never in moral elevation? Or will it lie in miserable mechanical inventions, which are harmful, injurious and demoralizing objects? [Why do we not seek] a greater unity with one another and in the subjugation of our lusts necesssary for such a unity? Why should we not suppose that men will rejoice and vie with one another not in riches and luxuries but in simplicity and frugality and in mutual kindness? Why should we not suppose that men will see progress not in seizing more for themselves but in taking less from others and in giving more to others; not in increasing their power, not in fighting more but in growing more humble, and in coming into closer union, man with man and nation with nation?

Instead of men unrestrainedly yielding to their lusts, breeding like rabbits, and establishing urban factories for the production of chemical foods to feed their increasing poulation, and living in these cities without plants or animals, we should imagine chaste people, struggling against their lusts, living in loving communion with their neighbors amid fruitful fields, gardens and woods, with tame, well-fed animal friends. But there will be differences: people will not consider the land to be anyone's private property and it will not belong to any particular nation, they will not pay taxes or duties, or prepare for war, or fight; but on the contrary, they will have more peaceful intercourse with every race.

To imagine the life of men like that, we need not invent, alter or add anything to the lives of the farming peoples of China, Russia, India, Canada, Algeria, Egypt, and Australia.

To picture such a life to ourselves, we need not imagine any kind of cunning or out-of-the-way arrangement, but only acknowledge the universal law expressed alike in the Brahmin, Buddhist, Confucian, Taoist, and Christian religions—the law of love of God and of one's neighbor.

In such a life men will not have to be a new kind of being such as virtuous angels. They will be just as they are now, with all the weaknesses and passions natural to them. They will sin, will perhaps quarrel, and commit adultery, and take away other people's property, and even slay; but all this will be the exception and not, as now, the rule. Their life will be quite different since organized violence will not be considered good and necessary, and [the claim] that evil government deeds are good will not be indoctrinated.

Their life will be quite different, because there will no longer exist that impediment to teaching the spirit of goodness, love, and submission to the will of God; we must no longer accept ciriminal and evil governmental violence as necessary and lawful.

Why should we not imagine that through long suffering, men may be aroused from the suggestion, [or rather] the hypnotism, and must submit only to Him and to their own consciences? All this is not difficult to imagine; but it is difficult to imagine that it will not take root.

17. "Except ye become as little children, ye shall in no wise enter the kingdom of heaven" refers not to individuals alone but also to societies. As a man, having experienced all the miseries caused by the passions and temptations of life, consciously returns to a state of simplicity, kindness towards all, and readiness to accept what is good (the state in which children unconsciously live) and with the wealth of experience and the reason of a grown-up man, so does society. Having experienced all the miserable consequences and aberrations of abandoning God's law in preference for human power, and attempting to arrange an industrial life, we must consciously reject the snares of human power, and must submit to the highest, Divine law and return to the soil.

To consciously reject human power, and to obey the supreme law of God alone, is to accept His eternal, universal law, which is alike in all teachings, whether Brahmist, Confucian, Taoist, Christian, and to some extent Islamic and Babist.[61] It is incompatible with man-made power.

[It means] to prefer living on the farm and to acknowledge it to be not an accidental and temporary condition but one which makes it easiest for man to fulfill God's will.

For such a return to farming and for a conscious disobedience of power, the Eastern nations (and among them the Russian) are most favorably situated.

The Western nations have already wandered so far on the false path of altering the organization of power, and supplanting agricultural for industrial work, that such a return is difficult and requires great effort. But, sooner or later, the ever-increasing annoyance and instability of their position will impel them to return to a sensible and truly free life, supported by their own labor and not by the exploitation of other nations. However alluring the external success of manufacturing industry and the showy side of such a life may be, the most penetrating thinkers among the Western nations have long pointed out how disastrous is the path they are following, and how necessary it is to reconsider and change their way, and to return to farming.

The majority of the Eastern peoples, including the Russian nation, will not have to alter their lives. They need only stop their advance along the false path they have just entered, and become clearly conscious of the negativeness of power and the close affinity to husbandry which were always natural to them.

We of the Eastern nations should be thankful to Fate for placing us in a position in which we can benefit by the example of the West: not by imitating it (but by avoiding its mistakes), not doing what it has done, or not traveling the disastrous path from which many nations are preparing to return.

This halt in the march along a false path, and this demonstration of the possibility and inevitability of a different way, easier, more joyful, and more natural than that of the West, embodies the major meaning of the Russian Revolution.

Notes

1. Tolstoy, *Ob obshchestvennom dvizhenii v Rossii* [Regarding the social movement in Russia] (1905), *PSS*, 36: 156-165. This work appeared in a pamphlet under the title *The Crisis in Russia* (London: The Free Age Press, 1905).
2. The zemstvo is a generic name for institutions of local self-government established in the 1860s. For more information see page 12.
3. A reference to Bloody Sunday. See page 34.
4. Tolstoy's condemnation of the militaristic and expansionist policies of democ-

racies bears striking resemblance to Lenin's views on imperialism as the highest stage of capitalism. The latter thought his views justified with the outbreak of World War I. The Abyssinian War (1895) began with an Italian invasion. For the Boer War see page 107 note no. 26. The Spanish-American War (1898) was held in disdain by Tolstoy for American expansionism. For the Boxer Rebellion in China see page 107 note no. 26. British involvement in Tibet eventually led to its independence from China in 1913. The carving up of Africa by European powers was also viewed with dismay by Tolstoy.

5. Luke 18: 10, 11, and 13. Note by Tolstoy.

6. Tolstoy, *The Great Iniquity* (1905), in *Collections & Essays By Tolstoy*, The World's Classics, trans. Aylmer Maude (London: Oxford University Press, 1952), 272-306 *(Velikii grekh, PSS*, 36: 206-230).

7. *The Public,* Aug. 19, 1905, 307, HGS. Another reviewer, H. W. Thomas, a month later, again in *The Public* for Sept. 16th on page 382, writes:

> The whole question of the land, of labor and capital, is at bottom a question of justice, of what is fair and right; and the appeal must be not alone to legal forms, but to the great law and life of love, of brotherhood. Tolstoy tells us that it was owing to the deep sense of the wrong and shame of holding their less favored brothers in servitude, that the serfs of Russia were set free; and [in] his great religious faith in man and God he believes the owners of the vast land estates will come to see the wrong, the *sin* of denying the rights of the suffering poor to use the earth that is the gift of God to all his children. This excommunicated, but Divinely ordained teacher of righteousness, may be mystical or extreme in some things; but in his self-forgetting and consecrated life he stands at the eternal centers of the true and the good, of the soul and God, from which alone can come the power to lift our world into the moral grandness of the life of Christ in the life of man.

8. A reference to the liberals working in the zemstvos.

9. The vast Russian Empire was multi-national in character. At times tsarist authorities deemed it wise to enforce policies of Russification (education, propaganda, etc.) to create a more homogenous and Christian character. See pages 10-11.

10. At this time the major socialist party in Russia was the Russian Social Democratic Labor Party founded in 1898. A party split in 1903 created two factions known as the Mensheviks and the Bolsheviks. There were numerous radical movements, such as the Marxists, the anarchists, the Social Revolutionaries, and various national-liberationists, among others. Within each one there was an array of different factions. The above-mentioned Mensheviks, as a rule, opted for political rather than revolutionary change. The Bolshevik party, although they espoused armed uprisings countenanced representation in the second, third, and fourth Dumas. The Constitutional Democrats (Cadets), firm believers in liberal reforms, also supported many of the people's demands during the 1905 revolution and from the viewpoint of tsarist authorities could be construed as radical. See pages 34-35 for Tolstoy's reaction to liberalism.

11. The revolutionary turmoil of 1905.
12. Henry George, *The Crime of Poverty* (Henry George Foundation of Great Britain), 10. This note and the following four were written by Aylmer Maude.
13. Ibid., 12.
14. Ibid., 13.
15. Ibid., 14 and 15.
16. Rods used on soldiers who had to run the gauntlet as punishment. Sometimes death resulted.
17. From 1715 to 1789 the population of France increased by 25%. With no improvement in agricultural methods, no appreciable increase in arable land, suffering from onerous taxes, coupled with much land speculation, an inflexible social hierarchy, and with omnipresent aristocratic privileges, a volatile situation was created.
18. George died in 1897. Tolstoy grieved this loss profoundly. See page 28.
19. Charles Stewart Parnell (1846-1891), an Irish nationalist leader elected to Parliament in 1875, who united different Irish factions. His agitation on behalf of the Irish Land Question helped pass the Land Act and the first Home Rule Bill.
20. Arnold Toynbee (1852-1883) was an English reformer and pioneer economic historian. William E. Gladstone (1809-1898) was a spearhead in the Liberal Party, an advocate of many reforms, and was prime minister four times. Herbert Spencer (1820-1903) was an English philosopher who attempted to correlate natural sciences with philosophy. He was best known for applying evolution to all phenomena including mankind, known as "social Darwinism."
21. A lecture Henry George gave at Oxford University in 1884 caused quite a furor.
22. Henry Labouchere (1831-1912) was a radical M.P. and journalist.
23. The Peasant Land Bank was established in 1883 by the Minister of Finance N. K. Bunge (1823-1895) to help peasants buy land through the granting of loans. By 1905 the peasants had acquired about one-third of their lands through this means.
24. See page 29. Tolstoy is probably using the term "scientific" here to refer to sociology in general and Comtean positivism in particular, with its matter of fact reliance on science (as we know it, that is, dealing with the physical world). Progress was to achieve reform but with a cold rejection of religion, faith, and philosophy. August Comte (1798-1857) was the founder of sociology.
24. Nikolai I. Novikov (1744-1818) was a publisher and journalist who attempted to spread education and improve social conditions during Catherine II's reign but was imprisoned. Alexander N. Radishchev (1749-1802) was the author of the influential *Journey from St. Petersburg to Moscow* which portrayed the cruelties of serfdom and was banished to Siberia for a decade. For the Decembrists see page 4.
25. *Obrok* was rent paid for the use of land in kind or in money. *Barshchina* was agricultural labor on the owner's estate in exchange for the use of land.
25. See Henry George's *Social Problems*, 242-243.
26. Henry George, Jr., *Henry George*, 296. This note was placed by Aylmer Maude.
27. Tolstoy, "Tolstoy on Land Ownership" (1905), in *The Public*, Aug. 12, 1905, 298-299, HGS. (Reprinted from the *Philadelphia Evening Bulletin*). It has been

slightly recast for smoother reading. This article is found, in part, in: *PSS*, 35: 154-157.

28. Tolstoy, *Tri nepravdi* [The three lies], 1905 (*PSS*, 36: 402-406). A second version of this unpublished piece is presented.

29. Originally the term *Pomeshchik* referred to a man who received land in exchange for services (usually military) rendered to the state. By 1900 it was used for any member of the gentry with landholdings.

30. Tolstoy, *The End of the Age* (1905), trans. V. Chertkov and I. F. Mayo (London: Free Age Press, 1905), 49, 53-57, 67, 68-70, 71-72, and 86 *(Konets veka, PSS*, 36: 231-277).

31. The Russo-Japanese War. See page 34.

32. For more on the mir see pages 7 and 36.

33. Tolstoy, *An Appeal to the Russians* (1906), trans. Aylmer Maude (London: The Free Age Press, 1906), 62-77 *(Obrashchenie k rysskomy liudiam. K pravitel'stvy, revoliutsioneram, i narody, PSS*, 36: 304-314).

34. See page 15 note no. 31.

35. A probable reference to the extreme measures used by Prime Minister Stolypin to quell peasant discontent and revolutionary activity.

36. A reference to Nicholas II's grandfather Alexander II.

37. The first Dume was prorogued in 1906, having met fro only seventy-three days.

38. Tolstoy associated these men with power hunger. During the French Revolution Georges-Jacques Danton (1759-1794) was a popular leader of the Cordeliers, the Revolutionary Tribunal, and the first Committee of Public Safety, but was guillotined by Robespierre. Jean Paul Marat (1743-1793) was a journalist and another revolutionist and member of the Cordeliers. He was stabbed to death by Charlotte Corday. Napolean Bonaparte (1769-1821) was the Corsican Emperor of the French and brilliant military leader. His machinations totally altered the history of Europe and the world. Charles Maurice de Tallyrand (1754-1838) was foreign minister under Napoleon and also Louis XVIII and served in other capacities. He was a moving force at the Congress of Vienna and obtained milder peace terms for France. Otto Fürst von Bismarck (1815-1898) through a policy of warfare and domestic readjustments of different German states became the architect of the German Empire of 1871 under Prussia's leadership.

39. A reference to the Soviets. See page 34.

40. An artel was a banding together of laborers in a cooperative form of association which was especially prevalent among those engaged in seasonal and itinerant work.

41. For more on the peasants' redemption payments see pages 6-7.

42. The Black Hundred was a generic name applied to extreme right-wing groups (beginning in 1905). They advocated a strong monarchy, a staunch nationalism, and anti-Semitism. A number of pogroms have been attributed to them.

43. Tolstoy, *Predislovie k rysskomu perevodu knigi Genri Dzhordzha "Obshchestvennye zadachi"* [Preface to Russian edition of Henry George's "Social problems"], Sept. 22, 1906 *(PSS*, 36: 300-303).

44. The original wording is to be found on page 209 in *Social Problems*.

45. Volost

46. Tolstoy, *The Meaning of the Russian Revolution*, (1906), trans. Louise and Aylmer Maude (London: The Free Age Press, 1906), 1-2, 4, 7-18, 21-26, 30-36, 40-41, 47-50, and 50-52 *(O znachenii rysskoi revoliutsii, PSS,* 36: 315-362). Selected sections are presented. Another piece entitled *Edinstvennoe vozmozhnoe reshenie zemel'nogo voprosa* [The only possible solution to the land question] which was penned shortly after this one, will be presented in *An Anthology of Single Land Tax Thought,* (Vol. III of *The Henry George Centennial Trilogy* in preparation).

47. Examples of absolute monarchs disliked by Tolstoy. Charlemagne's (742-814) large empire was created by incessant military struggle. He is known, however, for his concern for people and learning. The Holy Roman Emperor Charles V (1500-1558) through conquest (especially in the New World) ruled over an immense empire across the globe. As defender of the Catholic faith he struggled against a growing Protestantism. The Inquisition reached its height during the reign of the Spanish king Philip II (1527-1598), who was a fanatic Catholic. He also waged incessant wars throughout his vast realm. He launched the ill-fated Armada in 1588. His son Philip III (1578-1621) was noted for his rabid bigotry and expulsion of the Moriscos in 1609. Louis XIV (1638-1715) brought the French monarchy to its height. This quintessential absolute monarch initiated numerous wars, built Versailles, and persecuted the Protestant Huguenots. His reign witnessed an incredible flourishing of culture. Henry VIII (1491-1547) was famous for his six wives, his antipapal policy, and establishment of the Anglican Church.

48. Bourbons (1589-1789); Convention (1792-1795); Directory (1795-1799); Napoleon (1799-1814); Bourbons (1814-1830); Louis Philippe (1830-1848); Second Republic (1848-1852); Napoleon III (1852-1870); and Third Republic (1871-1940).

49. See note . . . The reference to "Johns" possibly refers to a number of Byzantine Emperors noted for intrigues. It could also refer to the excommunicated John (1167?-1216) of England, who signed the Magna Charta (1215) and was infamous for his cruelty and treachery.

50. Under the Bourbon *ancien régime* in France the *lettre de cachet* was a sealed document sent by the king to a group or an individual giving notice of imprisonment or exile. There was no appeal. It has been used as a symbol of tyranny.

51. A reference to the suffrage movement in Europe and America. Norway first received the vote in 1907; in the U.S., 1920 (19th Amendment). In New Zealand, women had the vote since 1893.

52. It was a common belief by many people in Europe and America, especially those with a strong religious bent, that the rapid advances in industrialization and urbanization, which drastically changed rural life, were detrimental. The newer forms of weaponry were also shocking. Social Darwinism used principles from the natural sciences such as the doctrine of evolution and the struggle for the fittest to become a unifying factor of knowledge and by extension human affairs. Such an application was regarded by these critics with horror, for in its extreme forms, poverty, war, and suffering, could be justified.

53. Probably Tolstoy, who learned Hebrew at the age of fifty, is referring to the word "sholom." This word has many meanings with numerous nuances. The Jewish tradition envisages God, through His divine grace, as seeking peace not only in the heavens but on our planet between nations and among people in daily life.

54. Examples of social critics who advocated greater reforms and freedom. Jean-Jacques Rousseau (1712-1778), the famed philosopher, projected a society with greater liberty and more enlightened education; Felicité Robert de Lamennais (1782-1854) was a liberal humanitarian; Thomas Carlyle (1795-1881) was a critic of British society; John Ruskin (1819-1900) attacked social and economic evils in England; William Ellery Channing (1780-1842) advocated religious tolerance, reform in education, and wrote against slavery on our shores; William Lloyd Garrison (1805-1879) was the noted American abolitionist; Ralph Waldo Emerson (1803-1882) defended greater intellectual freedom; for Herzen see page 6; Edward Carpenter (1844-1929) was a champion of much positive reform in England.

55. References to the French Revolution of 1789 and the English Revolution (1640-1660).

56. In Russia there were many sectarian Christian sects who were persecuted by the tsarist authorities, including the above-mentioned Dukhobors. Although there were variations, the Dukhobors had no church organization, no priests and the Bible was not considered sacred but believed that the spirit of Jesus is in every person. They were also extreme pacifists and rejected all external authority. As a means of protest devotees of other religious groups would resort to extreme measures such as bodily mutilation and suicide. The proceeds from *Resurrection* were used to finance the emigration of the Dukhobors to Canada.

57. Here is a rare example of Tolstoy's total rejection of the West and identification of the Russians as essentially Oriental. It could be construed as an extreme form of Slavophilism. For more on Slavophilism see pages 4-5.

58. Peter I, the Great (1672-1725) was noted for his promulgation of incessant warfare, enforced Westernization, the execution of his son for alleged treason, and personal cruelty. Ernst Johann Biron (1690-1772) was a favorite of Tsaritsa Anna Ivanovna (1693-1740). His great influence at court led to what Soviet historians have labeled as an era of German domination, great exploitation, and corruption. In reality, although he wielded great power, he did not control court life nor Russian domestic and foreign policy.

59. Names of famous anarchists. For Bakunin see pages 5-6; Pierre-Joseph Proudhon (1809-1865) proposed a system of mutualism with loosely federated groups; Jean Jacques Élisée Reclus (1830-1905) was a noted geographer turned anarchist; and Max Stirner (1806-1856), whose real name was Johann Kaspar Schmidt, advocated an extreme form of individualism; for Kropotkin see page 13 note no. 4. Ironically, what Tolstoy labels as Christian is also pure anarchism, but on a more spiritual plane.

60. Although George extolled the virtues of life on the land, unlike Tolstoy, he accepted technological improvement as a liberating force.

61. Babism was founded by Murzi Ali Muhammed of Shiraz in nineteenth-century Persia. He believed he was the the Bab, or Gateway to the hidden imam (the perfect embodiment of the Islamic faith), and the harbinger of the manifestation of Allah's will. He was put to death in 1850 with 20,000 of his followers as a threat to authority and the established religion. His disciple, Bahaullah, founded the Bahai religion.

Chapter 6

The Last Years: 1907–1910

Letter to Prime Minister Peter A. Stolypin[1]

Tolstoy was shocked over the brutalities perpetuated by the government in quelling disturbances. This letter to Stolypin of July 1907 begs the Prime Minister not to implement private property in land, and instead to apply the single tax throughout Russia, for the land hunger was the main cause of the revolution.

I write to you not as a minister, not as the son of my friend,[2] but as a brother: as a man whose destiny, whether he wants it or not, is to live his life in accordance with that [divine] will which has placed you in this world.

The matter about which I write to you is [the following]:

The reasons for the revolutionary horrors, which are now taking place in Russia, have very deep roots, but the most singular and immediate one is the people's dissatisfaction with the unjust land distribution.

If revolutionaries of any of the parties have success, then it is because they rely on this increasing bitterness of a disenchanted people.

Everyone, the revolutionaries and the government, is aware of this. Sad to say, none of them have conceived or suggested anything (except the greatest stupidities and injustices) for the solution to this problem. All these measures—from the socialists' demands to return all the land to the people, sales through banks, or the return of state lands to the peasants, as well as resettlement—all these are unrealizable fantasies or palliatives. They are so insufficient that the people's rage when they would recognize the injustice of these measures would be not eliminated, but increased.

What is now necessary for the pacification of the peoples in Russia, especially the peasants, is not such measures as would increase the quantity of land but rather the abolition of the centuries-old injustice.

This injustice according to my recollection is very similar to serfdom, the ownership of people, which is so antagonistic to the fundamental laws of good. The so-called right of private property in land, which now influences all peoples of Christendom, is especially blatant in Russia. The awareness of this sin gives rise to revolution and is also its main driving force. The greatest part of this realization, to be precise, is an unconscious vague and false understanding of the injustice.

Its injustice consists of the *right* of one man to own another (slavery). This [sin] should not exist, nor should the *right* of one man, no matter who he is, whether rich or poor, tsar or peasant, be able to possess property in land.

The land is the property of everyone, and all people have the same right to use it. To recognize this fact or to ignore it: that is exactly the same as occurred during the days of slavery. In spite of the antiquity of that institution with its basis in protective law, everyone knew that it should never have been a reality. Whether or not it will be established in the near future, everyone knows and feels that the land cannot be the property of any individual.

It is now the same with property in land.

It is necessary to actively destroy this [alleged] right, not to spread or transfer it from one class to another. Not only must we not acknowledge this [putative] right for any certain class, [but in particular] for the peasants [we must] not encourage its use. It would be contrary to peasant ways. Of course, to whoever understands this question in its genuine meaning it should be clear that the right to the possession of property, and for one of *osminnik* lands,[3] for the peasant owner with extended holdings as well as for the rich or the tsar with millions of desiatinas should be illegal and criminal. This question is therefore not of who owns the land or how much: it requires the abolishing the right of property in land and making it equally accessible to all.

And such a solution to the land question—the abolition of the property right and its equal use for everyone—the laying out of this foundation has already been clearly and definitely worked out in the study of the single tax by Henry George.

I will not preach this method to you. It was set forth with complete clarity, with irrefutable persuasiveness, in all the works of this remarkable man, in particular the terse and lucid book *Social Problems*. I am afraid that while you are reading what I write, you are saying what I have heard many times: "Oh, Henry George, I know." But you are not trying to recognize and understand the essence of this land emancipation. Under the influence of negative words about Henry George spread by uninformed people who refute him, you fail to take the time to explore the methodology of this proposal.[4]

What I suggest to you is a great matter. You and the government now treat the land problem with pitiful palliatives, which will amount to nothing. It must be presented in such a way that you do not placate any single class or make concessions to the demands of the revolutionaries. You should establish justice which will not violate our most ancient ways, not taking into consideration whether or not this is done in Europe. I do not know if you will immediately pacify the revolution (no one can know this) but certainly one of those major and legitimate causes of the people's anger will be removed from the revolutionaries.

I advise you to do this, having in mind not any state or political considerations but the most important matters in the world. If you will not destroy then you will weaken the hatreds, bitterness, and moral evils that the revolutionaries are now trying to impose onto people's lives and which the government is fighting.

There cannot be any doubt that all revolutionary activity continues because of this anger which is a result of the dissatisfaction of the peasants with the land system. And if this is the case, it can be undone by eliminating this discord, by pulling out from under the feet of the revolutionaries the root cause. It means having sufficient water on hand with which to douse the incipient fire, and not to drown the raging fire.

I think that for an energetic man such as you, it is possible.

You must begin working with the Duma so that it will be not your enemy but your ally.[5] All the best people, from the educated to those from the masses will be not your enemies but your helpers.

I write to you, Peter Arkadeevich, under the influence of love for the son of my friend, who is traveling a false path.

You are confronted with two roads. You can either continue the activity which you have just begun as a leader of exiles, hard labor, and prisons. Not having achieved your goals, you will retain the unpleasant memory, and more importantly, it will harm your soul. Or if you would place this problem before the nations of Europe, they will cooperate in the abolition of the ancient, great, and general cruelties of private property in land for all peoples and actively promulagate truly decent laws . . . commensurate with the people's wishes. You will reassure them by ending those terrible villainous evils which both the revolutionaries as well as the government now use.

Think this over, Peter Arkadeevich, think this over. The time for neglect is past. It is too late to return—there remains only repentance. If there is only one chance in a hundred, that you will succeed in this great undertaking, you are obliged to start it. But I think that the chance of success is greater than that of failure. You must begin this task and you will see that all the best people of every party will join you. On your side will be a hundred million peasants, who are now hostile to you. With you will be the most powerful force of social thought: and when that will be with you, very soon all the increasing exasperation and brutality of the people that the government had attempted in vain to suppress with great cruelty will be not only dispersed but wiped out.

Yes, my dear Peter Arkadeevich, whether you want this or not, you stand at the crossroads: the one way, which you sadly travel, is the road of evil deeds, stupid weaknesses, and in the main, sinful; the other is the road of noble strength, of meaningful work exerted, of a great and good deed for all mankind, full of glory and love of people. In case of vacillation, let God help you choose the latter path.

I know that if you choose the path that I have suggested, you and your associates will be faced with greater difficulties than all the grand princes, perhaps sovereigns, and all the peoples of our planet.

All these labors will be lightened for you, by the realization that you are doing this not for yourself, not for advantages, not for vainglory, but for your soul and for God.

Let God help you, and He will assist you, I am sure.

If you find this letter harsh, please forgive me. I have written it from my soul, which has been guided by love for you.

P.S. I have shown this letter to only one close friend and there is no possibility of anyone discussing it.

I am sending along with this letter George's book *Social Problems* translated into Russian, and one of my pamphlets, which concisely sets forth his basic principles.

Stolypin responded only after a second letter. "You consider evil what I consider good for Russia," he writes.

> It seems to me that the lack of "property" among the peasants creates all our unbalance—nature implanted certain inborn instincts in man . . . and one of the most powerful . . . is the sense of property. One cannot love what belongs to another as one does one's own, and it is impossible to tend, to improve land, which is only temporarily in one's possession, as [anyone] would one's own. The artificial emasculation of our peasantry in this regard, the destruction of his innate sense of property, leads to much that is bad and, above all, to poverty—and poverty, in my opinion, is worse than slavery. . . . It is ridiculous to talk to these people about freedom or about freedoms. First raise the level of his well-being to at least that smallest degree where a minimal prosperity makes a man free. . . . And that can be accomplished only by the free application of labor to the land, that is to say, under the existence of the right of ownership in the land—I do not reject the teachings of George, and I think that the single tax will in time help in the struggle against very large ownership of property, but now I do not see any purpose here in Russia of driving off the land the more developed class of landholders, but on the contrary I see the undoubted necessity of relieving the peasant by giving him the legitimate opportunity to acquire the piece of land he needs and granting him full ownership of it. . . .[6]

From "Tolstoy in the Twilight," by Henry George, Jr.[7]

In June Henry George, Jr. (1862-1916) set sail for the Old World. A major object of his visit was to meet the greatest disciple of his father. Tolstoy was overjoyed at the prospect. While on a train headed west across Russia Henry, Jr. was surprised to learn that soon after he had sent a telegram to Tolstoy expressing his wish to see him, the news had flashed through every car and everyone started to treat him with deference.[8] A simple response to a request for a visit, sent by wire to his beloved teacher's son, reads: "I will be very glad to see you, I am waiting."[9] So glad was Tolstoy, that very day he penned an article "Concerning the Arrival of Henry George's Son" which appeared in Russian newspapers and is included within this selection.[10] On June 5 the younger George did spend a memorable day at Yasnaya Polyana. The following article recounts this visit and its tearful parting.

As he sat there in the chair, age seemed to have placed its hand heavily upon him; yet he appeared not so feeble as delicate. But the eyes revealed the keen, buoyant, spirit within. It was a life joyously spending itself to the very end, undaunted by the approach of death.

Before he spoke, Tolstoy gave me a deliberate, searching gaze, mixed with a peculiarly kind expression; and then, as if not displeased, offered a very cordial and personal welcome, during which I noticed my father's portrait holding a post of honor on the wall.

"Your father was my friend," he said with a singular sweetness and simplicity.

I asked after his health. "I was troubled to read in a Japanese newspaper a report that you had not been so well," I ventured to say.

He answered with the frankness that I found to be a characteristic of the whole family:

"I am quite old—eighty-one. I do not expect to stay much longer. One of my feet has to be nursed. But I am keeping at work."

He gave me a smile as if the matter of his death was nothing at all; as if he said: "Tomorrow I die. Meanwhile, I have another book to write." . . .

As to the work, I said I had heard that there was another book under way. Did it deal with political economy?

"No," he answered; "this is not on political economy. It treats of moral questions, which your father put first."

This led him to refer to an article on my father's teachings, for which my visit had served as text and which he had just sent off to a St. Petersburg newspaper. "Perhaps the paper will fear to print it, for we have little freedom here, and there is little discussion. But if that paper will not print it, then I hope to get it into another."

He handed me a copy of the article. It was in the Slavonic language [Russian]. When translated, I found the following passages which throw a strong light upon social, governmental, and revolutionary conditions in Russia today, as well as showing the vigor and hope of this wonderful old man's mind:

[I have just received a telegram from the son of Henry George expressing a desire to visit me. The thought of meeting the son of one of the most remarkable men of the 19th century keenly reminded me of everything done by him. But also of the stagnation which exists, not only in our Russian government but in every government of the so-called civilized world, in regard to the radical solution of all economic questions and which was already set forth so many years ago with such irresistible clearness and conviction by that great man.]

The land question revolves around the deliverance of mankind from slavery produced by its private ownership, which to my mind, is now in the same situation in which the questions of serfdom in Russia and slavery in America were in the days of my youth. The difference is only that while the injustice of private land ownership is quite as flagrant as that of slave ownership, it is much more widely and deeply connected with all human relations. It extends to all parts of the world (slavery existed only in America and Russia) and is much more tormenting to the land slave than personal slavery. How strange, one might say how ridiculous, were they not so cruel, and did they not involve the suffering of the majority of the toiling masses, are those attempts at the reconstruction of society proposed and undertaken by the two inimical camps—the state and revolutionary. Both do so through all kinds of measures, with the exception of that one which alone can destroy that crying injustice from which the overwhelming majority of the people suffer, which when driven inwards is still more dangerous than when it outwardly appears. All these efforts for the solution of political questions by new enactments without the destruction of private land ownership, reminds one of the splendid comparison by Henry George, of all such enactments to the action of the fool, who having placed the whole of the burden on one of the two baskets that hung upon the donkey's back, filled the other with an equal weight of stones.

But, with or against the desire of those classes who profit by the existence of this injustice, and however much the learned people of those classes may strive against it, hiding it, or pretending that they do not understand it, it cannot fail to be—and very quickly—destroyed. It must be destroyed because it is already now clearly understood by all the Russian working classess, the majority of whom never have acknowledged these violations of justice.

And therefore I rejoice at the thought that, no matter how far may be the governmental and revolutionary workers from the reasonable solution of the land question, it nevertheless will be (and very soon), solved especially in Russia. It will not be done by those strange, groundless, arbitrary, unfeasible and, above all, unjust theories of expropriation, and the still more foolish state measures for the destruction of village communes and the establishment of small landownerships, that is, the strengthening and confirming of that system against which the struggle is to be directed.[11] But it will and must be solved in one way alone—by the recognition of the equal right of every man to live upon and be nourished by the land on which he was born—that same principle which is so invincibly proved by all the teachings of Henry George.

I think thus, because the thought of the equal right of all men to the soil, notwithstanding all the efforts of "educated" people to drive that thought by all kinds of schemes of expropriation and the destruction of the village communes from the minds of the Russian people, nevertheless lives in the minds of the Russian people of today, and sooner or later—and I believe sooner—will be fully realized.

It may be interesting to know that these vigorous utterances did appear in the St. Petersburg newspaper, and from that paper were quickly republished by many journals in many lands, thus showing the eagerness with which the utterances of the Sage of Yasnaya Polyana are caught up and spread throughout the world.

In connection with this unqualified espousal of what he was pleased to call the "teachings of Henry George," my host directed that the translations of the George books into the Slavonic tongue be brought to him. They proved to be all of the principal books except *The Open Letter to the Pope* (obviously inappropriate for Russia where the Greek Church holds sway),[12] and the unfinished *Science of Political Economy*.[13] He also showed me a large number of the translated pamphlets and lectures—all in cheap form for popular circulation. The translator and popularizer of the works is his intimate friend and neighbor, Sergei D. Nikolaev, who, he said, would come to the house in the evening.

Tolstoy talked with the utmost fervor and enthusiasm of the truth of these books as if the matter was impersonal to me, and he suddenly tossed the rug off his feet and got out of his chair to go over to a table and write his name in some of the copies. The ease and certainty with which he moved was quite bewildering. . . .

While we stood there in his workroom I asked him for a portrait of himself, with his autograph. He immediately produced a picture from a cupboard, and sat down at at table to write on it.

"Would it be good English to say, 'With best love?'" he asked.

"It would be the English that honors most," I replied.

"I loved your father," he rejoined simply. And then, after a pause, during which he wrote his name on the picture, he said: "They arrest men here in Russia for circulating my books. I have written them asking why they arrest such men, who are blameless. Why not arrest the man who wrote the books? But they did not reply, and they do not arrest me."

Then he said, rising: "If you will not stay and sleep with us, I must urge you to go at once to catch your train."

And at the head of the stairway he stopped and took my hand, saying simply, "This is the last time I shall meet you. I shall see your father soon. Is there any commission you would have me take to him?"

For a moment I was lost in wonder at his meaning. But his eyes were quietly waiting for an answer.

"Tell him the work is going on," I replied.

He nodded, and I departed, feeling that I had been privileged to talk with the greatest man on earth.

Letter to Peter A. Polilov (Tatiana L. Sukhotina)[14]

Despite the setback a few years earlier in her effort to establish a modified form of the single tax on her estate, Tolstoy's daughter Tatiana continued to interest herself in Georgist political economy. She read all of George's books and wished to write an exposition in a language accessible to as many people as possible. After finishing the first section of it in November 1909, she wanted her father to give a reading but, seeking impartiality signed it under the pseudonym of Peter A. Polilov. Tolstoy was so taken with it that he wrote a long response. He was quite surprised to learn that his daughter had written such a thoughtful presentation.[15]

Your article, with your letter to me, has given me great pleasure. I have long ceased to interest myself—and in fact I have never interested myself—in political questions. But the question of the land, that is of land slavery, though it is considered a political question, is, as you quite correctly say, a moral question, [addressing] a violation of the most elementary demands of morality, and therefore it not only occupies my thoughts but torments me. I am tormented by the stupid cynical decision of that question accepted by our unfortunate government, and by the complete misunderstanding of it by people who are considered advanced.[16] You can therefore imagine the joy I experienced when I read your admirable article, which so clearly and powerfully sets forth the essence of the matter. This question torments me so [much] that I recently had a vivid dream in which, while I was in the company of "the learned," I had disputed their views. I expounded the same opinion regarding the existing crying injustice of private property in land your article so admirably expresses. I roughly jotted down that dream and wished to have it printed after corrections but you and your article have realized my dream.[17]

God help you to complete your work, and the sooner the better. Do you know Nikolaev? Get to know him. He is such an expert and such a passionate partisan of Henry George's teaching, as well as an admirable man, as one seldom meets.

I am very grateful to you for the joy you have given me.

It seems to me that the injustice of land slavery, and the necessity of emancipation from it, now stand on the same stage of recognition on which the emancipation of the serfs stood in the eighteen fifties. There is the same conscious indignation on the part of the people, who were keenly aware of the injustice, and the same consciousness of it among the few best represenatatives of the wealthy classes, and the same coarse, partly unintentional and partly intentional misunderstanding by the government. The only difference is that during the emancipation of the serfs, the government had the example of Europe, and above all of America. Now such an example is lacking. If it does exist, it consists [conversely] in the formation of small private landed property, which not only does not free, but strengthens the people in land-slavery. The government people, standing as usual on the lowest moral and intellectual level, at the present time having become especially self-confident and bold, particularly after their triumph over the revolution, and being unable to think independently or to understand the immorality of property in land, are recklessly breaking up the age-long supports of Russian life.[18] They do this to bring the Russian people to that horrible, immoral, and ruinous condition in which the peoples of Europe exist. These groups with their limitations and immorality do not understand that now the Russian people are not in a position in which it would be natural to compel them to imitate Europe and America. Rather, from their perspective they should show other nations the path along which the emancipation from land-slavery can be accomplished. If the government were, I do not say wise or moral, but at least to some degree what it boasts of being, namely *Russian*, it would understand the Russian people. It has been ingrained in their consciousness that the land is God's and may be common property but never an object of private possession. It would understand that on this contemporary important question the Russians are far ahead of other nations. If our government were not a coarse and stupid institution and quite estranged from the people, it would understand not only the great role it is called upon to perform by formulating the advanced ideals of the people—but by also [living up to that role] as pacifiers of the people. It is now trying to attain [that pacification] by execution unheard of since the days of Ivan the Terrible, and by all kinds of horrors, but it would certainly be attained just by one thing, the realization of the general popular ideal: the emancipation of land from private ownership. It would then not be necessary for the tsar or for his ministers, like criminals, to hide themselves behind three rows of guards. Only announce a land manifesto, as was done at the time of the Emancipation of the serfs, and the people, better than any other guards, would defend the government, which they would then acknowledge as their own. The blindness of the people of our so-called highest society is amazing. The Duma? At all my encounters with its members I have considered it my duty to beg them at least to raise the question of land emancipation from the claims of private property and to introduce a land tax in the manner of Henry George.[19] Their reply is always one and the same: "We have not occupied ourselves with that question and are not acquainted with it. Above all, that matter would in no way be accepted for discussion." Evidently those gentlemen are too ardently occupied with thrashing empty straw to find leisure to think of that which *alone* is important and necessary. They are blind and—what is worst of all—are convinced that they see.

So how can I not help rejoicing in your activity!

Please write me of the success of your work.

I press your hand in friendship and gratitude.

Three Days in the Village and *A Dream*[20]

From the fall of 1909 to July 1910, Tolstoy worked on a series of short vignettes depicting the harsh realities of peasant life in his homeland. *Three Days in the Village* tells of Russians tramping across the vast country begging for handouts, people suffering in wretched huts, and of tax extortion by the authorities. Offering a glimpse of the real Imperial Russia of tens of millions humans under the surface pomp and circumstances of the Romanovs, Tolstoy also gives reminders of poverty elsewhere around the globe. A diary entry for October 22, 1909, notes a wonderful dream in which Tolstoy engages in an impassioned conversation with Henry George.[21] The appropriately entitled *Dream* was included as the final section of *Three Days in the Village*.[22]

1. First Day: Tramps.

Something entirely new, unseen and formerly unheard of has appeared lately in our country districts. To our village of eighty homesteads, from half a dozen to a dozen cold, hungry, tattered tramps come every day, seeking a night's lodging.

These people, ragged, half-naked, barefoot, often ill and extremely dirty, enter the village and go to the local policeman. So that they should not die in the street of hunger and exposure, he quarters them on the inhabitants, regarding only the peasants as "inhabitants." He does not take them to the pomeshchik, who besides his own ten rooms has ten others: office, coachman's room, laundry, servants, and upper-servants hall and so on. Nor does he take them to the priest or deacon or shopkeeper, in whose houses, though not large, there is still some spare room. He takes them to the peasants, whose whole family, wife, daughters-in-law, unmarried daughters, and children, live in one room [which could be] sixteen, nineteen, or twenty-three feet long. And the master of the hut takes the cold, hungry, stinking, ragged, dirty man, and not only does he give him a night's lodging but feeds him as well.

"When you sit down to table yourself," an old peasant householder told me, "it's impossible not to invite him too, or your own soul accepts nothing." So they feed him and give him a drink of tea.

Those are the nightly visitors. But during the day, not two or three, but ten or more such people call at each hut, and again it is: "Why, it is impossible . . . ," and so forth.

And for almost every tramp the housewife cuts a slice of bread, thinner or thicker according to the man's appearance even though she knows her rye will not last until the next harvest.

"If you were to give to all who come, a loaf [the peasants' large-sized black bread] would not last a day," some housewives said to me. "So sometimes you harden your heart and refuse!"

And this goes on every day, all over Russia. An enormous yearly-increasing army of beggars, cripples, administrative exiles,[23] helpless old men, and above all unemployed workmen exists in such a fashion (to shelter themselves from the cold and wet) and is in reality fed by the hardest-worked and poorest class, the country peasants.

We have workhouses, foundling hospital boards of public relief, and all sorts of philanthropic organizations in our towns. In all those institutions, located in buildings with electric light, parquet floors, neat servants, and various well-paid attendants, thousands of helpless people of all sorts are sheltered. But however many there may be, they are but a drop in the ocean of the enormous population which now tramps destitute over Russia and is not sheltered and fed by any institutions, but solely by the village peasants whose own Christian feelings induce them to bear this heavy and gigantic burden.

Just think what people who are not peasants would say if (even once a week) such a shivering, starving, dirty, louse-infested tramp were placed in each of their bedrooms! But the peasants not only house them but feed them and give them tea, because "your own soul accepts nothing unless you have them to table."

In the more remote parts of Saratov, Tambov, and other provinces, the peasants do not wait for the policeman to bring these tramps but always receive them and feed them on their own.

And, as is the case with all really good deeds, the peasants do this without knowing that they are doing a good turn. Yet it is not merely a good deed "for the soul," but is of tremendous importance for all of Russian society. If not for the peasants' strong Christian feeling, it is difficult to imagine what the fate would be, not only of these hundreds of thousands of unfortunate, houseless tramps but especially of all the well-to-do people who have country houses.

[It is diffciult] to imagine the mental condition due to the state of privation and suffering to which these homeless tramps have come to. It is only necessary to realize that it is only this help rendered by the peasants that restrains them from committing, upon those who possess a superfluity of the necessities these unfortunates lack, the violence that would be quite natural in their position.

So that it is not the philanthropic organizations, not the government with its police and all its juridical institutions, that protect us, the well-to-do, from being attacked by those who wander, cold, hungry, and homeless, who have been brought to the lowest depths of poverty and despair. [No], we are protected, as well as fed and supported, by that backbone of the Russian nation, the peasantry.

Yes! Were it not for a deep religious consciousness in Russia's vast peasant population of the brotherhood of all men, these homeless people, having reached the last stages of despair, would have not only long since destroyed the houses of the rich, in spite of any police force (there are so few of them in country districts) but even killed all who stood in their way. So we ought not to be horrified or surprised when we hear or read of people being robbed or killed, but should bear in mind that since they occur as seldom as they do, we are in debt to the unselfish help rendered by the peasants.

Every day from ten to fifteen people come to our house to beg. Some among them are regulars, who for some reason have chosen that means of livelihood, and having clothed and shod themselves as best they might, and having made sacks to hold what they collect, tramp the country. Among them some are blind, or have lost a leg or an arm and sometimes, though rarely, there are also women and children. But these are only a small part. Most of the beggars who come now are passers-by, without a beggar's sack, most of them young, and not crippled. All of them are in a most pitiable state, barefoot, half-naked, emaciated, and shivering from the cold. You ask them, "Where are you going?" The answer is always the same: "To look for work"; or, "Have been looking for work, but found none, and I am making my way home. There's no work; they are shutting down everywhere." Many of these people are returning from exile.

A few days ago when I was barely awake our servant, Ilya Vasileevich, told me:

"There are five tramps waiting near the porch."

"Take some money from the table and give it to them," I said.

Ilya Vasileevich took it, and, as is the custom, gave each of them five kopecks. About an hour passed. I went out to the porch. A dreadfully tattered little man with a sickly face, swollen eyelids, restless eyes, and boots falling to pieces, began bowing, and held out a certificate to me.

"Have you received something?"

"Your excellency, what am I to do with five kopecks? . . . Your excellency, put yourself in my place! Please, your excellency, look . . . please see!" and he shows me his clothing. "Where am I to go to, your excellency?" (it is "excellency" after every word, though his face expresses hatred.) "What am I to do? Where am I to go?"

I tell him that I give [the same amount] to all alike. He continues entreating and demands that I should read his certificate. I refuse. He kneels down. I ask him to leave me.

"Very well! That means, it seems, that I must put an end to myself! That's all that's left for me to do. . . . Give me something, if only a trifle!"

I give him twenty kopecks, and he goes away, evidently angry.

There are a great many such peculiarly insistent beggars, who feel they have a right to demand their share from the rich. They are literate for the most part, and some of them are even well-read persons on whom the Revolution [of 1905] has had an effect. These men, unlike the ordinary, old-fashioned beggars, look on the rich not as people who wish to save their souls by distributing alms but as robbers who suck the blood of the working classes. It often happens that a beggar of this sort avoids or does no work, and yet considers himself, in the name of the workers, not merely justified in hating the robbers of the people (the rich) but bound to hate them from the depths of his heart. And if, instead of demanding from them, he begs, that is only a pretense.

There are a great number of these men, many of them drunkards, to whom the inclination is to say, "It's their own fault"; but there are also a great many tramps of quite a different type, who are meek, humble, and very pathetic; it is terrible to think of their status.

Here is a tall, good-looking man, with nothing over his short, tattered jacket. His boots are bad and worn down. He has a good and intelligent face. He takes off his cap and begs in the ordinary way. I give him something, and he thanks me. I ask him where he comes from and where he is going.

"From St. Petersburg, to home in my village in Tula province."

I ask him, "Why on foot?"

"It's a long story," he answers, shrugging his shoulders.

I ask him to tell it to me. He relates it with evident truthfulness.

"I had a good place in an office in St. Petersburg, and received thirty rubles a month. I lived very comfortably. I have read your books War and Peace and *Anna Karenina*," he says, again smiling a particularly pleasant smile. "Then my folks at home got the idea of migrating to Siberia to the province of Tomsk." They wrote to him asking whether he would agree to sell his share of land in the old place. He agreed. His people left but the land allotted them in Siberia turned out to be worthless. They spent all they had and returned. Being now landless they are living in hired lodgings in their former village and work for wages. It so happened that just at the same time [my narrator] lost his job in St. Petersburg. It was not his doing. The firm became bankrupt and dismissed its employees. "And just then, to tell the truth, I came across a seamstress." He smiled again. "She quite entangled me. . . . I used to help my people and now see what a smart chap I have become!. . . . Ah well, God is not without mercy. Maybe I'll manage somehow!"

He was evidently an intelligent, strong, and active fellow, and it had taken only a series of misfortunes to bring him to this present condition.

Take another man. His legs are swathed in strips of rag, his clothing, girdled with a rope, quite threadbare and full of small holes, evidently not torn, but worn-out to the last degree, and his face, with its high cheekbones, is pleasant, intelligent, and sober. I give him the customary five kopecks, and he thanks me and we start a conversation. He has been an administrative exile in Viatka. It was bad enough there but it is worse here. He is going to Ryazan where he used to live. I ask him what he had been. "A newspaper man. I took the papers round."

"For what were you exiled?"

"For selling forbidden literature."

We began talking about the Revolution. I told him my opinion that the evil was all in ourselves and that such an enormous power as the government cannot be destroyed by force. "Evil outside ourselves will be destroyed only when we have destroyed it within us," I said.

"That is so but it won't be for a long time."

"It depends on us."

"I have read your book on the Revolution."

"It is not mine but I agree with it."

"I wished to ask you for some of your books."

"I would be very pleased. . . . Only I'm afraid they may get you into trouble. I'll give you the most harmless."

"Oh, I don't care! I am no longer afraid of anything. . . . Prison is better for me than this! I am not afraid of jail. . . . I even long for it sometimes," he said sadly.

"What a pity it is that so much strength is uselessly wasted!" I said. "How do people like you destroy your own lives! . . . Well, and what do you mean to do now?"

"I?" he said, looking intently into my face.

At first, while we talked about past events and general topics, he had answered me boldly and cheerfully. But as soon as our conversation referred to himself and he noticed my sympathy, he turned away and hid his eyes in his sleeve. I noticed that the back of his head was shaking.

And how many more people are there like him!

They are pitiable and pathetic, and they, too, stand on the threshold beyond which a state of despair begins and could even make a kindly man primed to go to any lengths.

"Stable as our civilization may seem to us," says Henry George, "disintegrating forces are already developing within it. Not in deserts and forests, but in city slums and on the highways the barbarians are being bred who will do for our civilization what the Huns and Vandals did for the civilization of former ages."

Yes! What Henry George foretold some twenty years ago is happening now before our eyes, and most glaringly in Russia. [It is due to] the amazing blindness of our government, which assiduously undermines the foundations on which alone any and every social order can stand.

We have the Vandals foretold by Henry George ready for action in Russia. And strange as it may seem [even] in our deeply religious population these Vandals, these doomed men . . . are so especially dreadful, because we do have not the restraining principles of convention, propriety, and public opinion that are so strongly developed among the European nations. We have either a real, deep religious feeling, or as with Stenka Razin and Pugachev, a total absence of any restraining principle.[24] And dreadful as it may be, this army of Razins and Pugachevs is growing greater. It is abetted by the recent jacquerie-like conduct of our government, with its horrors of police violence, insane banishments, imprisonments, exiles, fortresses, and daily executions.[25] Such actions release the Stenka Razins from the last remnants of moral restraint. "If the learned gentlefolk act like that, God Himself permits us to do so," they say.

I often receive letters from that class of men, chiefly exiles. They know I have written something about not resisting evil by violence and for the most part they retort ungrammatically, though with great fervor: that what the government and the rich are doing to the poor must be answered only in one way: "Revenge, revenge, revenge!"

Yes! The blindness of our government is amazing. It does not see that when it attempts to disarm its enemies it merely increases their number and energy. Yes! The government and the rich and those who live among the rich are in terror of these people. But besides the feeling of terror these people inspire there is also another feeling, much more pressing than that of fear, that we cannot help feeling towards those who, by a series of accidents, have fallen into vagrancy. That feeling is of shame and sympathy.

And it is not fear so much as these feelings that should oblige us, who are not in that condition, to respond to this new and terrible phenomenon in Russian life.

2. Second Day: The Living and the Dying.

As I sat at my work, Ilya Vasileevich entered softly and, evidently reluctant to disturb me, said that some wayfarers and a woman had been waiting a long time to see me.

"Here," I said, "please take this [money] and give it to them."

"The woman has come about some business."

I told him to ask her to wait a while and continued working. By the time I came out, I had quite forgotten about her, until I saw a young peasant woman with a long, thin face, and clad very poorly and too lightly for the weather, appear from behind a corner of the house.

"What do you want? What is the matter?"

"I've come to see you, your honor."

"Yes . . . what about? What is the matter?"

"To see you, your honor."

"Well, what is it?"

"He's been taken wrongfully. . . . I'm left with three children."

"Who's been taken and where to?"

"My husband . . . sent off to Krapivny."

"Why? What for?"

"To be a soldier, you know. But it's wrong—because, you see, he's the breadwinner! We can't get on without him. . . . Be a father to us, sir!"

"But how can this be? Is he the only man in the family?"

"Just so . . . the only man!"

"Then how is it they have taken him if he's the only man?"

"Who can tell why they've done it? . . . Here I am, left alone with the children! There's nothing for me to do but to die. . . . Only I'm sorry for the children! My last hope is in your kindness, because, you see, it was not right!"

I wrote down the name of her village, her name and surname, and told her that I would see to it and let her know.

"Help me, if it's only ever so little! . . . The children are hungry, and, as God is my witness, I haven't so much as a crust. The baby is worst of all . . . there's no milk in my breasts. If only the Lord would take him!"

"Haven't you a cow?" I asked.

"A cow? Oh, no! . . . Why, we're all starving!" she said, crying, and trembling all over in her tattered coat.

I let her go and prepared for my customary walk. It turned out that the physician, who lives with us, was going to visit a patient in the village the soldier's wife had come from, and another patient in the village where the district police station is situated, so I joined him, and we drove off together.

I went into the police station while the physician attended to his business in that village.

The district elder[26] was not in nor was the clerk. Only the clerk's assistant, a clever lad whom I knew. I asked about the woman's husband, and why, since he was the only man in the family, he had been taken as a conscript.

The clerk's assistant looked up the particulars, and replied that the woman's husband was not the only man in the family, for he had a brother.

"Then why did she say he was the only one?"

"She lied! They always do," he replied with a smile.

I made some inquiries about other matters I had to attend to and then the physician returned from visiting his patient, and we drove towards the village in which the soldier's wife lived. But before we were out of the first village a girl of about twelve came quickly across the road towards us.

"I suppose you're wanted?" I said to the physician.

"No, it's your honor I want," said the girl to me.

"What is it?"

"I've come to your honor, mother died, and we are left orphans. There are five of us. Help us! . . . Think of our wants!"

"Where do you come from?"

The girl pointed to a brick house, which was not badly built.

"From here . . . that is our house. Come and see for yourself!"

I got out of the sledge and went towards the house. A woman came out and asked me in. She was the orphans' aunt. I entered a large, clean room. All the children were there, four of them. Besides the eldest girl there were two boys, a girl, and another boy of about two. Their aunt told me all about the family's circumstances. Two years ago the father had been killed in a mine. The widow tried to get compensation but failed. She was left with four children and the fifth was born after her husband's death. She struggled on alone as best she could, at first hiring a laborer to work her land. But without her husband things became worse. They had to sell first their cow, then the horse, and at last only two sheep were left. Still they managed to live somehow but two months ago the woman herself fell ill and died. She left these five children and the eldest was twelve years old.

"They must get along as best they can. I try to help them but can't do much. I cannot think of what's to become of them! I wish they'd die! . . . If they could only be placed in some orphanage, or at least some of them!"

The eldest girl evidently understood and took in the whole of my conversation with her aunt.

"If at least little Nicky could be placed somewhere! It's awful because you can't leave him for a moment," she said pointing to the sturdy little two-year old urchin, who with his little sister was merrily laughing at something or other and evidently did not share his aunt's wish.

I promised to take steps to get one or more of the children into an orphanage. The eldest girl thanked me and asked when she should come for an answer. The eyes of all the children, even of Nicky, were fixed on me as on some fairy being capable of doing anything for them.

Before I had reached the sledge, after leaving the house, I met an old man. He bowed, and at once began speaking about these same orphans.

"What misery!" he said; "it's pitiful to see them. And the eldest little girl, how she looks after them—just like a mother! Wonderful how the Lord helps her! It's a mercy the neighbors don't forsake them, or they would have simply died of hunger, the dear little things! . . . They are the sort of people it does no harm to help," he added, evidently advising me to do so.

I took leave of the old man, the aunt, and the little girl, and drove with the physician to the woman who had been to see me that morning.

At the first house we came to I inquired where she lived. It happened to be the house of a widow I know very well. She lives on the alms she begs, and she has a particularly importunate and pertinacious way of extorting them. As usual, she immediately began to beg. She said she now needed special help to enable her to rear a calf.

"She's eating me and the old woman out of house and home. Come in and see her."

"And how is the old woman?"

"What about the old woman? . . . She's hanging on. . . ."

I promised to come and see not so much the calf as the old woman and again inquired where the soldier's wife lived. The widow pointed to the second house down, and hastened to add that while no doubt they were poor, her brother-in-law "does drink dreadfully!"

Following her instructions I went to that house.

Miserable as are the huts of all the poor in our villages it is long since

I saw one so dilapidated as that [hovel]. Not only the whole roof but the walls were so crooked that the windows were aslant.

Inside was no better than the outside. The brick oven took up one-third of the black, dirty little hut, which to my surprise was full of people. I thought I would find only the widow with her children. But here was a sister-in-law (a young woman with children) and an old mother-in-law. The soldier's wife herself had just returned from her visit to me and was warming herself on the oven top. While she was getting down her mother-in-law began telling me of their life.

Her two sons had lived together at first and all managed to feed themselves.

"But who remains together nowadays? All separate," the garrulous old woman went on. "The wives began quarreling, so the brothers separated, and life became harder. We had a little land and managed to live only by their wage labor; and now they have taken Peter as a soldier! So where is she to turn to with her children? She's living with us now but we can't manage to feed them all! We cannot think of what to do. They say he may return."

The soldier's wife, having climbed down from the oven, continued to implore me to help get her husband back. I told her it was impossible and asked what property her husband had left behind with his brother to keep her and the children. There was none. He had handed over his land to his brother to feed her and the children. They had owned three sheep but two had been sold to pay the expenses of getting her husband out. There was only some old rubbish left, she said, besides a sheep and two fowls. That was all she had. Her mother-in-law confirmed her words.

I asked the soldier's wife where she had come from. She came from Sergievskoe. Sergievskoe is a large, well-to-do village some thirty miles off. I asked whether her parents were alive. She said they were alive, and living comfortably.

"Why don't you go back to them?" I asked.

"I thought of that myself but am afraid they won't have the four of us."

"Perhaps they will. Why not write to them? Shall I write for you?"

The woman agreed and I noted down her parents' address.

While I was talking to the woman, the eldest child (a fat-bellied girl) came up to her mother and pulling at her sleeve, began asking for something, probably food. The woman went on talking to me and paid no attention to the girl, who again pulled and muttered something.

"There's no getting rid of you!" exclaimed the woman and with a swing of her arm struck her on the head. The girl burst into a howl.

Having finished my business there I left the hut and went back to the widow.

She was outside her house, waiting for me, and again asked me to come and look at her calf. I went in and in the passage there really was a calf. The widow asked me to look at it. I did so, feeling that she was so engrossed in her calf that she could not imagine anyone not being interested in it.

Having looked at the calf I stepped inside and asked:

"Where is the old woman?"

"The old woman?" the widow repeated, who was evidently surprised that I could still be interested in the old woman after having seen the calf. "Why, on the top of the oven! Where else should she be?"

I went up to the oven and greeted the old woman.

"Oh! . . . oh!" answered a hoarse, feeble voice. "Who is it?"

I told her and asked how she was getting on.

"What's my life worth?"

"Are you in pain?"

"Everything aches! Oh! . . . oh!"

"The physician is here with me. Shall I call him in?"

"Doctor!. . . . Oh! . . . oh! What do I want with your doctor?. . . . My doctor is up there. . . . Oh! . . . oh!"

"She's old, you know," said the widow.

"Not older than I am," I replied.

"Not older? Much older! People say she is ninety," said the widow. "All her hair has come out. I cut it all off the other day."

"Why did you do that?"

"Why, it had nearly all come out, so I cut it off!"

"Oh! . . . oh!" moaned the old woman. "Oh! God has forgotten me. He will not take my soul. If the Lord won't take it, it can't go of itself! Oh! . . . oh! It must be for my sins! . . . I've nothing to moisten my throat. . . . If only I had a drop of tea to drink before I die . . . Oh! . . . oh!"

The physician entered the hut. I said goodbye and went out into the street.

We got into the sledge and drove to a small neighboring village to see the physician's last patient, who had sent for him the day before. We went into the hut together.

The room was small, but clean. In the middle of it a cradle hung from the ceiling and a woman stood energetically rocking it. At the table sat a girl of about eight, who gazed at us with surprised and frightened eyes.

"Where is he?" the physician asked.

"On the oven," replied the woman, not ceasing to rock the cradle.

The physician climbed up, and, leaning over the patient did something to him.

I drew nearer and asked about the sick man's condition.

The physician gave me no answer. I climbed up, too, and gazing through the darkness gradually began to discern the hairy head of the man on the oven top. Heavy, stifling air hung about the sick man, who lay on his back. The physician was holding his left hand to feel the pulse.

"Is he very bad?" I asked.

Without answering me the physician turned to the woman.

"Light a lamp," he said.

She called the girl, told her to rock the cradle, went and lit a lamp and handed it to the physician. I got down so as not to be in his way. He took the lamp and continued examining the patient.

The little girl, staring at us, did not rock the cradle strongly enough and the baby began to cry piercingly and piteously. The mother, having handed the lamp to the physician, pushed the girl angrily aside and again began to rock the cradle.

I returned to the physician and again asked how the patient was. The physician, still occupied with the patient, softly whispered one word.

I did not hear and asked again.

"The death agony," he repeated, purposely using a foreign word. He got down and placed the lamp on the table.

The baby did not cease crying in a piteous and angry voice.

"What's that? Is he dead?" said the woman, as if she had understood the foreign word the physician used.

"Not yet, but there is no hope!" he replied.

"Then I must send for the priest," said the woman distressedly, rocking the screaming baby more violently.

"If only my husband were at home! . . . But who can I send now? They've all gone to the forest for firewood."

"I can do nothing more here," said the physician and we went away.

I heard afterwards that the woman had found someone to send for the priest, who had just enough time to administer the last sacrament to the dying man.

We drove home in silence, both, I think, experiencing the same feeling.

"What was the matter with him?" I asked at length.

"Inflammation of the lungs. I did not expect it to end so quickly. He had a very strong constitution but the conditions were deadly. With a 105 degree fever he went and sat outside the hut where the temperature was only twenty degrees."

Again we drove on in silence for a long time.

"I noticed no bedding or pillow on the oven," I said.

"Nothing!" replied the physician. And, evidently knowing what I was thinking about, he went on:

"Yesterday I was at Kroutoe to see a woman who has had a baby. For a proper examination, it was necessary that she would have to lie stretched out full length but there was no room in the whole hut."

Again we were silent, and again we both probably had the same thoughts. We reached home in silence. At the porch stood a fine pair of horses, harnessed tandem to a carpet-upholstered sledge. The handsome coachman was dressed in a sheepskin coat and wore a thick fur cap. The sledge belonged to my son, who had driven over from his estate. . . .

And here we are sitting at the dinner table laid out for ten people. One of the places is empty. It is my little granddaughter's. She is not quite well today and is having dinner in her room with her nurse. A special hygienic dinner has been prepared for her consisting of beef bouillion tea and sage.

At our large four-course dinner, with two kinds of wine, served by two footmen, and eaten at a table decorated with flowers, [the following] is the kind of talk that goes on:

"Where do these splendid roses come from?" asks my son.

My wife tells him that a lady, who will not divulge her name, sent them from St. Petersburg.

"Roses like these cost one and a half rubles each," my son says, and goes on to relate how such roses at some concert or play were showered on a performer until they covered the stage. The conversation passes on to music and then to a man who is a very good judge and patron of music.

"By the by, how is he?"

"Oh, he is always ailing. He is again going to Italy. He always spends the winter there and his health improves so wonderfully."

"But the journey is very trying and tedious."

"Oh, no! Not if one takes the express, for it is only thirty-nine hours."

"All the same, it is very dull."

"Wait a bit! We shall fly before long!"

3. Third Day: Taxes.

Besides my ordinary visitors and applicants, today there are some special ones. The first is a childless old peasant whose life is ending in great poverty. The second is a poor woman with a crowd of children. The third is, I believe, a well-to-do peasant.

All three have come from our village and have come about the same business. The taxes are being collected before the new year. The old man's samovar, the woman's only sheep, and one of the well-to-do peasant's cows have been noted down for seizure in case of nonpayment. They all ask me to defend them, assist them, or to do both.

The well-to-do peasant, a tall, handsome, elderly man, is the first to speak. He tells me that the village elder[27] came, noted down the cow and demanded twenty-seven rubles. This levy is for the obligatory grain reserve fund, and ought not, the peasant thinks, to be collected at this time of year. I know nothing about it and tell him that I will inquire at the district government office and let him know whether the tax payment can be postponed.

The second to speak is the old man whose samovar has been noted down. The small, thin, weakly, poorly clad man relates, with pathetic grief and bewilderment, how they came, took his samovar, and demanded three rubles and seventy kopecks, which he can't get.

I ask him what the tax is for.

"Some kind of government tax. . . . Who can tell what it is? Where are my old woman and myself to get the money? As it is, we hardly manage to live! . . . What kind of laws are these? Have pity on our old age and help us somehow!"

I promise to inquire, to do what I can, and I turn to the woman. She is thin and worn-out. I know her. I also know that her husband is a drunkard and that she has five children.

"They have seized my sheep! They come and say: 'Pay the money!' My husband is away working, I say. 'Pay up!' they say. But where am I to find it? I have only one sheep and they are taking it!" And she begins to cry.

I promise to find out and to help her if I can. First, I go to the Village Elder, to find out what the taxes are, and why they are collecting them so rigorously.

In the village street two other petitioners stop me. Their husbands are away at work. One asks me to buy some of her homespun linen and offers it for two rubles. "Because they have seized my hens! I had just reared them and live by selling the eggs. Do buy it; it is good linen! I would not let it go for three rubles if I were not in great need!"

I send her away, promising to consider matters when I return. Perhaps I may be able to lessen the tax.

Before I reach the elder's house a woman comes to meet me. Olga is a quick-eyed, black-eyed former pupil of mine, who is now already an old woman. She is in the same plight, for they have seized her calf.

I go to the elder. He is a strong, intelligent-looking peasant with a grizzly beard. He goes out into the street to me. I ask him what taxes are being collected so rigorously. He replies that he has had very strict orders to collect all arrears before the new year.

"Have you had orders to confiscate samovars and cattle?"

"Of course!" replies the village elder, shrugging his shoulders. "The taxes must be paid. . . . Take Abakumov, for instance," he says, referring to the well-to-do peasant whose cow has been taken in payment for some grain reserve fund. "His son is an *izvozchik* and they have three horses.[28] Why shouldn't he pay? He's always trying to get out of it."

"Well, suppose it is so in his case," I say, "but how about those who are really poor?" And I name the old man whose samovar they are taking.

"Yes, they really are poor and have nothing to pay with. But do you think such things get considered up there!"

I name the woman whose sheep was taken. The elder is sorry for her too, but, as if excusing himself, explains that he must obey orders.

I inquire how long he has been an elder and what pay he gets.

"How much do I get?" he says, replying not to the question I ask, but to the question in my mind, which he guesses: namely, why he takes part in such proceedings. "Well, I do want to resign! We get thirty rubles a month but are obliged to do things that are wrong."

"Well, and will they really confiscate the samovars, the sheep, and fowls?" I ask.

"Why, of course! We are bound to take them and the district government will arrange for their sale."

"And will the things be sold?"

"The people will manage to pay up somehow."

I go to the woman who came to me about her sheep. Her hut is tiny and in the passage outside is her only sheep, which is slated to support the imperial budget. Seeing me, she, a nervous woman worn out by want and overwork, begins to talk excitedly and rapidly, as peasant women do.

"See how I live! They're taking my last sheep while these brats and myself are barely alive!" She points to the bunks and the oven top where her children are. "Come down!. . . . Now then, don't be frightened!. . . . There now, how can you keep yourself and them naked brats?"

The brats, almost completely naked with nothing on but tattered shirts, not even any trousers, climb down from the oven and surround their mother.

The same day I go to the district office to make inquiries about this way of exacting taxation, which is new to me.

The district elder is not in. He will be back soon. In the office several people are standing behind the grating, also waiting to see him.

I ask them who they are and why they have come. Two of them have come to get passports in order to work in another region. They have brought money to pay for the passports. Another has come to get a copy of the district court's decision rejecting his petition that the homestead (where he has lived and worked for twenty-three years, which had belonged to his uncle and who had adopted him), now that his uncle and aunt are dead, should not be taken from him by his uncle's granddaughter. She is the direct heiress and taking advantage of the Law of the November 9, is selling the freehold of the land and homestead on which the petitioner lived.[29] His petition has been rejected but he cannot believe that this is the law and wants to appeal to some higher court, though he does not know which one. I explain that there is such a law and this provokes disapproval, confusion, and incredulity among all those who are present.

Hardly have I finished talking with this man when a tall peasant with a stern, severe face asks me for an explanation of his affairs. The business he has come about is this: "Not to dig on one's own land? What laws are these? We live only by digging the iron! We have been trying for more than a month and can't get anything settled. We don't know what to think of it, for they will ruin us completely and that will be the end of the matter!"

I can say nothing comforting to this man, and turn to the elder, who has just come back, to inquire about the vigorous measures which are being taken to exact payment for tax arrears in our village. I ask under which clauses the taxes are being levied. The elder tells me that there are seven different kinds of rates and taxes pertaining to the arrears of the peasants: (1) the imperial taxes, (2) the local government taxes, (3) the insurance taxes, (4) former grain reserve funds, (5) new grain reserve funds in lieu of contributions in kind, (6) communal and district taxes, and (7) village taxes.

The district elder tells me, as the village elder had done, that it was by order of the higher authorities that the taxes were being collected with special rigor. He admits that it is no easy task to collect them from the poor but he shows less sympathy than the village elder. He does not venture to censure the authorities, and above all, he has hardly any doubt of the usefulness of his office, or of the rightness of taking part in such activity.

"One can't, after all, encourage. . . ."

Soon after, I had occasion to talk about these things with a *zemskii nachalnik*.[30] He had very little compassion for the hard lot of the poverty-stricken people, whom he rarely saw, and just as little doubt of the morality and lawfulness of his participation. In his conversation with me he admitted that, on the whole, it would be pleasanter not to serve but he considered himself a useful functionary, because other men in his place would do even worse things. "And since one is living in the country, why not take the salary, small as it is, of a zemskii nachalnik?"

The views of a governor relating to the collection of taxes necessary to meet the needs of those who arrange the nation's welfare were entirely free from any considerations as to samovars, sheep, homespun linen, or calves taken from the poorest inhabitants of the villages: he too had not the slightest doubt as to the usefulness of his activity.

And finally, there are the ministers and those who are busy managing the liquor traffic,[31] those who teach men to kill one another, and those who condemn people to exile, to prison, to penal servitude, or to the gallows. All the ministers and their assistants are quite convinced that samovars and sheep and linen and calves taken from beggars are put to their best use in producing vodka, which poisons the people, making weapons for killing men, building jails and lock-ups, and, among other things, paying them salaries. [How else could they] furnish drawing rooms, buy dresses for their wives, and [go on] journeys and [engage in] amusements for relaxation after fulfilling their arduous labors for the welfare of the coarse and ungrateful masses[?]

4. Conclusion: *A Dream.*[32]

A few nights ago I had such a significant dream that several times during the following day I asked myself, "What has happened today that is so specially important?" And then I remembered that the important thing was what I had seen, or rather heard, in my dream.

It was a speech that struck me greatly, spoken by one who, as often happens in dreams, was a combination of two men: my old friend, now dead, Vladimir Orlov, with grey curls on each side of his bald head, and Nikolai Andreevich, a copyist who lived with my brother.

The speech was evoked by the conversation of a rich lady, the hostess, with a landowner who was visiting her house. The lady told of the peasants on a neighboring estate who had burned the landlord's house and several sheds which sheltered century-old cherry trees and duchesse pears. Her visitor, the landowner, said that the peasants had cut down some oaks in his forest, and had even carted away a stack of hay.

"Neither arson nor robbery is considered a crime nowadays. The immorality of our people is terrible. They have all become thieves!" someone said.

And in answer to those words, that man, combined of two, spoke:

"The peasants have stolen oaks and hay, and are thieves, and the most immoral class," he began, addressing no one in particular. "Now, in the Caucasus, a chieftain used to raid the *aouls*[33] and carry off all the horses. But one of them found the means to get back from the chieftain's herds at least one of the many horses stolen from him. And is it not the same with the trees, the grass, the hay, and all the rest of the things you say the peasants have stolen from you? The earth is the Lord's, and common to all; and if the peasants have taken what was grown on the common land of which they have been deprived, they have not stolen, but have only resumed possession of a small part of what has been stolen from them.

"I know you consider land to be the property of the landlord, and therefore call robbery when the peasants restore to themselves its produce. But, you know, that is not true! The land never was, and never can be, anyone's property. If a man has more of it than he requires, while others have none, then he who possesses the surplus land possesses not land but men—and men cannot be the property of other men.

"Because a dozen mischievous lads have burned some cherry tree sheds, and have cut down some trees, you say the peasants are thieves, and the most immoral class! . . .

"How can your tongue frame such words! They have stolen ten oaks. Stolen! To prison with them!

"Why, if they had taken not your oaks alone but everything that is in this house, they would only have taken what is theirs: made by them and their brothers, but certainly not by you! 'Stolen oaks!' But for ages you have been stealing from them, not oaks but their lives, and the lives of their children, their womenfolk and their old men, who withered away before their time only because they were deprived of the land God gave to them and all men in common, and they were obliged to work for you.

"Only think of the life those millions of men have been living and of how you live! Only consider what they do, supplying you with all the comforts of life, and of what you do for them. You deprive them of everything: even the possibility of supporting themselves and their families! All you live on including everything in this room, everything in this house, and in all your splendid cities, all your palaces, all your crazy luxuries have been made by them.

"And they know this. They know that these parks of yours, and your race horses, motor cars, palaces, dainty dishes and finery, and all the nastiness and stupidity you call 'science' and 'art' are purchased with the lives of their brothers and sisters. They know and cannot help knowing this. Then think what feelings these people would have towards you if they were like you!

"It might be supposed that, knowing all you inflict on them, they could only hate you from the bottom of their souls and could not but help wishing to revenge themselves on you. And you know there are tens of millions of them and only some thousands of you. But what do they do?.... Why, instead of crushing you as useless and harmful reptiles, they continue to repay your evil with good, and live their laborious and reasonable though hard life, patiently biding the day when you will become conscious of your sin and will amend your ways. But in place of that, what do you do? From the height of your refined, self-confident immorality, you deign to stoop to those 'depraved, coarse people.' You enlighten them, and play the benefactor to them, that is to say, with the means supplied to you by their labor, you inoculate them with your depravity, and blame, correct, and, best of all 'punish' them as unreasoning or vicious infants bite the breasts that feed them.

"Yes, look at yourselves, and consider what you are and what they are! Realize that they alone live, while you, with your Dumas, ministries, synods, academies, universities, conservatories, law courts, armies, and all such stupidities and nastinesses, are but playing at life and spoiling it for yourselves and others. They, the people, are alive. They are the tree and you are harmful growths like the fungi. Realize, then, all your insignificance and their grandeur! Understand your sin, and try to repent, and at all costs set the people free...."

"How well he speaks!" I thought. "Can it be a dream?"

And as I thought that, I awoke.

This dream set me to thinking again about the land question: a question for those who live constantly amid poverty-stricken, toiling peasants cannot help to do so. I know I have often written about it, but under the influence of that dream, even at the risk of repeating myself, I once more felt the need to express myself *Carthago delenda est*.[34] As long as people's attitude towards private property in land remains unchanged, the cruelty, madness, and evil of this form of enslavement cannot be pointed out too frequently. . . .

Notes

1. Tolstoy to Peter A. Stolypin, July 26, 1907, *PSS*, 77: 164-168.
2. Tolstoy served with Stolypin's father during the Crimean War at Sevastopol.
3. Osminnik was a parcel of land equivalent to one-fourth of a desiatina. It is equal to the amount of sowing that can be done by four chetveriks, or about a bushel and a half of grain.
4. "If you would care to have a better way to familiarize yourself with this matter, I advise you to invite my friend, the great expert [and translator], perhaps the best of all those engaged in Georgist studies, [Sergei D.] Nikolaev. He, I assure you, would not refuse visiting you and cooperate in all possible ways in this great matter." This note was in the original text.
5. At times Tolstoy was quite contradictory. Although he was as a rule against liberal concessions, such as the Duma, here he supports them. For more on his relations with the Duma see pages . . .
6. Peter A. Stolypin, Oct. 20-23, 1907, in Alexandra Tolstoy, *Tolstoy: A Life of My Father*, trans. E. Hapgood (New York: Harper & Brothers, 1953), 456.
7. Henry George, Jr., "Tolstoy in the Twilight," *Land Values*, March 1910, 208 and 210, HGS. A bracketed passage on page 227 has been added from "Tolstoy's Latest Word on George," in *The Public*, July 23, 1909, 714, HGS. The entire text of this letter is to be found in *PSS*, 38: 70-71.
8. Henry George, Jr., "A Visit to Tolstoy," *The Public*, Nov. 26, 1909, 1145, HGS. This article was a reprint from *The New York World* (Nov. 14, 1909).
9. Tolstoy to Henry George, Jr., June 2, 1909, *PSS*, 79: 214.
10. See Gusev, *Dva goda* [Two years], 262-263 and 265
11. A reference to the Law of November 9, 1906. This law and subsequent legislation allowed every head of the peasant household to leave the commune and to claim a share of its land in a consolidated plot, rather than in scattered strips. See page 36.
12. To be more precise, the Russian Orthodox Church, which is an independent part of the Orthodox Eastern Church. Greek Church is a term used in the West to collectively refer to the latter.
13. George's *The Science of Political Economy* was first published posthumously in 1898.

14. Tolstoy to P. A. Polilov (T. L. Sukhotina), Nov. 6-7, 1909, trans. Aylmer Maude, in *Land & Liberty*, July-Aug. 1926, 161-162, HGS. This letter is found in *PSS*, 80: 177-179.

15. See Tatiana L. Tolstoy [Sukhotina-Tolstaia], *Tolstoy Remembered*, trans. Coltman Derek (New York: McGraw-Hill Book Co., 1977), 268-271 and Ibid., *Vospominaniia* [Remembrances] (Moscow: Khudozhestvennoi literatury, 1976), 360-366.

16. A reference to Stolypin's land reforms.

17. Most likely a reference to *A Dream*, the concluding part of *Three Days in the Village*. See pages 247-249.

18. Another reference to Stolypin's land reforms.

19. See page 51 note no. 91.

20. Tolstoy, *Three Days in the Village* and *A Dream*, in *Three Days in the Village and Other Sketches* (1909-1910), trans. Louise and Aylmer Maude (London: Free Age Press, 1910), 7-53 *(Tri dnia v derevne* and *Son, PSS*, 38: 5-30).

21. Tolstoy, Oct. 21, 1909, *PSS*, 57: 155-156.

22. The final version is printed here.

23. Administrative exile (outside the court system) to different provinces or Siberia was a common form of punishment especially for political offenders. By 1900 there were approximately 150,000 of them out of a total of 300,000 exiles. This practice was expanded by the Bolsheviks.

24. Tolstoy's insight, which is shared by other observers, regarding the ambivalent nature of the Russian people, has been the subject of historical debate.

25. A reference to Stolypin's ruthless quelling of radical activity and peasant disturbances in the wake of the 1905 Revolution.

26. See next note.

27. The village elder was the executive officer of the commune elected for three years. His duties included the handling of various infractions and the collection of taxes. More often than not, he was regarded as an agent of the government rather than as a representative of communal interests. Other elders were at the head of different branches in the provincial bureaucracy, such as the district (volost) elder.

28. An izvozchik was a cabby.

29. See note no. 11.

30. The zemskii nachalnik (land captain) was established in 1889. This office was ostensibly created to end bureacratic disorder in the village and only a noble could hold it. It was, however, used to stifle any liberalism (since the 1860 reforms) at the local level with tighter control. Broad discretionary powers in overseeing peasant administration and justice (without appeal) were wielded until 1917. It was considered to be, in part, a return to the days of serfdom.

31. Vodka was a lucrative state monopoly established in 1894. It was probably the single largest source of revenue before World War I.

32. See pages 255-260 in the appendix for a translation of the first unused version.

33. An aoul was a village in the Caucasus or Central Asia.

34. "Carthage must be destroyed" was the famous line repeatedly used by the Roman statesman and author Cato the Elder, Marcus Portius (234-149 B.C.). He considered Carthage a threat to Roman security. During the third Punic War, three years after his death, this North African city and Cato's wishes were carried out.

Appendix

From *The Light That Shines Through the Darkness:* First Draft[1]

Stepan: (holds out a cigarette case) "Do you want one?"

Boris: (looking at the [tennis] players) "No thank you. I don't smoke."

Stepan: "When did you quit?"

Boris: "It has been eight months. I thought it was stupid, so I gave it up."

Stepan: "Why is it stupid? Why do you deprive yourself of an extra pleasure?"

Boris: "There's hardly any pleasure in it."

Mitrofan: "I think that the only [real] question is whether it is a legitimate or an unnecessary need."

Boris: "It seems to me unnecessary."

Mitrofan: "This [opinion] must be proven."

Boris: "That millions have lived without it shows that it is unnecessary. It is [also wasteful], since millions of desiatinas of land are sown with tobacco instead of grain and fruit."

Stepan: "If the land is used in this fashion, it could be advantageous."

Boris: "It is not proof enough. The reason the land is used for the production of tobacco is that it is in the hands of the large proprietors."

Stepan: "And how could it be otherwise? How could we distribute it?"

Boris: "I would do it so that the land would be in the possession of those who feed themselves by [working on] it."

Stepan: "How would you do this? You would destroy any progress that the economy has made. Then you will see, whether it is the peasants or the large landowners who can best cultivate the soil."

Boris: (Looks at Liuba and she looks at him) "Now we are arguing at a standstill. But what to do. I am sure that landownership is a crime, just like slavery."

Stepan: "How would you arrange it differently?"

Boris: "By Henry George's single tax plan. This means is certain [to work]."

Mitrofan: "But how would you do this?"

Boris: "There are various means. In Russia we have a sovereign who can do this, if he would [only] understand his prerogatives, and not be so backwards. Then all kinds of [reforms] could be effected. In a constitutional government this [plan] could be carried out only by a house; with a majority there would be . . . "

Stepan: "The Social Democrats [would create a fine mess]."

Boris: "Why not the Social Democrats?"

Mitrofan: "Neither a sovereign, or the Social Democrats, or the bourgeoisie will ever do this, for the ruler and the bourgeoisie are large landowners."

Boris: "How about a revolution?"

Mitrofan: "I did not talk about a revolution for the nationalization of the land. The problems of life are complicated and no nationalizaton of the land can resolve them."

Boris: "Surely the single tax is not quite like nationalization. Like the air and the sun's rays, the land cannot belong to anyone."

Stepan: "With this difference, that it is not necessary to cultivate the sun's rays so that they can warm [us], as it is necessary to cultivate the earth for it to produce."

Letter to Tsar Nicholas Alexandrovich Romanov:
Rough Draft[2]

. . . But you ask, is there now any kind of work similar and equal to the liberation of the peasants? In every historical period there is always a coming closer to the [ultimate] ideal, which humanity aspires to and can approach. In the last century this was the emancipation from slavery. In the present century it is [the awakening of] the workers' question, the root of which, in my opinion, is the obsolete and the revoltingly unjust right of landownership. This question was not only raised but theoretically solved a long time ago by Henry George in his works, especially *Progress and Poverty* (you probably know them, but if you do not, and if you would make a request I will send you their summary). According to this way of thinking, the land cannot be an object of property, that for organizing the use of the land it is necessay to transfer all the taxes onto it, by a tax commensurate to its value through gradations. In England, America, Germany, and France, the influence of the large landowners, capitalists, the parliaments, and the press has culminated in the rejection of Henry George's single tax plan. Therefore this project can be put into effect only by autocratic authority. Its realization is especially important and necessary in such an agricultural country as Russia, where up to this time the people have lived in the conviction that the land is God's and cannot be [owned as] property. It seems to me that the realization of this project is as probable as in your grandfather's time was the emancipation of the serfs. In the same precise way it is possible to introduce its major foundation and begin work by gubernias (as what was done for the freeing of the peasants) for valuating (assessing) the lands, imposing a tax on them, and working out corresponding laws. I am firmly assured that this is possible, and whoever the tsar may be who does it and shows that it is possible will do one of the greatest deeds for mankind's good.

Since I am not overly confident [of my own knowledge] and admit that [on details] I could be mistaken, and since there are people more informed and intelligent than I, it will be shown that this cannot be done. I know, however, that it can. For you to save yourself and the Russian people from the greatest misery, you must seek out that which approaches the solution of the world's foremost question, which would contribute to the good of not a single class, but all the people. You must make it your goal to lead them to its attainment. Only then will you escape not only from the danger which surrounds you, from the misfortune which menaces you, from the hatred your power brings, but with your friends, aids, and all the best people of Russia you will be actively loved by the people. You will then be in a [favorable] position for you will be able to rely on them [all] against a small group of backward egotistical people. As these [possibly] unconvincing arguments may not be based on the broadest considerations, they can be mistaken, but there is still a single agrument, leading to the same result, which cannot be mistaken and is undoubtedly just and self-sufficient, whether you perceive it or not.

This argument is that our life here is given to us only once and we can corrupt it, make of it a series of sufferings for ourselves and others, or do the greatest good for others and for yourself in this life and the future one to come.

You are in a special position in which the difference between the greatest good and the greatest evil for yourself and others is especially evident. . . .

Letter to a Peasant About the Land: Concerning Henry George's Project[3]

The project of Henry George stipulates that all the land, no matter where it is and whoever uses it, should be evaluated according to its income [assessed value], not by that income which the user receives from it or from what he garners from the land, but according to how much adavantage the land itself generates including the more remunerative lands. And then this income [rent] from the land is taken for the community from those who use it.

Such an approximate valuation of the land in Russia should yield from accessible field lands between three and ten rubles per desiatina, while kitchen gardens around villages and water meadows would be even more. In busy places and by wharfs on navigable rivers, in cities with establishments and factories, in places where there is ore, oil, gold, and so forth, payment for the land should be several thousand rubles a sazhen per year.

This money garnered from this valuation which belongs to all the people, Henry George proposes to use for community needs for everyone, in the same manner that any taxes and duties are now collected.

An advantage of such a restructuring [of land relations] is that the people who now possess the largest [portions] of land would give them up, because they would be unable to pay the rent. The people who themselves want to work on the land could then take it over.

The first advantage of such a system is that the present land would then be placed in the hands of people who would work it, and not be in the grip of the large landowners.

The second advantage is that the laboring people would stop being servants and factory slaves. Those who now live in the cities would begin to return to the countryside.

The third advantage would be that all the necessities of life, such as matches, tea, sugar, kerosene, iron, cloth, cotton, and any machinery, as well as the unnecessary things such as wine and tobacco, and everything else would be twice or [even] thrice cheapened. This advantage [would benefit] not only landowners but by all the people, who will receive their share of the [ground] rent although they do not work on the land.

So if such an order were to be established, two great lies from which the people suffer would also be destroyed.

The first one is that people are deprived of their natural and innate right to the land. The second one is that the taxes are collected not from the people's common property, the land, but from man's own labor, so that the more he works, the more that is collected from him.

The main advantage is that such a restructuring [of society] would save people from sin. They would no longer use someone else's labor for which they have been educated in idleness without having to work since childhood and for which, at times, they are not guilty. They would be liberated from the still larger sin of the lying and distortion by which people excuse themselves for this activity. [The new system] would save workers from the temptation and the sin of dependence, and from condemnation of those who do not work, and would thus destroy the major reason for the sin of keeping people separated.

It is possible to put Henry George's system into effect without noise, enmity, vexation, or with ruining people. It would cost very little to transfer taxes and duties form productive labor to the land, and only small portions of the land would be abandoned. People who acquire the land will be those who till it and love their work, not the ones who do not toil on it. And all the land will be in the hands of the real farmers—idle life in the cities will be reduced and everyone will become richer and more virtuous.

Such is Henry George's project.

A *Dream:* First Version[4]

The conversation began after dinner. It started when Maria Vasileevna Krasnopevtsova, the widow-owner of the house and the guardian of her young children, was having a discussion at dinner with her guest, the District Marshal of the Nobility Gertsenshtein, a genuine Russian man, [about what] Gertsenshtein himself considered should be done about the theft of timber in the forest, since it was the property of her children.

"The [peasants] came and cut seven oak trees as if they were in their own woods and then hauled them off. I will not be able to stop this unless I will be able to punish them: otherwise everyone will steal and nothing will remain. I do not have the right [to allow my children's property to disappear. But I do have an obligation to protect it.]"

"[Your presentation of] the whole situation is completely unnecessary, for it is primarily due to the severing of the householder-breadwinner families from their work. To put them in prison would be cruel."

"What would you suggest me to do, tell them 'thank you?'"

This ironic rebuff was aimed at Simeon Terenteich Prokofeev, the teacher of Maria Vasileevna's children. In his opinion, although he was unable to serve in a "decent" home, he nevertheless now saw himself as a good, obliging, modest man, and a good instructor, who helped children develop a love for their studies. They had studied so well that the two oldest ones passed their exams wonderfully in the third and fourth grades of the preparatory school.

Simeon Terenteich fell silent and only gave out a sigh. He knew well that in face of the decisive judgment of Maria Vasileevna and her total indifference to the opinions on the part of those who were talking, it was impossible to argue. Still silent, he cast his eyes on the tray with the compotes. They finished eating the last course.

"This behavior has recently increased," the marshal of the nobility F. I. Gertsenshtein said in support of the objections of Maria Vasileevna. "The last restraining principles of morality have disappeared. But now the ideas of the property rights have completely vanished among the people, so there is already no difference between yours and mine. There is a dreadful collapse of religion and morality."

"But Simeon Terenteich wants the peasants to be favorably treated."

Simeon Terenteich was silent. He was leaning closer to his plate and was choking on an apple which he had swallowed almost whole.

"I do not want anything," he seethed.

"I could not make it out. What were you saying?"

"I did not say anything."

"Well, Simeon Terenteich would not speak about the peasants. For him the peasants are holy," Maria Vasileevna said.

"Oh yes, if we did not have prisons for these holy ones or even more gallows," the genuine Russian man said. "The peasants are now through and through thieves."

Simeon Terenteich flushed, then he turned pale and with a labored voice and an unnatural smile said, "Through and through robbers is a very good expression, for it refers to you and not to those you speak of."

"That is something you would especially like," the genuine Russian man said.

"Nothing. Only the fact is, that those are the robbers who seize someone else's property and use it. I do not think that the people from whom property is taken get it back from the thieves could be called robbers."

"Is that what you mean."

The servant Taras suggested to the marshal of the nobility, who had already eaten his portion, to take another compote. The marshal of the nobility heartily refused. Heartily, because he wanted to express [his contempt] for this insolent little pedagogue (who was evidently hinting on something as rude.) Maria Vasileevna got up, and smiling said: "It will be better if we talk in the living room. Coffee will be served there."

"Wonderful," said the marshal, smiling at the mistress. And having gotten up in a grand manner, as becoming a Russian man, he crossed himself looking over to the corner.[5]

"You wait. I will show you up for those words you said," he thought, brooding about the impudence of all these scribblers.

"So, this is how you prefer to determine thievery anew," [he said] as he turned to Simeon Terenteich.

"Not in a new but in a very old common sense." Simeon Terenteich began to talk fervently. "There is no reason to be evasive, you know, I meant those robbers who seize someone else's property. I meant the landowners."

"Why is it that those who take over the land have seized it in violation of the rights of others?"

"Property in land is acquired like any other property, by labor. One man works on it and acquires it. The difference [between property in land

and other kinds of property] is that the acquisition of pearls, diamonds, and gold cannot [infringe] on the rights of others. On an island on which everyone lives off the land, if one person appropriates it for himself he takes it away from the others, rather than letting them maintain themselves. He impoverishes the others or makes them his slaves."

"But surely we are not on an island."

"As a matter of fact the land does have boundaries."

"So how is the land to be divided equally?" Maria Vasileevna joined in the conversation. "How much sugar would you like," she asked after Taras had placed the tray with coffee down on the table.

"It is not necessary to divide it. It is impossible, as it is impossible to identically divide the air for everyone," said Simeon Terenteich.

"How can it be done without dividing?"

"The way these very robbers know how, since they recognize the land as God's, as common, is to be used only by general agreement."

"So [now you are talking about] that dear mir with its two *arshin*-long fields.[6] Such is how your studies, your lofty ideas have driven the peasants to what they have all become."

"The mir will not drive them to poverty but the landowners and the government will."

"If it were not for the government, they would have definitely perished. Thank goodness the government has understood the situation. And the Law of November 9 can yet rectify the matter. A rock-solid property in land is the first and single condition for order and good organization."

"Yes, a well-organized society, based on illegitimate separate personal property in land."

"It exists throughout Europe and thanks to it throughout these countries there is order and a properly functioning society."

Simeon Terenteich began to get angry and quickly began to talk:

"What a horrible thing to say. Europe. Our government (excuse me) consists of stupid backwards people, incapable of thinking with their own minds and are [easily swayed] by life's circumstances. Europe. In Europe, there never was what we have had and still have—the land commune."

"This commune is good, like the praising of a pigsty. That is the commune."

"If you will permit me. There has lived and still lives in the consciousness of the Russian people that the land cannot be an object of property and this state of mind is far ahead of Europe's. Europe will sooner or later be introduced to it—it is [already] now beginning in England—and this is the foremost consciousness of the Russian people that we consider backwards and we hold Europe as an example, [a place] which has lost all consciousness."

"Yes, it would be fine if we could be at least a bit like Europe. The main thing is that everyone that we speak to [uses European] phrases. I ask, how is this property in land to be organized?"

"Strong people are not satisfied with loud words. We need action. But we still don't have it. It is exactly in this area that you and other dreamers like you, do not have the answer."

"Just the opposite. We have a very simple, clear, and definite answer."

"It should be interesting to listen."

"The answer is that land should be held in common."

"Yes, this is what we have heard. But how is it to be done? Some would want to work on the land but there are others who would rather play the violin."

"This arrangement could be effected since those who use the land would pay for that advantage and those who do not use it, like those who play the violin, would go their own way."

"How can this be worked out?"

"One would pay [for the use of the land to the community]."

"How much? How strange it is. It appears to you so easily."

"How much? As much as the violinist should pay in taxes for the social amenities the administration provides."

"Yes, such is Henry George. The single tax. Yes, Henry George, the single tax."

"But surely it is impractical."

"Why? The freeing of slaves seemed impractical. And how about our abolition of serfdom? That was even more impractical than freeing people from land slavery. And at that time they said exactly the same thing, [that it couldn't be done]. The entire matter consists in recognizing the criminality of landownership. You and Maria Vasileevna speak of thieves. But surely all the landowners are the robbers. You know, there was a time when the slaves did not recognize their slavery to be a falsehood and bore it submissively, and then there came a time when it was impossible to endure this any more. The better people among the slaveowners understood this, so did the slaves and only force could restrain them—but you cannot maintain force for long, the force [that now protects] land-slavery. There are also the same better people . . . "

"Such as you."

"The better people among the land-slaveowners understand that this cannot continue in such a manner and [must] recognize that they are robbers."

"Maria Vasileevna, can you believe that we are criminals?"

"Yes, thieves and, in the main, people who recognize themselves to have been deceived, admit that they and all landowners are criminals. And at such a time we cannot devise anything more intelligent than the Law of November 9, which is amoral and will corrupt the people. And we think that we are so behind Europe, although as the people see it, our consciousness is 1000 versts ahead of her. Yes, this is terrible."

"But I still do not see what we are to do."

"Assess the land and transfer all the duties and taxes onto it."

"Henry George. And what of the urban population?"

"The urban population will not be paying taxes. But the reform does not [entirely] consist of that. I would not even know how to carry out the freeing of the land slaves, as others could not know how to go about freeing the negroes, and the serfs in Russia. But I do know that it is impossible to continue to live by this flagrant injustice. And it is necessary not to conceal this from ourselves, but to know that stealing fifteen oak trees from Maria Vasileevna is not robbery. It means that for her and her children to possess the land on which these oak trees grow is illegitimate and criminal—such is what robbery is . . . "

"Thanks for telling me I'm a thief," Maria Vasileevna chimed in. "You, Simeon Terenteich, it seems to me, have been talking nonsense."

"Maria Vasileevna, surely this is not a joke." Simeon Terenteich began to talk disjointedly. "Surely you will understand. As sure as they know that the sun rises every day, the peasants know that the land is God's, and they know not as I do, by reasoning, but from their guts, that it is impossible for them to live without the land, so that their children can grow up and be [decent] people like us. They have been working on the land their entire lives and can hardly feed themselves. And suddenly, so they clearly understand, people who do not work this land have taken it from them and compel them to labor on it and do all kinds of unnecessary and stupid things. And they must pay taxes for which they have to sell their last cow or have to buy a horse, repair a hut or go cut down [someone else's] oak trees which are growing on God's land. The peasant addresses his needs quite directly: he is skillful at doing so, as he is deft in packing his cart to travel along a laborious road. He knows of no formula of words that will define his act as unjust. He knows, on which side is injustice, terrible injustice and cruelty, terrible cruelty."

"What strange thoughts you have," Maria Vasileevna began, and she started a long speech about her responsibility towards her children, about the fact that there are bad guardians, about the children of Prince Adashev, who was married to a Stroganov, who had [quite] a history with Bubnova, and about his own sister [married to someone] well known.[7]

Simeon Terenteich was silent, then got up and silently left.

"You know, I would have such a man around my children."

"I was thinking. Find me [another type of man like that]."

"Such muddleheadedness."

That evening the servant Taras, who had the habit of writing down his notes, wrote the following description of the day:

There was the marshal of the nobility, they ate late, they were waiting for the children. The lady of the manor was lecturing me for the problem with the curtains. But perhaps I am ready to explode. It was good that Simeon Terenteich spoke with the marshal of the nobility. The entire affair has been turned inside out but truth cannot be concealed. Yes, in great deception lives our peasant brotherhood. And then came my brother's daughter-in-law.

Notes

1. Tolstoy, *I svet vo t'me svetit* [Light that shines through the darkness],1896-1900 *(PSS,* 31: 216-243).
2. Tolstoy to Tsar Nicholas II, Dec. 26-31, 1901, *PSS,* 73: 194-196.
3. Tolstoy, "Pis'mo k krest'ianinu o zemle: O proekte Genri Dzhordzha," [Letter to a peasant about the land: Concerning Henry George's project," 1905 *(PSS,* 90: 75-76).
4. Tolstoy, *Son* [A dream], 1909-1910 *(PSS,* 38: 364-369). This first version was not used. The soft sign has been dropped in the patronymics in favor of an "e."
5. The corner in which the icons were located.
6. An arshin is equivalent to twenty-eight inches. This line is an obvious attack on the repartitional field system and the commune.
7. The Stroganovs were an immensely rich merchant, industrial, and landholding family. They were instrumental in the colonialization of Siberia and contributed quite a few noted statesmen.

Bibliography

Presented here are a number of pertinent selections. By no means exhaustive, this bibliography does contain all Tolstoy's writings in Russian (his complete works) and also all George's published books. Tolstoy's major works in English are not included since they are easily attainable. Some remembrances by people who had conversed with Tolstoy and useful secondary sources are also listed. Most of the former are, however, in Russian. Scholarship about Tolstoy in English is staggering, and, as with the primary material the reader should not have a problem locating suitable resources. There are also a reasonable number of books about George but a search in an academic library is advisable. Volume I of this Trilogy (*An Anthology of Henry George's Thought*) contains a bibliography with works about George which can also be consulted.

Primary Sources

Aikhenvald, Iu. I. *Lev Tolstoi*. Moscow: Izdanie tsentralnoe tovarishchestva "Kooperativnoe izdatel'stvo," 1920.

Annenkov, P. V. *The Extraordinary Decade: Literary Memoirs*. Translated by Irwin R. Titunik. Ann Arbor: The University of Michigan Press, 1968.

Aptekman, O. V. "Dve dorogie teni: Iz vospominanii o G. V. Plekhanove i M. A. Natansone kak semidestiatnikakh" [Two dear vestiges: The remembrances of G. V. Plekhanov and M. A. Natanson as participants in the 1870's]. *Byloe* [White] 16 (1921).

Bakunin, Michael A. "L'Empire knouto-Germanique et la révolution sociale" [The knouto-Germanic Empire and the social revolution] *Œuvres* [Works], ed. P.-V. Stock, Vol. 3, Paris: Tresse et Stock, 1895-1913.

Biriukov, P. ed. *Leon Tolstoi: Journal intime des quinze dernières années de sa vie: 1895-1910* [Lev Tolstoy: Secret journal for the last fifteen years of his life: 1895-1910]. Translated by Natasha Rostowa and Mgte. Jean-Debit. Paris: Agence Generale Librairie et de Publications, 1917.

———. *L. N. Tolstoi: Biografiia*. 3 Vols. Moscow: Posrednik, 1911-1913.

Bulgakov, V. F. *L. N. Tolstoi v poslednii god ego zhizn* [L. N. Tolstoy in the last year of his life]. Moscow: Khudozhestvennoi literatury, 1960.

———. *Lev Tolstoi, ego druz'ia i blizkie: vospominaniia i rasskazi* [Lev Tolstoy, his friends and acquaintances: remembrances and stories]. Tula: Priokskoe knizhnoe izdatel'stvo, 1970.

————. *O Tolstom: vospominaniia i rasskazi* [About Tolstoy: remembrances and stories]. Tula: Priokskoe knizhnoe izdatel'stvo, 1974.

Chernyshevskii, Nikolai Gavrilovich. "Chto delat'?: Iz rasskazov o novykh liudiakh" [What is to be done?: Tales about new people]. Vol. 11, *Polnoe sobranie sochinenii v pyatnatsati tomakh* [Complete works in fifteen volumes]. Moscow: Gosudarstvennoe izdatel'stvo khudozhestvennoi literatury, 1939-1953.

————.*What Is To Be Done?: Tales About New People*. Translated by Benjamin R. Tucker. New York: Random House, 1961.

Christian, R. F., ed. *Tolstoy's Letters, 1880-1910*. Vol. 2, New York: Charles Scribner's Sons, 1978.

Figner, Vera N. *Vospominaniia v dvukh tomakh* [Remembrances in two volumes]. Vol. 1, Moscow: Izdatel'stvo sotsial'no-ekonomicheskoi "Mysl'," 1964.

————. "Mark Andreevich Natanson." *Katorga i ssylka* [Hard labor and exile] 56 (1929).

George, Henry. *A Perplexed Philosopher*. New York: Robert Schalkenbach Foundation, 1988.

————.*The Land Question*. New York: Robert Schalkenbach Foundation, 1982.

————.*Our Land and Land Policy*. The Complete Works of Henry George. Vol. 8, New York: Doubleday, Page & Co., 1904.

————. *Protection or Free Trade*. New York: Robert Schalkenbach Foundation, 1992.

————. *The Science of Political Economy*. New York: Robert Schalkenbach Foundation, 1992.

————. *Progress and Poverty*. New York: Robert Schalkenbach Foundation, 1992.

————. *Social Problems*. New York: Robert Schalkenbach Foundation, 1992.

Gershenzon, M., ed. *P. Ia. Chaadaev: Filosoficheskie pis'ma i apologiia sumashedshego*. Moscow, 1913; reprint, Ann Arbor: Ardis, 1978.

Gol'denveizer, A. B. *Vblizi Tolstogo* [Close to Tolstoy]. Moscow: Khudzhestvennoi literatury, 1959.

Golubova, S. N. et al, eds.*L. N. Tolstoi v vospominaniiakh sovremennikov* [L. N. Tolstoy in the remembrances of his contemporaries]. 2 Vols. Moscow: Khudozhestvennoi literatury, 1960.

Gusev, N. N. *Dva goda c L. N. Tolstym* [Two years with L. N. Tolstoy]. Moscow: Khudozhestvennoi literatury, 1973.

————. *Lev Nikolaevich Tolstoi*. Moscow: Nauka, 1970.

———— and Chertkov, V. G. eds., *Tolstoi i o Tolstom* [Tolstoy and about Tolstoy]. 4 Vols. Moscow: Tolstovskii muzei, 1924, 1927, and 1928.

————. *Lev Nikolaevich Tolstoi: materiali k biografii s 1881 po 1885 god* [L. N. Tolstoy: material for a biography from 1881 to 1885]. Moscow: Izdatel'stvo "Nauka," 1970.

Herzen, Alexander Ivanovich. *My Past and Thoughts*. Berkeley: University of California Press, 1973.

————.*Sobranie sochinenii v tridsati tomakh*. 13 Vols. Moscow: Akademiia nauk SSSR, 1954-1964.

Kornilova-Moroz, A. I. "Perovskaia i osnovanie kruzhka chaikovtsev" [Perovskaia and the foundation of the Chaikovskii circle]. *Katorga i ssylka* [Hard labor and exile] 22 (1926).

Kropotkin, Peter A. *Zapiski revoliutsionera*. Moscow: Izdatel'stvo "Mysl'," 1966.

Lakshin, B. ed. *Interviu i besedy s L'vom Tolstym* [Interviews and conversations with Lev Tolstoy]. Moscow: Sovremennik, 1987.

Lenin, Vladimir Ilyich. *Polnoe sobranie sochinenii* [Complete works]. Vols. 17 and 20, Moscow: Gosudarstvennoe izdatel'stvo politicheskoi literatury, 1958-1965.

Makovitskii, D. P. *Iasnopolianskie zapiski* [Yasnaia Poliana notes]. 4 Vols. Moscow: Izdatel'stvo "nauka," 1979.

Marx, Karl. *Capital: A Critical Analysis of Capitalist Production*. Vol. 1, Moscow: Foreign Languages Publishing House, 1961.

───── and Engels, Friedrich. *Letters to Americans: 1848-1895*. New York: International Publishers, 1969.

Molochnikov, V. A. *Tolstoi i o Tolstom* [Tolstoy and about Tolstoy]. Moscow: Izdanie Tolstovskogo muzeia, 1927.

Pobedonostsev, Konstantin P. *Reflections of a Russian Statesman*. Ann Arbor: The University of Michigan Press, 1968.

Rousseau, Jean-Jacques. *Discours sur l'origine et les fondements de l'inégalité parmi les hommes*. Paris: Éditions Gallimard, Paris, 1965.

Semonov, S. T. *Vospominaniia o Leve Nikolaeviche Tolstom* [Remembrances about Lev Nikolaevich Tolstoy]. St. Petersburg: Obshchestvennaia pol'za, 1912.

Sergeenko, A. S. ed. *Kto byl Lev Tolstoi* [Who was Lev Tolstoy]. Moscow: Izdanie trud obshchiny "Trezvaia zhizn," 1920.

Sergeenko, Peter A. *How Count Tolstoy Lives and Works*. Translated by Isabel F. Hapgood. London: J. Nisbet & Co., Ltd., n.d.

───────. *Ocherki Tolstoi i ego sovremenniki* [Sketches about Tolstoy and his contemporaries]. Moscow: Izdanie V. M. Sablina, 1911.

───────. ed., *Mezhdunarodnyi tolstovskii al'manakh* [International Tolstoyan almanac]. Moscow: Kniga, 1909.

Sreznevskii, V. I. and Bem, A. L. eds. *Tolstoi: pamiatniki, tvorchestva i zhizni* [Tolstoy: memories, work, and life]. Vol. 1, Petrograd: Ogni, 1917.

Sukhotina-Tolstaia, T. L. *Dnevnik* [Diary]. Moscow: Sovremennik, 1979.

───────. *Sur mon père*. [About my father]. Paris: Institut d'Études Slaves de l'Université de Paris, 1961.

───────. *Vospominaniia* [Remembrances]. Moscow: Khudozhestvennoi literatury, 1976.

───────. *Tolstoy Remembered*. Translated by Coltman Derek. New York: McGraw-Hill Book Co., 1977.

───────. *Dnevniki v dvukh tomakh* [Diaries in two volumes]. 2 Vols. Moscow: Khudozhestvennaia literatura, 1978.

Tolstoy, A. I. and Popov, P. S. eds. *S. A. Tolstaia: Pis'ma k L. N. Tolstom, 1862-1910* [S. A. Tolstoy: Letters to L. N. Tolstoy, 1862-1910]. Moscow: Akademiia, 1936.

Tolstoy, Alexandra. *The Tragedy of Tolstoy*. Translated by Elena Varneck. New Haven: Yale University Press, 1933.

───────. *Tolstoy: A Life of My Father*. Translated by E. R. Hapgood. New York: Harper & Bros. Publishers, 1953.

Tolstoy, L. L. *Pravda o moem otse* [The truth about my father]. Leningrad: Izdatel'stvo knizhnyi ugol, 1924.

Tolstoy, Lev Nikolaievich. *Polnoe sobranie sochinenii* [Complete works]. 91 Vols. Moscow: Gosudartsvo izdatel'stvo khudozhestvennoi literatury, 1928-1964.

————. "Count Tolstoi on the Doctrine of Henry George." *American Monthly Review of Reviews*, 17 Jan. 1898.

————. "Count Leo Tolstoy, On the Single Tax: His Estimate of Henry George." *The Sterling Weekly* 4 Feb. 20, 1897.

Tolstoy, S. L. ed. *Dnevniki Sofi Andreevny Tolstoi, 1897-1909* [Diaries of Sofia Andreevna Tolstoy, 1897-1909]. Moscow: Kooperativnoe izdatel'stvo "Sever," 1932.

Yardley, Arthur ed. *Addresses at the Funeral of Henry George*. Chicago: The Public Publishing Co., 1905.

Secondary Sources

Ardens, Nikolai. *Zhivoi Tolstoi: zhizn L'va Nikolaevicha Tolstogo v vospomi- naniiakh i perepiske* [The living Tolstoy: the life of Lev Nikolaevich Tolstoy in remembrances and correspondence]. Moscow: Izdanie Tolstovskogo muzeia, 1928.

Avrich, Paul. *The Russian Anarchists*. Princeton: Princeton University Press, 1967.

Barker, Charles A. *Henry George*. New York: Oxford U. Press, 1955.

Bayley, John, ed. *The Portable Tolstoy*. New York: Viking Penguin, 1978.

Berdyaev, Nicolai A. *The Russian Idea*. New York: The Macmillan Co., 1948.

Bell, Stephen. *Rebel, Priest, and Prophet: A Biography of Dr. Edward McGlynn*. New York: Robert Schalkenbach Foundation, 1968.

Berlin, Sir Isaiah. *Russian Thinkers*. New York: Penguin Books,1986.

Billington, James. *The Icon and the Axe: An Interpretive History of Russian Culture*. New York: Random House, 1970.

Blum, Jerome. *Lord and Peasant in Russia: From the Ninth to the Nineteenth Century*. Princeton: Princeton University Press, 1972.

Broido, Vera. *Apostles Into Terrorists: Women and the Revolutionary Movement in the Russia of Alexander II*. New York: The Viking Press, 1977.

Brower, Daniel R. *Training the Nihilists: Education and Radicalism in Tsarist Russia*. Ithaca, N. Y.: Cornell University Press, 1975.

Byrnes, Robert F. *Pobedonostev: His Life and Thought*. Bloomington: Indiana University Press, 1968.

The Compact Edition of the Oxford English Dictionary, 1971 ed., S. v. "pogrom."

Copleston, Frederick C. *Philosophy In Russia: From Herzen to Lenin and Berdyaev*. Notre Dame: Notre Dame University Press, 1986.

Cord, Stephen B. *Henry George: Dreamer or Realist?* Philadelphia: University of Pennsylvania Press, 1965.

D'iakov, V. A. "L. N. Tolstoi o zakonomernostiakh istoricheskogo protsessa, roli lichnosti i narodnykh mass v istorii" [L. N. Tolstoy on the regularity of the historical process, the role of personality and the people in history], *Voprosy istorii* [Questions of history] 8 (Aug.1978).

Dole, Nathan H. *The Life of Lyof N. Tolstoi*. New York: Charles Scribner's Sons, 1923.

Dubnow, Simon. *History of the Jews in Russia and Poland: From the Earliest Times Until the Present Day*. Vol. 1, New York: Ktav Publishing House, 1975.

————. *History of the Jews, From the Congress of Vienna to the Emergence of Hitler.* Translated by Moshe Spiegel. Vol. 5, South Brunswick, N. J.: Thomas Yoseloff, 1973.

Dzhakupova, N. V. "Memuary kak istochnik dlia izucheniia organizatsionnoi splochennosti revoliutsionerov-razochintsev 1870-kh godov" [Memoirs as a source for the study of organizational solidarity of the revolutionary raz- nochintsy of the 1870's]. *Istoriia SSSR* [History of the USSR] 1 (Jan. 1984).

Efrusi, B. O. "Genri Dzhordzh, kak ekonomist" [Henry George as economist]. *Russkoe bogatstvo* [Russian wealth] 1 (Jan. 1898).

Emmons, Terence. "The Peasant and the Emancipation," in *The Peasant in Nineteenth Century Russia.* Edited by Wayne Vucinich. Stanford: Stanford University Press, 1968.

Filippov, M. M. "Sotsial'nyi vopros (po Genri Dzhordzhu)" [The Social question according to Henry George]. *Russkoe bogatstvo* [Russian wealth] 5-6 (May 1885).

Fillippov, R. V. "K otsenke programmnykh osnov 'Zemli i voli' 70-kh XIX veka" [An appraisal of the programmatic bases of "Land and liberty" of the 1870's]. *Voprosy istorii* [Questions of history] 5 (May 1982).

Fishman, William J. *Jewish Radicals: From Stetl to London Ghetto.* New York: Random House, 1974.

Frederic, Harold. *The New Exodus: A Study of Israel in Russia.* New York: G. P. Putnam's Sons, 1892; reprint, New York: Arno Press & The New York Times, 1970.

Frumkin, Jacob et al., eds., *Russian Jewry:1860-1970.* New York: Thomas Yoseloff, 1966.

Geiger, George R. *The Philosophy of Henry George.* New York: The Macmillan Co., 1933.

Georgieva, N. G. "Sovetskaia istoriografiia studencheskogo dvizheniia v Rossii na rubezhe XIX-XX vv" [Soviet historiography of the student movement in Russia at the turn of the twentieth century]. *Voprosy istorii* [Questions of history] 10 (Oct.1979).

Gershenzon, M., ed. *P. Ia. Chaadaev: Filosoficheskie pis'ma i apologiia sumashedshego.* Moscow, 1913; reprint, Ann Arbor: Ardis, 1978.

Ginev, V. N., ed. *Revoliutsionery 1870-kh godov: vospominaniia uchastnikov narodnicheskogo dvizheniia v Peterburge* [Revolutionaries of the 1870's: remembrances of the participants of the narodnik movement in St. Petersburg]. Moscow: Lenizdat, 1986.

Gleason, Abbott. *Young Russia: The Genesis of Russian Radicalism in the 1860's.* New York: The Viking Press, 1980.

Greenberg, Louis. *The Jews in Russia: The Struggle for Emancipation.* Vol. 1, New Haven: Yale University Press, 1965.

Grigoryan, M. *N. G. Chernyshevsky's World Outlook.* Moscow: Foreign Languages Publishing House, 1954.

Gudzii, N. K. *Lev Tolstoi.* Moscow: Khudozhestvennoi literatury, 1960.

Gustafson, Richard F. *Leo Tolstoy, Resident and Stranger: A Study in Fiction and Theology.* Princeton: Princeton University Press, 1986.

Harcave, Sidney. *First Blood: The Russian Revolution of 1905.* New York: The MacMillan Co., 1964.

Howe, Irving. *World of Our Fathers: The Journey of the East European Jews to America and the Life They Found and Made*. New York: Simon & Schuster, 1976.

Ianzhul, Ivan. "Otkrytoe pis'mo Genri Dzhordzha k pape L'vu XIII" [Open Letter of Henry George to Pope Leo XIII]. *Severnyi vestnik* [Northern messenger] 1 (Jan. 1892).

Itenberg, B. S. "P. L. Lavrov i revoliutsionnoe podpol'e Rossii pervoi poloviny 1870-kh godov" [P. L. Lavrov and the revolutionary underground of Russia in the first half of the 1870's]. *Istoriia SSSR* [History of the USSR] 2 (Mar. 1985).

————. *Dvizhenie revoliutsionnogo narodnichestva: Narodnicheskie kruzhki i 'khozhdenie v narod' v 70-kh XIX v.* [The Movement of the revolutionary narodniks: Narodnik circles and 'Going to the people' in the 1870's]. Moscow: Izdatel'stvo "Nauka," 1965.

Iuzhakov, S. "K Voprosu o bednosti, eia prichinaxh i ustranenii" [On the question of poverty, its causes and elimination]. *Otechestvenniya zapiski* [Notes of the fatherland] 266 (Jan. [?]1883).

"Izuchenie politicheskoi ekonomii Genri Dzhordzha" [The Study of of Henry George's political economy]. *Russkoe bogatstvo* [Russian wealth] 3 (1883).

Laktionova, N. Ia. "Nekotorye osobennosti narodnicheskogo dvizheniia scrediny 70-kh XIX v.: propagandistskaia deiatel'nost' kruzhka V. M. D'iakova" [Some features of the Narodnik movement of the mid-1870's: propaganda activity of the D'iakov circle]. *Vestnik Moskovskogo universiteta* [Bulletin of Moscow University] 5 (Sept.-Oct. 1985).

Lampert, E. *Sons Against Fathers: Studies in Russian Radicalism and Revolution* Oxford: The Clarendon Press, 1965.

Laserson, Max M. *The American Impact on Russia: Diplomatic and Ideological, 1784-1917*. New York: The Macmillan Co., 1950.

Lebedev, G. I. and Posse, V. A. *Zhizn' L. N. Tolstogo* [Life of L. N. Tolstoy]. St. Petersburg: Izdanie "Zhizni dlia vsekh," 1913.

Levin, Nora. *While Messiah Tarried: Jewish Socialist Movements, 1871-1917*. New York: Schocken Books, 1977.

L'vov-Rogachevskii, V. L. *Ot usad'by k izbe: Lev Tolstoi* [From the farm to the hut: Lev Tolstoy]. Moscow: Federatsiia, 1928.

Madison, Charles A. *Critics and Crusaders: A Century of American Protest*. New York: Henry Holt and Co., 1947.

Malia, Martin. *Alexander Herzen and the Birth of Russian Socialism*. New York: Grosset & Dunlap, 1965.

Masaryk, Thomas Garrigue. *The Spirit of Russia: Studies in History, Literature, and Philosophy*. Translated by Eden and Cedar Paul. 3 Vols. London: George Allen & Unwin, 1961.

Maude, Aylmer. *The Life of Tolstoy: Later Years*. Vol. 2, Oxford: Oxford University Press, 1987.

————. *Tolstoy and His Problems*. New York: Funk & Wagnalls Co., 1911.

Maynard, Sir John. *Russia in Flux: Before the October Revolution*. New York: Collier Books, 1968.

de Mille, Agnes George. *Henry George: Citizen of the World*. Chapel Hill: University of North Carolina Press, 1950.

Neilson, Francis. "Tolstoy's Message for Our Times." *The American Journal of Economics and Sociology* 7, 3 (Apr. 1948).

Offord, Derek. *The Russian Revolutionary Movement in the 1880's*. Cambridge: Cambridge University Press, 1986

Padover, Saul K. *The Genius of America: Men Whose Ideas Shaped Our Civilization*. New York: McGraw-Hill Book Co., 1960.

Pantin, I. K. *Sotsialisticheskaia mysl' v Rossii: perekhod ot utopii k nauke* [Socialist thought in Russia: the transition from utopia to science]. Moscow: Izdatel'stvo politicheskoi literatury, 1973.

Pascal, Pierre. *The Religion of the Russian People*. Translated by Rowan Williams. Crestwood, N.Y.: St. Vladimir's Seminary Press, 1976.

Pereira, N. G. O. *The Thought and Teachings of N. G. Chernyshevskij*. The Hague: Mouton, 1975.

Pomper, Philip. *The Russian Revolutionary Intelligentsia*. Arlington Heights, Ill.: Harlan Davidson, 1970.

Raeff, Marc. *Origins of the Russian Intelligentsia: The Eighteenth Century Nobility*. New York: Harcourt, Brace & World, 1966.

Ralli, Zamfir. "Mikhail Aleksandrovich Bakunin." *Minuvshie gody* [Past years] 10 (Oct. 1908).

Randall, Francis B. *N. G. Chernyshevskii*. New York: Twayne Publishers, 1967.

Redfearn, David. *Tolstoy: Principles for a New World Order*. London: Shepheard-Walwyn, 1992.

Robinson, Geroid T. *Rural Russia Under the Old Regime: A History of the Landlord-Peasant World and a Prologue to the Peasant Revolution of 1917*. Berkeley: University of California Press, 1969.

Rose, Edward J. *Henry George*. Edited by Sylvia E. Bowman. Twayne's United States Authors Series. New Haven: College & University Press, 1968.

Rosten, Leo. *Hooray for Yiddish: A Book About English*. New York: Simon & Schuster, 1982.

Rozanovoi, S., ed. *Lev Nikolaevich Tolstoi perepiska c Russkimi pisatel'iami* [L. N. Tolstoi, correspondence with Russian writers]. Moscow: Gosudartsvo izdatel'stvo khudozhestvennoe literatury, 1962.

Sablinsky, Walter. *The Road to Bloody Sunday: Father Gapon and the St. Petersburg Massacre of 1905*. Princeton: Princeton University Press, 1976.

Saiki, O. A. "Iz istorii 'Molodoi' partii narodnoi voli" [The history of the "Young" party of the people's will]. *Istoriia SSSR* [History of the USSR] 6 [Nov.-Dec.1971]: 76 and 81.

Simmons, Ernest. *Leo Tolstoy: The Years of Maturity*. Vol. 2, New York: Vintage Books, 1960.

———. *Tolstoy*. London: Routledge & Kegan Paul, 1973.

———. *Introduction to Tolstoy's Writings*. Chicago: The University of Chicago Press, 1968.

Slonimskii, L. "Genri Dzhordzh i ego teoriia progressa" [Henry George and his theory of progress]. *Vestnik evropy* [Messenger of Europe] 4 (1889).

Spence, G. W. *Tolstoy the Ascetic*. New York: Barnes & Noble, 1968.

Stampfer, Shaul. "East European Migration to the United States," in *Migrations Across*

Time and Nations: Population Mobility in Historical Context. Edited by Ira A. Glazer and Luigi De Rosa. New York: Holmes & Meier, 1956.

Thomas, John L. *Alternative America: Henry George, Edward Bellamy, Henry Demarest Lloyd, and the Adversary Tradition.* Cambridge: Harvard University Press, 1983.

Troyat, Henri. *Tolstoy.* Translated by Nancy Amphoux. New York: Dell Publishing Co., 1969.

Tschizewskij, Dmitrij. *Russian Intellectual History.* Translated by John C. Osborne. Ann Arbor: Ardis, 1978.

Tugan-Baranovskii, Michael I. "Genri Dzhordzh i natsionalizatsiia zemli" [Henry George and the nationalization of land]. *Novoe slovo* [New word] 6, 9 (June 1897).

Ulam, Adam. *In the Name of the People: Prophets and Conspirators in Prerevolutionary Russia.* New York: The Viking Press, 1977.

Utechin, S. V. *A Concise Encyclopedia of Russia.* New York: E. P. Dutton & Co., 1964.

V. V., "Genri Dzhordzh o protektsionizm" [Henry George on protectionism]. *Severnyi vestnik* [Northern messenger] 12 (Dec.1886).

Venturi, Franco. *Roots of Revolution: A History of the Populist and Socialist Movements in Nineteenth Century Russia.* Translated by Francis Haskell. New York: Grosset & Dunlap, 1961.

Volkovoi, T. N., ed. *L. N. Tolstoi i ego blizke* [L. N. Tolstoy and his acquaintances]. Moscow: Sovremennik, 1986.

Wedgwood, Ethel. *Tolstoy on Land and Slavery: A Selection.* London: Land Values Publication Department, 1909.

Weidle, Wladimir. *Russia: Absent and Present.* Translated by A. Gordon Smith. London: Hollis & Carter, 1952.

Wieczynski, Joseph L., ed., *Modern Encyclopedia of Russian and Soviet History.* Gulf Breeze, Fla.: Academic International Press,1976, S. v. "Alexander II," by Charles Timberlake.

———. *Modern Encyclopedia,* 1978. S. v. "Byzantine Influence on Russia," by George P. Majeska.

———. *Modern Encyclopedia,* 1978, S. v. "Bund," by Henry J. Tobias.

———. *Modern Encyclopedia,* 1981, S. v. "Mark Andreevich Natanson," by Richard Johnson.

———. *Modern Encyclopedia,* 1981, S. v. "Nicholas II," by Robert D. Warth.

———. *Modern Encyclopedia,* 1982, S. v. "Pale of Settlement," by Hans Heilbronner.

Yarmolinsky, Avrahm. *Road to Revolution: A Century of Russian Radicalism* New York: Macmillan Co., 1968.

Young, Arthur N. *The Single Tax Movement in the United States.* Princeton: Princeton U. Press, 1916.

Zaikin, Anton. *Apostol mira i liubvi: L. N. Tolstoi, ego zhizn' i trudy* [Apostle of peace and love: L. N. Tolstoy, his life and works]. St. Petersburg: Knigoizdatel'stvo smysl zhizn', 1911.

Zenkovsky, V. V. *A History of Russian Philosophy.* Translated by George L. Kline, Vol. 1, London: Routledge & Kegan Paul, 1953.

Single Tax Periodicals Cited:
The Commonwealth [London].
Land & Liberty [London].
Land Values [London].
Progress [Melbourne].
The Public [Chicago].
The Single-Tax Courier [St. Louis].
The Single Tax: A Journal Devoted to the Cause of Taxing Land Values [Glasgow].
Single Tax Review [New York]. Formerly the *The National Single Taxer* [Minneapolis and New York].
The Standard [New York].